Tsvetaeva's Orphic Journeys in the Worlds of the Word

Tsvetaeva's Orphic Journeys in the Worlds of the Word

Olga Peters Hasty

NORTHWESTERN UNIVERSITY PRESS / EVANSTON, ILLINOIS

Northwestern University Press
www.nupress.northwestern.edu

Printed in the United States of America

ISBN 978-0-8101-4321-0

The Library of Congress has cataloged the original, hardcover edition as follows:

Hasty, Olga Peters.
Tsvetaeva's Orphic journeys in the worlds of the word / Olga Peters Hasty.
p. cm. — (Studies in Russian literature and theory)
Includes bibliographical references and index.
ISBN 978-0-8101-1315-5 (alk. paper)
1. T͡Svetaeva, Marina, 1892–1941—Criticism and interpretation. 2. Orpheus (Greek mythology) in literature. I. Title. II. Series.
PG3476.T75Z69 1996
891.71'42—dc20

96-7332
CIP

For Christopher and Kate

. . . творчество и любовность несовместимы. Живешь или там или Здесь

[. . . creative work and amorousness are incompatible. One lives either there or here.]

Так, только в последний миг жизни сей, в предпервый—той мы понимаем, что куда вело.

[Thus only in the last moment of this life—which precedes the first moment of the next—do we understand what led where.]

Contents

Acknowledgments

ANY STUDY of Marina Tsvetaeva owes a debt of gratitude first and foremost to Simon Karlinsky for his pathbreaking work, which has served as the impetus for subsequent scholarship. Many other fine scholars have also devoted their attention to Tsvetaeva, and although I cannot list them all, I am indebted to them for their manifold contributions to my own understanding of this infinitely complex and rewarding poet.

I have benefited greatly from the generous attention paid my manuscript by various readers. I would like to thank Caryl Emerson for her penetrating reading, inspiring suggestions, and wise midwifery, which were instrumental in the materialization of this volume. I am also deeply grateful to Sibelan Forrester, Antonina Gove, and Christopher Hasty, who read the entire manuscript and provided generous commentary that significantly improved this study. I am very much obliged to Konstantin Azadovskii, Mikhail Gasparov, Natalia Medvedeva, Peter Scotto, Jane Taubman, and Ieva Vitins for their consideration of individual chapters. Many thanks go to Michael Wachtel for his unflagging determination to set things right and to Alexander Lehrman for his kind help in arriving at translations for many "impossible" passages.

In Susan Harris of Northwestern University Press I have found a supportive, enthusiastic editor. I also thank my keen-eyed copy editor, Kathy Lewis, and Nicole Monnier, who proofread and indexed the book. Princeton University deserves rich gratitude for its generous grant to Northwestern University Press to cover the costs of Cyrillic typesetting.

The support of friends and relations was invaluable throughout my work. I would like to thank Christine ("Die Muse") Dougherty for high spirits; Jack Dougherty for fine cooking and company; Susanne Fusso for friendship and faith; my mother, Z. E. Peters, for wise counsel; Aleksis Rannit and Tatiana Rannit for poetic inspiration; Omry Ronen for leading me deeper into poetry; and the Very Reverend Stefan Sabelnik for prayers and biblical references. Extra special thanks go to my dear friends at the Flounder Inn for keeping me afloat, to Christopher for *everything*, and to Kate for "concoctions" and shoulder rubs.

Preface

MARINA TSVETAEVA'S emotionally charged, contentious, and seemingly contradictory writings have focused critical attention on several qualities that are regarded in the twentieth century as the negative heritage of Romanticism. These qualities coalesce in a single image: the irrational, willful, unrestrained, and excessively emotional poet dependent on intense passion for creative productivity. Yet such a representation slights the Romantics' lucid, systematic thinking and habit of careful observation, of which Tsvetaeva was also an heir and avid student. The dynamic systems of process and, specifically, the Hegelian dialectic that typify poetic and philosophical inquiry of the Romantics are powerful forces that shape her artistic speculations and practice.

Compelled by a dialectic of generative contraries, Tsvetaeva attacks the phenomenal world of sense and mere appearance and yet insists that without sensuous incarnation poetry cannot exist. She sets out to subvert the conventional significance of perceived objects in order to expand the domain of sensibility. Her demand is for nothing less than the coincidence of all opposites, and it falls to the poet to enable such coincidences, indeed to comprise them herself: «Меня можно вести только на контрастах, то есть, на всеприсутствии всего» [I can be led only on contrasts, that is, on the all-presence of everything]. Tsvetaeva's recognition of the productive force of antinomy surfaces in her bisexual erotic analogies, in the dichotomy of body and soul, and, most compellingly, in the living poet's confrontations with death. The last in particular urge her to new connections that course through time and space to make the past endure in the future and to nullify the effects of physical separation.

The general philosophical notions that inform Tsvetaeva's poetry find precise, concrete expression in the material of her art—from minute detail and textual devices of individual poems to the ordering of entire collections. We must not let her Dionysian surface dazzle us. The emotional intensity

Tsvetaeva achieves in her verse is the product of highly consistent translations of large poetic concerns into the technical resources of poetry. To appreciate this consistency in her art is to recognize Tsvetaeva as a serious, intellectually responsible thinker whose avant-garde writings document a systematic and sustained engagement with fundamental questions of poetic discourse.

But her seriousness is of a different sort than that of her great Russian contemporaries. If for Boris Pasternak every poem tells of its own becoming, for Tsvetaeva poems testify to the coming-into-being of the poet herself. Her reflections center on defining the poet's lineage, her predicament, and her fate. The present study examines the complex representations of the poet in Tsvetaeva's writings. It illuminates her conception of the goals and responsibilities of her art and demonstrates the degree to which her thought *about* poetry is fully continuous with her thinking *through* poetry—a thinking which takes as its vehicle the material of her craft. Tsvetaeva's search for a definition of the poet and for an imagery adequate to the task of conveying her essential features is also an attempt to find, secure, and legitimize her own artistic identity.

In an inquiry of such breadth there can be no pretensions to exhaustiveness. The faces of the poet and the discussions of her art in Tsvetaeva's works are manifold and richly varied. Close readings of a selective series of texts reveal specific textual embodiments of her artistic ideals and broaden our understanding of the concepts of which Tsvetaeva's images are the imaginative correlative and vehicle. I trace here but one of the myriad courses that can be charted through her vast artistic legacy: the great tale of poetic enterprise embodied in Orpheus.

The myth of Orpheus, it has been said, is "poetry thinking about itself,"[1] and his history "in the modern world is an abbreviated version of the history of modern poetry in general."[2] The Greek bard, as he guides Tsvetaeva and leads our inquiry, has a "biography" with four distinct but interrelated moments. In the first, Orpheus moves stones, trees, and animals with his song and introduces an Apollonian order into his surroundings. Next, on the strength of his longing to be reunited with his beloved Eurydice after her death from the sting of a serpent, Orpheus defies the boundary between the living and the dead to enthrall the gods and successfully petition her return. Yet, in the third stage, the retrieval of Eurydice fails when Orpheus disobeys the condition that he refrain from looking back at his beloved until they have attained the upper world. Finally, the Maenads—hostile to Orpheus's constancy to Eurydice and enflamed by Dionysian festivities—drown out his voice with frenzied shrieks and tear him to pieces. His severed head is thrown into the Hebrus, where, borne along by the current, it continues to sing. Of these four stages—the transformation of the natural world, the descent or catabasis, the failure of Orpheus's quest, and the *sparagmós* or dismemberment—Tsvetaeva pointedly rejects the first, which demonstrates the power of poetry over natural objects. She focuses instead on the three that represent the poet's struggle to subvert the existing order and show the inevitable consequences of his transgression of established norms.

These aspects of the myth influence Tsvetaeva's definition of the poet, generate a complex of expanding associations that demonstrate her creative process, and shape the poetic identity she seeks to project. In following connections that the Orpheus myth suggests to Tsvetaeva, we must learn to move freely through Greek myth, Western literature, and biographical detail in a consideration of personae metonymically related to his myth. Thus, for example, we observe how the ties Tsvetaeva establishes between Aleksandr Blok and Orpheus in the lyric «Как сонный, как пьяный» [Like One Somnolent, Intoxicated] are extended to Rainer Maria Rilke, whom, like Blok, she designates as an incarnation of the Greek bard. Orpheus also stimulates Tsvetaeva's own mythos of self-realization. Through his myth she asserts her own poetic identity vis-à-vis these two poets.

Tsvetaeva's contemplation of Orpheus and Eurydice in the lyric «Эвридика—Орфею» [Eurydice to Orpheus] prompts an examination of Hamlet's relationship with Ophelia. In the context of the configuration of eros, poetry, and death highlighted by the myth of Orpheus, the Danish prince emerges as a negative example. In the poems «Офелия — Гамлету» [Ophelia to Hamlet], «Офелия — в защиту королевы» [Ophelia—in Defense of the Queen], and «Диалог Гамлета с совестью» [Hamlet's Dialogue with His Conscience], Hamlet—who represses the erotic impulse that Orpheus successfully transforms into creative process—plays the role of antipoet.

Even as Tsvetaeva recognizes Orpheus as the prototypal poet, she contemplates personae appropriate to her own gender. Identifying with both Ophelia and Eurydice, she gives these traditionally passive women an active role and an authoritative voice. In the cycle *Сивилла* [The Sibyl] the myth of the Cumaean Sibyl, which shares significant themes with the Orphic legend, augments Tsvetaeva's definition of poet and poetry. The prophetess joins Eurydice and Ophelia in the series of women through whom Tsvetaeva offers correctives to the male stance represented by Orpheus and Hamlet. It is significant that Tsvetaeva represents these female personae in a disembodied state—Eurydice appears as a shade, Ophelia comes as a ghost to haunt Hamlet, while the Sibyl emphasizes the loss of body that accompanies the mortal woman's transformation into immortal prophetess. The empowerment of these female personae is consequential to their disembodiment as the power of eros is drawn into an analogical relation with the poetic imperative. Although Tsvetaeva does privilege the female body as current gender readings have shown, it is important to stress that implicit in her identification with the incorporeal Eurydice, Ophelia, and Sibyl is an attempt to define the impetus for the creative process in terms other than the erotic, an undertaking whose success erodes the issue of gender.

Central to Tsvetaeva's project is the hostility of the mundane toward the poet. In the Orpheus myth this hostility is precipitated by the poet's longing for the other world and becomes for Tsvetaeva the basis for establishing a confederacy of poets in which conflicts of gender are subsumed by the poet's grimmer confrontation with inimical mundane surroundings and violent death. The cycle *Поэты* [Poets] demonstrates the denigration to which the creator of verse is subjected by his antipoetical surroundings and asseverates the bonds that link all poets as self-sacrificial victims of a hostile world. The fact that their disparagement is played out on the surface of the text while their empowerment is established in the "elsewhere" of the subtexts imbedded in it makes the cycle a model of Tsvetaeva's cosmogony.

Tsvetaeva herself undertakes an Orphic quest in *Новогоднее* [New Year's], the great *poèma* written on the death of Rainer Maria Rilke. Here death, the ultimate disembodier, is vanquished when it is made to replace eros as the inciter of creative activity.

Orpheus continues to inform Tsvetaeva's conception of the role of the poet in prose memoirs of the thirties, where she describes her craft more explicitly and retraces her emergence as a poet. Thus, for example, in « Живое о живом » [The Living about the Living] Tsvetaeva describes a Crimean outing to a spot purported to be the entrance to Hades and reveals its symbolic significance to her life as a poet. In the essay « Дом у Старого Пимена » [The House at Old St. Pimen's] she registers a confrontation with the death of a loved one in her childhood as a cardinal point in her maturation as a poet. The expressly poetical norms of perception demonstrated in this essay reverse the workings of death set into motion by a specifically historical apprehension of existence.

As Tsvetaeva moves toward her own death, she represents the Apollonian gift of song as an onerous burden. The lyrics « Разговор с гением » [Conversation with a Genius] and « Есть счастливцы и счастливицы » [There Are Fortunate Men and Women] plead for escape no longer from the limitations of the mundane and from her human form, but rather from the inexorable poetic imperative. In these poems the human side of the divinely bestowed bard comes to the fore, and the very antinomies that generate poetry now indicate the fated tragedy of the poet's end.

Introduction

> Denn Mythologie und Poesie, beide sind eins und unzertrennlich.
> [For mythology and poetry, the two are one and indivisible.]
> —Friedrich Schlegel, "Discourse on Mythology"

> Все было встарь, все повторится снова,
> И сладок нам лишь узнаванья миг.
> [All has been of old, all will repeat anew,
> And only the moment of recognition is sweet to us.]
> —Osip Mandelstam, "Tristia"

THE CENTRALITY assigned to Orpheus in Tsvetaeva's poetic system is both cause and consequence of the overarching metaphor which she uses to establish her artistic vision—the poet's translation between a limited physical world and an abstracted "elsewhere" for which the poet longs.[1] The ideal "elsewhere" is defined as the absence of commonly construed boundaries or limitations which fragment that wholeness of vision the poet seeks to recover and make endure. Entailed in the very postulation of the two essentially incompatible realms is the imperative that they be truly reconciled by the poet, for otherwise the champion of wholeness effects yet a new fragmentation. Poetry becomes the means toward this reconciliation, and its mediatory role is stressed consistently in Tsvetaeva's accounts of her art. Already in her « Отрывки из книги *Земные приметы* » [Excerpts from the Book *Earthly Signs*, 1919] she maintains « Искусство — не самоцель: мост, а не цель » [Art is not an end in itself: it is a bridge, not a goal].[2] Accordingly, the "other world" toward which the poet is drawn is described in « Герой труда » [A Hero of Labor, 1925] not as the realm of poetry, but as the « страна, куда стихи только ход » [realm to which poetry is but a path] (*IP* 1:178). In the same essay she stresses both mediation and wholeness in her formulation of the poet's responsibility: « творить мир тот — в мирах сих » [to create the other world in these worlds] (*IP* 1:184). In a letter of January 1927, she explains, « и самое *небесное* из вдохновений — ничто, если не претворено в *земное* дело» [and the most *heavenly* of inspirations is nothing if it is not transformed into an *earthly* deed].[3] In the essay «Поэт о критике» [A Poet on Criticism, 1926] she rejects the notion of the poet's flight into the abstracted ideal world in an elaboration of the nature of that "translation" in which the poet engages:

> Нельзя о невесомостях говорить невесомо. Цель моя — утвердить, дать вещи вес. А для того, чтобы моя «невесомость» (душа, например) весила, нужно нечто из здешнего словаря и обихода, некая мера веса, миру уже ведомая и утвержденная в нем.
>
> [It is impossible to speak of weightless things weightlessly. My goal is to anchor, to give an object weight. And in order for my "weightless thing," (the soul, for example) to have weight, something of the vocabulary and custom of this world is needed, some measure of weight already known to this world and anchored in it.] (*IP* 1:229)

Later in this passage she summarizes: «Поработить видимое для служения незримому — вот жизнь поэта . . . незримое перевести на видимое» [To subject the visible to serve the invisible—this is the life of a poet . . . to translate the invisible into the visible] (*IP* 1:229). In the essay «Поэт и время» [The Poet and Time, 1932] this definition of the poet's responsibility is couched in temporal terms: «Отстаивать у времени то, что в нем вечного, либо увековечивать то, что в нем временного — как ни повернуть: времени — веку мира сего — противуставляется век тот» [To defend from time what is eternal in it, or to immortalize what is temporary in it—however you turn it: to time—the era of this world—is juxtaposed the era of the other] (*IP* 1:379).

The emphasis on the in-between—a direct consequence of the postulation of the two worlds—is instrumental in eroding those insidious conventional divisions and boundaries the poet seeks to counteract. The definition of poet and poetry that emerges from this model is applied systematically and with impeccable consistency in an impressive demonstration of the potential afforded by analogical thinking, which in Tsvetaeva's system displaces the logical.

The mediatory nature of poetry, which is foregrounded so clearly in her model of the universe, informs Tsvetaeva's positioning of poetry vis-à-vis the visual arts and music and shapes her descriptions of the inherent characteristics of the word. She secures for poetry a privileged position which derives precisely from its capacity to affect translations between the quotidian and the transcendent. This is the distinctive feature that sets poetry apart from the visual arts, which Tsvetaeva regards as too dependent on the surrounding world, and from music, which she finds too abstracted from it. Particularly in the context of the vast probings of the art movements that emerged in Russia in the early part of this century, it is difficult to concur with her refusal to acknowledge in the visual arts the potential for transcending the limitations of mundane perception. This view—one she expressed on many occasions—above all indicates her attempts to erode the primacy accorded the sense of sight. In what she considered to be a visually dominated world, Tsvetaeva chose to champion aural perception. Although it is possible to find occasional indications of her awareness of how a word looks on a page, the visual plays a relatively minor role in her poetics.

Tsvetaeva's mistrust of the sense of sight was predicated on a conviction that the eye gathers only surface impressions which serve to impede rather than to foster a genuine understanding of the essential nature of things. Hers was a deep antipathy to what Wordsworth called "the most despotic of our senses," which can serve only "to lay the inner faculties asleep." Accordingly she rejected emphatically any ties between poetry and the visual arts. The intransigence of this rejection must have sprung at least in part from antipathy to attempts on the part of members of Russian avant-garde movements to wed eye and ear. Yet the implications of Tsvetaeva's position extend well beyond such polemics.

Tsvetaeva had a marked tendency to align the visual with that mundane perception against which the poet struggles and the aural with the possibility of attaining new, enlightened cognizance. It is through intense listening—ideally with closed eyes—that genuine comprehension comes about. The visual and the aural convey impressions of different worlds and are thus at odds with one another. The blocking out of deceptive visual stimuli in favor of the true, aurally perceived ones is a gesture that appears regularly in Tsvetaeva's writings, even as blindness to the surrounding world serves repeatedly as a sign of clairvoyance.

Yet, if in her insistence on the supremacy of ear over eye Tsvetaeva goes counter to the prevailing tendency of Russian modernist movements to integrate poetry and the visual arts, neither does she evince any desire to have poetry aspire to the nonrepresentative state of music. For all the importance accorded music in her family and upbringing, Tsvetaeva does not share in the melomania of the German Romantics and Russian Symbolists, who nurtured her early poetic development. However strong her emphasis on aural perception and the acoustic properties of her medium, she refuses to acknowledge in the nonrepresentational nature of music a mark of superiority over poetry. Indeed, Tsvetaeva jealously guards that very "failure" of poetry to remain aloof from all reference to the external world. It is precisely in this Achilles' heel detected by the German Romantics in their juxtaposition of poetry with music that she saw the virtue and the superiority of her art.

If for Tsvetaeva the visual arts were too closely representative of the external world, music was too far removed from it. Poetry was the art that stood at the center, privileged by its capacity to refer simultaneously to an objectified surrounding world *and* to the intuited internal space of the poet projected as a poetic "elsewhere" or "beyond."

Although that very aural perception that Tsvetaeva champions in poetry is also the domain of music, the difference inherent in the type of hearing necessary to each of these arts serves to distinguish rather than to reconcile them. Thus, for example, in the opening paragraph of the autobiographical essay « Мать и музыка » [Mother and Music, 1935], the mother's insistence that Marina's superb ear destines her to become a musician is systematically undercut by Tsvetaeva's demonstration that her hearing is that of a poet and not, as her mother would have it, of a musician (*IP* 2:172).

The difference lies in the overwhelmingly associative nature of the poet's hearing, which, undaunted by conventional limits, fosters connections that extend far beyond the boundaries of word, text, and genre in a synesthetic riot of detours and digressions. An exploration that goes no further than the fourth degree of the scale leads the poet to weave connections with other languages, tales, and senses. The associations are linked specifically to our world and yet are, as Tsvetaeva demonstrates, virtually illimitable. The associative potential of its acoustic properties, which removes poetic language from the constraints of the mundane, operates simultaneously with a referential capacity that links it to this world. Herein lies the superiority of the language of poetry over that of music. The innate abstractness of poetic language allows a great suppleness and range of expressivity that need not run the risk of losing its moorings in the recognizable world. If Tsvetaeva's rejection of the visual arts is predicated on foregrounding specifically acoustic potentialities, her insistence on underscoring the distinction between poetry and music demonstrates her high regard for the semantic, referential function of language.

Underlying the permutations of the descriptive metaphors marshaled to depict her conception of her art is the central image of a divided universe that demands integration. This vision is reproduced analogically in all aspects of poet and poetry. The profound interrelationship that must be wrought between sound and meaning and that lies at the heart of Tsvetaeva's poetics is one such reproduction. The acoustic properties of the word are aligned with the soul and become a metonymy of the "other," invisible world, while its semantic attributes are construed as analogues for the poet's body and as representative of "this" visible world. The poet's voice, although dependent on the body for production, moves beyond it. So too the acoustic aspect of the word is projected by visual representations and linked to semantics, and yet ranges outside their scope. The attributes of the word emerge as correlative not only with her cosmogony, but with the poet herself. Poet, voice, and poetry mediate between this world and the other, between body and soul, between the semantic-referential and the acoustic-associative.

Such a definition of poetry, poet, and word is directed against the acceptance of divisions which ultimately inhibit the recognition of productive interrelationships. It is the chief function of poetry to deploy the generative power of opposites in order to replace existing boundaries and delimitations with interconnections that expand the reader's perceptual possibilities. Central to this project are analogy and its horizontal manifestation, metamorphosis. Both deny significance to discrete entities and deflect attention from completion toward the infinite processes of transmutation and becoming. The capacity of poetry to draw otherwise random shards of existence into ever new configurations and interrelationships is crucial to Tsvetaeva's definition of her art. In a letter to Boris Pasternak of 11 February 1923, she provides a compelling metaphor that we may isolate as the root image not only for the process of lyric verse to which it is applied, but for all facets of poetic activity:

> Лирические стихи (то, что называют) — отдельные мгновения *одного* движения: движение в прерывности. Помните в детстве вертящиеся калейдоскопы? . . . Тот же жест, но чуть продвинутый: скажем — рука. Вправо, чуть правей, еще чуть и т.д. Когда вертишь — двигается.
>
> [Lyric poems (so-called) are separate moments of *one* movement: an intermitted movement. Do you remember those turning kaleidoscopes from our childhood? . . . The same gesture, but slightly protracted: a hand, let us say. To the right, a bit more to the right, a bit more, and so on. As you turn it, it moves.][4]

What would appear to be an excruciatingly limited and fragmentary state—discrete shards of fixed quantity and quality confined within a rigidly defined space—opens into dynamic and virtually illimitable interconnectedness into which the separate pieces can be drawn. To subsume fragmentation by the act of interrelating is to open new perceptual possibilities and to replace the notion of finality with that of expectation and ceaseless becoming. The poet's creative process is not one of invention, but rather of instauration of the capacity to structure discrete units into meaningful wholes which are in turn prevented from imposing their particular boundaries on perception. The central task of the poet is to create ever new connections, as poetry aspires to indicate from within the limitations of language the infinite and uncharted realm of creative potential.

Out of the centrality that Tsvetaeva accords mediation, interrelation, and the (re)integration of contraries springs the image of Orpheus. Like the German Romantics, whom Walter Strauss aptly characterizes as "intoxicated with mythological and symbolic thinking,"[5] Tsvetaeva discerns an essential unity between poetry and myth. Hence, for example, the formulaic, acoustically supported parallel she establishes between « миротворчество » [world-creation] and « мифотворчество » [myth-creation] in her essay « Живое о живом » [The Living about the Living, 1933] (*IP* 2:53).[6] Hence too the primacy Tsvetaeva accords mythic thinking in the memoir « Дом у старого

Пимена» [The House at Old St. Pimen's, 1933] where she writes, «все — миф, так как не-мифа — нет, вне мифа — нет, из-мифа — нет, так как миф предвосхитил и раз навсегда изваял — все» [everything is myth, since there is no non-myth, no extra-myth, nothing that falls outside myth, since myth has anticipated and shaped everything once and for all] (*IP* 2:221). These formulations appear in the latter stages of Tsvetaeva's artistic development, but the central position they assign to myth springs from her earlier writings. Hers is a position that accords well with Walter Strauss's definition of modern mythopoeia as "a private fabrication utilizing traditional personae and details . . . to protect a personal vision of the world that expresses a certain notion about man and his reality, the world, and some power or destiny that lies beyond or within it."[7]

In Tsvetaeva's writings myth assumes a paradigmatic function specifically within the process of ordering the signs of the surrounding world. Apparently random and chaotic details of the quotidian crystallize around mythic plots into coherent, well-integrated structures. Myth, in other words, serves for Tsvetaeva not as a source of specific allegorization, but rather as an incentive for typological thinking. It provides the creative framework, the pattern, and the formulae by means of which various facets of existence are interrelated into a comprehensible whole.[8]

It is precisely the propensity of the mythological text to undergo typological transformations, as discussed, *inter alios* by Jurii Lotman, that enables it to serve as the means for imaging the universe in terms of ever recurring cycles rather than disjointed linear segments.[9] Tsvetaeva moves beyond the notion of recurrence to arrive at a spatial and temporal synchrony in which there and here, then and now, are made to interpenetrate and ceaselessly to inform one another. For her, myth provides the basis not only for the recognition of a repeated form or gesture, but also for the recognition of enduring presence.

In the movement from the specific to the universal necessary to the discernment of mythic patterns, complexities of being are reduced to their elemental components, making possible the recognition of connections, parallels, and similarities among apparently disparate phenomena. Conversely, in its extraordinary concentration, myth carries vast associative and interpretive potential that can be unfolded into endlessly expanding networks of connection and meaning. In the course of this process, Tsvetaeva's mythopoeia comes to serve as a corrective to the distortions and limitations of the barren, disordered, nontypological and nonsymbolic perspective of the mundane. The constant reassertion of the validity of essential mythic structures argues for Tsvetaeva's concept of an immense, unbroken poetic force that underlies all poetic utterance and that participates in evolving comprehension in which discovery lies in the ever new regroupings to which a finite set of elements is subjected.

In her mythologization Tsvetaeva makes no distinction between literary and biographical details, which become indistinguishable within the constructs of the predetermined mythic plot into which they are drawn. To text and life are applied the same organizing principles, the same sort of readings. Here myth and mythopoeia also carry the function noted by Mircea Eliade as central to myth: evaluating human actions and canonizing value systems.[10]

Like the Acmeists, who, in Omry Ronen's description, "prized especially those myths in which they could perceive a metapoetic potential,"[11] Tsvetaeva too was attracted to myths which could be drawn into explicating poet and poetry. The myth of Orpheus, to which poets have ever recurred in considering their art, its linguistic medium, and their own powers, assumes a central position in her quest. The myth encapsulates a series of antinomies, trenchantly summarized by Charles Segal, which beset existence and which the poet as mediator seeks to address:

> As a potent mythic symbol, Orpheus spans life and death; order and emotionality; animate and inanimate forms; fertility and sterility; man's control over nature and sympathetic fusion with nature; the power of art over death and its futility before death; the malleability of harmony with natural processes and hopeless protest against the most basic law of existence; the transience of human creation and the yearning for participation in eternal forms. Located at the fringes of the civilized world, the son of the god of order and light or of an obscure Thracian barbarian, he embodies the marginal, "liminal" position that art and the artist, and artful language too, have always held.[12]

The myth urges a confrontation of the difficult question of the poet's own power as tied specifically to the power of his medium, for, as Segal has observed, the myth may be understood to "celebrate . . . the poetic inspiration and the power of persuasive language" but also to "express . . . the intransigence of reality before the plasticity of language." It falls ultimately to the poet to "seek to understand and incorporate the two polarities of Orpheus."[13]

The complexity of the Orpheus myth and the vast interpretive field it opens make it particularly amenable to the exploration of poetry and to the exercise of poetic thinking. In the introduction to a study of permutations of the Orpheus myth, John Block Friedman observes: "Each age has fashioned Orpheus in its own image, giving him new attributes, emphasizing certain of his deeds at the expense of others and even changing the course of the narrative to make the Orpheus myth conform to the values of the day."[14] What Friedman says of each age holds true for each of the many poets who have engaged this myth. Tsvetaeva too, in incorporating the myth of Orpheus into her poetic system, singled out aspects she considered relevant to her own quest.

Orpheus became for her the prototypal poet, an embodiment of that mysterious power that ever reappears in poets of different times and places:

> ибо поэзия не дробится ни в поэтах, ни на поэтов, она во всех своих явлениях — одна, одно, в каждом — вся, так же как, по существу, нет поэтов, а есть поэт, один и тот же с начала и до конца мира, сила, окрашивающаяся в цвета данных времен, племен, стран, наречий, лиц, проходящая через ее, силу, несущих, как река, теми или иными берегами, теми или иными небесами, тем или иным дном.
>
> [For poetry is not fragmented in poets or among poets, it is, in all its manifestations, one, the same, complete in each—just as there are in essence no poets, but only the poet, one and the same, world beginning to world end, a force that takes on the hues of given times, tribes, countries, dialects, individuals, flowing through those who carry it, this force, like a river between these or other banks, under these or other skies, over one riverbed or another.] (*IP* 2:7)[15]

Irina Shevelenko has observed that for Tsvetaeva "the poet" emerges as "both that generalized 'force' which embodies the creative capacity of 'poetry' and a particular appearance of the creator who 'carries' this 'force.' " Her Orpheus too is a distinct manifestation of this tendency to endow the concept of "poet" with both of these meanings.[16]

Privy to the world of the living and the world of the dead, the poet belongs entirely to neither. This intermediary position is for Tsvetaeva the source of poetry. It permits, indeed demands, that translation between the two realms of existence which she determines to be the poet's task. Yet it is also a source of the mortal danger that accompanies the pursuit of poetry. The longing for the other world expressed in poetry is fulfilled by the poet's sacrificial death in the *sparagmós*, dismemberment.

A consideration of the interpretive processes to which Tsvetaeva subjects the myth provides a fruitful starting point for the explication of her artistic values and for the investigation of how these values are translated into specific poetic detail. In Tsvetaeva's Orpheus we discriminate definitive characteristics of the poet and observe how they function within her poetic universe. We cannot, of course, speak exclusively in terms of her shaping of the Orpheus myth, for the myth itself affected her understanding of her art. Above all, the analysis of any of Tsvetaeva's images must take into account the flexibility of their functions and meanings within the contexts of the ever shifting, dynamic configurations into which they are drawn and which they draw toward themselves. In tracing the potential for metamorphosis that Tsvetaeva uncovers in the Orpheus myth, we trace also her creative process.

Chapter One

The Emergence of Orpheus

Wir stellen im Wechsel das Vollendete dar.
[In change we represent the completed.]
—Friedrich Hölderlin, *Hyperion*

ORPHEUS, HIMSELF a constellation of images crucial to Tsvetaeva's definition of self and poetry, is one of many nexuses that draw us into the complex world of her art. This chapter records the emergence of Orpheus and with him themes that were to engage Tsvetaeva for the rest of her life. The sources of her early Orpheus and the interrelationships into which he is immediately absorbed fuel the metamorphoses of the prototypal poet that persist in her writings. Tsvetaeva's recognition of Orpheus in Aleksandr Blok, announced in the lyric « Как сонный, как пьяный » [Like One Somnolent, Intoxicated, 12 November 1921], establishes criteria vital to the poetic act and lays the groundwork for her subsequent hypostases of the bard. The lyric « Так плыли голова и лира » [Thus Floated Head and Lyre, 18 November 1921] emblematizes the poet's intermediary situation between life and death and the proximity of the creative process to the process of dying. The creation of the individual poem is here represented as correlative to the large gesture of lyric poetry, and the violent dismemberment of Orpheus is subsumed by the transcendent unity of his art. Both of these Orpheus lyrics receive close attention in this chapter.

Tsvetaeva was introduced to Greek mythology in her childhood, spent in a home where her mother's passion for German Romanticism intersected with her father's scholarly work on Greek and Roman culture. As late in her career as 1926, Tsvetaeva continued to refer to two rudimentary texts that she had read in her youth that provided a naive, Romantically infused recounting of the Greek myths. Thus even after completing *После России* [After Russia, 1922–25, pub. 1928], her last volume of lyric poetry, in which her thorough familiarity with Ovid's *Metamorphoses* is evident, Tsvetaeva continued to rely on retellings of the Greek myths for young readers as sources for her own writings. In a letter to Anna Teskova of 9 May 1926, she requests a copy of

Gustav Schwab's *Die schönsten Sagen des klassischen Altertums* for her work on the second part of *Theseus*. The importance Tsvetaeva ascribed to this book of myths is summed up in the inscription in her copy: « книга на всю жизнь » [a book for one's entire life].[1] In August of 1926, Tsvetaeva wrote to Rainer Maria Rilke in connection with her plans to begin work on *Phaedra*: "Schenke mir eine griechische (deutsche) Mythologie—ohne Philosophie, ganz einfach und ausführlich Mythen. Ich glaub, in meiner Kindheit hatte ich ein Buch von *Stoll*" [Give me a Greek (German) mythology—without philosophy, just myths—simply and in detail. I think in my childhood I had a book by *Stoll*.].[2] The book to which Tsvetaeva refers here is H. W. Stoll's *Die Sagen des klassischen Altertums*, which together with Schwab's book *Die schönsten Sagen des klassischen Altertums* had accomplished her earliest introduction to Greek mythology. Her requirement that her sources provide details of the Greek myths "without philosophy" indicates her need for a basic plot free from interpretive accretions—a skeletal structure around which elements of her own "philosophy" could be made to cohere. The events recorded in the myth were treated as facts that became points of departure for Tsvetaeva's creative work. As late as 1933, she continued to cite Schwab as the primary source for her own recasting of the Greek myths:

> Источники моей Федры и вообще всей моей мифики — немецкий пересказ мифов для юношества Густава Шваба. Верней (источники то я сама, во мне) — материалы.
>
> [The sources of my Phaedra and in general of all my mythicism is the German retelling of myths for young readers by Gustav Schwab. More accurately (the sources are I myself, in me)—materials.][3]

Both Stoll and Schwab presented the Orpheus myth—characteristically for their time—as a romantic tale concerned primarily with the tragically parted lovers and their eternal reunification after Orpheus's tragic death. Tsvetaeva saw the failure of Orpheus and Eurydice to be united in this world and their lasting, incorporeal union in the other as consummately exemplifying the imperative that earthly gratification be foregone in favor of loftier ambitions. She based the opening of her own poetic career on this model by translating the realm of death where Eurydice and Orpheus are conjoined into the domain of the poetic text where the eschewed meetings of a fleeting, superficial world could be similarly transformed into profound, indissoluble unions. Her first poetry collection, *Вечерний альбом* [Evening Album, 1910] signaled an emphatic foreclosure of marriage to the philologist Vladimir Nilender, not for lack of love, but out of an urgent need to sacrifice gratification to a higher cause. Orpheus's forced parting from Eurydice led him to the underworld. Tsvetaeva effected for herself a parting that led her into poetry.

Tsvetaeva designated Nilender as both her first love and the person who drew her into the myth of Orpheus. In the 1933 essay « Живое о живом » [The Living about the Living] she relates:

> Об Орфее я впервые, ушами души, а не головы, услышала от человека, которого, — как тогда решила — первого любила . . . это был переводчик Гераклита и Гимнов Орфея.
>
> [I heard about Orpheus for the first time with the ears of my soul rather than of my head from a person who, as I then decided, was my first love . . . This was the translator of Heraclitus and the Hymns of Orpheus.] (*IP* 2:58)

The particulars of Tsvetaeva's relationship with Nilender have received attention in the memoirs of her sister Anastasia and in the works of her major biographers.[4] Here it is sufficient to recall that Tsvetaeva, apparently in love with Nilender, rejected his proposal of marriage (or, perhaps more accurately, the concept of marriage itself) and conveyed her feelings to him in poems of *Evening Album*.

Encoded in the public space of this volume, whose publication Tsvetaeva construed as a means for communicating with Nilender, are intensely personal messages to him. At the same time *Evening Album* presents a general statement of her position in which we may recognize the seeds of her subsequent development. Thus, for example, in the poem « Невестам мудрецов » [To the Brides of Sages] Tsvetaeva proclaims the paltriness of marriage in the face of the eternal wisdom of Heraclitus and the shade of Orpheus.[5] In the latter part of the collection which bears the heading « Только тени » [Only Shades], Nilender himself is transformed into one of the disembodied beings she praises.

The collection concludes with a poem titled « Еще молитва » [Another Prayer, 1910] (*SP* 1:71–72). Although ostensibly addressed to Christ, this "prayer" is informed by the myth of Orpheus and is directed specifically to Nilender. It opens with an assertion of the human needs and desires of the eighteen-year-old Marina: « Дай не тень мне обнять, наконец! » [Let me at last embrace something other than a shade!] (I,4) and « Можно тени любить, но живут ли тенями / Восемнадцати лет на земле! » [One can love shades, but does one live by shades at eighteen in this world?] (II, 3–4). In the final three stanzas these earthly pleas give way to a recognition of the superiority of unearthly attachments: « Кроме мертвых, ведь нету друзей » [There are, after all, no friends but the dead] III, 4). Physical gratification is represented as incompatible with the loftier strivings to which she proclaims devotion. The poem culminates with an entreaty that she be granted the strength to remain faithful to the incorporeal ideals she has adopted. The ambivalent decision to renounce the desires of the flesh announced in this early lyric proceeds from lack of experience, as Tsvetaeva—even at eighteen possessed of remarkable self-knowledge—herself recognizes with the supplication « Дай понять мне, Христос, что не всё только тени » [Let me comprehend, Christ, that not everything is merely shades] (I, 3). In her poem she pleads, in other words, not for innocence of the surrounding world, but for the capacity to renounce it after having experienced it fully.

The uneasy configuration of eros, poetry, and death around which the Orpheus myth revolves emerges early to assume a central position in Tsvetaeva's writings. What was perhaps initially a flight into poetry prompted by apprehension of sexual maturation developed over the years into an unshakable conviction that loss and renunciation constitute an integral part of the poetic imperative, that unsatisfied longing gives rise to poetry, and that the defining act of the poet is self-sacrifice.

The Orpheus-inspired notions apparent in *Evening Album* and the interest in the Greek bard which Nilender had apparently sparked in Tsvetaeva could only have been strengthened by her immersion in the works of German Romantics during her sojourn in Germany in the summer of 1910.[6] It is difficult to overestimate the significance ascribed to Orpheus by the German Romantics. In writing of the "new seriousness regarding mythology" and "the deepening of the mythological consciousness" that characterize this period of German literary development, Walter Strauss describes their shaping of the myth and the powerful influence Orpheus exerts on definitions of the poet:

> [Orpheus] has been radically transformed into an instrument of the imagination whereby the poet can assess himself and his mission in a new way; the myth, losing its classical and neoclassical grounding, now becomes *the* myth of regeneration, and it is interpreted so as to account for the modern situation of the poet (that is, his growing alienation from the world) and for the experience of his psyche (his inner self-division and his quest for self-integration).[7]

The central position of Orpheus in the mythopoeia of the German Romantics is perhaps best exemplified—to note a poet particularly dear to Tsvetaeva—by Novalis, who "reads his own pitifully brief life as an Orphic experience and structures all of his thought and work around this experience."[8]

Here it is helpful to recall that it was primarily through the German Romantics, with their tendency toward a Dionysian vision of the Hellenistic world, that Russians perceived Greek myth, culture, and philosophy and that this view is reflected particularly in the writings of Tsvetaeva's most immediate predecessors, the neo-Romantic Russian Symbolists. Dorothy Zayatz Baker has observed that in the treatment of the Romantics the heroic image of Orpheus gave way to one of tragedy and failure: "Most frequently, such prototypes of the poet appear to be disabled by the intense anguish that results from the very act of poetic creation."[9] The Symbolists were, as Baker also notes, the first Russian poets to use Orpheus extensively in their writings.[10]

The role assigned the Greek bard in their intense reexamination of the identity of the poet and the power of his art closely resembled that projected by the German Romantics in their preoccupation with the poet's alienation from the surrounding world and in their questioning of his effectiveness. From them Tsvetaeva inherited the abject Orpheus as the prototypal poet. She assimilated also the extension of mythopoeia to personal biography characteristic of the Romantics and Symbolists alike. Although she did not go as far as Novalis, the myth provided her with a framework around which to structure accounts of her own emerging poetic identity.

Tsvetaeva devotes considerable attention to the source of Orpheus's anguish. Because the poet is human he remains, for all his strivings, subject to those very laws of the material world and desires of the flesh which it is his mission to overcome. His internal conflict is projected in the negotiations between the two realms of existence in terms of which Tsvetaeva defines the writing of poetry. At the same time the duality that impels creative activity determines the poet's death, for this duality internalizes that acute enmity between poets and nonpoets which finds its ultimate expression in the dismemberment of Orpheus.

Tsvetaeva locates the source of poetry specifically in the unresolved tension between the capacious world of the gods and the narrow one of mortals, between the transpersonal demands of the divine art and the personal desires of the mortal poet. In Orpheus's descent she discerns two features, each of which is aligned with one of the poet's aspects. The first is the imperative of absence which generates the longing that is translated into song and which transcends the boundaries of mortality. The second aspect of the catabasis is Orpheus's physical desire for Eurydice: the need for actual presence that leads flesh to prevail over spirit. Orpheus's praiseworthy descent into Hades is offset by his untoward desire to recapture Eurydice's shade in its earthly form.

Initially, Tsvetaeva's primary focus was on Orpheus's descent and the force of the desire that prompted it. In a passage from « Отрывки из книги *Земные приметы* » [Excerpts from the Book *Earthly Signs*, 1919] which marks a relatively early stage in the evolution of her reading of the myth, Tsvetaeva compares Orpheus with Lazarus to the Greek bard's advantage in a chiasmic juxtaposition of images characteristic of her mode of thought and logical argument:

> Лазарь, возвращающийся *оттуда*: мертвый к живым, и Орфей, спускающийся *туда*: живой — к мертвым . . . Разверстая яма и Елисейские поля. — Ах, ясно! — Лазарь *оттуда* мог принести только тлен: дух, в Жизнь воскресший, в жизнь не « воскресает ». Орфей же из жизни ушел — в Жизнь. Без чужого веления: жаждой своей.

> [Lazarus, returning *from there:* the dead to the living, and Orpheus, descending *there*: the living to the dead . . . A gaping pit and the Elysian Fields.—Oh, now I see!—*From there* Lazarus could bring only decay: a spirit, resurrected into Life, cannot "resurrect" into life. Orpheus, on the other hand, departed from life into Life. Not at someone else's bidding: on the strength of his own desire.] (*IP* 1:112; ellipsis in original)

The question of Eurydice or even the poet himself returning to the realm of the living is not yet addressed, and a parallel between Eurydice and Lazarus (and thus by analogy also between Orpheus and Christ) has yet to be recognized. Here Tsvetaeva speaks only of the felicitous descent: Orpheus's attainment of a realm far preferable to that of the living. The return of Lazarus from the dead is described in unequivocally negative terms as a transition from incorporeal existence in a supramundane realm ("Life") to bodily presence among the living ("life"). The imperative of Orpheus's return from Hades which was to become crucial to Tsvetaeva's definitions of the poet does not yet arise, but the inappropriateness of his attempt to retrieve Eurydice is already implicit in the commentary on Lazarus.

Even after she explicitly points out the error of Orpheus's attempt to retrieve his beloved in the lyric "Eurydice to Orpheus" (1923), considered in the following chapter, Tsvetaeva continues to praise the power and the infallibility of the longing that drew Orpheus to the underworld. Thus, for example, in the 1925 address « Бальмонту » [To Bal'mont] she writes:

> Двое, Бальмонт, побывали в Аиде живыми: бытовой Одиссей и небесный Орфей. Одиссей, помнится, не раз спрашивал дорогу, об Орфее не сказано, доскажу я. Орфея в Аид, на свидание с любимой, привела его *тоска*: та, что всегда ходит — своими путями! И будь Орфей слеп, как Гомер, он все равно бы нашел Эвридику.
>
> [Two, Bal'mont, have been in Hades alive: the mundane Odysseus and the heavenly Orpheus. Odysseus, as I remember, had to ask the way a number of times; we are not told about Orpheus, but I will fill in. Orpheus was led to Hades for a meeting with his beloved by his *longing:* that which always takes its own paths. And were Orpheus blind as Homer he still would have found Eurydice.] (*IP* 1:171)

As in the Lazarus passage, here too it is not Orpheus's attainment of Eurydice but his independent, unique, and extraordinary progress that is the focus of Tsvetaeva's attention.

The first poet Tsvetaeva identified directly with Orpheus was Aleksandr Blok. The import of her equation of Greek bard and Symbolist poet can best be appreciated in light of the tremendous significance Blok held for her. In her memoirs, Tsvetaeva's daughter Ariadna Efron writes:

> Блок в жизни Марины Цветаевой был единственным поэтом, которого она чтила не как собрата по «струнному рукомеслу», а как *божество* от поэзии, и которому, как *божеству*, поклонялась.
>
> [In Marina Tsvetaeva's life Blok was the only poet whom she honored not as a brother in the "stringed craft," but as a poetic *deity* and whom she worshiped as a *deity*.][11]

Associations with Blok surface at important moments in Tsvetaeva's life, and she frequently quotes his verse to substantiate her own ideas. Whether she writes about poetry in general or a specific artist, be it Rainer Maria Rilke, Valerii Briusov, Natal'ia Goncharova, Andrei Belyi, Boris Pasternak, Anna Akhmatova, or herself, Blok the « сплошная совесть » [utter conscience] (*IP*, 1:182) serves as the ultimate measure of artistic integrity and achievement.[12]

In aligning Blok with Orpheus, Tsvetaeva was perpetuating the German Romantic and Russian Symbolist penchant for creating reincarnations of Orpheus. She was doing so, however, on the basis of a personally drawn connection. Viktoria Schweitzer notes that Tsvetaeva's work on a series of poems to Blok coincided with her reading of Greek myths with her daughter. She cites a letter of 8 November 1921, in which Alia (Ariadna Efron) writes, « Мы с Мариной читаем мифологию . . . А Орфей похож на Блока: жалобный, камни трогающию . . . » [Marina and I are reading mythology . . . And Orpheus resembles Blok: pitiful, touching stones . . .].[13]

The recognition of Orpheus in Blok may well have been triggered specifically by the coincidence of her own poetic activity and her perusal of myths with her daughter, but the association has deeper roots. It emerges in the midst of Tsvetaeva's own distinctly Orphic process of confronting Blok's death.[14] In the series of poems she wrote to Blok in 1916, while he was still alive, Tsvetaeva aligned Blok with Christ and emphasized the poet's sacrificial meekness, proximity to death, and unearthly qualities. Given her propensity for typological thinking, little effort was required to discern in Orpheus another suitable embodiment of these attributes of the poet. The parallels between Greek bard and Christian Messiah were noted already by the Gnostics and emphasized in the Middle Ages when recognition of Orpheus as the pagan precursor to Christ gave rise to the designation "Orpheus-Christus."[15] The German Romantics with their strong interest in the Middle Ages perpetuated this alignment. The coincidence of abject mortality and radiant divinity and the theme of self-sacrifice represented by Christ in Tsvetaeva's 1916 poems to Blok modulate readily into the image of Orpheus. In April of 1920, Tsvetaeva compared Blok's voice to a shaft of light penetrating the gloom of Hades in the poem « Как слабый луч » [Like a Weak Ray], which describes Blok's Moscow reading at the Polytechnical Museum. The coincidence of the poet's helplessness and vulnerability before his audience with his incontestable purity in the realm of poetry suggests an intersection between the images of Christ and Orpheus and prompts the emergence of Tsvetaeva's Orpheus-Blok.

The link of Blok to both Orpheus and Christ highlights the sacrifice which is exacted for the transcendence of the boundaries between life and death. In *Poems to Blok* the interrelated figures are complementary: the image of Christ underscores the divinely preordained sacrifice consequent to the embodiment of the divine Word in flesh; that of Orpheus highlights the hostility of the mundane that results in the death of the poet. Thus the images of Orpheus and of Christ emphasize the twofold necessity of the poet's sacrificial death—divine ordination and mortal hostility—and stress too the divine and the human aspects of the poet himself. Where the demands of poetry and the desires of its human vessel are at odds, it is inevitably the fulfillment of the sacred poetic imperative that takes precedence.

Tsvetaeva's vision of Orpheus-Blok found specific embodiment in « Как сонный, как пьяный » [Like One Somnolent, Intoxicated, 12 November 1921]. This lyric provides the opportunity to observe Tsvetaeva's translation of the thematic material of the myth into a particular instance.[16] Blok's identity with the Greek bard is based here on his fulfillment of a preordained, ever repeating poetic destiny. In this lyric, Tsvetaeva focuses on Orpheus's failure to retrieve Eurydice and on the aftermath of his dismemberment. The poem takes us from the onset of the creative urge to the poet's death and the transcendence of that death. This progression is projected onto one specific poet—Blok—and then, by virtue of his established identity with Orpheus, is extended to all poets. The suggestion implicit in this intersection of the specific with the universal is that each poet retraces Orpheus's fate and that this fate is replicated within the creation of each individual poem.

Как сонный, как пьяный,
Врасплох, не готовясь.
Височные ямы:
Бессонная совесть.

Пустые глазницы:
Мертво и светло.
Сновидца, всевидца
Пустое стекло.

Не ты ли
Ее шелестящей хламиды
Не вынес
Обратным ущельем Аида?

Не эта ль,
Серебряным звоном полна,
Вдоль сонного Гебра
Плыла голова?

[Like one somnolent, intoxicated, unawares, without preparing, the hollows of the temples: sleepless conscience.

Empty eye sockets: dead and light. The dreamer's, the clairvoyant's empty glass.

Was it not you who failed to bring back her rustling chlamys by way of the return crevice of Hades?

Was it not this head, filled with silver resonance, that floated along the sleepy Hebrus?] (*SP* 2:50)

The urgency of the first stanza is conveyed by the staccato of its rapid tempo. The two opening lines describe the necessary dissolution of the poet's conscious self as the poetic imperative precludes any individual volition. The poet resembles someone overcome by sleep or intoxication, but the simile suggests a semblance that precludes identity. Whatever loss of self is brought about, the poet's responsibility remains intact and ready to be engaged. The ever wakeful (« бессонная ») conscience stands out in the context of the poet's own somnolence (I, 1 and II, 3) and the "sleepy" Hebrus (IV, 3).

In the description of the poet's entrance into a creative state are portents also of his death. The reference to intoxication in the first line suggests both Orpheus's fertile ties with Dionysus and his destruction by worshipers celebrating the festival of that god. The emblem of Blok's artistic integrity—his sunken temples—suggests the poet's impending death. At Blok's reading in the spring of 1920 in Moscow Tsvetaeva had observed the poet's unconscious gesture of rubbing his temple as he stood before the assembled audience and recorded this detail in the poem "Like a Weak Ray." In Gustav Schwab's account, the first stone hurled by Orpheus's enraged attackers to hit its mark draws blood from the bard's temple. In the context of this detail from the myth, Blok's unconscious gesture emerges as a sign of his vulnerability before the gathered crowd and his presentiment of impending death. In "Like One Somnolent, Intoxicated" Blok's sunken temples become emblems of the purity of the poet who is destined to become the sacrificial victim of his audience.

The poet's self-surrender notwithstanding, Tsvetaeva insists on his assumption of responsibility even in the face of his inevitable end. The temple—locus of the poet's vulnerability—is aligned with the wakeful conscience that ensures his guiltlessness. An image that hints at Orpheus's death is made an integral part of the force that enables him to transcend it.

In the second stanza intimations of death emerge more palpably. The stanza opens with an insistence on the poet's emptiness—the untrammeled perceptual state from which the creative process springs.[17] This is the emptiness not of exclusion, but of unlimited potential: a plenum of all possible determinations and distinctions. Departure from the perceptual limitations of the mundane world and from that self which is bound to the quotidian has a deathly quality (« мертво »), but also entails illumination (« светло »). The dream state is a Romantically inspired metaphor on which Tsvetaeva frequently draws in delineating the creative space of the poet who dispels the norms of the quotidian from that supramundane state between waking and sleep, between life and death. In this state the poet is a clairvoyant—an "all-seer" (« всевидец ») in the sense that the potential for seeing everything is vouchsafed in the elimination of predetermined constructs. A perceptual slate wiped clean (« пустое стекло ») opens the way for writing poetry.

The poet's compliance with the demands placed on him by his art is signaled by the ever greater fluidity to which the staccato quality of the first stanza gives way for the remainder of the poem. In stanza two an enjambment overarches the break between lines three and four and only line three is punctuated by a comma. Each of the two sentences of that stanza ends with a truncated foot. The unrealized final weak beat makes the ends of the lines and sentences less pronounced.

The two concluding stanzas that identify Blok with Orpheus are characterized by a particularly carefully crafted smoothness that suggests the appropriateness and inevitability of Orpheus's descent and dismemberment. Each of these stanzas consists of one sentence rather than of two. The enjambments in stanza three are enhanced metrically by the transference of one amphibrachic foot from lines one and three to lines two and four, respectively. The boundaries separating the mundane and the eternal, the mortal and the divine, are transcended by the coming-into-being of the poem. Orpheus's dismemberment gives way to the perpetual flow of song, and divisiveness is absorbed into unity. The metrical fluency of the two final stanzas is superimposed on what are two moments of anguish for Orpheus: his failure to retrieve Eurydice and the *sparagmós*.

Tsvetaeva creates not an exultant Orpheus who overcomes the laws of nature, but rather one who surrenders himself to song at the expense of his own desires and of his very life. His failure to retrieve Eurydice transforms Orpheus's earthly longing into an unearthly one, one that arouses the hostility of the women it leads him to disregard. Yet this "failure" and the workings of that hostility—implicit in the image of the severed head floating down the Hebrus—are prerequisites for the ultimate victory of the voice whose tones endure unabated.

The frustrated retrieval and the dismemberment lead to the consummation of the poetic act that brings peace: a union that marks the end of hostility. The "silver resonance" (« серебряный звон ») that describes transcendent song is an image derived from Blok's own poetry and is to be perceived as a resonance of his voice in this poem. The epithet « сонный » [somnolent] reappears, applied now to the river that bears the head and song. The calm, lyrical tone in which the head floating down the Hebrus is described draws attention away from the violence underlying this situation to focus instead on the inevitability of the poet's destiny and his resignation to it. Indeed, the entire poem prepares us for his inescapable end: the vulnerability in the first stanza, the deathly trance in the second, and finally the bard's own journey to the bourne of death and back suggest his familiarity with the other world. The message here and throughout Tsvetaeva's poems to Blok is that, however tragic, the poet's departure from this world is inevitable and correct.

The poet's severed head is an image that Blok too had used in describing himself, and this strengthens and perhaps to some degree even motivates Tsvetaeva's equation of him with Orpheus. In the prologue to his great *poèma Vozmezdie* [Retribution], on which he worked from 1910 to the last days of his life, Blok similarly juxtaposes the eternity of song to the mortality of the poet. Although Blok does not explicitly invoke Orpheus, the severed heads of St. John the Baptist and André Chénier suggest a strong metonymic link to his myth—particularly in light of the dedication to perpetuating song regardless of the tragic consequences.

Но песня — песнью всё пребудет,
В толпе всё кто-нибудь поет.
Вот — голову его на блюде
Царю плясунья подает;
Там — он на эшафоте черном
Слагает голову свою;
Здесь — именем клеймят позорным
Его стихи . . . И я пою, —

[But song will yet remain song,
In the crowd someone keeps singing.
See—the dancing woman presents
His head to the king on a platter.
There—he lays down his head
On the black scaffold.
Here—his poems are branded
With an ignominious name . . . And I sing,—][18]

Within a week Tsvetaeva opened the poem « Так плыли голова и лира » [Thus Floated Head and Lyre, 18 November 1921] with the very image that had concluded "Like One Somnolent, Intoxicated." This poem too requires close attention for what it contributes to our understanding of Tsvetaeva's Orpheus. The entire lyric is devoted, as its title suggests, to the contemplation of Orpheus's head and lyre floating down the Hebrus—the poet's ultimate translation between worlds. The silver resonance of voice and lyre to which the very banks of the river respond marks the transition between the ephemeral and the eternal and the juncture of the poet's ultimate defeat and his ultimate victory.[19] Although this lyric was not included in *Poems to Blok,* the alignment of Blok with Orpheus endures in the coincidence of theme and overlapping imagery.

"Thus Floated Head and Lyre," like "Like One Somnolent, Intoxicated," is not only Tsvetaeva's account of the destiny of Orpheus and by extension of all poets, but also a metaphorical representation of the writing of each individual poem imbedded in the larger context of poetry itself. Prominent here is the link of life, blood, and poetry that she was later to develop more explicitly.[20]

As in "Like One Somnolent, Intoxicated" in this second lyric Orpheus is evoked not by name but by a constellation of attributes crucial to Tsvetaeva's representation of the essential poet.[21] Head, lyre, and song are commingled with the poet's blood. The tension resulting from the poet's simultaneous ties to mortality and to divinity emerges here in the painful discord of a dialogue between the head and lyre. The poetic imperative—expressed by the lyre—draws the poet inexorably to the other world. The mortal poet—represented by Orpheus's head—follows obediently but with an expression of profound regret for the familiar surroundings of the world of the living which he must leave behind. The mundane world and the body of the poet are thus brought into an analogical relationship, even as the voice is aligned with the other world. The process of entering death that Tsvetaeva records in this lyric is analogous to the process of the creation of each individual poem. The Hebrus is the river of poetry that carries the lyrics together with Orpheus's head in the wholeness and mutability of its stream. Once again Tsvetaeva presents Orpheus's death not as escape, relief, or the fulfillment of his longing to be reunited with Eurydice, but as engagement in poetic activity.

With her emphasis on the difficulty with which the poet departs from the realm of the living, Tsvetaeva provides a counterbalance to the anguish described in the myth that Orpheus experiences when he is forced to leave Hades for the world above after his failed quest to retrieve Eurydice. The imperative of moving between the realms of existence is born of the longing for an elsewhere and yet also generates the pain attendant on departure from the here-and-now. The transition is fraught with inescapable pain, yet within the creative process the divergent orientations of the human poet and the divine demands of his art are ultimately resolved and the two become indistinguishable. Song prevails. The fate of the human remains of the poet is denied significance.

Так плыли: голова и лира,
Вниз, в отступающую даль.
И лира уверяла: мира!
А губы повторяли: жаль!

Крово-серебряный, серебро-
Кровавый след двойной лия,
Вдоль обмирающего Гебра —
Брат нежный мой, сестра моя!

Порой, в тоске неутолимой,
Ход замедлялся головы.
Но лира уверяла: мимо!
А губы ей вослед: увы!

Вдаль-зыблящимся изголовьем
Сдвигаемые как венцом —
Не лира ль истекает кровью?
Не волосы ли — серебром?

Так, лестницею нисходящей
Речною — в колыбель зыбей.
Так, к острову тому, где слаще
Чем где-либо — лжет соловей . . .

Где осияные останки?
Волна соленая — ответь!
Простоволосой лесбиянки
Быть может вытянула сеть?—

[Thus floated: head and lyre, down into the receding distance. And the lyre persuaded: peace/world! And the lips repeated: pity!

Spilling a blood-silver, silver-bloody double trail along the horror-struck Hebrus—my gentle brother, my sister!

At times, in unquenchable longing, the progress of the head slowed. But the lyre persuaded: pass by! And the lips after it: alas!

Drawn together into the distance by the rippling headrest as by a wreath, is it not the lyre that flows with blood? Not the hair with silver?

Thus, along the descending staircase of the river—into the cradle of swells. Thus, to that island where the nightingale lies more sweetly than in any other place . . .

Where are the illumined remains? Salty wave—reply! Perhaps the net of the bare-headed woman of Lesbos has drawn them out?—] (*SP* 2:137; ellipsis in original)

The poem opens with a description of the head and lyre floating downstream into the receding distance, a final trip together that is analogous to the whole life of the poet. Both appear to be transmitters of essentially the same voice: their utterances join to create one phrase as the lyre insists on « мира » [peace/world] while the lips repeat « жаль » [pity]. They are also linked by contiguity.

The second stanza continues to interrelate the images of head and lyre. The stream of blood flowing from the severed head and the stream of silvery sound issuing from the lyre are commingled by an inversion of the epithets applied to the trace they leave: "Blood-silver, silver-bloody." Their consanguinity is reenforced further by the concluding line of this stanza, where the head and the lyre address one another as brother and sister. The Hebrus in which the two streams are united is horror-struck by what it bears along. The application of the epithet « обмирающий » to the river creates a counterbalance for the lack of volition entailed in the downstream course of the head and lyre, as the river is itself overwhelmed and rendered helpless by what is transpiring in its course. As this metaphor leads us to understand, the individual poet, the individual poem, does affect the great stream of poetry by which it is absorbed.

In the third stanza Tsvetaeva focuses on the poet's pain when he is forced to relinquish his ties with the world of the living. When the head, filled with inconsolable longing, slows its progress down the river, the lyre insists that they must proceed, eliciting yet another expression of regret from the lips (« Но лира уверяла: мимо! / А губы ей вослед: увы! » [But the lyre persuaded: pass by! / And the lips after it: alas!]). Here the discord that underlies the apparent unity of head and lyre emerges explicitly. This discord throws a tragic light on the confluence of life's blood and the silver sound presented in the immediately preceding stanza. The horror suggested by the epithet « обмирающий » applied to the Hebrus now appears to derive from the disunity between the urgings of the lyre and the desires of the head, a disunity that is correlative with that between the poet and the nonpoetical mob which precipitates the violence to Orpheus. The application of the epithet "gentle" to Orpheus is now understood to signal not only fraternal affection, but also the meekness of self-sacrifice.

The suggestion of discord introduced in stanza three throws new light on the opening stanza as well. Its subdued, acoustically and rhythmically harmonious tone suggests that the lyre and the poet's lips are in concert as they cooperate to produce one phrase expressing a mutually shared regret at leaving the world behind—« мира жаль ». Yet this is not actually the case. As we can determine from the old orthography in which this poem was written and originally published, the lyre, in its half of the phrase, is saying not "world"—« мiр », but "peace"—« мир ». This distinction, however, cannot be determined aurally and Orpheus, like the modern reader considering this poem in new orthography, perceives only a homonym that can carry either of these meanings. He decodes the lyre's utterance as signifying "world" and accordingly expresses regret at parting from it. He does not realize that he has misunderstood the lyre, which urges him on to the peace of the realm of death and not to a contemplation of the world from which he is departing. In this seemingly small misunderstanding Tsvetaeva imbeds the tension between the poet's human desires and the dictates of his art. The poet, his apparent submissiveness notwithstanding, is pained by the destiny he must fulfill: he is reluctant to depart from the world of the living at the lyre's ineluctable demand. The epithet « обмирающий » that characterizes the Hebrus enhances the representation of the poet's singular and uneasy situation inasmuch as it contains both an echo of « мир » and clear semantic and acoustic ties to « умирающий » (dying), a word which although absent from the poem describes its central action.

Tsvetaeva's use of the ambiguity of « мир » provides an example of the subtle and complex function of polysemy in her writings. Her virtuosic manipulation of context and the associative capacity of language enable her to engage a panoply of meanings in her texts in very specific ways. This hallmark of Tsvetaeva's poetics is given particular attention in the later discussion of her cycle *Poets* and the *poèma New Year's*, but here we can already observe that she uses semantic ambiguity to reveal the effects of different perspectives on both the encoding and the decoding processes. The function assigned to the polysemy of language is a weighty one, for the way ambiguity is dealt with can be made to reflect both the encoder's and the decoder's points of vantage. Here the divergent meanings the word « мир » conveys to the lyre and the head reflect the different perspectives of the mortal and the eternal, the human and the poetic—antithetical states which the single word, like the poet himself, is capable of comprising.

The fourth stanza of the poem opens with a comparison of the river Hebrus to a gently rocking bed, a metonymically prompted simile reenforced in the second line of the subsequent stanza where the sea into which the river flows is referred to as the "cradle of swells" (« колыбель зыбей »). In this river, head and lyre are drawn steadily together, rounded into a circle of wholeness in which the fragments now participate and which subsumes the dismemberment of Orpheus, who returns to his origin.[22]

The noun « венец » introduces a panoply of images that expand the poem. « Венец » can be a crown or crowning point of something; it can refer to a wedding ceremony, a wreath, a garland, or a halo. These various meanings override the disunity of head and lyre, which are ultimately wedded to the same end, and also suggest the complexity of their interrelationship. They indicate, moreover, that the achieved unity of head and lyre is the ultimate moment of poetry in which life and death touch, and the ephemeral and the eternal come together.

In the last two lines of this stanza it is the lyre that flows with blood and the hair of the head that flows with silver. Here we observe the coincidence of opposites and the interrelation of unity and multiplicity that Tsvetaeva effects in poetry. The head and lyre are not simply conjoined in a circle of perfect and harmonious poetic unity. The reversal of their attributes indicates that each is immanent in the other and that this immanence is now fully revealed. The inevitable confluence of life's blood and poetry is underscored, yet the difficulty underlying that confluence remains ever in the forefront.

In the penultimate stanza the "descending staircase" of the river flows into the sea. The head and lyre move out of the river and out of the poem to come to rest on an island Tsvetaeva designates as the home of a mellifluously mendacious nightingale. This unnamed island is Lesbos, where, according to popular accounts of the Orpheus myth, the head was buried and the lyre enshrined in a temple. We may recognize in this detail of the myth a metonymic representation of the descent of Orpheus's shade into the underworld and the celestial commemoration of the lyre in the constellation Lyra. Tsvetaeva, however, opts for a literal reading that provides her with the opportunity to question what transpires after the poet's death. The detail of the sweetly singing nightingale does not appear in Ovid's *Metamorphoses*, but is found in the retellings of Schwab and Stoll, both of whom ascribe the exceptional quality of the bird's song on the island of Lesbos to the presence of Orpheus's remains.[23] Tsvetaeva adopts the image of the nightingale but characterizes the bird's outpourings as untruths. The impact of the verb « лжет »—already startling in this context—is accented by the emphatic pause that precedes it. Tsvetaeva's accentuation of this verb, the anonymity of the island, and the suggestive ellipsis with which she concludes the stanza signal her refusal to restrict the Orphic sphere of influence to a specific place and to equate the poet's essential being with his remains. This idea—one Tsvetaeva articulated frequently—found consummate expression in the *poèma New Year's* (1927), to which chapter 7 is devoted. In *New Year's*, confronting the death of Rainer Maria Rilke, Tsvetaeva asserts, « как места / Несть, где нет тебя, нет есть: могила » [just as there is / No place where you are not, no, there is: the grave] (*SP* 1:264). In "Thus Floated Head and Lyre" this notion is projected by the question that opens the concluding stanza and the question with which the poem ends. Tsvetaeva's reluctance to accept those details of the myth that specify and thus limit the whereabouts of Orpheus's remains indicates doubt not in the veracity of this information but in its significance. Only the confluence of blood and silver within the river is of consequence, for this confluence is a victory over the mortality symbolized by those remains, a victory over time and place.

The transition to eternity is prepared in the penultimate stanza where the river is described as a staircase descending into the "cradle of swells" (« колыбель зыбей »). This metaphor conveys most immediately the sea into which the river flows, an image supported by the arrival of head and lyre at an island in the third line of the stanza and by the salt wave which is addressed in the second line of the final stanza. At the same time, however, the image of the descending staircase suggests a descent into the underworld—here designated as the source of Orphic song. Thus a single metaphor indicates the separate progress of Orpheus's spirit and of his remains. As the head and lyre disappear from the field of vision in the penultimate stanza, the recognition of the subtly implied other world in this dual metaphor enables the reader to chart a course that leads beyond Orpheus's mortal remains to the realm where end and origin meet.

Popular recounters of the myth—and Schwab and Stoll are among these—generally conclude their narratives with the descent of Orpheus's shade into Hades, where the curtain falls on a happily reunited couple locked in eternal embrace. Tsvetaeva, however, focuses her attention, as we have observed, on the process of dying, which is here also the process of the coming-into-being of the individual poem within the broad lyrical current of the Hebrus. Orpheus's final attainment of Eurydice is of no more interest to her than the fate of his remains. The enactment of a transpersonal poetic destiny supersedes the gratification of personal desires.

In his reading of this poem Michael Makin recognizes in "the bare-headed woman of Lesbos" Sappho, with whom Tsvetaeva identifies. He notes "that the dismembered body of Orpheus the poet has been pulled from the waves by another poet" and describes this as an act of appropriation.[24] From the perspective of this study we may say that the concluding lines of Tsvetaeva's poem center the eternal return of Orpheus in the incorporation of poetic fragments into ever new texts that reconstitute the whole.[25] Yet even as the poet's remains are transformed into a metaphor for poetry, the poet, as Sibelan Forrester notes, is herself "caught in the 'net' of the paradigmatic Orphean 'fate.' "[26]

Like the lyric "Like One Somnolent, Intoxicated," "Thus Floated Head and Lyre" centers on the tragic destiny of the poet and the proximity of the creation of song to death. The difficulty of the poet's intermediary situation is underscored as he is ever torn between the mortal and the eternal, between life and death, between his human desires and the poetic imperative.

Tsvetaeva continued to avoid all those moments of joy, power, and glory which the myth affords Orpheus to focus instead on his apparent failures. It is possible to construe this representation as an attempt on her part to disenfranchise Orpheus and thus also those male poets she designates as his embodiments in order that they be more readily overcome. Indeed in the poem «Эвридика — Орфею» [Eurydice to Orpheus], to which the following chapter is devoted, an assertive female persona whom we may identify with Tsvetaeva herself reproaches Orpheus and emphasizes the error of his descent. Thus too Ophelia and the Cumaean Sibyl, discussed in chapters 3 and 4, are endowed with powerful voices to counter prevailing male attitudes.

Yet it is erroneous to regard Tsvetaeva's treatment of the myth exclusively as an attempt to establish her own supremacy. Her image of the abject, disenfranchised poet is emblematic of the difficult, tragic task to which he is called: to bridge two essentially incompatible realms both within himself and in the surrounding universe. The image is derived from the German Romantic tradition that teaches us to recognize in the poet's dejection an unmistakable sign of ascendancy. For Tsvetaeva the ultimate victory of the poet is relegated to a supramundane poetic space. As we shall find expressed in even stronger terms in the cycle *Поэты* [Poets], the focus of chapter 5, what appear to be signs of the poet's lowliness, weakness, or helplessness are to be construed as powerful indicators of his superior status.

Accordingly, in the lyrics just considered Tsvetaeva responds to the two moments of Orpheus's myth when he appears to be at his nadir—his failure to retrieve Eurydice and his death—to asseverate the victory of the poet in his struggle with the mere human.[27] Conspicuously absent from her treatment of the myth is Orpheus's legendary ability to move animals, trees, and stones with his song. Her only reference to this detail appears in a letter to Rilke of 12 May 1926, as a sarcastic comment on the absence of well-developed, individualized poetic perception among her readers: "Die alte Fabel von Orpheus und den Thieren, zu denen auch—Schaafe gehören?" [The old fable of Orpheus and the animals among which were also sheep].[28] Tsvetaeva refused to recognize in this detail of the myth a possible allegory of the poet's civilizing effect on primitive instincts or a demonstration of the poet's ability to fuse with and affect his natural surroundings. For her it represented a highly inappropriate, indeed dangerous, physical manifestation of the power of poetry. The admission of such proof displaces the poet's faith in his intangible art and runs counter to the selfless and even self-sacrificial aspect of the poet Tsvetaeva develops. Her remarks on Christ in "Excerpts from the Book *Earthly Signs*" reflect this position and are also directly applicable to the poet:

> Как мне жаль Христа! Как мне жаль Христа за его насильственные чудеса! Христос, пришедший горы двигать — словом! « Докажи, тогда поверим! »— « Верим, но подтверди! » Между чудом в Кане (по просьбе Марии) и испытующим перстом Фомы — странная перекличка. Если бы Мария была зорче, она бы, вслед за превращением воды в вино, увидела другое превращение: вина — в кровь . . .
>
> [How I pity Christ! How I pity Christ for his forcible miracles! Christ, who came to move mountains with a word! "Prove it, then we will believe!" "We believe, but reaffirm it!" There is an eerie correspondence between the miracle in Cana (at the request of Mary) and the probing finger of Thomas. Had Mary been more keen-eyed she would have seen on the heels of the transformation of water into wine another transformation: of wine into blood . . .] (*IP* 1:112; ellipsis in original)

In this context Orpheus's turn of the head to determine whether Eurydice is following him out of the underworld emerges as a gesture of doubt on the part of the poet, who seeks physical manifestation of the power of his song. The incompatibility of such proof and faith is correlative with the conflicts of flesh and spirit and of personal desire and the poetic imperative with which the poet is ever confronted.

The catabasis, as has been noted, is emblematic of the poet's privileged and yet impossible situation between two antithetical worlds of existence. On the strength of this duality Tsvetaeva successfully engages moments of Orpheus's apparent failure to proclaim the victory of the poet over the mere mortal who houses him. From the vantage point of the eternal-poetic, Orpheus's attempt to retrieve Eurydice is an error which must be rectified by the failure of the project. In this context, the fateful turn of the head emerges as a sign of the poet's recognition—whether conscious or unconscious—of the stern necessity that Eurydice be lost to him forever. The failure of the man to regain Eurydice marks the victory of the poet who sacrifices his gratification to his art.

However commendable, Orpheus's descent into Hades to retrieve Eurydice marks a confrontation with death that results in only temporary victory over it. It is his dismemberment—once again an apparent defeat—that leads to the complete and permanent transcendence of ultimate unity. Thus Strauss explains that Orpheus's "deepest meaning is to be found in his dismemberment by the Maenads and in the perpetuity of song that issues from his lips even after the *sparagmós:* he is divided and yet he is one, and so he guarantees the possibility of reassembling the shattered fragments."[29]

Tsvetaeva discerns in the dismemberment a coincidence of the poet's martyrdom with his ultimate victory over death. In her insistence on the poet's movement between the two worlds, Tsvetaeva offers a corrective to the Symbolists' longing to dissolve altogether their ties with this world. She recognizes that the impetus for poetry springs precisely from the restrictiveness of this markedly narrow world. The poet's intense frustration—whether the consequence of Eurydice's absence or of the limitations of his surroundings—generates the intense longing that impels him toward the other world. To remain in the other world, however, would obviate the need to engage in poetic activity. This notion is implicit in the myth of Orpheus, where the possibility that the bard simply remain with Eurydice after his initial entry into the underworld is never seriously entertained. Whether or not accompanied by Eurydice, he must return to the realm of the living. Back in the sensible world, he makes no attempt to take his own life in order to regain the coveted admission to the underworld.

Orpheus's apparent reluctance to die in order to join his beloved leads Plato, in the opening discussion of love in the *Symposium,* to write disparagingly of his emotions. Tsvetaeva, however, discerns in this element of the myth a sign not of cowardice or dearth of feeling on Orpheus's part but the fulfillment of the poetic imperative and the poet's destiny. Orpheus's translation into death, like Eurydice's into life, would preclude the intense longing out of which his mediating song is born. On the strength of Orpheus's unfulfilled desire, the urge to unite opposites implicit in heterosexual eros is expanded by the poet into a need to conjoin life and death.

Yet Orpheus's songs of longing for the other world inevitably entail rejection of the world around him and thus arouse the hostility that culminates in the *sparagmós*. The dismemberment realizes his metaphorical inner split and fulfills both his longing for the other world and his sacrificial destiny. In order for poetry to continue unabated after this fulfillment it is necessary for Orpheus to return. After the "final" descent attained through the dismemberment, Orpheus is made to reappear on our earth in ever new incarnations that ensure the perpetuation of song.

Chapter Two

Eurydice

> The hint half guessed, the gift half understood, is Incarnation.
> Here the impossible union
> Of spheres of existence is actual.
>
> —T.S. Eliot, *Little Gidding*

RECOGNIZING ORPHEUS as the prototypal poet, but barred by gender from identifying with him herself, Tsvetaeva entered the myth in the guise of Eurydice, whose voice resounds in « **Эвридика — Орфею** » [Eurydice to Orpheus], a poem written in 1923 and included in *После России* [After Russia, 1922–25, pub. 1928], Tsvetaeva's last collection of lyric verse.

In the poetry of *After Russia* the self-assurance of the full-fledged poet replaces the anxieties attendant on Tsvetaeva's entry into the poetic arena. As Antonina Gove observes, "No longer does the poet claim that the world bars her from self-affirmation as in the poems of the juvenile period. Her problem, indeed, appears to be the opposite—she can find virtually no one who is her equal in range and power."[1]

In Simon Karlinsky's judgment it is in the lyrics of *After Russia* that Tsvetaeva's "poetic craft reaches its highest peak, and her human and poetic stature its most awesome dimension and sweep."[2] Tsvetaeva's conception of the poet develops in proportion to her own artistic growth and the expanded range of literary sources that inform her lyrics. Karlinsky writes:

> Now her points of reference are Homer, Ovid, the Nibelungenlied, Shakespeare, Racine and Goethe. She remains in this collection her own passionate and rebellious self, but she is now also capable of a detachment that is almost Olympian. And, while using her personal experience and literature as her point of departure as she had always done, she now writes philosophical poetry that probes the nature of time, of space, of human speech and of communication.[3]

The lyrics discussed here and in the following three chapters come from this collection and reflect the verity of Karlinsky's assessment.

By the time Tsvetaeva wrote the poems of *After Russia,* Ovid's *Metamorphoses,* with its artistically more satisfying accounts of Greek myths, had joined Stoll and Schwab to provide the underpinning for the ancient Greek personae, images, and motifs that course through this collection of lyric verse. Like Stoll and Schwab, Ovid relates that Eurydice was stung by the serpent very soon after her marriage to Orpheus—so soon, in fact, that it remains uncertain whether their union was consummated. Unlike those retellings of the myth that describe Orpheus as losing his voice with the death of his beloved and recovering it only after his descent, in these versions Orpheus's longing for Eurydice finds expression in song and wins him admission to the underworld. Unfulfilled sexual desire throws into sharper relief the distinction between flesh and spirit that is central to the lyric "Eurydice to Orpheus."

"Eurydice to Orpheus" is focused entirely on the catabasis, now described from the perspective of the underworld by Eurydice, whom Orpheus comes to reclaim. In this lyric, as in the Ophelia-Hamlet poems discussed in chapter 3 and the *Sibyl* cycle analyzed in chapter 4, the woman is given a commanding presence and a powerful voice with which to articulate her view. Tsvetaeva frees Eurydice from her traditionally silent, passive role to endow her with an intelligent consciousness and replace acquiescence with self-assertion. Unlike Orpheus, who enters the other world without paying the price of death, Eurydice knows full well what has been exacted for her new existence. It is because she knows this that she desires no return. She expounds on existence from her newly attained perspective and faults Orpheus for the inappropriate intrusion of his physical desires into her incorporeal realm. Expressing her joy at being freed of her body she, like the Eurydice of Gluck's *Orfeo ed Euridice,* insists that she does not want to surrender her newly won eternity.[4]

Eurydice offers the perspective of one who is freed from the very body and erotic desire that lead Orpheus to Hades to retrieve her. She indicates a transvaluation of physical love. At the same time her reference to Orpheus as brother at the conclusion of the poem acknowledges the poet's close ties to the underworld. In the course of the poem it is Eurydice who instructs the silent Orpheus in the duality of perspective that is the prerogative of the poet. The vantage point on existence the underworld has afforded her is one that the poet must comprehend.

Tsvetaeva was not the first to give Eurydice a lyrical voice. Besides Gluck's opera she would have been familiar with Valerii Briusov's lyric « Орфей и Эвридика » [Orpheus and Eurydice, pub. 1904]. Briusov's Eurydice too is reluctant to follow Orpheus, whom she calls her brother, but she is a pale, feebly protesting creature who, in spite of her reservations, obediently trails after her erstwhile beloved. By contrast, Tsvetaeva's Eurydice is possessed of authority, a strong sense of self, and a clear voice with which to articulate her concerns. Her incorporeality argues for the surcease of erotic engagement but does not mitigate her recognition and understanding of the physical desire that motivates Orpheus.

This chapter focuses on "Eurydice to Orpheus," but the analysis of this lyric is postponed until Tsvetaeva's motivation for creating the Eurydice who emerges in her poem has been considered and the evolution of this persona has been described. To this end we shall first reconsider Tsvetaeva's attitude toward Orpheus-Blok to explore underlying reasons for her need to assert herself specifically vis-à-vis this profoundly admired poet. Then we shall examine Eurydice's principal antecedent, Jairus's daughter, whose resurrection Tsvetaeva considers in the lyric «И сказал Господь» [And the Lord Said, March 1917] and the two-poem cycle *Дочь Иаира* [Jairus's Daughter, 1922]. These preliminary excursions deepen our understanding of the function Eurydice assumes both in Tsvetaeva's lyric and in her artistic self-definition.

"Eurydice to Orpheus" provides the opportunity to trace concomitantly with the developing image of Orpheus Tsvetaeva's own mythos of self-realization and to recognize the extent to which she sought to structure her own life on the principles she expressed in her poetry. To a significant measure this lyric constitutes Tsvetaeva's reestablishment of the poetic self she had dissolved in praise of Orpheus-Blok in her earlier poems. Abandoning the anonymity of humble worshiper, she now assumes, in the guise of Eurydice, a superior stance which counterbalances her earlier self-effacement.

Tsvetaeva's need for self-assertion vis-à-vis Blok stems specifically from the failure of her project to effect a meeting with him. It is important to consider this failure because among the roles her Eurydice plays is that of avenger. Tsvetaeva's dissatisfaction with the stance she had herself adopted toward Blok is clearly heard in a letter written to Boris Pasternak on 14 February 1923, some five weeks before the genesis of "Eurydice to Orpheus":

> Пастернак, я в жизни — волей стиха — пропустила большую встречу с Блоком (встретились бы — не умер), сама — 20-ти лет — легкомысленно наколдовала: — « И руками не потянусь ». И была же секунда, Пастернак, когда я стояла с ним *рядом*, в толпе, плечо с плечом (семь лет спустя!), глядела на впалый висок, на чуть рыжеватые, такие некрасивые (стриженый, больной) — бедные волосы, на пыльный воротник заношенного пиджака. — Стихи в кармане — руку протянуть — не дрогнула. (Передала через Алю, без адреса, накануне его отъезда.)

> [Pasternak, in life I—at the will of a verse—missed a momentous meeting with Blok (had we met—he would not have died), I myself—at 20—frivolously augured: "And I will not reach out my hands." And yet there was a second, Pasternak, when I stood *next* to him, in a crowd, shoulder to shoulder (7 years later!), gazed at his sunken temple, at his slightly reddish, so ugly (he was shorn,

ill)—thin hair, at the dusty collar of his worn coat.—My poems in my pocket—I had only to reach out my hand—I didn't waver. (I sent them via Alia, with no [return] address, on the eve of his departure.)][5]

The moment Tsvetaeva describes in this passage occurred during Blok's 1920 Moscow visit. Her enigmatic and rather disturbing observation that, had they met, Blok would not have died appears to be in the words of Tsvetaeva's own Eurydice a « превышение полномочий »—an "exceeding of authority"—yet above all it signals the emotional intensity Tsvetaeva invested in the unrealized relationship.[6] The line she cites in her letter to Pasternak is from the lyric « Ты проходишь на Запад Солнца » [You Pass to the West of the Sun] which she had written to Blok in May 1916. Its subtext is « Свете Тихий », a Russian Orthodox prayer addressed to Christ, which is drawn into the service of deifying Blok. In it Tsvetaeva, in the guise of a humble, anonymous worshiper, promises to refrain from intruding on his sacred space by seeking his attention. Its fourth stanza opens with the avowal, « И по имени не окликну, / И руками не потянусь » [And I won't call you by name / And I won't reach out my hands] (*SP* 1:228). It is Tsvetaeva's fulfillment of the promise made in these lines that, according to her explanation to Pasternak, prevented her from approaching Blok when he was in Moscow.

Strictly speaking, this account is accurate, for Tsvetaeva did in fact refrain from introducing herself to the poet whose attention she would have prized. Yet what she neglects to mention to Pasternak is that she appears to have seriously expected Blok to seek her out when he visited the old Russian capital. A casual but revealing remark in a letter Tsvetaeva wrote to Anna Akhmatova on 26 April 1921—shortly before Blok's Moscow visit—indicates that she was not only anticipating a personal meeting with Blok, but apparently expected this meeting to draw her into closer contact with Akhmatova as well. Tsvetaeva's full-fledged membership in the Russian Parnassian community would thus be assured. In this letter Tsvetaeva, having delivered herself of hyperbolic praise of Akhmatova, writes,

> Пусть Блок (если *он* повезет рукопись) покажет Вам моего Красного Коня. (Красный, как на иконах.) — И непременно напишите мне, — больше, чем тогда! Я ненасытна на Ваши души и буквы.
>
> [Have Blok (if it is *he* who conveys the manuscript) show you my Red Steed. (Red as on icons.)—And write me without fail—more than that other time. I am insatiable for your souls and letters.][7]

Tsvetaeva had apparently envisioned a situation in which a poetic deity would not merely grant an audience at her request but would be impelled by the strength of her poetry to single her out. She sought recognition not as yet another admirer, but as a poet in her own right. Her poetic voice rather than her physical presence was to engage Blok.[8]

It is important to note here that even at moments of utmost reverence or glorification Tsvetaeva retains at least a tenuous link to the self she dissolves in praise. A jealously guarded life line, an anchor to the world of her inmost self, is what ultimately enables her to regain her equilibrium even after the most exhaustive of surrenders, which ultimately strengthen her voice. Thus we can observe that just as Tsvetaeva uses her lyric "You Pass to the West of the Sun" to explain to Pasternak the impossibility of reaching out for Blok's hand, so may we use another poem she dedicated to Blok to prove her certainty that their meeting would take place. In the poem « У меня в Москве — купола горят! » [In My Moscow Cupolas Blaze], also written in 1916, Tsvetaeva engages in some subtle poetic subterfuge or, perhaps more accurately, encodes in the public space of the poem an urgent personal message to Blok.

У меня в Москве — купола горят!
У меня в Москве — колокола звонят!
И гробницы в ряд у меня стоят, —
В них царицы спят, и цари.

И не знаешь ты, что зарей в Кремле
Легче дышится — чем на всей земле!
И не знаешь ты, что зарей в Кремле
Я молюсь тебе — до зари!

И проходишь ты над своей Невой
О ту пору, как над рекой-Москвой
Я стою с опущенной головой,
И слипаются фонари.

Всей бессонницей я тебя люблю,
Всей бессонницей я тебе внемлю —
О ту пору, как по всему Кремлю
Просыпаются звонари . . .

Но моя река — да с твоей рекой,
Но моя рука — да с твоей рукой
Не сойдутся, Радость моя, доколь
Не догонит заря — зари.

[In my Moscow—cupolas blaze! In my Moscow—bells ring! And sepulchres stand in a row,—in them sleep tsaritsas and tsars.

And you do not know that at dusk in the Kremlin it is easier to breathe than anywhere else in the world! And you do not know that at dusk in the Kremlin I pray to you until dawn!

And you pass over your Neva at the time when I stand over the Moscow River with my head bowed, and the streetlights flow together / grow heavy with sleep.

With all my insomnia I love you, with all my insomnia I heed you—at the time when throughout the Kremlin the bell-ringers awaken . . .

But my river—and your river, but my hand—and your hand will not come together, my Joy, until dusk catches dawn.] (*SP* 1:229–30)

In this poem Tsvetaeva once again proclaims her adulation of Blok. At the same time, however, she already moves toward establishing herself as a separate entity not completely subsumed by him like the one Eurydice was to become. Her own dictum that prohibited her from reaching out to Blok—that "deadly game" she describes bitterly in her letter to Pasternak—appears to be in full effect.

The first stanza demarcates her own Muscovite space (« У меня в Москве ») which she describes as the best place to be (« Легче дышится, чем на всей земле ») and which, her devotions notwithstanding (« Я молюсь тебе — до зари »), sets her apart from Blok's Petersburg.[9] The theme of their geographical distance, inseparable from the historical and cultural differences of which those two cities are emblematic, is continued in the third stanza. Here, however, all distinctions are undermined by the temporal simultaneity into which Blok in his Petersburg and Tsvetaeva in her Moscow are drawn. In stanza four the rapprochement of the two poets continues as Tsvetaeva proclaims her insomniac love for Blok and the intensity with which she heeds him:

Всей бессонницей — я тебя люблю,
Всей бессонницей — я тебе внемлю —

[With all my insomnia I love you, / with all my insomnia I heed you—]

The verb « внимать » [heed] places Tsvetaeva in the position of addressee and emphasizes the intensity with which she listens to Blok. The awakening bell-ringers mark the new day into which Tsvetaeva's nocturnal vigil has led.

The poem concludes with what appears to be an assertion that neither their rivers nor their hands can join: that there can be no meeting between the two poets. In fact, however, it is this very stanza that projects alternate forms of contact that transcend temporal and spatial norms. Tsvetaeva's river and Blok's river have come together in this poem. Moreover, if their "rivers" are understood in the metaphoric sense frequently assigned to them by Tsvetaeva of "poetry" (cf., e.g., the two Orpheus poems considered in the preceding chapter), the confluence has already been accomplished by the Blokian images, references, and subtexts that prevail in her *Poems to Blok*. The hand of the second line of the stanza is an image metonymically aligned with that of the river of poetry. The hand guides the flow of verse. Its fingers suggest by shape the tributaries of a river, and—perhaps more importantly—the tracery of veins in the hand resembles waterways. The prerequisite for the joining of rivers and of hands that this poem sets is the meeting of dawn and dusk. Although this condition may seem impossible to fulfill, this is not in fact the case. In Russian this meeting has already taken place within the single word « заря » that designates both times of day. Moreover, in the white nights of northern summers dawn and dusk do indeed converge, as Blok himself records in the poem « В северном море » [In the North Sea] in the lines

> . . . Руки
> Одна заря закинула к другой,
> И сестры двух небес прядут один —
> То розовый, то голубой туман.
>
> [One dawn/dusk has thrown its hands out to the other. And the sisters of two heavens spin one, now rose, now azure mist.][10]

Blok himself had bridged that space between Moscow and Petersburg that Tsvetaeva presents as an ostensible separation between them. Thus, for example, the 1909 poem « Все это было, было, было » [All This Was, Was, Was] includes an exuberant stanza describing a clear, crystal morning by the walls of the Moscow Kremlin. Even more apparent is the connection to Blok's poem « Утро в Москве » [Morning in Moscow], which begins just at that moment of the day to which Tsvetaeva's poem brings us and which affords a transparent opportunity for her to identify with its addressee. Thus, even as Tsvetaeva projects her artistic identity by aligning herself with Moscow, it is a Moscow from which Blok is not entirely absent.

Tsvetaeva's poem "In My Moscow" emerges as a declaration not only of the impossibility of her contact with Blok, but also of a fervent desire for its realization and the suggestion that their meeting has been preordained—in part by Blok's own verse. Yet however intense Tsvetaeva's own longing, in the vision she developed it was Blok who had to stretch out his hand to her. The subtexts to her poem suggest that Blok has already initiated this gesture in his own writings and now has only to recognize in her the rightful addressee of those lyrics. Tsvetaeva's dedications to him encourage this recognition.

The stipulation that Blok seek her out emerges from an anguished combination: a great need for recognition that bespeaks insecurity and a great pride that reflects certainty in her calling. Tsvetaeva's poetic renderings of the imaginative process habitually rely on personae who must wait to be singled out by the divine—be it a god or poetic inspiration. Thus, as we have seen, for example, in the poem "Like One Somnolent, Intoxicated," Tsvetaeva emphasizes the unexpectedness with which the poetic imperative manifests itself (« врасплох, не готовясь ») and the absence of personal volition in the poet himself. Similarly, the Sibyl considered in chapter 4 and the Virgin Mary with whom she is compared do not summon the divine. They are chosen. Although Tsvetaeva demonstrated somewhat less than perfect passivity she was waiting for Blok's divine recognition.

That Blok failed to play the part Tsvetaeva had assigned to him was a bitter disappointment that could only have contributed to her need to assert herself as she does in "Eurydice to Orpheus," where the Greek bard is cast as the silent pupil of a chastising Eurydice. Tsvetaeva was later to refer to the lyric "Eurydice to Orpheus" in a letter to Pasternak dated 25 May 1926, at a crucial juncture in her correspondence with another Orpheus—Rainer Maria Rilke. At that point she capitulated to a profound and painful sense of rejection when Rilke intimated that it might not prove possible for him to respond to all her letters and admitted that his Russian was insufficient for reading her poetry.[11] In that letter to Pasternak, Tsvetaeva cites "Eurydice to Orpheus" and ascribes to Eurydice full responsibility for the outcome of the catabasis:

> Оборот Орфея — дело рук Эвридики. (« Рук » — через весь коридор Аида!) Оборот Орфея — либо слепость ее любви, невладение ею (скорей, скорей!), либо — о Борис, это страшно — помнишь 1923 год, март, гору, строки:
>
> Не надо Орфею сходить к Эвридике,
> И братьям тревожить сестер —
>
> либо *приказ* обернуться — и потерять.
>
> [Orpheus's turning is the work of Eurydice's hands. ("Hands"—through the whole length of the corridor of Hades!) Orpheus's turning is either the blindness of her love, her lack of control over it (faster, faster!), or—oh, Boris, this is terrifying—remember the year 1923, March, the mountain, the lines:
>
> Orpheus must not descend to Eurydice
> And brothers disturb sisters—
>
> or the *command* to turn around—and lose.][12]

We shall return to this issue in the chapter Orpheus-Rilke. Here it is sufficient to note the degree to which the lyric "Eurydice to Orpheus" figures in Tsvetaeva's self-assertion specifically vis-à-vis male poets.

Yet however strongly Tsvetaeva's concentration on the error of Orpheus's attempt to retrieve Eurydice is motivated by a need to assert herself, it is important not to lose sight of the broader implications of this theme in her poetic world. Given that Tsvetaeva defines the responsibility of the poet in terms of moving between two worlds, it is inevitable that she subject the implications of this definition to strict scrutiny and that she seek to explicate what those necessary peregrinations entail. Were self-assertion the sole reason for its existence, "Eurydice to Orpheus" would be a far smaller poem than it is.

If we turn now to the poems in which Tsvetaeva addresses Christ's miracle of raising Jairus's daughter we can recognize that those earlier poems prefigure the main objections to returning the dead to the world of the living that Eurydice advances. The lyric « И сказал Господь » [And the Lord Said,

March 1917] from *Версты*, 2 [Versts, 2], and the two-poem cycle *Дочь Иаира* [Jairus's Daughter, 1922] from *Ремесло* [Craft] help us trace the evolution of her reading of the Orpheus myth—a reading that is both syncretic and exegetic—and deepen our understanding of "Eurydice to Orpheus."

We have noted already the parallel between Orpheus and Christ implicit in Tsvetaeva's *Poems to Blok* and have seen her juxtaposition of Orpheus's descent with the resurrection of Lazarus in "Excerpts from the Book *Earthly Signs*." In the lyric "And the Lord Said" the girl who has died, a precursor of Tsvetaeva's Eurydice, is granted her plea to be spared the return to earth to which Christ summons her:

И сказал Господь:
— Молодая плоть,
Встань!

И вздохнула плоть:
— Не мешай, Господь,
Спать.

Хочет только мира
Дочь Иаира. —

И сказал Господь:
— Спи.

[And the Lord said: "Young flesh, arise!"

And the flesh sighed: "Lord, do not disturb my sleep.

Jairus's daughter wants only peace."

And the Lord said: "Sleep."] (*SP* 2:19)

The child in this poem is described not as a disembodied spirit, but as "youthful flesh" (« молодая плоть »), a designation that argues for the appropriateness of her return to life on earth, as does the reference to her death as sleep, with its suggestion of immanent awakening. Tsvetaeva, however, construes this "appropriateness" as merely apparent and proceeds to undo Christ's miracle. Contrary to biblical accounts of the resurrection of Jairus's daughter (Matthew 9:18, 23–25; Mark 5:22–24, 35–42; Luke 8:41–42, 49–56), Tsvetaeva's poem gives the young girl a voice with which to express her desire to remain in the realm of death. This wish is countenanced by Christ and prevails over His initial command. The absence from the poem of the girl's father, whose bereavement prompted Christ to intervene, enables Tsvetaeva to focus more specifically on the clash of flesh and spirit, of mortality and eternity.

Already in this relatively early poem Tsvetaeva uses equivoques to demonstrate that the decoding process is correlative with the perspective of the decoder. Besieging the line describing the child's wish, « Хочет только мира », is that very ambiguity we have already observed functioning in the lyric "Thus Floated Head and Lyre": the coincidence of "world" and "peace" in the noun « мир ». This poem appeared even in its original publication in new orthography, and only contextual clues guide the reader's decoding of this word. Alexander Sumerkin, editor of the Russica edition of Tsvetaeva's poetry, felt that the awkwardness of the ambiguity here demanded commentary. The notes to this poem explain that intended here is the girl's desire for *peace* and that to decode « мир » as *world* is to misapprehend her request that her slumber remain undisturbed (*SP* 2:343).

At the time she wrote this poem Tsvetaeva had not yet attained that virtuosity at deploying the potential of polysemy that characterizes her later writings. Nonetheless, we note that Christ in this poem experiences no difficulty in understanding correctly what the girl intends. Responding without hesitation, He grants her the « мир » she wants. His immediate comprehension of the situation derives from the recognition that the girl uses "sleep" metaphorically to mean "death." If the word "sleep" were understood literally, the girl's request to be permitted to sleep could be construed as indicating a desire to be spared death, particularly in light of the Gospel accounts where Christ insists that the child is asleep *rather* than dead ("for the maid is not dead, but sleepeth," Matthew 9:24; "the damsel is not dead, but sleepeth," Mark 5:39; "she is not dead, but sleepeth," Luke 8:52). If sleep were intended as a literal rather than a figurative replacement for death, the subsequent line « Хочет только мира » would signal the girl's allegiance to the world of the living rather than her longing for the peace of death.

The mixed signals of the text in which Tsvetaeva imbeds Christ's decoding and which prompt Sumerkin's commentary suggest the difficulty of the choice that confronts Him and the child. The ease and certainty with which Jairus's daughter decides between life and death and with which Christ decodes her utterance reflect the perspective lent them by their knowledge of the other world. Were Jairus present in this poem he would doubtless have thought his daughter was pleading for return to the world of the living. Thus even as the child and Christ readily make the analogous choices between worlds and between meanings of the word « мир », it is given to the reader to experience an inkling of the difficulty entailed in deciding between them.

With "And the Lord Said" Tsvetaeva conveys a twofold rejection: first, of the desirability of life over death and second, of Christ's concretely realized miracle itself. Like Orpheus's ability to move trees, stones, and animals with his song, such miracles can only replace genuine faith with the shallow certainty of tangible proof.

Some five years later, in 1922, Tsvetaeva returned once again to Jairus's daughter. Her two-poem cycle *Дочь Иаира* [Jairus's Daughter] anticipates more closely the themes, imagery, and poetic mastery of the poem "Eurydice to Orpheus." In *Jairus's Daughter* Tsvetaeva considers the consequences of the accomplished miracle. Here neither Jairus's daughter nor Christ has a voice. We hear only a narrator who describes and evaluates the recorded events from a perspective that is markedly superior to that of both child and Savior. This narrator reproaches Christ for His "indifference" because He heeds the pleas of the bereaved rather than the dictates of the soul as He had in the earlier poem. Although in this cycle the girl is brought out of death to rejoin the living, Christ's miracle falls painfully short of complete success. Tsvetaeva's lyric represents the failure to reconcile the girl who has tasted death with the world of the living, a failure that would have attended also Eurydice's retrieval from Hades had it been accomplished.

Дочь Иаира

1

Мимо иди!
Это великая милость.
Дочь Иаира простилась
С куклой (с любовником!) и с красотой.
Этот просторный покрой
Юным к лицу.

2

В просторах покроя —
Потерянность тела,
Посмертная сквозь.

Девица, не скроешь,
Что кость захотела
От косточки врозь.

Зачем, равнодушный,
Противу закону
Спешащей реки —

Слез женских послушал
И отчего стону —
Душе вопреки!

Сказал — и воскресла,
И смутно, по памяти,
В мир хлеба и лжи.

Но поступь надтреснута,
Губы подтянуты,
Руки свежи.

И всё как спросоньица
Немеют конечности.
И в самый базар

С дороги не тронется
Отвесной. — То Вечности
Бессмертный загар.

Привыкнет — и свыкнутся.
И в белом, как надобно,
Меж плавных сестер . . .

То юную скрытницу
Лавиною свадебной
Приветствует хор.

Рукой его согнута,
Смеется — всё заново!
Всё роза и гроздь!

Но между любовником
И ею — как занавес
Посмертная сквозь.

Jairus's Daughter

1

Go past! This is a great mercy. Jairus's daughter has bid farewell to her doll (her lover!) and to beauty. This expansive cut (of garment) suits the young.

2

In the expanses of the cut the body is at a loss, after-death transparency.

Maiden, you cannot conceal that bone wanted to part from bone.

Why, indifferent one, contrary to the law of the rushing river,

Did you listen to women's tears and father's moaning, as opposed to the soul!

You spoke—and she was resurrected, and dimly, by memory, into the world of bread and falsehood.

But her gait is broken, her lips compressed, her hands cool.

And her extremities continue to grow numb as if half-asleep. And she won't stir from the precipitous road

Into the very midst of the bazaar—That is the immortal sunburn of eternity.

She'll grow accustomed and they will get used to her. And in white, as is proper, among her smooth sisters . . .

That is a choir greeting the young reticent with a bridal avalanche.

She is bent by his arm, laughs—everything anew! Everything is rose and cluster.

Yet between her lover and her—like a curtain—after-death transparency.] (*SP* 2:156–57; ellipsis in original)

In the first brief poem, a prologue for the more extended second, the narrator exhorts Christ to forego the resurrection of the girl. Death is described as a great boon that removes her from the chain of procreation. In the image of the doll—a metonymic representation of the realm of the living—Tsvetaeva conflates sexuality and maternity to highlight the domination of physicality and procreation in the world the girl has left behind. Thanks to the « великая милость » [great mercy] of death, the constraints of the body are replaced with freedom—the « просторный покрой » [expansive cut], a trope which subsequently opens the second poem of this cycle and which also finds its way into Eurydice's description of the underworld in the lyric "Eurydice to Orpheus." With the disappearance of the body, the confines of the spirit are removed and permit its expansion to the infinite proportions of the other world.

In the second poem the speaker addresses both the child and Christ before returning to an account of the events. The superfluity of the body in the other world is reasserted, and the child's own secret desire to be rid of it is revealed. As in the lyric "Jairus's Daughter," the girl is once again privileged—now on the strength of her prepubescence. She has not yet been enslaved by sexual desire and the biology of reproduction and is thus nearer to incorporeality. All the more reason, then, to level reproof at Christ, who remains unnamed in the poem, for His resurrection of the child. The accomplished miracle is described in expressly negative terms as a return of the girl "into the world of bread and falsehood" (« в мир хлеба и лжи »). This is the great "lie" of physicality on which Eurydice expounds in Tsvetaeva's later poem.

The girl's experience with death has altered her profoundly and she is now, for all of Christ's efforts, irrevocably alienated from the "bazaar" of the flesh-and-blood world. Contact with eternity has left an indelible mark that distinguishes her from those around her and demands a readjustment on both sides: « Привыкнет — и свыкнутся » [She'll grow accustomed and they will get used to her]. The configurations of enjambments and caesuras of stanza eight lend it a palpable awkwardness which is emblematic of the difficulties ensuing from the girl's return to life, where she can be neither content nor assimilated.

Even the passage of time—which must seem illusory from the perspective of eternity which the child has glimpsed—cannot eradicate the profound differences between Jairus's extraordinary daughter and the denizens of the sensible world. The intimation of the first poem that her doll presages the lover who will ensure maternity is here fulfilled. Her wedding, depicted as an unstoppable, crushing force, is to provide a new beginning for her recently recovered and now pubescent physical self. Death is to be replaced with sexuality. The girl is to be reborn into the realm of flesh and procreation—that life with a lowercase *l* Tsvetaeva had referred to in connection with Lazarus.

The facile assurances that her wedding will effect the girl's return to "normal" life presented in stanzas nine and ten and the promise of a new beginning given in stanza eleven are annihilated by the weighty "yet" which opens the final stanza of the poem. Tsvetaeva explicitly intensifies the sexuality of the girl's nuptials by referring to the girl's marriage partner as her lover and not as her spouse. The moment of heightened physicality projected in the consummation of her marriage is to bring about the girl's complete readjustment to life. Yet it is precisely at this crucial moment that her allegiance to the other world reasserts itself. The loss of body characterized in the opening stanza of poem 2 as «Посмертная сквозь» [After-death transparency] reappears in the final line to intervene between her and the expectant lover. In a creature who has once experienced what it is to be spirit the flesh cannot successfully regain ascendancy. For Jairus's daughter eros has been subsumed by death. Her union with death overshadows earthly coupling.

The implications of this poem extend beyond the immediate circumstances of Christ's raising of Jairus's daughter from the dead. The miracle provides Tsvetaeva with an opportunity to consider variations on the Orpheus myth and the new perspectives these variations open on the model for poetic activity she was developing. The first variable is the absence of eros: the retrieval of Jairus's daughter is free from the sexual desire that motivates Orpheus's transgression of the boundary separating life from death. Christ's purpose in performing the miracle is both transpersonal and aphysical. Accordingly, Orpheus's bodily descent into the underworld is superseded by Christ's voice bridging the two realms to accomplish the retrieval of the deceased: « Сказал — и воскресла » [You spoke—and she was resurrected]. Tsvetaeva's emphasis on the replacement of the body with the voice motivates her to omit from this poem the detail described in the Gospels of Matthew, Mark, and Luke that Christ grasped the girl's hand to lead her back into this world,[13] although elsewhere in her writing she accords considerable significance to this gesture.

At the same time, however, Tsvetaeva does not lose sight of the necessity of incarnation, a necessity Christ Himself exemplifies. Of particular importance to her is the opportunity the miracle provides to focus, now from the vantage point of an inhabitant of the other world, on the conflict between flesh and spirit that besieges Orpheus. In *Jairus's Daughter*, the child's imperfect return demonstrates what would have transpired had Orpheus returned Eurydice to life and highlights the error of such an undertaking. Although in the second poem Tsvetaeva states that Christ ought not to have reversed the girl's death at the behest of her mourners, the remainder of the poem reveals that this reversal has not in fact been fully accomplished. The girl is now among the living, but she has not been entirely resubjugated to the flesh. Christ's selfless, chaste, and "successful" return of the maiden to life is ultimately a failure, in contrast to which Orpheus's selfish, erotically inspired descent culminates in true, albeit paradoxical, victory: the failure of Eurydice's retrieval.

The parallel between Orpheus and Christ is obvious, but not exhaustive. In the girl's alienation from the surrounding world we recognize an essential feature of Tsvetaeva's poet. Because this alienation is consequent to her sojourn in and return from the other world, her situation is in this regard analogous to that of Orpheus himself. Yet despite the similarity of their positions, Jairus's daughter remains without voice even as she remains without name. In the absence of desire she remains completely passive and cannot develop into an adequate female counterpart to the Greek bard.

Just as she had done with the myth of Orpheus, Tsvetaeva ignores the larger interpretive framework that surrounds Christ's miracle. Thus she does not reflect on Christ's raising of Jairus's daughter as a literal prefigurement of that greater metaphorical transformation of death into eternal Life He was to accomplish with His own death and resurrection. Although such an understanding of the miracle expands dramatically any reflections on the relationship between the two realms of existence and, in fact, comes closer to Tsvetaeva's own views, she chooses to entertain only the narrative thread the miracle provides. The value she places on the process of developing connections and interrelations, coupled with a fierce independence of thinking, makes her reluctant to adopt any readings that have already been enshrined and at which she has not arrived through direct personal experience and contemplation. Tsvetaeva herself insists on tracing that unique, solitary path she describes Orpheus pursuing in her 1925 address to Konstantin Bal'mont cited in chapter 1.

Having considered the self-assertive function Tsvetaeva assigns to her Eurydice and the themes raised by her lyrical antecedent, Jairus's daughter, we are in a position to examine the lyric "Eurydice to Orpheus," giving particular attention to the way the poem's technical resources reproduce its thematic concerns. Orpheus's error in "Eurydice to Orpheus" parallels that of Christ in the *Jairus's Daughter* cycle. In this lyric, however, the retrieval fails as the passive, silently obedient child is replaced by an assertive Eurydice, who voices her objections and instructs the misguided male who seeks her return.

Эвридика — Орфею

Для тех, отженивших последние клочья
Покрова (ни уст, ни ланит! . . .)
О, не превышение ли полномочий
Орфей, нисходящий в Аид?

Для тех, отрешивших последние звенья
Земного . . . На ложе из лож
Сложившим великую ложь лицезренья,
Внутрь зрящим — свидание нож.

Уплочено же — всеми розами крови
За этот просторный покрой
Бессмертья . . .
До самых летейских верховий
Любивший — мне нужен покой

Беспамятности . . . Ибо в призрачном доме
сем — призрак *ты*, сущий, а явь —
Я, мертвая . . . Что же скажу тебе, кроме:
— « Ты это забудь и оставь! »

Ведь не растревожишь же! Не повлекуся!
Ни рук ведь! Ни уст, чтоб припасть
Устами! — С бессмертья змеиным укусом
Кончается женская страсть.

Уплочено же — вспомяни мои крики! —
За этот последний простор.
Не надо Орфею сходить к Эвридике
И братьям тревожить сестер.

Eurydice to Orpheus

[For those who have divorced themselves from the last shreds of the shroud (neither lips nor cheeks! . . .) Oh, is not Orpheus's descent into Hades an exceeding of authority?

For those who have relinquished the last ties with the earthly . . . For those who have laid aside on the bed of beds the great lie of beholding with one's own eyes, for the inward seeing—a meeting is a knife.

After all, this expansive cut of immortality has been paid for with all the roses of the blood. You who have loved to Lethe's very sources—I need the peace

Of amnesia . . . For in this ghostly house, *you*, the extant one, are a shade, and I, the dead one, am real . . . What then can I say to you but "Forget and abandon this!"

You know you can't disquiet me! I won't follow! No hands, after all, nor lips to press against lips! Female passion ends at immortality with the bite of a snake.

After all, this ultimate expanse has been paid for—recall my outcries! Orpheus must not descend to Eurydice, and brothers disturb sisters.] (*SP* 3:56; ellipses in original)

As in the second poem of *Jairus's Daughter,* the argument against return to the physical world is presented in a juxtaposition of its limitations to the expanse of the underworld. The « последние клочья / Покрова » [the last shreds / Of the shroud] which designate the body in the first stanza are replaced in the underworld with the acoustically similar « просторный покрой » [expansive cut] (stanza three)—an image also found in *Jairus's*

Daughter—and «последний простор» [ultimate expanse] (stanza six) of nonphysical being. Death, designated as a final resting place by «ложе из лож» [bed of beds] (stanza two), eliminates the enormous «ложь» [lie] of physical encounters. In "Eurydice to Orpheus" the argument against what in *Jairus's Daughter* is designated as «мир хлеба и лжи» [the world of bread and falsehood] is developed acoustically, upheld by that aspect of language whose ties to the physical world are the least fixed. The paronomastic chain created in stanza two with the lines «На *ложе* из *лож* / С*лож*ившим великую *ложь* лицезренья» (my emphasis) underscores the lie inherent in the realm of the flesh, where the excessive significance ascribed to visually verifiable presence and the consummation of love is correlative with the sovereignty of the fleeting moment. In the underworld the absence of both physical and temporal constraints obviates this lie. Eurydice's unsuitability to be Orpheus's flesh-and-blood wife is signaled by the archaism (an Old Church Slavic root with a modern ending) «отженивших» that marks her separation from her body, whose impermanence and insignificance are underscored by the metaphor «последние клочья / Покрова». Even as the moment of death eliminates eros, death itself ceases to be as mortality gives way to immortality—«бессмертье»—literally, deathlessness.

Eurydice recalls her moment of death and reminds Orpheus that her "deathlessness" is hard-earned: «Уплочено же — всеми розами крови / За этот просторный покрой» [After all, this expansive cut has been paid for with all the roses of the blood] and «Уплочено же — вспомяни мои крики!—За этот последний простор» [After all, this ultimate expanse has been paid for—recall my outcries!]. For her the surrender of flesh-and-blood and the concomitant disappearance of desire is a newly won freedom rather than a loss. With the sting of the very serpent who leads Eve to carnal knowledge, Eurydice is freed from the desires of the flesh: «С бессмертья змеиным укусом / Кончается женская страсть» [Female passion ends at immortality with the bite of a snake].

From the perspective of Eurydice's infinite realm of disembodied spirits, Orpheus's spatially and temporally restricted physical world cannot but appear ephemeral and unreal. For her the shard of realized potential of being that is granted the living is not possessed of any reality. It is Orpheus who is the ghost, and Eurydice who is fully realized—"real." In this context Orpheus's audacious, much-sung deed pales to become merely an error in judgment. Eurydice's ascendancy is indisputable. It is she who opens before him the unearthly perspective on existence that he must transmit in song.

At the same time, however, Orpheus's untoward appearance in her realm compels Eurydice to take stock of and comprehend her own situation. The antinomy male-female is subsumed by that of living-dead, and a new, unprecedented knowledge of existence is attained. As she comes to understand herself more fully, Eurydice also comes to know more of the poet, to draw nearer to being a poet herself. In the opening of her address to Orpheus she describes his flesh-and-blood appearance in the underworld as an act that exceeds the power vested in him. Yet by the end of the poem, even as she concludes with an admonition that Orpheus not descend to her, Eurydice acknowledges their kinship: «Не надо Орфею сходить к Эвридике / И братьям тревожить сестер» [Orpheus must not descend to Eurydice, and brothers disturb sisters]. Intimated here is the transgressive nature of Orpheus's descent. Yet at the same time there is a rightness in what Orpheus does: the familial ties Eurydice describes derive logically from her incorporeality which dictates the replacement of matrimonial love with fraternal. More significantly, Eurydice acknowledges Orpheus's ties with her insubstantial world and answers her initial question, «О, не превышение ли полномочий, / Орфей, нисходящий в Аид?» [Oh, is not Orpheus's descent into Hades / an exceeding of his authority?]. Orpheus's presence in the underworld is in and of itself proof of his right to be there. The plural of the final line of the poem signals the expansion of Eurydice's frame of reference and the admission of all poets' ties with the spirits of the other world.

Orpheus, possessed of a body and the desires it dictates, gains access to the underworld on the strength of a longing born specifically of the absence of Eurydice's body. Her sojourn in Hades perpetuates this situation and ensures the poet's continued translation of body into song. There is no way out for the poet. To return Eurydice to life is to recapture the body whose absence is necessary to the creation of song. For Orpheus to die is to lose the body that dictates the fertile longing for Eurydice. The production of poetry is dependent on the poet's impossible situation. The difficulty and the necessity of the poet's relations to the two complementary but mutually exclusive states remain central to Tsvetaeva's characterization of the poet. If we now examine "Eurydice to Orpheus" more closely we can observe how the poem itself models specifically this material and, more broadly, Tsvetaeva's cosmology.

In Boris Pasternak's lyrics of the twenties we can discern a concentrated effort to create a lyric landscape that, Cubist-like, presents simultaneously, and with no attempt at differentiation on the part of the poet, a variety of irreconcilable perspectives. Tsvetaeva exposes the Cubist conceit of presenting all options in simultaneity. Unlike Pasternak, she demands not an apprehension of several perspectives functioning simultaneously in a celebration of or mourning for our three-dimensional world, but rather the perception of one perspective at a time—always in full awareness that it is neither the only nor the ultimate one. Tsvetaeva's poetic urgency is fed precisely by the impossibility of sustaining perspectival simultaneity. Only at the moment of death, as we shall see in chapter 7, can this possibility be realized. Tsvetaeva's poet (and with her the reader) must ever change the position from which the word, the poem, and the universe are regarded. To this end the fluidity of signs is underscored and the myth of Orpheus is juxtaposed with the resurrections of Lazarus and Jairus's daughter, while Orpheus's own perspective is offset by Eurydice's view of existence.

If we turn now to a close reading of "Eurydice to Orpheus" we recognize that Tsvetaeva replicates her cosmogony in the composition of the poem. A complex structure of disruptive caesuras and unexpected enjambments recreates the collision of two mutually exclusive perceptual realms in the confrontation of Eurydice and Orpheus in the underworld. From her position Eurydice remonstrates with Orpheus for wanting to wrest her from her new capacious realm. Yet even as she recounts the hard-earned advantages of her space over the restricted world to which Orpheus seeks to return her, she begins to regain an awareness of her erstwhile physicality. Orpheus's presence overrides the effects of Lethe, and Eurydice is thrown into confusion by the interpenetration of their two distinct realms. As the strict, geographically articulated division between the world of the living and that of the dead is thrown into question by Orpheus's "unlawful" appearance before her, the formal boundaries and divisions of the poem undergo an analogous disruption. The sustained discrepancy between metrical lines and syntactic phrasing that Tsvetaeva effects is analogous to Orpheus's disruption of the demarcation between worlds. After Eurydice succeeds in putting the two incompatible realms of existence back into perspective, her agitation subsides and the metrical lines are realigned with syntactical units.

Tsvetaeva's principal strategy in this poem can be described as a complex manipulation of formal properties of lyric verse that create and/or emphasize divisions and those that function to smooth over or obviate them. This takes place in the climate of a dense, paronomastic texture that accentuates the thematic concerns of the lyric and acts as a forceful cohesive element, particularly at junctures of metrical and syntactic confusion.

The interactions Tsvetaeva sets up among technical elements of her poem capture the difficulty of the transition between the worlds of flesh and of spirit. The problem of reconciling these two realms is foregrounded with a series of enjambments that serve to emphasize rather than to override the divisions between the lines and stanzas that they bridge. These enjambments thus take on an iconic function: the heightened awareness of line boundaries reflects a heightened awareness of the distinction between the realms of the living and the dead. Concentrated in the first half of the poem, these occur after lines 1, 5, 10, and 13.[14] The most striking appears at the very center of the poem—between stanzas three and four, where Eurydice insists that Orpheus not rob her of the peace of amnesia (« беспамятность ») that accompanies her hard-earned deathlessness (« бессмертье »). The deliberate disruption of the flow of the poem that occurs here conveys the agitation Eurydice experiences upon encountering Orpheus. Yet Eurydice's recollection focuses not on what she has left behind in his world, but rather on the price exacted for her release from it (« Уплочено же — всеми розами крови » and « Уплочено же — вспомяни мои крики!— »), which is to say, on the imperium of the boundary between life and death. The sacrifice of body which was demanded of Eurydice is not exacted from Orpheus at that all-powerful dividing line which he crosses not with screams but with song. His oxymoronic presence in Hades *in corpore sano* is incomprehensible to Eurydice and elicits the turmoil represented in the crafted awkwardness of these stanzas.

The emphasis on the division between lines two and three of the third stanza and between stanzas three and four is accomplished by a false closure—an analogue to the "false closure" of the life from which Orpheus temporarily departs. The end of the second line in the third stanza brings the reader to what is perfectly acceptable as the end of a sentence: « Уплочено же — всеми розами крови / За этот просторный покрой ». The fact that this fully comprehensible syntactical unit coincides with the end of a line leads the reader to pause. Because the two immediately preceding lines coincide with syntactical units the expectation of a break here is particularly strong. Yet the subsequent line opens with an unexpected genitive that demands a reopening: Бессмертья—which is, appropriately enough, the genuine conclusion of the sentence—must be admitted into the phrase. This accomplishes an emphatic stress on "deathlessness" and demonstrates Eurydice's discomfort at having to admit Orpheus into her field of vision.

« Бессмертья » opens the penultimate line of stanza three and is followed by a pause. Six lines in the poem have pauses in precisely this position (after the first amphibrachic foot: I, 2; II, 2; II, 4; III, 3; V, 2; V, 3). Here the break is given special prominence by the ellipsis and the dropping of the continuation one line lower. (The persistent regular amphibrachic meter ensures continuity.) The length and intensity of the pause after « Бессмертья » is such that the severely retarded continuation of the line comes to sound like the opening of a new one. Aurally perceived, « До самых летейских верховий любивший » [You who have loved to the very sources of Lethe] would constitute one four-foot amphibrachic line fully in keeping with the metrical expectations engendered by the poem. The likelihood of perceiving this as one line is further increased by the conjunction of two additional circumstances: the smoothness of the enjambment between « верховий » and « Любивший » that overrides the line break and the emphatic pause immediately after « Любивший », which approximates the intensity of a line break. This creates a disjunction between actual line boundaries and aurally perceived units as a result of which the aural and visual perceptions of the poem come to be at odds here. In light of Tsvetaeva's tendency to align the aural with the other world and the visual with this world, we can recognize in this strategy another reflection of Orpheus's displacement of the division between life and death.

The boundary between the third and fourth stanzas is similarly problematic. Immediately after the word « Любивший », which opens the final line of stanza three and constitutes its first amphibrachic foot, we arrive at a pause signaled by a dash. The end of this line appears to coincide with the end of a sentence. This impression is intensified by the fact that it is also the end of the entire stanza and fulfills the rhyme anticipated in this position. This conjunction of the end of the line, the end of the stanza, and the accomplished rhyme with what appears to be a complete syntactical unit brings about a weighty stop that even the absence of punctuation cannot override. Because « До самых летейских верховий любивший » [You who have loved to the very sources of Lethe] could be heard as one line, the possibility is created that « мне нужен покой беспамятности » [I need the peace of amnesia] may be similarly regarded as one line. Yet this possibility is obviated by the weighty pause after « мне нужен покой ». Even as a readjustment of the perceiver's ordering process is demanded by the line break here, the confusion is prolonged by the fact that the strong sense of closure after « мне нужен покой » is undone by the genitive « Беспамятности » that ushers in stanza four. Just as after « Бессмертья », after « Беспамятности » a full stop is signaled. Yet here the fact that this stop is indicated by an ellipsis rather than a period undermines the sense of completion offered by the termination of the sentence.

This series of conflicting signals brings about a marked disjunction between the formal properties and the syntactical units of this poem precisely at those junctures of the lyric that depict Eurydice's disconcertion. At the same time, Tsvetaeva deliberately creates closures which are subsequently revealed as false and creates situations in which termination and (re)opening overlap, as, for example, when the word that ends a sentence also begins a new line or stanza. Thus, for instance, « Беспамятности » opens stanza four even as it completes the sentence begun in stanza three. These features operate in concert with the thematic material of the poem to represent the dissolution of boundaries which is the prerogative of the poet and to signal the fact that Eurydice is speaking from beyond. Implicit here is the replacement of the notion of death as termination with the concept of death as new beginning, an idea which is realized more fully in the *poèma New Year's*, where Tsvetaeva reconsiders the boundaries of existence in light of Rainer Maria Rilke's death.

The fourth stanza is less disorienting than the immediately preceding one, but the poetic lines do not yet fully recover their fluency. Eurydice's uncertainty is still palpable in the number and the intensity of pauses in this stanza. There are seven pauses within lines (three of which are particularly strong), and the breaks at the end of lines two, three, and four are emphasized by punctuation. Line four begins with a dash that magnifies the break between it and the preceding line. Yet although these stops give the stanza a halting quality, the clear, unambiguous articulation of the line boundaries allays the confusion found in the preceding stanza. The only enjambment in this stanza smoothly joins its first two lines. Eurydice moves now toward regaining her equilibrium as she comes closer to understanding and formulating the nature of her altered relationship with Orpheus.

Eurydice's contemplation of herself vis-à-vis Orpheus is emphasized metrically by two spondees. In line two of stanza four the italicized « ты » gains a hypermetrical stress which is followed immediately by the anticipated ictus—here the first syllable of « сущий ». The « Я » that opens the following line also claims a stress (albeit a weaker one)—unprecedented in this position in the poem—on the strength of the comma-dictated pause that comes after it. There follows the expected ictus—the first syllable of « мертвая ». The emphatic metrical isolation of the "you" and the "I" underscores their singularity and the impossibility of reestablishing those ties that had joined Eurydice and Orpheus while she was yet alive.

Eurydice fully regains her equilibrium only in the fifth stanza. Here anaphorae accelerate the tempo of the poem. Eurydice's assertion in the opening of this stanza that Orpheus cannot upset her has been gainsaid already by the structural turmoil of her utterances in stanzas three and four. Yet with her analysis of the situation, her agitation subsides and is gradually replaced with conviction. Her concluding exclamations reflect no longer a struggle to convince herself, but rather an urgent attempt to convey to Orpheus the particular point of view of which she is now fully cognizant. The lines are no longer structured disruptively or incongruously.

In the final stanzas Eurydice reiterates more firmly the arguments with which she began. Her earlier reminder to Orpheus that she has neither lips nor cheeks is now augmented with the observation that she has neither arms to embrace Orpheus nor lips to press against his (« Ни рук ведь! Ни уст, чтоб припасть / Устами! »). The awkward enjambment between lines two and three—the only one in the stanza—proves again Eurydice's capacity to distinguish between the two realms of existence and the needs of spirit and of flesh. The line break separating « припасть » and « Устами » simulates the impossibility of a physical encounter with Orpheus. Yet even as Eurydice insists on the incongruity of Orpheus's desire in the underworld, it is clear that her confrontation with this incongruity has deepened her awareness of herself and the new world she inhabits.

The two opening lines of the final stanza echo those of stanza three. Regression to a state of agitation threatens only briefly in the metrical and intonational disruption that marks her recollection of her own transition from life to death articulated by her screams (« вспомяни мои крики! »). But now Eurydice is not to be put out. Even as her discomposure was conveyed by the disjunctive incongruity developed among syntactical units, caesuras, enjambments, and line and stanza breaks, here Eurydice's certitude is demonstrated in an unprecedented harmony among these very elements. Her final exhortation to Orpheus derives from the perspicacity she gains from meeting his challenge. Couched as a smoothly flowing statement, it carries a forceful authority in the context of the turbulent exclamatory outcries that lead up to it: « Не надо Орфею сходить к Эвридике / И братьям тревожить сестер » [Orpheus must not descend to Eurydice, / and brothers disturb sisters].

The extraordinary circumstances with which she has been confronted have led Eurydice to a multifaceted conclusion. Her reference to herself in the third person reasserts that, together with that "shroud" of her body, she has cast off the earthly identity which Orpheus's sudden appearance made her recall and underscores her distance from that erstwhile Eurydice whom Orpheus seeks. The absence of body on which physical passion depends leads her to describe their new relationship as that of sister and brother. This conclusion is not unexpected: Eurydice has emphasized the incorporeality which obviates eros throughout the poem. Significant here, as we have observed, is Eurydice's transformation of the specificity of her own situation into a statement of universal acknowledgment of the kinship of all poets with the bodiless, immortal shades. The concern articulated in the opening of the poem that Orpheus may be exceeding his authority in defying the formidable boundary between life and death gives way here to a recognition of his ties with the underworld that retroactively justifies his appearance. Orpheus is banned not from making the descent, but from seeking to return Eurydice from aphysicality to eros.

In "Eurydice to Orpheus" the full-voiced Eurydice initiates the silent Orpheus into the infinite and eternal perspective of her realm. The poem implies that it is her instruction that persuades Orpheus to abort his project with the turn of his head. Credit for the consequent victory of poet over man thus rightfully goes to Eurydice, who issues the « *приказ* обернуться — и потерять » [the *command* to turn around—and lose] that Tsvetaeva speaks of in her 25 May 1926 letter to Pasternak.[15]

In the course of her work on the poems of particularly the first part of *After Russia*, Tsvetaeva was absorbed in the writings of both Rainer Maria Rilke and Friedrich Hölderlin, a poet who also influenced Rilke's artistic development. These two poets in particular guided Tsvetaeva in her own translations of an intense, unfulfilled longing for Boris Pasternak into some of the most powerful lyrics of *After Russia* and provided artistic and spiritual guidelines crucial to her deliberations on the nature of the poet.

Having considered Tsvetaeva's Eurydice as she evolved out of her antecedent, Jairus's daughter, we must note another poetical Eurydice whom Tsvetaeva's persona of Orpheus's beloved resembles in important ways. This Eurydice appears in Rilke's much anthologized "Orpheus. Eurydike. Hermes" (1904), a lyric included in *Neue Gedichte,* a collection Tsvetaeva read in Prague in 1922. In connection with Tsvetaeva's Eurydice it is important to note Rilke's—both because his image of Orpheus's beloved affected the one that emerges in Tsvetaeva's lyric and because, as described in chapter 6, he was himself destined to become an incarnation of Orpheus for Tsvetaeva. (Chapter 4 touches on the influence of other lyrics of *Neue Gedichte* on Tsvetaeva's Sibyl.)

Because Rilke's poem is written in the third person, none of its characters has an individual voice. His serenely self-contained Eurydice seems very unlike Tsvetaeva's dynamic persona, and yet there is a distinct similarity: Rilke's lyric represents a woman who is, like Tsvetaeva's Eurydice, fully self-sufficient. Rilke achieves for his female persona that allegiance to a superior existence that Tsvetaeva herself sought both in her art and in personal relations. Both poets accord an indisputable ascendancy to the female, characterized by a wholeness of vision inaccessible to the male.

In her penetrating discussion of "Orpheus. Eurydike. Hermes" the poet Elizabeth Sewell remarks on Rilke's identification with Eurydice rather than with Orpheus and notes his "long, loving, cherishing, utter rejection of sex and fertility" and "the rejection of sex between man and woman in marriage . . . in favor of restored, insulated self-hood for the woman."[16] Tsvetaeva's close identification with Jairus's daughter and particularly with Eurydice generates a new perspective on the narratives of both miracle and myth. Recounted specifically from the point of view of the conventionally passive, often silent women, the tales imply an innate capacity on the part of the female to relinquish ties with the physical world and to translate loss into gain. Tsvetaeva's reading of Rilke contributed significantly to her own achievement of this.

Charles Segal, who has called "Orpheus. Eurydike. Hermes" "modern poetry's richest retelling of the classical myth as a single sustained narrative," notes that the shift from a male to a female point of view is paralleled by "Rilke's shift of perspective from exteriority to interiority, from relation to enclosure."[17] These correlative shifts of perspective are implied in Tsvetaeva's Eurydice lyric and are fully realized in her Sibyl cycle, the focus of chapter 4.

The effect of Rilke's lyric on Tsvetaeva is indisputable. At the same time, however, Tsvetaeva's Eurydice differs significantly from both her image of Jairus' daughter and Rilke's representation of Orpheus's beloved. For Tsvetaeva's Eurydice, complete indifference to the upper world is replaced by dynamic self-assertiveness and a direct engagement of the implications of Orpheus's appearance in the underworld. This Eurydice is not contented in her knowledge and demonstrates a distinct need to draw what she has learned to the attention of the male. Her Eurydice, although ultimately preferring the netherworld, is not so completely and irrevocably separated from the land of the living or from the sway of love as is Rilke's—hence her palpable agitation at Orpheus's appearance. Tsvetaeva was not prepared to surrender Eurydice's capacity to affect and be affected by Orpheus. In her remarks on this poem in the letter to Pasternak of 25 May 1926, she writes:

> Все, что в ней еще любило — последняя память, тень тела, какой-то мысок сердца еще не тронутый ядом бессмертья, помнишь?
> . . . С бессмертья змеиным укусом
> Кончается женская страсть!
> все, что еще отзывалось в ней на ее женское имя — шло за ним, она не могла не итти, хотя, может быть, уже не хотела итти.
>
> [Everything in her that still loved—the final memory, shade of her body, corner of her heart not yet touched by the poison of immortality, remember?
> . . . Female passion ends at immortality
> With the bite of a snake!
> everything in her that still responded to her woman's name—followed him, she couldn't not follow, although, perhaps, she no longer wanted to follow][18]

Tsvetaeva's reluctance to relinquish completely that physical desire for whose abandonment both Jairus's daughter and Eurydice so eloquently plead derives from the relationship between poetry and eros she perceives the Orpheus myth to document. The myth lends a particularly fertile space for the exploration of this complex relationship, particularly as it is thrown into question in the realm of death. In his study of Orpheus, Segal points out that "the early Greek vocabulary for the appeal of song draws a parallel between the literally fascinating (Latin *fascinum,* magical charm) power of language and the power of love, between erotic seduction and the seduction exercised by poetry."[19] This association persists throughout Greek literature and is central also to Tsvetaeva's deliberations on her art. Eurydice's responsiveness to Orpheus's presence reflects the interdependency of eros and poetry.

We have observed that in her treatment of the Orpheus myth Tsvetaeva represented poetry as emerging from the translation of the eros that characterizes the desires of the mortal individual, the "mere human," into the transpersonal, transcendent language of poetry. The confrontation between Eurydice and Orpheus suggests that, although interdependent, eros and song are not interchangeable. Orpheus is wrong to seek an exchange of the poetry that has gained him admission into Hades for the erotic fulfillment implicit in his retrieval of Eurydice. This too, however, is as it should be, for neither can poetry successfully replace eros, the source of and motivation for its generation. Tsvetaeva allows the power of death to negate the ascendancy of eros, but not to deny it participation in the act of transcendence.

Here the question arises as to what then, if not Eurydice, the poet must bring back with him as he makes his own necessary return to the upper world. The retrieval of Eurydice from the other world would appear to be a highly appropriate metaphor for the act of translation between the invisible and the visible worlds in terms of which Tsvetaeva defines poetry. That this is not the case is made clear in her lyrics about Jairus's daughter and in the response that Orpheus's appearance in the underworld elicits from Eurydice. If the embodiment of the otherworldly is a perversion of the poetic imperative, what then does that imperative demand? What is the purpose of the Orphic descent and return?

Tsvetaeva's Eurydice reminds the poet that like any good translator he dare not overlook the powerful forces of context and perspective in determining essential meaning and in considering the appropriateness of his rendering. To bring Eurydice herself back into the limited world would be a translation so literal as to lose meaning. From the arguments Tsvetaeva projects in the cycle *Jairus's Daughter* and the lyric "Eurydice to Orpheus" we may educe that the poet is to return from his journey to the beyond with two intangible, closely interrelated qualities: an intense longing for that mysterious, unbounded realm into which he has been granted insight and—consequent to that insight—a new perspective from which to regard the world to which he returns, a new light in which to appraise his surroundings.

Tsvetaeva's emphatic denial of Christ's raising of Lazarus and Jairus's daughter and her forceful rejection of Orpheus's attempt to retrieve Eurydice specify that although embodied in "earthly signs" the intimations of the beyond that the poet brings to our world are not to undergo a substantive transformation. The poet's translations must not reimpose the spatial, temporal, causal, and physical boundaries of the mundane. The immaterial is to be indicated but is not itself to become part of the material world. The otherworldly must instead be recreated by signs chosen, ordered, and presented so as to point beyond themselves. Flesh must be replaced by the word which, like the poet, mediates between worlds. After the catabasis the generative force of eros is replaced by that of death. The songs of longing, loss, and mourning inspired by Eurydice's death are thus exemplary poems in Tsvetaeva's definition.

Eurydice's proscription together with Orpheus's felicitous failure to retrieve her are indicative of those precarious negotiations between body and spirit, between the ephemeral and the infinite, between the personal and the transcendent, and ultimately between life and death which the poet must ever conduct. In Tsvetaeva's poetic universe these opposing forces do not find resolution. They must instead remain engaged in a dynamic tension that safeguards against stasis and leads to an active comprehension of that universe. It is because he is a poet that Orpheus gains audience with Eurydice in Hades, and yet it is also because he is a poet that he must return to the realm of the living without her.

The expansion of Eurydice's understanding results from her struggle to resolve the apparently irreconcilable antinomies that are activated by Orpheus's appearance in the underworld. In this Eurydice approximates the poet. So too the agitation Tsvetaeva makes so palpable in "Eurydice to Orpheus" is comparable to that of the poet entering the creative state, as described, for example, in "Like One Somnolent, Intoxicated." In considering the coming-into-being of the Sibylline prophetess in the opening poem of the *Sibyl* cycle, we shall encounter a pattern similar to that of "Eurydice to Orpheus": the Sibyl's temporary state of discomposure—occasioned by an unexpected simultaneity of antipodes—gives way to a forceful certitude as her struggle to encompass them leads to expanded comprehension. In the *poèma New Year's* (chapter 7) it is Tsvetaeva herself who recapitulates this process.

Yet before we extend our exploration to those works and what they contribute to defining the poet, it is necessary to make a brief detour to consider a persona Tsvetaeva engages to project what the poet must *not* be. From the simple exercise of consulting an alphabetized index of Tsvetaeva's poems we can quickly recognize the tremendous energy she invested in considering what something is *not*, for the number of lyrics that open with "no," "not," or "no, not" is remarkably high. As Tsvetaeva herself observed in the essay « Световой ливень » [A Downpour of Light], « Только путем нет можно установить наличность да: отдельность » [Only by means of no is it possible to determine the presence of yes: distinctiveness] (*IP* 1:137). Our detour is thus a well-motivated excursion intended to throw into relief the attributes Tsvetaeva ascribes to the poet. Moreover, this sally into the realm of the "antipoet" is dictated specifically by the lyric just considered.

Less than a month before writing "Eurydice to Orpheus" (23 March 1923) Tsvetaeva completed the poem « Офелия — в защиту королевы » [Ophelia—in Defense of the Queen, 28 February 1923], a monologue in which Ophelia's tone is strikingly similar to the one in which Eurydice chastises her male counterpart. Moreover, the meter of the two poems is nearly identical, a circumstance that compellingly urges the reader to consider the two poems side-by-side. Upon doing so it is not difficult to recognize in "Ophelia—in Defense of the Queen" a situation that complements the one projected in "Eurydice to Orpheus." In the latter poem Orpheus leaves the realm of the living to confront the dead Eurydice who controverts his physical desires. In the former Ophelia leaves the realm of the dead to confront the living Hamlet to argue fervently for the consummation of love. The juxtaposition of these two lyrics urges us to counterpose Orpheus, the genuine poet, with Hamlet, the antipoet, the focus of the following chapter.

Chapter Three

Hamlet the Antipoet and Ophelia

So much for him.
—Shakespeare, *Hamlet* (I, ii)

OVID'S *METAMORPHOSES* provided Tsvetaeva with more than another version of the Orpheus myth to complement the accounts of Stoll and Schwab. Ovid's recasting of the Greek myths demonstrates brilliantly the power of context to effect metamorphosis. Central to Ovid's work are not only the various mythic and metaphorical transformations of its fabulous creatures, but also the transformations of our readings of its tales accomplished by the ever changing configurations into which he draws the narratives. This characteristic leads Charles Segal to comment on the broad spectrum of readings of the *Metamorphoses* and to conclude that Ovid's "use of the narrative frame creates multiple refractions (though not infinite possibilities) for each myth and lets us draw more than one possible conclusion or a single, simple moral."[1]

Tsvetaeva too insists on creating her own contexts. Her rejection of existing interpretations frees her to draw myths into configurations that accentuate their potential signification. Clearly this is not something Tsvetaeva learned only from Ovid. We have already witnessed her own propensity for topological thinking—the recognition of constants in disparate narrative contexts—on the strength of which she connects, for example, the myth of Orpheus with Christ's raising of Lazarus and Jairus's daughter. In *After Russia* kaleidoscopic groupings and regroupings of recurring personae, motifs, and images create a dynamic contextual environment that generates ever widening interrelationships among these elements, thus bringing to light ever new aspects of their particularity. The Orpheus myth too is shaped and reshaped by its environment and must be considered in light of the configurations into which Tsvetaeva draws it. Although, as Tsvetaeva herself maintains, chronology is crucial to an understanding of her poetic development, her exploration of possibilities afforded by the Orpheus myth is best pursued with an achronological approach modeled on her kaleidoscope metaphor of constant regroupings of given elements.[2] One such configuration involves Hamlet, a persona whose failings highlight Orpheus's success, and Ophelia, whose argument complements that advanced by Tsvetaeva's Eurydice.

Because Tsvetaeva's Hamlet serves as an example of what the poet must not be, the negative characteristics he embodies help to define the qualities that she ascribes to the genuine poet. Her Hamlet lyrics explore from another perspective the interrelation of eros, poetry, and death that is central to the Orpheus myth. If in Orpheus's desire for physical gratification Tsvetaeva saw a struggle between man and poet, in Hamlet's rejection of erotic desire she sees the failure of both. Hamlet's denial of sexuality spills over into a mistrust and dislike of words. Opposed to Orpheus's productive transformation of erotic desire into transcendent song that spans the upper and nether worlds is Hamlet's denial of love and language that leaves him cut off from both the living and the dead. Orpheus's specifically poetic urge to comprehend antinomies—flesh and spirit, man and poet, life and death—is not operative in Hamlet. Confronted with similar antinomies, the prince of Denmark fails to recognize their interdependency. He erroneously assumes that they are fixed in eternal opposition and that he can therefore remain constant to only one *or* the other. The impossibility of making such a choice leaves him stranded between them. The very tension that propels the poet is the source of the antipoet's paralysis. Having denied eros and language, Hamlet is left without the means either to live or to transcend life.

This chapter examines the antipoetical nature of the prince of Denmark as he appears in Tsvetaeva's three Hamlet poems: « Офелия — Гамлету » [Ophelia to Hamlet], « Офелия в защиту королевы » [Ophelia in Defense of the Queen], and « Диалог Гамлета с совестью » [Hamlet's Dialogue with His Conscience].[3] Originally published in 1924 as a cycle titled *Гамлет* [Hamlet],[4] these lyrics appear in *After Russia* as individual poems and are so treated in this discussion.[5]

Russian readings of both Greek mythology and Shakespeare were shaped primarily by the Romantics. The Romantic era is characterized by Dorothy Zayatz Baker as one "of transition in which the poet gradually abandons the pastoral, vatic image of . . . Orpheus and begins to confront the tragic aspects of the mythology."[6] The shift of emphasis from Orpheus as vatic bard to Orpheus as hapless victim was inherited by modern poets whose search for a self-image reflected a growing uncertainty in the power of the poetic word and the relevance of poet and poetry. The image of an ineffectual, tragic Orpheus that came to the foreground modulated smoothly into the Greek bard's eventual identification with Hamlet, who was similarly engaged to project the poet's self-perpetuated alienation from the surrounding world. As German Romantic, French Symbolist, and Russian Symbolist poets reshaped both the myth and the tragedy, enlisting each in the service of representing the poet's situation in a hostile, uncomprehending environment, the Greek bard and the Danish prince were steadily drawn into ever closer proximity. Thus, for example, Walter Strauss notes the unmistakable ties between Orpheus and Hamlet in the poetry of Stéphane Mallarmé.[7]

The interweaving of myth and tragedy makes an early appearance also in the literary career of Tsvetaeva's "Orpheus," Aleksandr Blok. Thus, for example, in his poems « **Я шел во тьме к заботам и веселью** » [I Walked in Darkness toward Cares and Merriment, 2 August 1898] and « **Дома растут, как желанья** » [Houses Arise, Like Desires, 5 November 1902], Orpheus and Hamlet are virtually indistinguishable. Eleanor Rowe observes that "like so many other Russian writers, Blok identified personally with Hamlet."[8]

In shaping the image of this new representative of the poet who assumed a place next to Orpheus, Blok, like other Russian Symbolists, drew on readings of *Hamlet* richly and abundantly supplied by the German Romantics to complement earlier assimilations of that tragedy that had been used to articulate both literary and sociopolitical concerns in nineteenth-century Russia.[9] Rowe succinctly describes the prevailing images of the Danish prince at that time:

> A Hamlet who is either weak of will, overactive of intellect, or decadent in character (to oversimplify the respective positions of Goethe, Friedrich Schlegel, and August Wilhelm Schlegel) reappears continually in the literature of nineteenth century Russia. Frequently two, and occasionally all three, of these qualities are operative in the "Hamletism" which seems to have pervaded large segments of Russian culture and life.[10]

The Symbolists distinguished in these attributes the signs of a distinctly poetic nature. Tsvetaeva, however, regarded these very traits as expressly antipoetical. For all her admiration of Blok, she refused adamantly and pointedly to align Hamlet with Orpheus or to admit him into her gallery of personae of the true poet. The proximity of Orpheus and Hamlet in Blok's poetry and his own identification with the Danish prince may well have prompted Tsvetaeva's self-assertion in the voices of both Eurydice and Ophelia as she sought to create a poetic dialogue with him.

However prominently alienation from the surrounding world figures in Tsvetaeva's definition of the poet, she remains convinced that to focus exclusively on that alienation itself is to lose touch with the perceptual advantages it affords. Indeed, in Tsvetaeva's eyes, the estrangement of the poet makes the poetic imperative all the weightier and demands not a Hamlet-like vacillation, resignation, or withdrawal, but an energetic counterattack on the tyranny of those perceptual norms that effect the alienation. For her an unpoetical environment is a demand for poetic activity and not an excuse for ineffectuality. Ultimately Tsvetaeva sees Hamlet's situation as a reflection not of alienation that impels the poet to launch attacks on his surroundings, but rather of abstraction that severely restricts his scope of vision, removes him from language, and traps him—divided from himself—in a divided world.

This view left Tsvetaeva with little sympathy for Hamlet as a poetic model. For her he became a representative not of the poet, but of his antithesis. In an attempt to counteract the growing tendency to focus on the poet's ineffectuality, Tsvetaeva insists on Hamlet's inadequacy as a poetic model through Ophelia, whom he has wronged. Thus her Hamlet is cast in the role of antipoet, while her Ophelia plays a role analogous to Eurydice's in instructing her male counterpart. Yet where Orpheus was chided for misdirected love, Hamlet is reproached for the absence of emotion.

Given Ophelia's ascendancy in Tsvetaeva's lyrics, it is helpful to note that, for all their preoccupation with both Orpheus and Hamlet, the German Romantics do not overlap these personae in the service of representing the poet. For them it is Ophelia who is linked closely to poetry. Thus, for example, Heinrich Heine, who ranks high on the list of Tsvetaeva's favored poets, saw in Ophelia, as Stefan Bodo Würffel convincingly argues, an allegory of poetry informed by the Romantically conceived, irresoluble conflict between art and life that the image of Ophelia extends also into the realm of death.[11] Würfel writes: "Independently of the drama in which she plays an important but nevertheless secondary role, and independently of Hamlet, she has emancipated herself after a singular manner, not so much as a character, but as an image. . . ."[12]

Tsvetaeva's Ophelia too is emancipated and becomes the spokeswoman of poetic truth; it is she rather than Hamlet who invites comparison with Orpheus. Certainly the image of Ophelia floating downriver toward the other world, absorbed in song, is suggestive of the Greek bard's final descent. Nor would the acoustic proximity, particularly strong in Russian, of the names Orpheus and Ophelia (« Орфей »—« Офелия ») be lost on Tsvetaeva. Yet she grants Ophelia an autonomy and certitude that take her well outside the male poetic tradition. Her Ophelia bears no vestiges of the helpless victim portrayed by the Romantics or by Tsvetaeva's more immediate predecessors, the Russian Symbolists.

Russian Symbolists devoted considerable attention to Ophelia and Hamlet. Even a cursory survey of some of the major lyrics devoted to the unhappy pair reveals that this relationship was construed to suggest at least implicitly the relationship of muse and poet, the poet identifying with Hamlet and thus acknowledging a sense of guilt and ineffectuality before his muse.

Blok, who in an amateur production in the summer of 1898 played Hamlet opposite his wife-to-be, Liubov' Dmitrievna Mendeleeva, devoted an entire series of poems to Hamlet and Ophelia. Among these are « Она молода и прекрасна была » [She Was Young and Beautiful, 27 July 1898],

« Есть в дикой рощи у оврага » [In the Wild Grove by the Ravine There Is, 3 November 1898], « Офелия в цветах, в уборах » [Ophelia in Flowers and Adornments, 30 November 1898], « Песня Офелии » [Ophelia's Song, 23 November 1899], « Прошедших дней немеркнущим сияньем » [By the Undying Glow of Bygone Days, 28 May 1900], « Песня Офелии » [Ophelia's Song, 23 November 1902], and « Я — Гамлет. Холодеет кровь » [I Am Hamlet. The Blood Grows Cold, 6 February 1914].[13] The Ophelia of these poems, like the Ophelia of the German Romantics, is an unhappy, beautiful victim whose voice—in those relatively few instances when it is heard—gives gentle and melancholy expression to longing and regret. Hamlet is overburdened with the weight of existence and suffers from a sense of helplessness, inadequacy, and guilt before Ophelia.

Hamlet's guilt is also central to the only one of Pasternak's poems on this subject with which Tsvetaeva was familiar when she created her own version of the Danish prince: « Уроки английского » [English Lessons, 1919] from *Сестра моя жизнь* [My Sister Life], a collection that won Tsvetaeva's exuberant praise. Implicit in the parallel between Desdemona and Ophelia which Pasternak's lyric projects is Hamlet's responsibility in the death of the unhappy maiden, which is construed as murder.[14]

Valerii Briusov modernizes Ophelia's image in an eponymous poem written in 1911. The distinctly twentieth-century suicide, which he describes ironically as a gesture of self-assertiveness, shows Ophelia to be a victim of the cold indifference of the surrounding world. The epigraph—the opening stanza of the third poem from A. A. Fet's cycle *To Ophelia*—carries an oblique reference to the indelibility of Ophelia's death from the soul of the author of the poem.

Although the focus in these various lyrics is on Ophelia, the identification of their authors remains, predictably, with Hamlet. Dominant is the all-pervasive guilt of the male poet before his female muse and before poetry itself. Ironically, this overwhelming male guilt becomes the means of subjugating Ophelia, who is overshadowed and silenced by its immensity.

Tsvetaeva perceived inherent dangers to both poet and poetry alike in such a Hamlet-Ophelia allegory. The poet's sense of inadequacy before the poetic ideal can give rise to a self-destructive, paralyzing guilt that saps the energy required for continual striving toward the unattainable and leave the poet alienated not only from life, but ultimately from poetry itself, a crisis designated by Ihab Hassan as playing "on a lyre without strings."[15]

Tsvetaeva's Ophelia is no longer the exquisite passive victim of Hamlet, derangement, fate, or of that projection of male guilt that subdues her. This new Ophelia marks a radical break with the image of the unfortunate creature that German Romantics and Russian Symbolists projected. She is a dynamic, dominant, self-assertive, and unquestionably superior character who is accorded her own voice not in madness or song, but in forcefully and logically articulated argument. As such she becomes—together with Eurydice and the Cumaean Sibyl—part of a coalition of female personae who interject correctives into male conceptions of poetry and the norms for poetic discourse.

The acquiescence to male readings of Hamlet and Ophelia of Anna Akhmatova's two-poem cycle *Читая Гамлета* [While Reading Hamlet, 1909] is entirely alien to Tsvetaeva. In Tsvetaeva's poems a powerful Ophelia addresses a weak, silent Hamlet. Her madness and the passive horizontality of her entry into death are replaced by the vivacious rectitude of her intrusion into the world of the living. Her sojourn in the bourne of death has apparently expanded that virginal perspective on life with which she left this world to encompass the claims of physical passion.[16] If Eurydice chides Orpheus for his inappropriate search for the gratification of erotic longing in the underworld, Ophelia faults Hamlet for renouncing and condemning sexuality in the domain of the living. The sterility of Hamlet's chastity emerges in sharp contrast to the fertile desire which leads Orpheus to defy the boundary between life and death. For all Eurydice's protestations, it is those very desires of the flesh that has no place in the underworld that gain him entry into it. It is because he refuses to regard eros and death as mutually exclusive that Orpheus attains the other world. Tsvetaeva's Hamlet is incapable of making such daring connections, and this task falls to her Ophelia. Ophelia's return from the dead to champion sexuality is not only a reproach to Hamlet but also a defense of the silent Orpheus of "Eurydice to Orpheus." It is, accordingly, Ophelia rather than the reticent Hamlet who comes to be aligned with Orpheus. In the lyric « По набережным, где седые деревья » [Along the Embankment, Where the Gray-Haired Trees, 28 September 1923] (*SP* 3:133) Tsvetaeva makes this parallel explicit.

Tsvetaeva had been invited to work on the poetic aspects of a new production of *Hamlet* undertaken by Vsevolod Meyerhold at the end of 1919 and the beginning of 1920. Although this cooperative effort, which was to have included the director Valerii Bebutov and the poet Vladimir Mayakovskii, did not materialize, the plans for it led Tsvetaeva to a serious study of Shakespeare's tragedy.[17] Her Hamlet and Ophelia derive from a profound and original assimilation of the play.

Although Tsvetaeva's treatment of Hamlet is to an important extent a polemic with the increasing tendency to approximate the Danish prince to Orpheus and to recognize in him an image of the poet, it has at the same time a personal dimension. The themes of unrequited love, of sundered lovers, of unconsummated love—always strong in Tsvetaeva's writings—are particularly prominent in her lyrics of the period in which the Hamlet poems were written. These themes are forcefully projected by the personae of Ariadne,

Phaedra, and Eurydice and are the core of the cycle *Provoda* dedicated to Boris Pasternak. Here Tsvetaeva was working through the miscarriage of an intensely desired meeting with Boris Pasternak in Berlin in the spring of 1923 which, Eurydice-like, she helped to derail.[18] Charted in her lyrics that analyze the consequences of their parting of ways is a progression from eros to psyche that has been compellingly documented by Ieva Vitins.[19] In those lyrics the need for direct physical encounter is surrendered to the creative force of unfulfilled longing. Indeed, Tsvetaeva's less than wholehearted attempts to secure that actual meeting with Pasternak suggest that she was once again reenacting the Orphic transformation of erotic energy into creative urge, as she had done in connection with Nilender, but now from the position of full sexual maturation.

Jane Taubman observes that "genuine as was her grief and disappointment at Pasternak's unexpected departure, Tsvetaeva was also glad to avoid a face-to-face encounter."[20] The missed meeting with Pasternak provides the stimulus for an exploration of the generative force of eros that is central to Tsvetaeva's poetic inquiry of this period. Impelled by the emotion unvented in direct encounter, she subjects to lyrical analysis the interrelationship of eros, psyche, and poetry. Ophelia takes her place in the series of personae dedicated to this examination. Her forceful exposition of the grave consequences of Hamlet's denial of erotic impulses complements the struggles with misdirected desire in which Ariadne, Phaedra, and Eurydice engage. United by their distinctly female perspective, each of these personae provides a particular point of vantage on the significance of eros.

Of these female personae only Ophelia can move between the bounds of the living and the dead. In Tsvetaeva's first Hamlet poem, "Ophelia to Hamlet," Ophelia comes from beyond the grave to chastise the prince. Her reproaches are centered on Hamlet's passive bookishness, a distinctly negative characteristic that marks his attempt to disengage himself from direct contact with life. To his « тяжеловесная хроника » [weighty chronicle], Ophelia opposes the chronicle of the stream (« ручьевая хроника ») in which she met her end and which she now seeks to resurrect in Hamlet's memory.

Офелия — Гамлету

Гамлетом — перетянутым — натуго,
В нимбе разуверенья и знания,
Бледный — до последнего атома . . .
(Год тысяча который — издания?)

Наглостью и пустотой — не тронете!
(Отроческие чердачные залежи!)
Некоей тяжеловесной хроникой
Вы на этой груди — лежали уже!

Девственник! Женоненавистник! Вздорную
Нежить предпочедший! . . . Думали ль
Раз хотя бы о том — что сорвано
В маленьком цветнике безумия . . .

Розы?.. Но ведь это же — тссс! — Будущность!
Рвем — и новые растут! Предали ль
Розы хотя бы раз? Любящих —
Розы хотя бы раз? —Убыли ль?

Выполнив (проблагоухав!) тонете . . .
— Не было! — Но встанем в памяти
В час, когда над ручьёвой хроникой
Гамлетом — перетянутым — встанете . . .

Ophelia to Hamlet

Hamlet, tightly clinched, in an aura of disillusionment and knowledge, pale to the last atom . . . (An edition of the year one thousand what?)

You can't touch me with your impudence and emptiness! (Adolescent fallow attic remains!) You have already lain on this breast like some weighty chronicle.

Virgin! Misogynist! Who preferred a frivolous spirit! / Who preferred to caress the frivolous one! . . . Have you ever once thought about—what is plucked in the little flower garden of madness . . .

Roses? But that is, after all—shh!—The future! We pluck and new ones grow! Have roses ever once betrayed? Lovers—Have roses ever once?— decreased?

Having fulfilled (having expended your fragrance!) you sink . . . —Never existed!—But we will arise in your memory at the hour when you arise over the chronicle of the stream as tightly clinched Hamlet . . .] (*SP* 3:52–53; ellipses in original)

Hamlet's distance from life is emphasized by the metaphor that makes him an old, weighty tome, suggested in the question « (Год тысяча который — издания?) » [An edition of the year one thousand what?] (I, 4) and in the lines « Некоей тяжеловесной хроникой / Вы на этой груди — лежали уже » [You have already lain on this breast / like some weighty chronicle] (II, 3–4). This image derives from the vow of Shakespeare's Hamlet to his father's ghost, "And thy commandment all alone shall live / Within the book and volume of my brain" (I, v). Ophelia's application of this metaphor to Hamlet in Tsvetaeva's poem betokens the excess of Hamlet's intellectuality, which he allows to prevail over his emotions. The semantic field within which these bookish references operate emphasizes severe restriction (« перетянутым — натуго » [tightly clinched]) and all-pervasive pallor (« Бледный до —

последнего атома . . . » [Pale to the last atom . . .]). Hamlet appears in an aura that conjoins his undermined faith (« разуверенье ») with the certitude of knowledge (« знание »). The former describes his disillusionment in love, the latter his need for absolutes with which he misguidedly hopes to replace life's uncertainties. Hamlet's loss of faith derives from the manifestations of both his mother's and Ophelia's sexuality in the immediate context of his father's death. The simultaneity of eros and death that had led Orpheus to the underworld precipitates Hamlet's highly appropriate turn to language. Yet in language he erroneously seeks a haven from the antinomies of existence rather than the realization of their generative power demonstrated by Orpheus. The books of "Words, words, words" into which he retreats serve only to isolate him from both life and death.

Ophelia accuses Hamlet of lingering in an adolescent state characterized by obnoxious behavior and a fear of sexual maturation. « Залежи » refers both to unwanted goods and fallow land. Thus the designation « Отроческие чердачные залежи » captures Hamlet's immaturity, inutility, alienation, and barrenness. The fear of direct sexual engagement is closely interrelated with the insecurity that inhibits creativity and with his lack of vitality.

Ophelia's accusations become increasingly pointed and intense in stanza three. Her exclamatory branding of Hamlet as virgin and misogynist focuses on his denial of sexuality and his failure to respond to her. This leads into the accusation that he favors a lifeless spirit (« нежить ») over vivacious flesh-and-blood. The reproach « Вздорную / Нежить предпочедший! » is an ambiguous one that complicates Ophelia's assessment of Hamlet's rejection of her love. Its ambiguity pivots on the word « нежить », which as a noun means "spirit" but as a verb means "to fondle, coddle, or caress" and thus encapsulates the dilemma confronting Hamlet when he finds himself torn between death and eros. The deployment of the first of these meanings gives rise to the accusation that Hamlet has given precedence to the demands of the spirit of his father over the love Ophelia proffers. If, however, « нежить » is regarded as a verb, « вздорную » becomes a feminine substantivized adjective to suggest Hamlet's preference for "caressing the frivolous one," a phrase that intimates his preoccupation with Queen Gertrude.

Although the first of these readings is perhaps the more obvious, the second is strongly encouraged by the line break that intervenes between « вздорную » and « Нежить ». The ensuing pause is one more likely to occur between subject and verb than between an adjective and the noun it qualifies. Although we can recognize the spirit of Hamlet's father in « вздорную нежить »,[21] its gender also suggests a feminine signified. With the equivoque « нежить » Ophelia provides a double perspective on Hamlet's behavior. He slights Ophelia not only because he is so absorbed in the cause to which his father's ghost has exhorted him, but also because of his preoccupation with Queen Gertrude's sexuality, which is implied here and discussed explicitly in the poem « Офелия — в защиту королевы » [Ophelia—in Defense of the Queen], considered below. Hamlet looks back to his parents, rather than forward to his own parenthood. Like Orpheus, he confronts eros in the context of death. He responds, however, not by embracing one and the other as does the Greek bard, but by denying both.

Tsvetaeva's Ophelia takes Hamlet to task for his denial of sexuality and accordingly replaces conventional censure of the female for loss of maidenhood with censure of the male who preserves it. The question that has continued to preoccupy readers of the tragedy as to whether or not Ophelia died a virgin gives way in Tsvetaeva's account to the more compelling issue of the causes and consequences of Hamlet's denial of eros.

The prince is directed to contemplate just what is plucked "in the little flower garden of madness." In Shakespeare's tragedy Ophelia's disarranged thoughts are presented in a complex bouquet of flower symbolism. Her madness is projected in the plucking and distribution of wild flowers, which are, however, singularly appropriate to their recipients. Her death too is linked with flowers; it is described as the consequence of her attempt to suspend her "fantastic garlands" from the limb of a willow that "grows aslant a brook." Yet in Tsvetaeva's poem the "flower garden of madness" to which Ophelia refers indicates not her own plight, but rather Hamlet's counterfeit derangement, which, like the ponderous tomes he peruses, is for him an avenue of escape from direct confrontation of sexuality and life. The "roses" to which she alludes are the very "roses of the blood" Eurydice describes. They stand for life's blood and for physical passion. The plucked roses of stanza four suggest a common trope for the loss of virginity, which in this context underscores Hamlet's sexual reticence. The nascent protestation « Но ведь это же » [But that is, after all] that intimates the transgressive nature of this "plucking" is immediately countered by Ophelia, who designates the termination of virginity a new beginning: « Будущность » [The future]—the unfolding temporal expanse of procreation. The past of virginity becomes the future of new generations. Ophelia's description of the ever new roses that appear and are "plucked" emphasizes the ingemination of sexual union and the issue of subsequent generations it ensures. The "loss" of virginity is thus revealed to be a gain from which Hamlet is barred. With the first person plural Ophelia uses here—« рвем » [we pluck]—the female is transformed from a passive victim of "deflowerment" by the male into an equal partner in the procreative act.

In Shakespeare's tragedy roses do not appear among the flowers gathered by Ophelia. Laertes refers to his sister as a "rose of May" (IV, v), but Hamlet's only mention of a rose is in reference to Queen Gertrude and not Ophelia. In the fourth scene of act III, having killed Polonius in his mother's bedchamber, he condemns Gertrude's behavior with the words "Such an act / . . . takes off the rose / From the fair forehead of an innocent love / And sets a blister there." Hamlet's rose is a sign denoting not virginity, but matrimonial fidelity. Thus when Ophelia shifts to the first person plural to align herself with all women and tells Hamlet that in time new roses grow to replace those plucked, he is reminded of something that he has already observed with considerable bitterness in his mother's behavior: that the object of love can be supplanted. Ophelia insists, however, that this "perfidy" is in fact an avowal of the regenerative force of love which counteracts death. Roses may be plucked or can fade away, but the blooming rose is itself ever blameless. The rose opens out into the complexity and perfection of love in the full bloom of consummation.

Once again erotic love emerges as a positive counterexample to Hamlet's untoward virginal behavior. The loss of virginity is construed not as an end to maidenhood but as the entry into procreation and thus also into the cycle of life-and-death. An alternate means to procreation for entry into this cycle is provided by death. Thus the dead, virginal Ophelia is in sympathy with a living, sexually experienced woman who would appear to be her antithesis. The unfulfilled physical potential of her virginal state is subsumed by death, which displaces the limits of the body and permits Ophelia to comprehend both the physical and the insubstantial world. By contrast, the living, virginal Hamlet's denial of death and eros alienates him from both realms.

Yet, although death overrides the distinction between maidenhood and maternity, Hamlet is by no means relieved of guilt for failing Ophelia in love. In the concluding stanza of the poem Ophelia turns from the prince to address the roses: « Выполнив (проблагоухав!) тонете . . . » [Having fulfilled (having expended your fragrance!) you sink . . .]. Attention shifts now from the eternally self-replenishing blooms of love she has championed to the ephemerality of the individual blossom. As Ophelia identifies with the discarded roses sinking into oblivion, her own barrenness at death emerges in stark contrast to the fully accomplished blooms she has described.

The last three lines of the poem retrieve the short-lived flowers from eternal oblivion. Fertile memory replaces the barren womb and also retrieves the dead. Ophelia, like the other discarded blossoms, will surface in Hamlet's consciousness whenever he contemplates the brook that records her death. The "chronicle" of the stream appears here in contrast to the "weighty chronicle" that described the prince in stanza two and demands Hamlet's direct confrontation of his multifaceted guilt, which comprises the Orphic configuration of eros, life, song, and death. The concluding line echoes the opening of the poem and trails off into ellipsis of unaccomplishment. Yet the recumbent Hamlet of stanza two is now replaced with an erect one who is forced to confront the rose that has resurfaced in his mind's eye.

The concluding image of the tightly belted Hamlet contemplating the chronicle-stream prompts a contrast with Orpheus. Hamlet stands apart—

contemplating, but not entering the stream that carried Ophelia away from life and that swept the dismembered Orpheus to his beloved, to death, and to the transcendence of earthly restrictions. He does not seek his beloved as did Orpheus; instead, she must come to him. For Hamlet Ophelia's existence is extended into the perpetual present not by the creative force of unquenchable longing, but by the inevitably destructive force of guilt. He remains contemplating an unfulfilled past, trapped in a present that is haunted by the consequences of his self-perpetuated alienation.

Tsvetaeva's second Hamlet poem, « Офелия — В защиту королевы » [Ophelia—in Defense of the Queen], was written on the same day as "Ophelia to Hamlet." Here the sympathy between Ophelia and Gertrude suggested in the first lyric is made explicit when Ophelia appears before Hamlet to defend the queen from his opprobrium. Echoing the « чердачные залежи » [fallow attic remains] of the preceding poem, Ophelia exhorts Hamlet to abandon his preoccupation with the « червивая залежь » [wormy remains] of the dead and to acknowledge instead the roses of the flesh-and-blood world. She seeks to engage Hamlet's desires in an effort to overcome his denial of eros. Accordingly she urges him—in a reversal of the arguments Eurydice advanced to Orpheus—to remember her as she was in that life she left so recently.

Офелия —В защиту королевы

Принц Гамлет! Довольно червивую залежь
Тревожить . . . На розы взгляни!
Подумай о той, что---единого дня лишь ---
Считает последние дни.

Принц Гамлет! Довольно царицыны недра
Порочить . . . Не девственным — суд
Над страстью. Тяжеле виновная — Федра:
О ней и поныне поют.

И будут! — А Вы с Вашей примесью мела
И тлена . . . С костями злословь,
Принц Гамлет! Не Вашего разума дело
Судить воспаленную кровь.

Но если . . . Тогда берегитесь! . . Сквозь плиты —
Ввысь — в опочивальню — и всласть!
Своей Королеве встаю на защиту —
Я, Ваша бессмертная страсть.

Ophelia—in Defense of the Queen

Prince Hamlet! Enough of disturbing worm-eaten remains . . . Glance at the roses! Think of her, who but a day hence counts her last days.

Prince Hamlet! Enough of defaming the queen's depths . . . It is not for virgins to judge passion. The more heavily guilty Phaedra—they sing of her to this day.

> And will!—While you with your admixture of chalk and dust . . . Malign with the bones, Prince Hamlet! It is not for your reason to judge inflamed blood.
>
> But if . . . Then beware! Through the slabs—up—into the bedchamber—and to my heart's content! I, your immortal passion, rise to the defense of my Queen.] (*SP* 3:53; ellipses in original)

Ophelia bases her defense of Gertrude not on the Queen's innocence, but rather on the guilt attendant on Hamlet's denial of eros, which disqualifies him from judging erotic passion. Ophelia's reference to the "even guiltier" (« тяжеле виновная ») Phaedra is an acknowledgment that Queen Gertrude's behavior is not above reproach. Yet Ophelia is preoccupied not with guilt or innocence, but with the transcendence of the limitations of time and space. This is accomplished on the strength of those very passions Hamlet is at pains to deny, translated according to the Orphic model into song. Ophelia emphasizes in the opening of stanza three that the songs born of Phaedra's tragic desire for Hippolytus will continue to be sung. The argument is compelling in light of Tsvetaeva's conviction that the registering of an event in song serves as a measure of its intrinsic value: « Годность или негодность вещи для песни — может быть, единственное непогрешимое мерило ее уровня » [The appropriateness or inappropriateness of something for song may be the only true measure of its level].[22]

The introduction of Phaedra into Ophelia's argument is significant. Tsvetaeva herself joined Eurypides, Seneca, and Racine in the perpetuation of Phaedra's passion in song. The two poems of her *Phaedra* cycle were completed very soon after "Ophelia—in Defense of the Queen" (7 and 11 March of the same year) and appear in *After Russia* immediately after this poem. The *Phaedra* tragedy (the second play in Tsvetaeva's projected *Theseus* trilogy) that was to follow in 1927 is colored by the tragedy of the Danish prince. As Simon Karlinsky has pointed out, "the death of Phaedra is told in terms that recall Ophelia's death in Shakespeare's Hamlet," while Hippolytus takes on characteristics of Hamlet.[23]

In the poem under discussion Ophelia compares Phaedra and Queen Gertrude on the strength of their incestuous passions. The juxtaposition is a revealing one that highlights not only the intensity of their transgressive passion, but also the difference between the two queens: Gertrude's desire for her erstwhile brother-in-law is vigorously consummated, while Phaedra's desire for her stepson remains unrequited and unfulfilled. The replacement of erotic fulfillment with death that is Phaedra's lot aligns her with the Ophelia who speaks in Tsvetaeva's poem and intensifies the parallel noted by Karlinsky between Hamlet and Hippolytus, who reject the women's love. With the introduction of Phaedra every possible configuration of life, death, virginity, and sexual fulfillment finds representation in this lyric: Gertrude is living and sexually fulfilled, Ophelia is dead and sexually unfulfilled, Phaedra is, like Ophelia, dead and unfulfilled and yet like Gertrude no longer a virgin. It falls to Hamlet to represent the barren category of the virginal and living which Ophelia decries.

The alignment of Queen Gertrude with Ophelia and Phaedra shifts the emphasis from fulfillment of desire to acknowledgment of its imperative. Hamlet's problem is now more specifically located not in his failure to consummate his love, but in his determination to repress it. Not only does his misguided refusal to admit erotic desire into his discourse with the surrounding world lead to Ophelia's death, but, more gravely, it prevents him from transforming that death into a creative impulse. The reference to Phaedra implies an incestuous desire beneath his condemnation of his mother's sensuality that may well contribute to his fear of confronting his emotions. In an article devoted to "Ophelia—in Defense of the Queen" Aleksandar Flaker perceptively notes that "in the poem there is no hint at the fact that Queen Gertrude is the Prince's mother."[24] Flaker sees this as a means of heightening the female erotic passion in the text, but does not note that leaving the kinship of Hamlet and Gertrude unnamed opens the way for Hamlet's emotional or physical attraction to Gertrude as well. With her positive reference to Phaedra, Tsvetaeva's Ophelia indicates that it is not the object of desire, but rather the desire itself that is of consequence. Tsvetaeva's scope here is broader than Flaker would have it when he writes, "Here a woman rises to defend female eros, while refuting male eros."[25] Ophelia's defense of Queen Gertrude is in fact a defense of the desires Hamlet represses. Ophelia aligns herself with and champions the generative force of eros, neither distinguishing between male and female nor passing judgment on its source. The surrender to erotic passion that she advocates is analogous to the poet's surrender to the dictates of her art. Lover and poet answer not for the origin of the force by which they are possessed, but only for the completeness and intensity of their surrender to it.

In the third stanza Ophelia describes, in a disdainful, unflattering tone, Hamlet's relegation of emotions to the highly inappropriate domain of the intellect. The intellect acts as an impenetrable boundary between body and spirit and estranges Hamlet from both the flesh-and-blood world his mother exemplifies and the insubstantial realm his father represents. Thus Ophelia suggests the companionship of bones—neither flesh nor spirit—for his tirades against the pleasures of the body. Hamlet's admixture of chalky pallor and dust evokes not the realm of death itself but rather the corpse left behind among the living. Hamlet's bloodlessness and the aridity of his reason stand in stark contrast to the inflamed blood (« воспаленная кровь ») of the queen. Hamlet's compass is too narrow to comprehend the intensity of passion. Restricted and restrictive reason cannot replace direct experience and is insufficient to judge urges to which he himself has never responded.

Ophelia vows to defend her queen should Hamlet persist in his malignity and threatens to rise from her grave to penetrate the bedchamber. In her analysis, Tamarchenko assumes that Ophelia is speaking of the queen's bedchamber where in Shakespeare's tragedy the ghost of Hamlet's father interrupts the prince's attack on his mother.[26] Yet it would appear that it is rather Hamlet's chamber that the importunate Ophelia threatens to enter. The final step of her plan to avenge her Queen entails fulfillment—« и всласть » [to my heart's content]. Ophelia intends to ravish her reluctant prince and thereby initiate him into the passion of "inflamed blood" which he is now incapable of appreciating.

Paradoxical as it may appear, Ophelia comes to Hamlet from beyond the grave not to advance an argument on the uselessness of the flesh like the one Eurydice elaborates to Orpheus, but rather to win him over to life and eros. Correlative with her reversal of conventional male and female roles is her reversal of the roles of the living and the dead. The insubstantial Ophelia possesses a vitality sorely lacking in the living Hamlet. In speaking to him she could well echo and lend new meaning to Eurydice's words « призрак *ты*, сущий, а явь — / Я, мертвая . . . » [*you*, the extant one, are a shade, and I, the dead one, am real . . .]. Ophelia is far more engaged in and understanding of the realm of the flesh than is the pallid prince. With the exception of the subtle reference to her own death in « Сквозь плиты — / Ввысь » [Up / through the slabs], Ophelia's only allusions to death occur in her descriptions of Hamlet rather than of herself. Her designation of the prince's bedchamber as « опочивальня » —with its link to the obsolete verb « опочить » [to sleep] that refers figuratively to death—underscores the lifelessness of his virginal existence.

In the concluding line of the poem Ophelia proclaims herself to be Hamlet's "immortal passion." This aligns her with that memory of living passions described in the preceding poem, which must be rescued from repression. Having counterposed herself to the worm-eaten remains of Hamlet's father (« Довольно червивую залежь / Тревожить . . . На розы взгляни! ») in that lyric, she now vivaciously encourages Hamlet to recognize that, rather than mitigate his emotions, her physical absence can invigorate them and cause them to endure. On the strength of a desire for Ophelia Hamlet could ostensibly extend the compass of his straitened existence between being and not being to one that could effectively and productively engage both life and death as did Orpheus. Fully cognizant of this, Ophelia offers him help. In defending her queen, she also charts the course for her prince's liberation.

Hamlet's condition is indeed pitiable. King Claudius, who throughout Shakespeare's tragedy articulates thoughts specifically applicable to Prince

Hamlet's situation, speaks of the guilt that weighs on his own conscience in terms that summarize Hamlet's dilemma:

And, like a man to double business bound,
I stand in pause where I shall first begin,
And both neglect. (III, iii)

The "double business" to which Hamlet is bound derives, like that of Orpheus, from the coincidence of eros and death. Confronted simultaneously by his now insubstantial father and his sensual mother, Hamlet remains trapped between the two realms of existence, although there is no reason why, urged by Ophelia's love and the exhortations of his father's Ghost, he should not respond to the promptings that issue from both. Yet "the book and volume" of Hamlet's brain is too narrow to encompass the breadth of their combined charges. Hamlet cannot, as did Orpheus, entertain eros and death in simultaneity.

Because Tsvetaeva's Ophelia conjoins and represents both death and eros, she not only instructs Hamlet, but also serves as a model for him. Hamlet's admission of his own eros would not only inspire his compassion for the queen, but would also transform the destructive power of his guilt into the generative, transcendent force of longing.

Ophelia's arousal of Hamlet's desire would transform the barren scholar into a productive poet. For this to become possible the prince must first recognize and confront the source of his guilt. Tsvetaeva's next Hamlet poem, "Hamlet's Dialogue with His Conscience," urges him to do so. Although Ophelia's voice, heard in the two earlier Hamlet poems, is replaced in this lyric by that of Hamlet's grammatically feminine conscience, the focus is once again on the guilt that derives specifically from his rejection of eros. The inexorable conscience repeatedly evokes the image of the drowned Ophelia to emphasize the tragic consequences of this repression. Hamlet's ineffectual attempts to placate his conscience with protestations of love for the deceased maiden are steadily eroded and he is finally forced to confront the flaw in his defense.

Диалог Гамлета с совестью

— На дне она, где ил
И водоросли . . . Спать в них
Ушла, — но сна и там нет!
— Но я ее любил
Как сорок тысяч братьев
Любить не могут!
— Гамлет!

На дне она, где ил:
Ил! . . И последний венчик
Всплыл на приречных бревнах . . .

— Но я ее любил
Как сорок тысяч . . .
                    — Меньше,
Все ж, чем один любовник.

На дне она, где ил.
— Но я ее —
        (*недоуменно*)
                — любил??

Hamlet's Dialogue with His Conscience

"She is at the bottom where the silt and weeds are . . . She went there to sleep, but there is no sleep even there!"
"But I loved her as forty thousand brothers cannot love!"
"Hamlet!"

"She is at the bottom where the silt is. Silt! And the last garland has surfaced on the riverside logs."
"But I loved her as forty thousand . . ."
"Less, however, than one lover."

"She is at the bottom where the silt is."
"But I" (*perplexed*) "loved her?"] (*SP* 3:79; ellipses in original)

Hamlet's conscience perpetuates the arguments advanced by Ophelia in the two earlier poems by pointing out that, however many fraternal loves Hamlet's emotions may outweigh, he still falls short of attaining the status of even one lover. Tamarchenko has argued persuasively that Tsvetaeva's three Hamlet poems represent three stages in Hamlet's confrontation of his guilt and that it is neither Ophelia nor even Tsvetaeva, but a part of Hamlet himself that levels the accusations and reproaches made in them.[27] There is indeed a progression from Ophelia's address to Hamlet in the first poem to her identification of herself as his "immortal passion" in the second and finally to the voice of Hamlet's own conscience in the last, where he comes closest to raising his guilt to a conscious level.

Yet, particularly in the context of the Eurydice poem considered earlier, it is difficult to deny any autonomy whatsoever to Tsvetaeva's outspoken Ophelia, who successfully reverses not only traditional gender roles, but even those of the living and the dead. To say that Ophelia is entirely the product of Hamlet's imagination is to return her to the fold of passive Ophelias against whom Tsvetaeva counterposes her own outspoken persona. It was doubtless in order to free Ophelia from direct identification with Hamlet and to preserve her individuality that Tsvetaeva, who originally published these three poems as a cycle, included them in *After Russia* as autonomous lyrics. In that collection the first two poems stand side by side, while "Hamlet's Dialogue" appears later in its chronologically determined place. Because Tsvetaeva did not hesitate to disrupt the otherwise strictly chronological arrangement of *After Russia* to create other cycles, it is not likely that mere adherence to chronology motivates her disposition of the Hamlet poems. It seems, rather, that she sought to prevent the similar but distinct voices of Ophelia and of Hamlet's conscience from merging.

In "Hamlet's Dialogue" the autonomy given the conscience emphasizes Hamlet's inner discord. Yet although it is separate enough to address Hamlet by name, it is indisputably a part of Hamlet himself and not, like Ophelia in the earlier poems, the voice of an outside judge. (Dmitrii Shostakovich recognizes this when he sets this poem for one voice rather than two in his opus 143).[28] The lyric, in Michael Makin's apt summary, "presents the schizophrenic or double-voiced musings of Hamlet about Ophelia's death."[29] Clearly it is the wiser part of Hamlet that urges him to confront the consequences of his denial of eros: the destruction of Ophelia's life and the acute constriction of his own. Hamlet is sundered that he may be regenerated with expanded comprehension.

Within the bounds of the poem the conscience is characterized by greater freedom of movement than is afforded Hamlet. Its speeches cross stanzaic boundaries, contain more enjambments, and are endowed with greater thematic and rhythmic variety than are Hamlet's. Hamlet can only repeat ever smaller parts of his argument as if, in Sibelan Forrester's felicitous formulation, "he has turned Echo to his own Narcissus."[30] This reflects the narrowness of the prince's outlook and indicates that the upper hand the conscience maintains for the duration of the poem results not only from the moral superiority of its position, but also from its ability to cross boundaries and override divisions, something Hamlet himself must yet learn to do.

At each of Hamlet's attempts to deflect it, his conscience intensifies its attack. Its laconic arguments derive from specific references to Shakespeare's tragedy, which lend weight and depth to what transpires on the surface of this lyric. These references foreground Hamlet's flaws and illuminate the complex of their effects. To better understand both the poem under discussion and the psychological makeup of the antipoet, it is necessary to take the allusions to Shakespeare's text into account. We shall do so in the subsequent examination of "Hamlet's Dialogue with His Conscience." Guided by what the poem tells us and by the specific way in which it engages the tragedy, we shall undertake concomitantly with a reading of "Hamlet's Dialogue with His Conscience" a reading of Shakespeare's tragedy through Tsvetaeva's eyes.

In the "Dialogue" the past moment of Ophelia's death is drawn into the perpetual present of Hamlet's guilt: « На дне она, где ил » [She is at the bottom, where thc silt is]. Initially the horror of Ophelia's "muddy death" is mitigated by the explanation « Спать в них / ушла » [She went there to sleep], a phrase that emerges from the Shakespearean Hamlet's contemplation of the relative merits of being and not being in the first scene of Act III in what is perhaps his best-known soliloquy.

> To die: to sleep;
> No more; and, by a sleep to say we end
> The heart-ache and the thousand natural shocks
> That flesh is heir to, 'tis a consummation
> Devoutly to be wish'd.

Yet this is clearly not the consummation demanded of Hamlet in his relationship with Ophelia. His conscience does not permit him the consolation of regarding her death as an attainment of that enviable peace from the "slings and arrows of outrageous fortune." The gentle image of Ophelia in the sleep of death is dispelled by the reminder « но сна и там нет » [but there is no sleep even there], a condensation of the subsequent musings of Shakespeare's Hamlet:

> To die, to sleep;
> To sleep: perchance to dream: ay, there's the rub;
> For in that sleep of death what dreams may come
> When we have shuffled off this mortal coil,
> Must give us pause. (III, i)

Ophelia's death must give Hamlet special pause, for his father's ghost has already acquainted him with the torments that must be endured by one who dies "unhousel'd, disappointed, unanel'd," (I, v) as does Ophelia. There can be no doubt that her "sleep" is troubled.

There is more at stake here than the implication of Hamlet in Ophelia's death, for however construed, Ophelia's departure from life is above all a condemnation of Hamlet's estrangement from existence. If we concur in our reading of the tragedy with the first clown, who claims that Ophelia "willfully seeks her own salvation" (V, i), we recognize that she has not shied away from the "bare bodkin" and has in fact taken that step into death from which Hamlet was restrained by his fear of "dreams." If Ophelia's death is seen as the direct consequence of derangement which rendered her, as Queen Gertrude describes, "incapable of her own distress" (IV, vii), we note that her madness is genuine and not the "counterfeit" that Hamlet assumes in order to evade direct engagement in life. The image of the drowned Ophelia is thus both a powerful evocation of Hamlet's responsibility for her death and a galling reproach for his inability to come to grips with his own life.

In the "Dialogue" that Tsvetaeva creates, Hamlet responds to the weighty accusations implicit in the words of his conscience with a hyperbolic avowal of love for Ophelia: "But I loved her as forty thousand brothers cannot love." This response—the only one Hamlet can muster—bears the seeds of his guilt and cannot therefore placate his conscience. It is curtailed in each of its subsequent repetitions and rather than deflect only intensifies the shattering blow that the conscience finally delivers. This "defense" echoes the words Shakespeare's Hamlet cries out at Ophelia's funeral when he leaps into her grave to grapple with Laertes:

> I lov'd Ophelia: forty thousand brothers
> Could not, with all their quantity of love,
> Make up my sum. (V, i)

Shakespeare emphasizes how disconnected this exclamation is from the emotion it purports to convey. Having made this hyperbolic assertion, Hamlet challenges Laertes with the question "What wilt thou do for her?" and proceeds to enumerate a variety of gestures that are presumably to be interpreted as signs of love, but which very quickly degenerate into the ridiculous: "Woo't weep? woo't fight? [woo't fast?] woo't tear thyself? Woo't drink up eisel? eat a crocodile?" (V, i).

This rehearsal of possible means of expressing emotion is indicative of a problem that besieges Hamlet for the duration of the tragedy: his inability to reconcile himself to the disparity between signatum and designatum and the consequent mistrust of signs that ultimately paralyzes him. Hamlet's destructive tendency to abstract culminates in crippling anxiety. The certitude expressed in Hamlet's protestation to Queen Gertrude in the early stages of the play, "Seems, madam! Nay, it is; I know not 'seems' " (I, ii) steadily gives way to an overpowering fear of the ambiguity, inadequacy, and treachery of signs. His anxiety is exacerbated by the realization that the indeterminacy of any sign system is complicated further by the interpretive process to which it must be subjected: "for there is nothing either good or bad, but thinking makes it so" (II, ii). In his despair of arriving at fixed, unequivocal meaning, and of ensuring its unambiguous transmission, Hamlet intentionally intensifies the unsettling uncertainty of the communicative process. His assumption of madness in which his outward and inner selves are drawn into disjunction is both a consequence of and an analogue for his intense preoccupation with the disparity between sign and meaning. His feigned derangement is a protest that hypocritically intensifies the situation that precipitates it.

Here we may note parenthetically that the misguided expectation of a fixed, invariant relationship between signatum and designatum is a source of madness in nineteenth-century Russian prose (cf. especially Gogol' and Dostoevskii). Poets of the subsequent century, however, realized the rich associative potentialities generated by the indeterminacy of the linguistic sign system. We have already noted Tsvetaeva's dependence on the polyvalence of signs to achieve a radical expansion of existing norms. Hamlet, however, fails to recognize in the indeterminacy of language the vast potential for expressivity and the expansion of perception and understanding on which the poet draws. He sees in it only treachery and deceit. His description to Laertes of his emotions for Ophelia as exceeding those of forty thousand brothers, like the series of possible manifestations of love that follows, is the expression not of his love for Ophelia, but of his many unwholesome broodings on the disparity between professions of love and the feelings they are intended to convey. The very emotions that demand expression are suffocated by his excessive preoccupation with the vehicle of their communication.

In the tragedy Hamlet explains to his confidant Horatio that his precipitous leap into Ophelia's grave was prompted not by his anguish at learning of her death, but rather by her brother's response to it: "But, sure, the bravery of his grief did put me / Into a towering passion" (V, ii). Hamlet is jealous not of Laertes's affection for Ophelia, but of the spontaneity and lack of constraint with which he expresses his feelings. That his own utterances are divorced from genuine meaning is evident from his outcry as he grapples with Laertes in Ophelia's grave: "Nay, an thou'lt mouth, / I'll rant as well as thou" (V, i).

The forty-thousand-brother defense in "Hamlet's Dialogue with His Conscience" amounts similarly to a manifestation not of Hamlet's love, but of his inability to escape from the no-man's-land between sign and meaning. The conscience remains bent on driving home the tragic consequences of remaining in this situation. Its second evocation of the drowned Ophelia carries stronger reproach. In place of the aquatic plants is an emphasis on the mud: the word « ил » [silt] concludes the first line and opens the second. The new image of Ophelia's wreath that surfaces here is heavily laden with guilt. In Shakespeare's tragedy it is an image that interweaves Ophelia's unconsummated love, madness, and death—all products of Hamlet's failings.

As Queen Gertrude laments at Ophelia's burial, flowers of love become emblems of death.

> I hop'd thou shouldst have been my Hamlet's wife;
> I thought thy bride-bed to have deck'd, sweet maid,
> And not have strew'd thy grave. (V, i)

Here is a richness of the indeterminacy of signs that must give Hamlet pause, for it is he who has transformed what might have been Ophelia's bridal wreath into a token of death. Queen Gertrude's overlapping of love and death in the same image is captured by Tsvetaeva with the word « **венчик** » that signifies both a garland of flowers and the paper band placed on the forehead of the deceased in Russian Orthodox tradition.

In the tragedy Ophelia's wreath is singled out as one of the few marks she is conceded in a ceremony severely curtailed by the church because of the doubtful circumstances of her death. Confronted with Laertes's insistent demand, "What ceremony else?" the priest conducting the funeral rites responds:

> Her obsequies have been as far enlarg'd
> As we have warrantise: her death was doubtful,
>
> . . . .
>
> Yet here she is allow'd her virgin crants,
> Her maiden strewments, and the bringing home
> Of bell and burial. (V, i)

Here the wreath ("virgin crants"), an emblem of virginity, reminds us of Hamlet's sexual inadequacy vis-à-vis Ophelia. The image appears, moreover, in a context emphasizing that Ophelia's madness does not free her from accountability for her death. This intensifies the suggestion of the passage from Tsvetaeva's poem that Ophelia's "sleep" will not be dreamless. Furthermore, it throws into sharp relief the fact that Hamlet, by his forgery of madness, has enjoyed untoward success in evading answerability for his actions, including the murder of Polonius, which precipitates Ophelia's madness and untimely death.

Given the seriousness of the charge, the conscience is not prepared to rest satisfied with Hamlet's renewed attempt at self-justification with an avowal of love purported to exceed so dramatically the fraternal. When Hamlet begins to reiterate his single ineffectual defense, the conscience cuts him off to crush his preposterous hyperbole with a riposte that has been prepared by the immediately preceding reference to Ophelia's virgin/wedding/funeral wreath: « Меньше, / Все ж, чем один любовник ». This response situates Hamlet's guilt specifically in his rejection of eros. That he cannot be exonerated is driven home by the inexorable repetition of « На дне она, где ил ».

In the course of the poem « ил » remains a constant in the accusations the conscience levels at Hamlet. Its fourfold repetition is well motivated, for it is central to the concerns of poem and tragedy alike. Shakespeare's description of Ophelia's death as "muddy" refers to the site of her drowning, her clouded mind, and the ecclesiastical doubts raised by the circumstances of her death. In "Hamlet's Dialogue with His Conscience" this image is assigned another function: « ил » is the first half of the only rhyme that occurs between Hamlet and his conscience: « ил-любил ». This thrice-repeated, perfect rhyme stands out from the imprecise rhymes that predominate in this lyric. Its importance in eroding Hamlet's defense lies in the emphatic stress it places on the past tense he uses to describe his love. That by his own tacit admission Hamlet's affections do not endure beyond Ophelia's death underscores the tyranny of his reason over his emotions, a tyranny that prevents him from recognizing the capacity of love to extend beyond the bounds of earthly existence. Here we are at a great remove from that intensity of feeling that leads Orpheus to seek his beloved in the underworld. Hamlet's repression of eros precludes both the fulfillment of desire and its protraction. His leap into Ophelia's grave is a trivialization of Orpheus's descent to Eurydice that reflects the prince's limitations. Hamlet is to Orpheus what this leap into Ophelia's grave is to the catabasis. Hamlet, as the "Dialogue" drives home, cannot claim the role of bereaved lover; nor can he join the list of lovers who, having been parted by death, overcome that separation, be it by descent, by suicide, or by song.

Hamlet is perhaps himself not fully cognizant of the depth of meaning that lies in the question he poses in the tragedy, "What should such fellows as I do crawling between heaven and earth?" (III, i). His link to Ophelia is not the fertile one of longing, but the destructive one of guilt, which can only contract his already narrow compass. His final and weakest response to his conscience marks some progress in raising to consciousness the sources of his limitations. The parenthetic stage direction « (*недоуменно*) » [*perplexed*] that precedes the final « любил » [loved] of the poem and the two question marks that follow it indicate that Hamlet has been forced to recognize that the verb любил is not an appropriate designation for his relations with Ophelia. Certainly « убил » [killed] would come closer to describing what actually transpired, and the conscience demands that he acknowledge this. The nascent recognition that he has failed Ophelia brings him a step closer to comprehending the controlling idea of Tsvetaeva's Hamlet poems—that the rejection of erotic love results inevitably in alienation from both life and death.

The very image of Ophelia that is conjured up in the "Dialogue" reflects Hamlet's entrapment. The failed lover does not envision her as she was in life. Nor does he contemplate her tuneful, flower-bedecked progress downstream toward death or see her as she was in that grave into which he leapt. Instead, he situates her at the bottom of the stream and thus separates her not only from that life of which she was once a part, but also from the realm of death into which she has now entered. Hamlet's image of Ophelia is the product not only of his guilt, but also of his own entrapment in the crawlspace between heaven and earth.

Tsvetaeva's Ophelia returns from the dead to condemn Hamlet for his ineffectuality in the realm of the flesh. That the prince fails with equal ignominy in the realm of the spirit demonstrates that these failings are interdependent. Hamlet's denial of eros breeds an obsessive preoccupation with the flesh and inhibits him from penetrating beyond the constraints of the sensual world. Seeing in death only the decomposition of the body, he remains insensible to the spirit that is freed from its confines. Indeed, even the ghost he sees has not yet attained this freedom, for its sins have yet to be "burnt and purg'd away" (I, v). Hamlet's reference to the afterlife as "the undiscover'd country from whose bourn / No traveller returns" in his famous soliloquy (III, i) comes after his conversation with the ghost of his father, who, albeit briefly, does in fact effect such a return, as does the Ophelia of Tsvetaeva's poems. Hamlet's rejection of the possibility of return is directly linked to his inability to follow the departed. The Orphic mission is doubly frustrated. Projecting onto death his attitude toward life, Hamlet considers it to be not a release from the flesh, but the ultimate accomplishment of its denial. His thoughts of escape fail to go much further than that his "too, too solid flesh would melt" (I, ii), a formulation that denies existence beyond the physical world. Consequently, he regards the cycle of life and death as an entrapment in a series of metamorphoses of the flesh: "a king," as he observes, "may go a progress through the guts of a beggar" because "a man may fish with the worm that hath eat of a king, and eat of the fish that hath fed of that worm" (IV, iii). Along the same lines he traces "the noble dust of Alexander" until it is found "stopping a bung-hole" (V, i).[31] Tsvetaeva's Hamlet poems insist that it would have been better for Hamlet to consummate flesh-and-blood love than to fantasize about the stopping of bung-holes after that flesh has been reduced to dust. Hamlet's denial of eros not only removes him from life, it also prevents him from transcending its limitations to comprehend death. His inability to come to terms with flesh and blood bars him also from spirit.

Correlative with this disavowal of body and spirit is the disdain Hamlet repeatedly expresses for the word in the course of Shakespeare's tragedy. Unsettled rather than gratified by the ambiguity of signs, Hamlet fails to see in the indeterminacy of language the potential for a plethora of perception-expanding connections on which the poet draws. Hamlet is right to mistrust his father's ghost. His skepticism is a mark of a praiseworthy awareness of the ambiguity of signs that sets him apart from the other *dramatis personae* of Shakespeare's tragedy. For his cognizance of the ambiguities that beset him, Hamlet is a step closer to being a poet than is, for example, Laertes, whose decisive actions stem from a happy obliviousness to the complexity of signs. Yet Hamlet's misguided demand for unequivocal meaning precludes the perceptual breadth that is gained by the admission of multiple meanings. For Hamlet the polyvalence of signs is a source of doubt and anxiety rather than of freedom and creative potential. Accordingly, his own use of language is dangerous and antipoetical: he exploits the polysemy of language for deception and obfuscation rather than for revelation and illumination. It becomes for him the means for avoidance rather than the incentive for direct confrontation. Thus Hamlet kills a father, but it is Ophelia's hapless parent and not his stepfather, the king. The brother he attacks and then kills is Ophelia's kinsman and not his murdered father's pernicious sibling. The prince feels keenly the ambivalence of signs for although, like his father, he bears the name Hamlet, he is neither the ruler of the realm nor wedded to the queen.

In his frustrated desire that words remain permanently and unequivocally fixed to what they designate, Hamlet denies their capacity to point beyond themselves. He remains trapped between signifier and signified, a crawlspace which, like that between heaven and earth, is too narrow for action. Correlative with Hamlet's rejection of eros is his rejection of "words, words, words" (II, ii).For Tsvetaeva Hamlet's failure as a lover is a function of the very failings that prevent him from being a poet: a fear of admitting physical desire into his discourse with the surrounding world and a parallel fear of language. Whatever the outward similarity of the consequences, repression and sublimation are not at all the same thing. Simply stated, denial precludes the possibility of transcendence.

The conclusion to be drawn from the juxtaposition of Orpheus and Hamlet is clear. Despite the obvious dominance of flesh in this world and of spirit in the other, they cannot be divorced from one another. Tsvetaeva's Phaedra insists on this and Tsvetaeva herself summarizes it in a letter of 25 July 1923: « Все эти деления на тело и дух — жестокая анатомия на живом, выборничество, эстетство, бездушие » [All these divisions into body and spirit are cruel vivisections, selectivity, aestheticism, soullessness].[32] The reaffirmation of the complex interdependency of body and soul is also a reassertion of the poet's analogous linkage of the two realms of existence and the mysterious relation between the sound and sense of words. Just as Eurydice pleads that physical passion is out of place in Hades, Ophelia argues that in the world of the living it is crucial. Orpheus is wrong to seek erotic fulfillment in the realm of the dead, but the force of eros that leads him to it is a productive one. The flesh leading beyond itself is eros; language leading beyond itself is poetry. Thus, while Eurydice speaks for Tsvetaeva herself in rejecting the flesh, so too does Ophelia in reaffirming it.

By way of concluding this chapter and preparing to consider the Cumaean Sibyl in the next, it is helpful to take stock of and to augment the configurations we have thus far regarded in Tsvetaeva's Orphic kaleidoscope. In her letter to Boris Pasternak of 25 May 1926, already cited, Tsvetaeva is led by her discussion of Eurydice and Orpheus to an association of the mythical couple with the hero and heroine of her *poèma Молодец* [The Swain], written at the end of 1922. In that letter Tsvetaeva explains:

> В Эвридике и Орфее перекличка Маруси с Мóлодцем — не смейся опять! — сейчас времени нет додумать, но раз сразу пришло — верно. Ах, может быть просто последнее « не бойся »— *мой* ответ на Эвридику и Орфея. Ах, ясно: Орфей за ней пришел — *жить*, тот за моей [Марусей] — не жить. Оттого она (я) так рванулась. Будь я Эвридикой, мне было бы . . . стыдно — назад!
>
> [In Eurydice and Orpheus is an echo of Marusia and the Swain—again, don't laugh!—I don't have time to think it through just now, but since it came to me

in a flash it is true. Oh, maybe it is simply that the final "don't be afraid" is *my* response to Eurydice and Orpheus. Oh, I see: Orpheus came for her *to live*, the other for mine [Marusia]—to not live. That's why she (I) rushed forward. Were I Eurydice I would be . . . ashamed to go back!][33]

The Swain is Tsvetaeva's recasting of a folktale from Aleksandr Afanasiev's collection augmented by elements of the Gretchen-Faust relationship of Goethe's great tragedy. In Tsvetaeva's *poèma* the heroine, Marusia, with whom Marina identifies, prefers to sacrifice the lives of her brother and her mother and finally to die herself rather than to betray her knowledge of the identity of the vampire swain who courts her. When, in the second part of this work, Marusia is returned to life, her passive obedience—comparable to that of Jairus' daughter in the cycle of that name—underscores her alienation from her surroundings and her inability to be reconciled to the world of the living. In spite of her marriage, her sensually gratifying relations with her husband, and the son she bears, Marusia's flight back to the other world is inevitable. The *poèma* ends with the lines, « До-мой / В огнь синь » [Home / Into the blue flames] (*SP* 4:151).

Tsvetaeva's juxtaposition of Orpheus and Eurydice with the Swain and Marusia isolates—for all the surface discrepancies in their tales—the demand placed on both Eurydice and Marusia to choose between life and death, between sensual and insubstantial existence. Marusia, like Eurydice and Jairus's daughter, prefers the dominion of death. Yet a significant difference prevails in her choice. In *The Swain* the eros that both Jairus's daughter and Eurydice reject in their assertion of freedom from sensual incarnation leads directly into death rather than procreation. The paradoxical freedom from the body that Marusia wins by surrendering to erotic desire underscores the capacity of eros and death to effect a transcendence of the limits of the self. Unlike Orpheus, whose erotic desire leads him still living into death, Marusia attains the other world to which the power of eros leads her, only at the cost of her life.

The ill-starred Marusia and her horrific lover highlight another aspect of the Orpheus myth that is absent from the narrative of Jairus's daughter—the transgressive aspect of Orpheus's intrusion into the realm of death as emphasized, for example, in the conclusion of Virgil's fourth *Georgic*. To the interrelationship of eros and poetic language which the context of life and death throws into high relief is added the implication of wrongdoing. What can be described positively as a transcendence of boundaries may also be regarded negatively as the guilty penetration of forbidden space—be it the realm of death, of virginal purity, or of incestuous relations. Marusia abandons herself without question to her overwhelming desire. Tsvetaeva's Hamlet remains mired in ratiocinations. His negative example teaches that the poet must not stop to discriminate between transgression and transcendence, but must instead, like Orpheus and Marusia, surrender unreservedly to the force by which he is possessed. Indeed, as Tsvetaeva was to elaborate at some length in the essay « Искусство при свете совести » [Art in the Light of Conscience, 1932], the principal criterion in evaluating the poet is the intensity of his surrender to the creative urge, an urge which is represented in her Hamlet poems by its analogue eros. « Гений: высшая степень подверженности наитию » [Genius is the highest degree of susceptibility to inspiration] (*IP* 1:383).

Tsvetaeva's Hamlet is characterized by a fear of transgression and an oppressive sense of guilt that inhibit his surrender and thus exclude him from the league of poets. The negative example of the prince of Denmark teaches that the poet must embrace both creative and destructive potential. Hamlet's timidity before the antinomies that confront him alienates him from the living and the dead. It impedes action and emotion and bars him from both the procreative love demanded by the living Ophelia and the murderous hate exacted by his dead father. The dead vampire of *The Swain* depends necessarily on the living for his existence while Marusia/Marina surrenders herself completely to the love that leads her to death. It is meet and proper that the living demand life (Jairus, Orpheus) and that the dead demand death (Jairus's daughter, Eurydice, Hamlet's father's ghost), but the poet who creates them must comprehend both. The poet must ever respond to that powerful longing for the other which leads him to his own death even as it gives birth to song.

The ambivalence inherent in Orpheus's descent has been regarded alternately as transcendence and as transgression in the countless readings of the myth over the ages. This ambivalence was not lost on Tsvetaeva, who juxtaposes Orpheus alternately with Christ—an emblem of grace—and with the vampire swain—an emblem of damnation. Both are true guises of the prototypal poet. The antithesis to the all-embracing poet is neither Savior nor demon, but Hamlet the antipoet.

Chapter Four

The Sibyl

Die Poesie der Dicter bedürfen die Frauen weniger, weil ihr eigenstes Wesen Poesie ist.

Women have less need for the poetry of poets because their very essence is poetry.

—Friedrich Schlegel, *Ideas*

TSVETAEVA RECOGNIZED Orpheus as the prototypal poet whose embodiment she saw in Aleksandr Blok and would come to see also in Rainer Maria Rilke. Yet although the myth of Orpheus informed her understanding of poetry and served to structure her own close ties with those two poets, her choice to retain gender in exploring poetic identity prevented her from fusion with that prototype. The vociferous Eurydice and Ophelia were engaged to interject a female voice into that male realm. These female personae instruct Orpheus and Hamlet, yet neither is herself a poet. Eurydice cannot simultaneously retain full cognizance of both the world of the living and the realm of the dead and must instead insist on their distinction. Ophelia, whose arguments complement Eurydice's, projects a perspective that accommodates eros and death in simultaneity. She thus comes closer to representing the poetic vision that must embrace both life and death. Yet her instruction to Hamlet emphasizes not surrender to the transcendent force of unfulfilled desire, but rather the erotic fulfillment demanded by the corporeal realm that seeks its own perpetuation. This chapter focuses on an image of the poet projected by the Cumaean Sibyl, a female counterpart more commensurate to Orpheus's stature than either Eurydice or Ophelia.

Antonina Gove has persuasively argued that the "theme of an equality between a man and a woman" that appears in *After Russia* expresses Tsvetaeva's self-affirmation and concomitant denial of the exclusivity of gender in determining poetic identity.[1] Tsvetaeva herself insists that the question of gender pales before the essential nature of the poet. Thus, for example, in the essay «Живое о живом» [The Living about the Living, 1933] she asserts the priority of being a poet over being a woman with a demonstrative correction of a statement she herself makes, a didactic device she often uses when emphasizing a point: « . . . когда женщина оказывалась поэтом, или, что вернее, поэт — женщиной » [. . . when a woman turned out to be a poet, or, more precisely, a poet turned out to be a woman] (*IP* 2:39). To say that being a woman is secondary to being a poet, however, is not to underplay the significance of gender. The expressly female imagery, thematics, and perspective of Tsvetaeva's writings and her rebellious challenges to the male poetic establishment bespeak a profound awareness of her womanhood.[2] Indeed, earlier in the essay just cited Tsvetaeva privileges the female over the poet when she observes that only « большие, совсем большие поэты » [great, truly great poets] can equal a woman's capacity to love a disembodied spirit (*IP* 2:36). The implication—an echo, incidentally, of male Romantic notions—is that women are by their very nature closer to poetry than are men. Orpheus's legendary capacity to love a disembodied spirit is described by Tsvetaeva as a feature common to all women.

The Cumaean Sibyl provides Tsvetaeva with a female alternative to the traditional male image of the prototypal poet. Her source is again Ovid's *Metamorphoses*. In book XIV, Aeneas approaches the aged prophetess in her cave with the entreaty that he be allowed to visit his father's shade in the underworld. The Sibyl grants his request and leads him to Hades. On their return trip she recounts her story to Aeneas. Courted as a young maiden by Phoebus Apollo, she was offered any gift she desired by the amorous god. Indicating a heap of dust, she requested as many years of life as there were grains of dust in it, but forgot to ask for youth to complement her longevity. Rather than secure that overlooked gift by acceding to Phoebus's desires, she chose to suffer the ravages of old age. She explains to Aeneas that she is destined to wither away completely. Only one thing will remain to her: the voice by which she will be recognized.

John Block Friedman has noted that the *Testament of Orpheus* and the *Sibylline Oracles* share a number of common features.[3] Whether or not Tsvetaeva was familiar with these texts, she readily recognized important similarities between the myths of the bard and the prophetess that were relevant to her definition of poetry. Both Orpheus and the Sibyl were mortals bestowed with gifts by Phoebus Apollo that win them unique and privileged positions between mortality and eternity. The Sibyl, like Orpheus, travels to the underworld, and her voice, like that of Orpheus, supersedes the limitations of the mortal body. Tsvetaeva's preliminary outline of a project for a nine-poem cycle about the Sibyl underscored the link between these two myths:

> Сивилла (когда-нибудь!). Сивилла, когда-то любимица Феба, забыла испросить у него вечную молодость. И вот — стареет. Любовь к Фебу пребыла, Сивилла — голос Феба . . . Сивилла давно не слышит

людей . . . Встреча Сивиллы с сыном Феба, *их узнавание*. Сын Феба не видит Сивиллы, он только слышит ее голос: это говорит скала! Но по мере его возглаасов голос Сивиллы (вечный!) нежнеет: это говорит трава! это говорит ручей! Юноша влюбляется, хочет видеть, настаивает, наконец врывается в пещеру и разбивает себе грудь о скалу (Сивиллу). Сивилла над телом юноши.

[The Sibyl (someday!). The Sibyl, once the beloved of Phoebus, forgot to request from him eternal youth. And so—she ages. The love for Phoebus abides, the Sibyl is the voice of Phoebus . . . For a long time now the Sibyl hears no humans . . . The Sibyl's meeting with Phoebus's son, *their recognition*. Phoebus's son does not see the Sibyl, he only hears her voice: this is a cliff speaking! But in accordance with his exclamations the Sibyl's voice (eternal!) becomes gentler: this is grass speaking! a brook speaking! The youth falls in love, wants to see her, insists, finally bursts into the cave and shatters his chest against the cliff (Sibyl). The Sibyl over the body of the youth.] (*SP* 3:439–40; ellipses in original)

Orpheus's capitulation to the desire for visual verification as he leads Eurydice to the upper world appears here as the fatal inability of Phoebus-Apollo's son to recognize the essential superiority of aural perception over the visual. Here once again the error is committed by a male, and the truth is revealed by a disembodied female voice. In this plan the Sibyl is both muse and poem—the absent body that engenders desire and an instance of desire transcended.

As Tsvetaeva plumbs the myth of the Sibyl for what it can reflect of the poet's identity, important moments of the Orpheus myth assume new guises. The uneasy relationship of absent body, eros, and voice which remained central to Tsvetaeva's treatment of the bard undergoes realignment in the Sibyl's legend. The prophetess-to-be eschews physical vigor rather than submit to Phoebus-Apollo's attentions. Like Tsvetaeva's Eurydice, she is prepared to sacrifice her body in order to be freed of erotic desire. With the elimination of eros, the transgressive aspect of poetic creation is placed in abeyance, and disembodiment replaces dismemberment. Her voice does not replace a desired, absent other body, but rather displaces her own body. The quest for personal gratification that launches Orpheus's enterprise is translated into its surrender. Accordingly, ascent rather than descent characterizes the pythia's departure from the mortal world. The topography of Hades gives way to a lofty mountain, symbol of unity between the upper and the nether worlds that dispels the tensions confronted by Orpheus and Hamlet. The Sibyl assumes a mediatory position between mortality and divinity, between temporality and eternity, and between the external and the internal.

Of the nine Sibylline books only three survive, and of the nine Sibyl poems Tsvetaeva planned only three materialized. In the first poem of her *Sibyl* cycle, the bard's descent is replaced by a radical alteration of the Sibyl's perceptual state that makes possible the transition between the mortal and the eternal. The Sibyl departs from the perceptual dictates of the phenomenal world of sense and mere appearance. The blocking out of external stimuli signaled by the lowered eyelids—an image that recurs persistently in Tsvetaeva's lyrics—effects a transition from exteriority to interiority. Analogous to Orpheus's journey to the underworld is the Sibyl's inward journey. The kenosis or "emptying out" of the Sibyl that is described in this poem marks her departure from the ready-made world which can at best be a stimulus to reality, but not reality itself. This departure culminates in her apprehension of divinity—the creative, intuitive realms of imaginative thought. The "entry" of the god signals the appearance of the divine within the Sibyl's newly cleared perceptual field, a divinity that may be apprehended when the limits of the finite world are superseded. The Sibyl discovers another realm of existence not in consequence of a journey to the domain of death, but rather on the strength of a metaphorical voyage that takes her from the narrow conditions of the outside world to the vastness of the inner self.

In the second poem the Sibyl's separation from her surroundings is emphasized as she appears in the guise of an impenetrable cliff that looms in isolation over the mundane world. From this perspective she recognizes the insignificance of the events of the world below her. This phase is as close and as sympathetic as Tsvetaeva gets to the abstraction she condemns in Hamlet. Accordingly, in the final poem of the cycle the Sibyl is engaged in direct response to the world from which she has departed. The Sibyl's voice is now heard directly as she consoles an infant whose crying she understands as the distress of a spirit being forced into the burdensome existence of which she herself has been almost entirely freed: the correlative confines of the world of the living and the body. She comforts the child with the promise of death, construed as a rebirth into the untrammeled light and world (« свет ») of aphysical being.[4]

СИВИЛЛА

1

Сивилла: выжжена, сивилла: ствол.
Все птицы вымерли, но бог вошел.

Сивилла: выпита, сивилла: сушь.
Все жилы высохли: ревностен муж!

Сивилла: выбыла, сивилла: зев
Доли и гибели! — Древо меж дев.

Державным деревом в лесу нагом —
Сначала деревом шумел огонь.

Потом, под веками — в разбег, врасплох,
Сухими реками взметнулся бог.

И вдруг, отчаявшись искать извне:
Сердцем и голосом упав: во мне!

Сивилла: вещая! Сивилла: свод!
Так Благовещенье свершилось в тот

Час не стареющий, так в седость трав
Бренная девственность, пещерой став

Дивному голосу . . .
— так в звездный вихрь
Сивилла: выбывшая из живых.

2

Каменной глыбой серой,
С веком порвав родство.
Тело твое — пещера
Голоса твоего.

Недрами — в ночь, сквозь слепость
Век, слепотой бойниц.
Глухонемая крепость
Над пестротою жниц.

Кутают ливни плечи
В плащ, плесневеет гриб.
Тысячалетья плещут
У столбняковых глыб.

Горе горѐ! Под толщей
Век, в прозорливых тьмах —
Глиняные осколки
Царств и дорожный прах

Битв . . .

3

СИВИЛЛА — МЛАДЕНЦУ:

К груди моей,
Младенец, льни:
Рождение — паденье в дни.

С заоблачных нигдешних скал,
Младенец мой,
Как низко пал!
Ты духом был, ты прахом стал.

Плачь, маленький, о них и нас:
Рождение — паденье в час!

Плачь, малеький, и впредь, и вновь:
Рождение — паденье в кровь,

И в прах,
И в час . . .

Где зарева его чудес?
Плачь, маленький: рожденье в вес!

Где залежи его щедрот?
Плачь, маленький: рожденье в счет,

И в кровь,
И в пот . . .

Но встанешь! То, что в мире смертью
Названо — паденье в твердь.

Но узришь! То, что в мире — век
Смежение — рожденье в свет.

Из днесь —
В навек.

Смерть, маленький, не спать, а встать,
Не спать, а вспять.

Вплавь, маленький! Уже ступень
Оставлена . . .
— Восстанье в день.

Sibyl

1

Sibyl: burnt out, sibyl: a tree trunk. All the birds have died out, but a god has entered.

Sibyl: drunk dry, sibyl: aridity. All her veins have dried out: the man is zealous!

Sibyl: departed, sibyl: mouth of fate and destruction!—A tree among maidens.

Like a sovereign tree in a bare forest—fire first roared through the tree.

Then, beneath the eyelids—swiftly, unexpectedly, god surged up through the dry rivers.

And suddenly, in despair of seeking without: heart and voice fallen: within me!

Sibyl: soothsayer! Sibyl: vault! Thus the Annunciation was accomplished in that

Unaging hour, thus into the grayness of grasses ephemeral maidenhood, become a cave

For the divine voice . . . —thus into an astral whirlwind Sibyl: departed from the living.

2

Like a stone gray cliff, having severed ties with the age. Your body is the cave of your voice.

With your very depths—into the night, through the blindness of eyelids, with the blindness of battlements. Deaf-mute fortress above the motleyness of the reaping women.

Downpours envelop your shoulders in a cloak, fungus molders. Millennia splash by the rigidly immobile cliffs.

Woe to the mountain! Under the thickness of eyelids, in the discerning obscurities—clay shards of kingdoms and roadside dust

Of battles . . .

3

The Sibyl to the Infant Child:

Cling to my breast, infant child: birth is a fall into days.

From the nonexistent cliffs beyond the clouds, my infant child, how low you have fallen! You were a spirit, you have become dust.

Cry, little one, for them and us: birth is a fall into the hour.

Cry, little one, both henceforth and anew: birth is a fall into blood,

And dust, and time . . .

Where is the afterglow of its miracles? Cry, little one: it's a birth into weight!

Where are the fallow lands/accumulations of its munificence? Cry, little one: it's a birth into counting/birth counts!

Into blood, into sweat . . .

Yet you will rise! What is called death in the world is a fall into the firmament.

Yet you will see! What is a closing of eyelids in the world is birth into light.

From today—into forever.

Death, little one, is not to sleep, but to rise, not to sleep, but return.

Swim, little one! Already the step is left behind . . . —Resurrection into day.

(*SP* 3:24–26; ellipses in original)

A close consideration of these poems permits us to trace the coming-into-being of the prophetess of this cycle and of the poet of Tsvetaeva's imaginative realm. The opening lyric depicts the maiden's preparation for and entry into her divinely ordained role. The incantatory ninefold repetition of the name **Сивилла** emphasizes the inexorability of the summons and inevitability of her destiny. The nine stanzas of the poem fall into three equal sections, each of which describes one step of this transformation: her summons and preparation, her comprehension of what is exacted from her, and, finally, her attainment of oracular status. The conclusion of each section is set off by a temporary shift in meter and a concomitant deceleration of tempo that mark the Sibyl's progress. The poem culminates with her completed departure from the mundane world.

The first section of the poem (stanzas one to three) marks the result of the systematic annihilation of the Sibyl's restrictive self. The opening stanza describes the burning out of the tree and the dying out of its birds: only a hollow tree trunk survives for the god to enter. The second stanza emphasizes the consequent aridity. The metonymies of the tree trunk and the birds give way to a metaphoric representation of the Sibyl as a "tree among maidens." The first stage of her metamorphosis is complete.

Crucial to the becoming of the prophetess is the radical readjustment of her relationship to her surroundings, predicated on an alteration of her inner state. It is, in other words, not the surrounding world that must undergo transformation or replacement, but the Sibyl's perception of it. The Sibyl must eradicate all preconceived, ready-made perceptual norms, as is emphasized in the insistent recurrence of the prefix « вы- », which appears no fewer than five times in the first three stanzas of the poem: « выжжена, вымерли, выпита, высохли, выбыла ». The exhaustive emptying thus indicated is counteracted by a single « во- » prefixed verb that signals the entry of the divine: « но бог вошел ». In place of the twittering, short-lived birds, the Sibyl is to house eternal divinity. The drying up of her veins suggests the desiccation of her own vitality in total surrender to the divine "zealous man" by whom she is now possessed. The erotic undercurrents of the action serve only to underscore the degree to which sexuality has been superseded.

The Sibyl's departure from the temporally limited mundane occurs precisely at this juncture. Stanza three is pivotal: it asseverates that her self-surrender results not in the annihilation of the self, but in its dramatic expansion. It is here that we encounter for the first time an act that bespeaks the Sibyl's own volition: « Сивилла: выбыла » [Sibyl departed]. Individual responsibility is activated by her surrender to the suprapersonal force by which she is invaded. Having been emptied, she now vacates the world of the living.

The completion of the first section is marked by an elevation of tone that brings the poem to its first climax. Punctuation makes the caesuras which occur regularly in the first three stanzas increasingly pronounced in the second line of each couplet: a comma in line two, a colon in line four, and finally an exclamation mark in conjunction with a dash in the sixth line. The increased length of these pauses decelerates the tempo and indicates the gravity of what is transpiring. The enjambment in stanza three enacts the Sibyl's transcendence of boundaries. Because the punctuation and metrical pattern of the two preceding stanzas create emphatic stops at the end of each line, and because stanza three is identical in meter to the earlier ones, the enjambment that occurs here is unexpected and all the more pronounced. It helps to underscore the thematically delineated progress made by the Sibyl as she is transformed into a soothsayer—the mouthpiece of fate.

The image of the tree, which appears frequently in Tsvetaeva's works of the twenties, is one that has been symbolically aligned with poetry since ancient times. The growth of a tree proceeds simultaneously toward the chthonic and the celestial, which interact in its nurture and resultant growth, development, and fruition. As such it comes to be a powerful emblem of the poet. In Tsvetaeva's works too trees convey a specifically poetic ethos.[5] Thus, for example, in the nine-poem cycle *Деревья* [Trees] she writes of the power of trees to heal the ill effects of the mundane. The concluding lyric of that cycle represents the Cumaean prophetess in the guise of a tree and echoes the motif of discovery and insight transpiring beneath lowered eyelids.

Tsvetaeva's alignment of the Sibyl with a tree appears to have been prompted by a lyric of a poet she revered no less than Blok—Rainer Maria Rilke's "Eine Sibylle," written in 1907 and included in *Neue Gedichte II* [New Poems II], a collection with which Tsvetaeva was thoroughly familiar. In this poem Rilke describes the Sibyl's replacement of a human temporal scale with the far broader one of the forest: "Und man änderte die Maße, / und man zählte sie wie einen Wald // nach Jahrhunderten" [And one changed the scale / and one counted her like a forest // in centuries].[6] In the poem flocks of birds—Rilke's metaphor for words—circle about her and return to her branches to roost. As we shall see presently, this arboreal metaphor leads also to Tsvetaeva's comparison of the Sibyl with the Virgin Mary in the latter part of her poem. The incineration she describes in the opening of the poem under discussion and the fortresslike cliff that represents her Sibyl in the second lyric of the cycle also derive from Rilke's "Eine Sibylle," where the prophetess is described as "schwarz wie eine alte Citadelle / hoch und hohl und ausgebrannt" [Black as an aged citadel / high and hollow and burned out] (1:568).

The second section of «Сивилла: выжжена» (stanzas four to six) develops the images of the first part as the Sibyl enters the next phase of her transformation that culminates with her recognition of the source of her clairvoyance. The steps of her progress are outlined in sequence and with absolute certitude. Although the metric regularity with which the poem opened persists here, the decrease in the number of caesuras and the cessation of the incantatory invocation of the Sibyl's name give this section an entirely different tonality.

The metaphor of the tree dominates the opening of the second section, where it is characterized by a paronomastically related epithet «державным деревом» [sovereign tree]. The instrumental case proclaims the tree to be a medium of the god. Through it the divine—here represented as that all-consuming fire whose effects are described in the preceding stanzas—can manifest itself. The dry rustling of the flames and the burning tree are conveyed by the sibilants that predominate in the first four stanzas of the poem.

In the fourth stanza the particularity of the event being recorded is imbedded in a vast temporal framework that reflects its universality. Divinity, fire, and the sacrificial tree are described as participating in the production of primal sound. The communication of divine with mortal is ever repeated and yet ever new. Divine revelation is destructive of the physical world.

The fifth stanza continues the process of the Sibyl's coming-into-being and returns to the specific situation at hand. As the emptying and the burning out are completed, attention is drawn inward, where the god's dynamic course is traced through the "dry rivers" of the tree branches, which recall the Sibyl's desiccated veins of stanza two. Another important step in the Sibyl's becoming is completed with the transition from the external to the internal, signaled here by the Sibyl's lowered eyelids. The closed eyes are emblematic in this cycle and elsewhere in Tsvetaeva's writings of a perceptual transvaluation. The tyranny of phenomenal vision is replaced by transcendent imaginative perception. The image of blind clairvoyance is central also to the second poem of this cycle. It expresses a dominant concern of the Romantics that was ever at the heart of Tsvetaeva's artistic strivings. This concern is cogently described by M. H. Abrams:

> "Single vision," the reliance on the "bodily," "physical," "vegetable," "corporeal," or "outward eye," which results in a slavery of the mind to merely material objects, a spiritual sleep of death, and a sensual death-in-life—to this way of seeing poets opposed the liberated, creative, and resurrective mode of sight "thro', and not with the eye," or of sight by means of the "inward eye," the "intellectual eye," the "imaginative eye," or simply "the imagination."[7]

In Tsvetaeva's poem the inward concentration indicated by the lowered eyelids makes possible the sudden appearance of the god (« в разбег, врасплох »).[8] The god's upward rush through the "dry rivers" of the tree branches signals that the internal and the external have now been brought into conjunction and can be depicted simultaneously. This image is motivated by the description of the Sibyl's veins in line 4, « Все жилы высохли » [All her veins have dried out], and the appearance of the expanding branches of the tree which has become her metaphoric representation. It appears at a particularly appropriate juncture of the poem, for it is here that the Sibyl's dramatic emptying out culminates in her inner awareness.

The kenotic annihilation of the self and the exclusion of all external stimuli open the way for entry of the divinity, which in the second line of the poem had been described by the verb вошел and is now represented as an upsurge: « взметнулся ». The possibility emerges that the "entry" is to be regarded figuratively and that the "divinity" is an ever present attribute to be perceived if and whenever the boundaries of the self and the surrounding world are superseded. The contradance of Sibyl and divinity in this poem can thus be seen as emblematic of the ever shifting relationship of the external and the internal, and of the processes of internalization and externalization that are attendant on prophetic and poetic states. These transitions between interiority and exteriority constitute an analogue for the Orphic negotiation between the upper and the lower worlds.

The opening line of stanza five portrays rhythmically the inner turmoil that is consequent to the Sibyl's comprehension of the divine. The established metrical organization of the poem is perpetuated here—a caesura appears just as in stanzas one to three. The punctuation in this line, however, breaks up the feet—heretofore clearly ternary—into groups of two: xx, xxxx—xx, xx (« Потом, под веками — в разбег, врасплох »). The ternary feet dictated by the Sibyl's trisyllabic name are, like her sense of self, temporarily disrupted, only to be resumed in the subsequent line as the Sibyl regains her stability.

In stanza six the comprehension of the true situation comes swiftly and suddenly to her: she must seek within her newly emptied, instaurated self. The prepositional phrase in which this realization is couched—« во мне »—echoes the prefix « во- » of the opening stanza and reenforces that redirection of energies signaled by the lowered eyelids. The Sibyl now enters the other world of the inner self. The magnitude of what has transpired is emphasized by the hypermetrical stress with which the line opens: « Сердцем и голосом упав: во мне! » [Heart and voice fallen: in me!]. The strongly articulated pause that precedes « во мне! » lends particular weight to the exclamation and the fact that it breaks up an anticipated amphibrachic foot makes it all the more prominent. Once again, a deviation from the metrical norms set in the lyric demands a deceleration of tempo.

The intense inward concentration that leads the Sibyl to comprehend the divinity inside her leads to a dramatic expansion of her perceptual scope. In stanza seven she is described as a soothsayer (« вещая ») and a « свод », an image which by virtue of its meanings of "collection," "arch," or "vault" and its kinship with the verb « сводить » [to bring together] suggests drawing and holding together, supporting. « Свод » also refers to the vault of heaven. The Sibyl's severance from her former self and from her surroundings leads to a transcendent state of connectedness. She can now join past, present, and future in her prophecies and can overarch the fragmentation and divisiveness of the mundane world. She becomes the clairvoyant unifier of the mortal and the divine within her.

It is at this point that the strong articulation of the meter ceases and the pronounced stops at the ends of lines give way to a series of enjambments that erode line breaks and even the stanzaic boundaries that have up to now been inflexibly maintained. Absent from the two final stanzas of the poem are the internal rhymes that accentuate the meter of stanzas three, five, and seven.[9] This blurring of formal divisions makes palpable the Sibyl's transcendence of the boundaries of her previous self that leads to her expanded yet unified vision.

The foregrounding of ever repeating patterns of mythic plots is, as we have seen, a characteristic feature of Tsvetaeva's mythopoeia. Even as Christ arises in connection with Tsvetaeva's Orpheus, so the image of the Virgin Mary is drawn into her representation of the Sibyl. The Annunciation to which the Sibyl's admission of the divine is likened underscores the replacement of the importunate eros of Orpheus's myth with the transcendent asexual self-surrender typified by the Sibyl.

In her childhood diary Tsvetaeva's daughter Ariadna Efron notes that the Annunciation was her mother's favorite holiday.[10] Characteristically, Tsvetaeva favors even over Christmas and Easter a holiday that prefigures the birth, death, and resurrection of Christ. She consistently accords promise a higher status than completion or accomplishment. Anticipation expands time beyond a given moment to endow an event with eternal presence and to conflate past, present, and future in a fertile synchrony. The « час не стареющий » [unaging hour] of the Annunciation is not a finite event, but one that is drawn into perpetual being. Here the powerful creative stimulus of Orpheus's anticipation of personal gratification gives way to the anticipation of the fulfillment of divine ordinance. Filled with the divine Word, the Virgin Mary comprises the ephemeral and the eternal, the human and the divine. Her inner space expands to become, as a Russian Orthodox hymn of praise describes, "more expansive than the very heavens."

The Sibyl's submission to the divine imperative similarly removes her from mundane time and space as her surrendered self attains infinite and eternal proportions. She arrives at those vast reaches praised by Eurydice not through death, but through the annihilation of the self. This transcendence of the self expands what remained for Orpheus a quest for personal satisfaction into a transpersonal fulfillment of divine service.

Tsvetaeva does not distinguish here between the pagan and the Christian. She is concerned only with the parallels between ancient soothsayer and bearer of Christ, who conjoin the mortal and the divine. Those parallels highlight the crucial similarity between Orpheus and the Sibyl: the totality of their surrender to the force that impels their radical break with the existing order. At the same time the link of the Sibyl with the Virgin Mary throws into relief the selflessness that distinguishes these women from the Greek bard.

The interrelation of the Sibyl with the Virgin Mary is a productive one. It evolves directly out of Rilke's comparison of Mary with a tree in his lyric titled "Verkündigung" [Annunciation] and subtitled "Ein Engel spricht" [An Angel Speaks] from *Das Buch der Bilder* [The Book of Images]. In that poem the Virgin Mary is the "tree among maidens," as is emphasized by the angel's fourfold repetition of "Du aber bist der Baum" [You, however, are the tree] (1:409–10). This refrain marks the Virgin Mary's electedness, yet also reaffirms her real presence in the physical world, which, as the angel notes with regret, is outside the scope of his own existence.[11]

Tsvetaeva draws on the Annunciation to underscore the Sibyl's similar position. Although in the *Sibyl* lyrics she summarily dispenses with the body, she nonetheless places the prophetess firmly in the physical world—first in the image of the tree and then as the gray cliff that dominates the landscape of the second poem of the cycle. This imagery bespeaks not departure but mediation, as exemplified by the Virgin Mary.

In the context of the parallel that Tsvetaeva draws between the Sibyl and the Virgin Mary, the relationship between eros and poetic language that is central to the Orpheus myth undergoes significant redefinition. We have already noted that for Orpheus eros motivates the drive to effect a union of opposites, among which are male-female, mortal-immortal, and living-dead. Tsvetaeva follows the promptings of the myth when she recognizes the correlativity of these paired antinomies. In the *Metamorphoses* Ovid recounts that upon returning from the underworld Orpheus rejects women and engages in homoerotic relations with boys. This detail—absent, predictably, from the retellings of both Schwab and Stoll—is generally construed as Orpheus' ostensible adherence to a vow of fidelity to his lost beloved. Yet its implications go beyond commendable matrimonial fealty. It would appear that, having failed in his descent to reconcile the antinomies male-female and life-death, Orpheus withdraws from seeking their direct, literal union to conjugate them in song. The untoward presence of the mortal body among the shades is replaced by the mediating voice of the poet, an option, as we shall see in the conclusion of this study, which Tsvetaeva was to consider in the 1935 lyric « Есть счастливцы и счастливицы » [There Are Fortunate Men and Women]: « Если б Орфей не сошел в Аид / Сам, а послал бы голос / Свой » [If Orpheus had not descended into Hades / himself, but had sent his voice] (*SP* 3:184).

The myth of the Sibyl provides another perspective on the relation of eros and language, specifically in the context of the antinomies confronted by Orpheus. In the myth of the prophetess the body is no longer the locus or the object of desire. Instead, it is transformed into a sacred space of resonance for the mediating voice. With the reference to the Virgin Mary, Tsvetaeva underscores the elimination of eros and jubilates in the ultimate victory of the word that has replaced direct physical engagement. Even as it conjoins the mortal with the immortal and the ephemeral with the eternal, the image of a mortal woman pregnant with a divine male child represents an alternative synthesis of that antinomy of male and female that heterosexual union briefly reconciles.

The Virgin Mary, as representative of genuine supersession of eros and not merely its circumvention, is an ideal counterexample to Hamlet. For Tsvetaeva the Annunciation proclaims above all the victory of the word over the flesh, a momentous event underscored in Annunciation services when the Virgin is hailed repeatedly as Eve's replacement. The Sibyl and the Virgin Mary represent a situation in which the gratification of the flesh and the focus on the body it generates are superseded by the dedication of that body to mediation between the mortal and the divine. Thus, paradoxically, the body expands beyond the purely physical.

The Annunciation and the myth of the Sibyl do more than suggest an alternative to the erotic union of male-female. They serve also to override the antinomic relationship between life and death. Mary's womb houses the Child who is to accomplish the ultimate transformation of death into eternal Life. In the Sibyl myth the voice displaces body, eros, and birth. The replacement of mortality with eternity is accomplished directly by the unaging voice, not by a divine offspring.

As the process of the Sibyl's transformation is completed, it is not arrival but rather newly opened potential that Tsvetaeva emphasizes. The prefix « вы- », which is used so emphatically in the opening of the poem to signal the emptying of the Sibyl, now describes her vacation of the familiar world: « Сивилла: выбывшая из живых ». The « выбыла » of line 5 now becomes a participle showing that her departure has become an attribute of the Sibyl. « Выбывшая » extends across metrical feet, which previously had coincided with word boundaries and had been emphasized by punctuation and rhyme. The second pause that occurs in each of the other lines that invokes the name of the prophetess is absent here, and this variation creates a cadence for the poem.

The Sibyl has accomplished in her own way that paradoxical task that Orpheus too confronted and that Hamlet could not comprehend: she has left the world of the living without having died. Orpheus accomplishes in song the spatial comprehension of the upper and lower worlds. In her enigmatic prophecies the Sibyl achieves an analogous temporal comprehension of past, present, and future. The Sibyl's privileged vantage point comprises the vast antinomies of mortality and divinity, of life and death, of ephemerality and eternity that define existence. She simultaneously overarches them with her being (« Сивилла — свод ») and unites them within herself.

The Sibyl's individual development also reenacts universal poetic evolution. The certitude of immutable law does not preclude the freshness and unexpectedness of the individual moments of its manifestation. The "suddenly" of the Sibyl's self-realization and the astral whirlwind (« звездный

вихрь») with which she departs from our world echo the «**врасплох, не готовясь**» [unawares, without preparing] of Orpheus-Blok's entry into the creative state in the lyric "Like One Somnolent, Intoxicated."

The second poem of the cycle focuses on the transfiguration that reflects newly attained perceptivity. The Sibyl of the first poem no longer exists. The absence of her name—invoked nine times in the preceding lyric—acknowledges her departure from the mundane. The "tree among maidens" is here represented in the guise of an ageless cliff that emblematizes the profound interiority at which the prophetess has arrived and the distance of this interiority from the human spatio-temporal scale. Solitary, she now towers above the concerns of the everyday world, her senses tightly sealed against it.

The dynamism of the first lyric gives way here to slow, ponderous lines that communicate the Sibyl's remove from the hurried pace of the day-to-day. In the wake of the dactylic foot that opens each line, the two trochees that regularly follow it in the odd lines seem particularly drawn out. The ictuses—especially those that terminate each catalectic even line—arrest the momentum of the metrically regular lines of this poem. This gray uniformity also extends to the unvarying rhyme scheme. Verbs disappear almost entirely, replaced by the instrumental case. Each of the first three stanzas of the poem consists of two two-line sentences, and it is not until the concluding stanza that the lyric departs from this norm. The conjunction of these features and their inflexible regularity lend a concentrated gravity and immutability to the portrait of the clifflike Sibyl.

The Sibyl's liberation, her inspiration, and her comprehension of the divine appear to have culminated in an inert state in which she remains impervious to all signs of change and vitality. The fact that this representation is couched in a metrical form and rhyme scheme that are as weighty and monotonous as the gray, unchanging face of the cliff can only make it more difficult to discern any positive value in the Sibyl's radical transformation, which seems to have left her in circumstances more restricted than those she abandoned in the first place. It appears that the fluid relationship between inner and outer space that obtained in the first poem has ossified in this lyric into strict, impenetrable demarcations, a situation that appears to go against the grain of Tsvetaeva's own definition of her art. Yet, predictably, the contradiction is merely apparent. The image of the Sibyl underscores the vast difference between the prophetess and the mere mortal. The reader is urged to penetrate the outward visage of lyric and prophetess to recognize the deeper significance they shelter.

We may begin this penetration by recalling that the mountain has been an important poetic image aligned with the imaginative process. Thus, for example, as an image that, like the tree, suggests the drawing together of chthonian with celestial, it is a frequent metaphor in Friedrich Hölderlin's thinking about poetry. Even as it indicates ascent, the mountain encourages descent into the hidden spaces that harbor its riches. The separation of the Sibyl from the world is marked by the image of the solitary cliff. Yet what bears stronger testimony to this separation is not the image itself, but the vantage point that generates it. It is to the outside world whose denizens cannot penetrate her concealed and fortified interiority that the Sibyl presents an immobile rock face. This is implied by Tsvetaeva's choice of the instrumental case (« Каменной глыбой серой », etc.) over a direct equation of the prophetess with the cliff. Those who cannot penetrate outward appearances and who remain subject to the spatial and temporal constraints of their immediate world are insensible to the tremendous forces that bring a mountain into being, to the gradual changes of its exterior and the great, slow process of the mineral life within it.

The sharp separation of outer and inner states described in this poem is characteristic of Tsvetaeva herself. « В минуты потрясений », Ariadna Efron recalls about her mother, « она опускала веки » [In moments of intense emotion she would lower her eyelids.].[12] This detail of Tsvetaeva's personal body language reflects the control exercised by the poet over inner experience that finds expression in poetry. Her own immobility in moments of emotional intensity, the cliff face of the Sibyl, and the strictness of the form in which this poem is realized are emblematic of the poet's and the prophetess's strict control over the expression of inner turmoil.

Ultimately, the Sibyl's detachment from her surroundings accomplishes a unified vision of the fragmented world below her. The prevalence of the instrumental case functions additionally to underscore that her newly attained interiority is not an end in itself, but a means toward something greater: the penetration beyond physical boundaries indicated by the phrase « сквозь слепость / Век » [through the blindness / of eyelids].

The description of the prophetess opens with a reaffirmation of her break with temporality. The gray cliff that houses her voice is an image that, unlike the once-living tree of the preceding poem, represents her as immobile and impervious to change. The second stanza emphasizes further the Sibyl's break with and distance from her surroundings: she is both blind and deaf-mute. The battlements and the fortress characterize the hostility of her surroundings and the imperative that the inimical outside world be prevented from penetrating her isolation. Alienated from the surrounding world, the gray Sibyl stands above the varicolored, active reapers below her. The image of the reapers suggests the body's immediate need for sustenance and the unvarying cycle of life, death, and rebirth. It is an image suggestive of change, transience, and impermanence, which contrasts sharply to the indomitable sameness of the cliff. That the reapers are women reminds us that, had it not been for her removal beyond the limits of this world, the Sibyl would have been among them. As it is, she now stands, childless, distanced from the agricultural and generational cycle.

The third stanza records the cliff's allegiance to the natural elements and removes her further still from the temporal frame of the world she has vacated. The amplified temporal scale of the tree expands here to that of the mountain. The Sibyl now dominates not only the ephemeral scene of the bright harvesters, but the millennia that splash at the foot of her monumental bulk.

The spatial remove and the temporal expansion of the Sibyl's perspective determine the way she regards the mundane world in the conclusion of the poem. The last stanza opens with a suggestion of the pain and difficulty attendant on the Sibyl's all-seeing solitude: « Горе горѐ » [Woe to the mountain]. The paronomastic kinship of these words suggests the woe already implicit in the very word for mountain. A disruption of the established metrical pattern heralds the revelation of what transpires beneath the Sibyl's impenetrable eyelids. The consistent division of each stanza into two sentences gives way here to a flow of enjambed lines that overwhelm the stops the reader has been taught to expect at the end of the second and fourth lines of each stanza. Here even the last line of the stanza spills over into the opening of a new one. We have already observed a similar erosion of anticipated boundaries by the force of the Sibyl's transformation at the conclusion of the preceding poem of this cycle. The redrawing of expected divisions is, as we have seen, a powerful resource for Tsvetaeva's depictions of altered perceptual states. Here it signals that the focus of this poem, which has thus far concentrated on the impenetrability of the division between the Sibyl and the surrounding world, now shifts to the unfragmented interior space of the prophetess herself. That clairvoyance originates in the Sibyl's dark inner recesses can come as no surprise—the necessity for such a paradoxical outcome has been established by the preceding poem.

The Ozymandian shards of civilization and the roadside dust of battles that appear to the Sibyl's inward eye hold the totality of past, present, and future that defies temporal linearity. The paltry remains that the cliff overshadows indicate simultaneously what has become of past glory as well as the impending fate of the glories of the present and the future. The conclusion of the poem opens into what the Sibyl sees, but it is not given to the reader to follow very far the vision to which she is privy. The final stanza trails off—unrealized—in ellipsis and, just as in the preceding poem, the reader is left behind in the world from which the Sibyl has departed. The absence of closure also suggests the futility of any attempt at complete enumeration of the world's myriad trivialities in which we remain. In the bustle of the fragmented existence the Sibyl surveys, we recognize the stasis of ceaseless, futile repetition. Opposed to this teeming world is the profound mutability of the mountain's inner growth.

It was probably Tsvetaeva's reluctance to leave the Sibyl in her lofty isolation from the mundane that prompted her to conclude the cycle with « Сивилла — младенцу » [The Sibyl to the Infant Child], a poem written nearly a year after the first two Sibyl lyrics. In a note appended to this poem she explains: « Стихотворение перенесено сюда из будущего, по внутренней принадлежности » [The poem has been moved here from the future on the strength of its internal belonging] (*SP* 3:25). This lyric represents the final step in the Sibyl's development. In it the prophetess articulates her new perspective on existence once she is reconnected with the world from which she had been so far removed in the preceding poem.

The Sibyl consoles a newborn child with the promise of death, which she extols not by describing the enticing qualities of the afterlife, but by focusing on the negative characteristics of life to which birth subjects the child. Echoing the sentiment of Lermontov's « Ангел » [The Angel], the Sibyl describes birth as a fall from a superior edenic realm. Rather than comfort the infant, she repeatedly encourages it to cry. The poem is focused on the abjuration of enemies familiar to readers of Tsvetaeva: habit, quantification, linear temporality, weight, measure, and physicality—all of which we shall encounter again in the cycle *Поэты* [Poets] and which are presented here as the benchmarks of life on earth. The alternative to the restrictiveness and divisiveness characteristic of the mundane is the unbounded and unparceled expanse of death that Jairus's daughter and Eurydice were unwilling to replace with life.

The poem falls into two unequal parts. The first eight stanzas are devoted to a highly unflattering representation of the realm of the living. The remaining five offer consolation with the promise of death, redefined as an escape from that bondage of life on earth which the first part of the lyric condemns.

Just as inner and outer space undergo dramatic realignment in the opening poem of the cycle, the relationship between birth and death is subjected to radical revision in « Сивилла — младенцу ». Birth becomes the cessation of being, while death reopens the potential for that higher existence. The ascendancy of the state the infant must leave behind over the one into which it is born is conveyed spatially by its placement above our world. Birth is described insistently as a fall, and Tsvetaeva exploits the rhyme pair « рожденье-паденье » [birth-fall] to stress this alignment. Indeed, in the course of the poem the two words become virtually synonymous, while their paronomastic link with « день » [day] emphasizes the rule of temporality that they usher in. The child's plummet into "days" marks its departure from eternity and its entry into the strictly measured, fragmented time of mortality. In the second stanza the child's fall is described as its descent from the literally utopian « заоблачные нигдешние скалы » [nonexistent cliffs beyond the clouds] into the excessively defined placeness of this world. Correlative with the spatial and temporal limitations of the child's new surroundings is the embodiment of the spirit whose newly imposed corporeality is aligned with nouns that underscore both its burdensome quality and the brevity and futility of its existence: dust, hour, blood, and sweat (« прах », « час », « кро́вь », « пот »).

The Sibyl's brief but dramatic summary of the disadvantages attendant on birth may well move the child to cry in both regret and protest as it is urged to do. Her prompting « Плачь, маленький, о них и нас » [Cry, little one for them and us] suggests the twofold significance of the child's plaint: pity for "them," the denizens of the mundane whom this pronoun disassociates from the Sibyl and the child, and the longing for "us," the realm from which birth separates the child but to which the Sibyl herself remains connected. The Sibyl urges not a primal scream but a cry of cognizance.

The negative consequences of birth receive further elaboration in a series of conditions that develop out of the larger categories of spatial and temporal restrictions noted in the beginning of the poem. The Sibyl's repeated insistence that the child cry becomes more intense here. The sweat, dust, hour, and blood that characterize earthly existence are emphasized by the deceleration that occurs in stanzas five and eight, which are reduced to two lines of only one iambic foot each and which make palpable the oppressive weight of earthly existence.

Anticipating the predictable objections to the position she takes, the Sibyl counters hypothetical protestations to her stance with two questions that deny the commonly touted advantages of birth: « Где зарева его чудес? » [Where is the after glow of its miracles?] and « Где залежи его щедрот? » [Where are the fallow lands/accumulations of its munificence?]. Her response denies the "miracle" of birth which she calls a fall into weight (в вес), which is to say, into physicality and quantification. Similarly, any association of the giving of life with generosity is counteracted by the accountability and countability birth exacts: « рожденье в счет » [birth into counting/birth counts]. Stanza eight adds "blood" and "sweat" to the list of negative characteristics begun in the seventh, thus further discrediting any association of birth with miracle or munificence. The first section of the poem ends at stanza eight, which trails off into an ellipsis which suggests that the list is far from complete.

The ninth stanza opens the second section of the poem, which is devoted to praise of death characterized as a release from the onerous conditions of life. Enjambments, which were absent from the first section of the poem, now dominate. Although the basic metrical pattern remains unchanged, the conjunction of these enjambments with the strongly articulated breaks that also occur here makes this section sound entirely different from the first. As in the lyric "Eurydice to Orpheus," here too a realignment of formal boundaries signals a radical shift in vantage point. The downward movement emphasized up to now is reversed suddenly and dramatically by the exclamatory assurance that the child will rise again. « То, что в мире смертью / Названо » [What is called death in the world] is redefined by the Sibyl. The child's fall into corporealiy is to be undone by the oxymoronic upward fall into the firmament promised by death.

The exclamation « Но узришь! » [Yet you will see] bespeaks an enhanced vision: the blindness of the physical world to the privileged space of the soothsayer is to be replaced with the Sibyl's clairvoyant blindness to the physical world. Death's closing of the infant's eyes is thus "birth into light"—« рожденье в свет ».

A line break intervenes between these lids and their closing (« век / Смеженье ») to represent that this is in fact their opening into a new state. Tsvetaeva's subversion of the notion of death's finality is intensified by the temporary misapprehension of « век » that this line break prompts. In the position in which it occurs, « век » is initially more likely to be understood as "age" or an appointed life span than as "eyelids," particularly in light of the prevalent temporal motif in this cycle. The opening of the following line rectifies this misapprehension, but the homonymic relationship of the nominative of "age" and the genitive plural of "eyelid" is thus drawn to the reader's attention and enhances the notion that lowered lids transform temporality—« век »—into « навек »—forever.

The equation of lowered lids with the opening of new perceptual realms figured prominently, as we have observed, in the Sibyl's departure from the constraints of the physical world. Its appearance here in a description of death underscores her own proximity to death. In the mountainous topography of the world from which the child falls, we recognize an image of the Sibyl herself. The infant's transition from life to death is analogous to the Sibyl's transition from an outward state to an inward one. The death of the child is the literal equivalent of the Sibyl's metaphorical death to this world.

In a virtuosic paronomastic unfolding the Sibyl goes on to describe the child's welcome reawakening to the eternal from the quotidian: « не спать, а встать, / Не спать а вспять » [not to sleep, but to rise, / not to sleep, but return]. However distinct the two opposing realms, in the space of language they are nevertheless coterminous. In each case it takes only slight phonemic adjustment to rectify the erroneous, commonly held assumptions about "what is called death in this world" and to reveal its true significance.

« Вплавь, маленький! » [Swim, little one!] the Sibyl exhorts the infant in the concluding stanza. The replacement of the measured tread of the mundane world with the unbroken flow of eternity espoused here has already been made palpable by the enjambments that dominate this section of the lyric. The poem culminates with the infant's « Восстанье в день » [Resurrection into day]. The verb conveys both upward movement and insurrection and thus transforms passive acquiescence to death into active rebellion against the restrictions of life. The singular "day" at which the poem arrives has nothing in common with the numerous "days" into which the flow of eternity is broken in the piecemeal existence of the mundane. Rather, it is—like the « час не стареющий » [unaging hour] of the first poem of the cycle—an emblem of the cessation of time and entry into eternity.

"The Sibyl to the Infant Child" reverses the significance of the paired antinomies of birth and death. Inevitably this draws attention not only to the ascendancy of the realm of spirit over that of flesh, but also, and more importantly, to the interdependency of those contraries in the shaping of existence. This interdependency is demonstrated with particular cogency by the fluidity of Tsvetaeva's imagery and her use of the same trope, image, or word to represent apparently antithetical phenomena. Thus, for example, a fall signals entry both into life and into death, while the closing of eyelids designates a new opening into enlightenment. Death becomes entry into new life, and the days of life indicate the end of the day of eternity. Paronomasia and polysemy are used for similar ends. Thus, for example, the great antinomy "life and death" is mitigated by the acoustic similarity of the words describing those vastly different states observed in stanza twelve: « не спать, а встать, / Не спать, а вспять ». The coincidence of antithetical signifieds in a single signifier is deployed to show the subsumption of antinomies by language, as we have already seen, for example, in « мир » and « свет », which Tsvetaeva uses alternately to designate both this world and the other. Demonstrated here is the Orphic capacity of poetry both to describe and to accomplish the true interrelation of the visible world with the invisible.

The negative assessment of the infant's birth parallels Tsvetaeva's account of the raising of Jairus's daughter and the retrieval of Eurydice. The positive value of maternity is forcefully displaced by the Sibyl's incantatory rehearsal of the limitations into which any newborn child enters. Given this emphasis, there can fall to the child's mother only censure like that directed at Orpheus and at Christ when they attempt to translate spirit into the corporeal world.

The situation of the infant whom the Sibyl addresses is analogous to that of a poem, whose realization similarly involves translation from the realm of illimitable possibility into the restricted specificity of linguistic and poetic form, a realization that must inevitably fall painfully short of the potential from which it emerges. The three poems of the *Sibyl* cycle may be seen as an outline of the coming-into-being of the poet and of the individual poem. The first step in this process is removal from the external world of physical sense perception to the creative inner space of poetic vision. Yet although fortified against incursions from the outside world, that interior can be described only in the terminology of the outer, rejected world. The result can only indicate rather than recreate the potential from which it emerges. The return of the infant to death, which is, according to the Sibyl's account, also the locus of preexistence, suggests metaphorically the failure of any poem to exhaust the limitless potential of poetry. This failure returns the poet to the beginning of ever new attempts at fulfillment.

In defining her art Tsvetaeva projects "the self-sustained condition of yearning for the inaccessible" that Brigitte Peucker isolates as a "typical romantic impulse."[13] The ceaseless striving demanded by the ever imperfect (as signaled by the verbal aspect) attempts to « творить мир тот — в мирах сих » [to create (continually) the other world in these worlds] (*IP* 1:184) is conveyed in the image of ascent rather than descent. The mountain, Hölderlin's preferred poetic image, which reconciles subterranean forces with those of the upper reaches, is for Tsvetaeva too a guise of the poet. As she was to formulate in the essay « Кедр » [The Cedar, January 1923], written shortly after the Sibyl poems, « Превосходство горы над равниной в том, что ей открыты *все* дали » [The supremacy of a mountain over a plain is that *all* expanses are open to it.] (*IP* 1:164). Tsvetaeva's stress on "all" indicates that the vista to which she refers here is not limited to the topography of our own world. As we shall see also in the *poèma New Year's*, ascent, which Tsvetaeva aligns with death, opens the way for continually renewed perception.

Her vertical orientation follows closely the one charted by the German Romantics and succinctly summarized by Novalis: " . . . und wenn der unerfüllte Trieb in die unermeßliche Höhe will, so versinkt die glückliche Liebe gern in die endlose Tiefe" [. . . and if unfulfilled desire seeks immeasurable heights, so does happy love sink gladly into the endless deep].[14]

Just as no single poem can recreate the limitless potential from which it derives, no single representation of the poet is adequate to portray him wholly. Tsvetaeva draws definitive features of this complex persona into ever new configurations that intimate the scope of the venture in which he is engaged. It is instructive therefore to consider the Sibyl side by side with Orpheus specifically in the context of Hamlet, Ophelia, and Eurydice, all of whom illuminate different aspects of the poetic enterprise.

Orpheus and the Sibyl shape two distinct but complementary accounts of the origin and expression of poetic utterance that are drawn implicitly along the lines of gender. Although their differences are ultimately absorbed into the ineffable complexity of poetry, the bard and the prophetess nevertheless remain discrete representations of the poet's dedication to the poetic task.

We may begin the comparison by recalling that Apollo's gift to Orpheus is given freely and that Orpheus encounters no difficulties in practicing his art.

Quite the contrary, all that surrounds him makes manifest the beneficence of his song, and he himself derives gratification from his gift. In setting out for the underworld, Orpheus launches an intensely personal quest on the strength of his own desire and not at the behest of an outside power exhorting him to the fulfillment of a mission. Yet, as we have observed already, Tsvetaeva overlooks the happier moments of the bard's legend to turn instead to the latter part of the myth where loss, alienation, and a violent end are the poet's lot.

The Sibyl provides a contrast both to the guise of Orpheus which Tsvetaeva ignores and to the one she chooses to project. She is not a singer but a soothsayer. Her utterances are not harmonious strains of song, but enigmatic outcries that shatter complacency with their demands for interpretation that must go far beyond a commonplace understanding of both our world and its everyday language. The hearers of her prophecies are not, like the auditors of Orpheus's song, enthralled into passive or involuntary response, but are actively engaged in discovering their meaning. For the Sibyl herself, personal desire is subsumed by self-surrender.

After his initial sojourn in the underworld, Orpheus is forced to return to the world of the living, for to remain *in corpore sano* among the dead is, as Tsvetaeva's Eurydice eloquently argues, a paradox too great to be sustained. Plato, who appears not to have thought much of Orpheus, sternly reminds him in the *Symposium* that death is the appropriate means for effecting a departure from the world of the living. Yet to die means also to cease being a poet. The Sibyl is privileged in that, like Orpheus, she too succeeds in leaving the mundane world without suffering death. Hers, however, is an alternative model for that departure: rather than cross into death she discovers within herself a space where both realms of existence interpenetrate. The impossibility of choosing between them that prevents Orpheus from resting content in either and that leaves Hamlet in a space too narrow to admit one or the other leads the Sibyl to unite both. She represents not the momentary displacement of the boundaries between life and death of poetic inspiration, but rather the abeyance of death through poetic endurance.

The relationships of the Sibyl and Orpheus to their respective mortal coils replicate their situations vis-à-vis the world of the living. The Sibyl's departure from this world is concurrent with her gradual disengagement from the constraints of the flesh. In this respect too Orpheus is less fortunate. Even as he must return to the upper world, so must he remain confined to that body that houses both his desire for Eurydice and his divine voice. The very voice that gains the Orphic poet access to the other world also keeps him tethered to this one. Orpheus's ultimate break with this world is accomplished by a dismemberment that runs considerably deeper than a sundering of the flesh: the loss of his body divorces him from the erotic impulse on which his song depends and, above all, from his voice, the instrument of his song. The Orphic voice cannot exist apart from the body and thus seeks ever new embodiment in the world of the living. Its eternity is that of endless succession.

The Sibyl is freed of her body not by violent dismemberment, but by gradual atrophy. Moreover, she retains her voice even after the body has disappeared. The awkward pairing of immortal voice with mortal body is thus resolved and the need for Orphic peregrinations between worlds obviated. The paradoxical inappropriateness in the underworld of that very eros that leads the bard into it is for the Sibyl replaced with a surrender of the self that gains cessation of desire without the intervention of death. The Sibyl's utterances are produced independently of any need for personal gratification. Orpheus's search for completion outside himself gives way to an intense concentration of the inward self. The Orphic paradox is displaced by the paradoxical growth of that self that has been relinquished. The Sibyl's transcendence of eros suggests an alternative also to Hamlet's disastrous repression of desire.

Like Ophelia and Eurydice, Tsvetaeva's Sibyl derives her ascendancy from her incorporeality. The disembodiment of these three women metaphorically removes them from the sphere of personal gratification to a superior, detached position from which the futility of bodily existence is evident. Eurydice in the underworld champions death over eros; Ophelia leaves the bourne of death to arouse Hamlet's erotic desire of which she herself can no longer partake; the Sibyl assumes a position that supersedes both. Specifically, she advocates the replacement of the body with the mediating voice. Her visible presence gives way to one that is aurally perceived. Just as the serpent's sting liberates Eurydice from the constraining desires of the world and the flesh, so too is the pythia freed from them by her inward journey. Her concentrated interiorization suggests an alternative to death for effecting a departure from both the phenomenal world and the constraints of the body.

The elevation of the Sibyl marks the superiority of her position. Whereas Eurydice in the underworld can retain only perturbing intimations of a world left behind forever, the Sibyl's departure from the mundane improves her vision of that world by enlarging the context in which she perceives it. Her disposition between the heaven of Phoebus-Apollo and the world of mortals bespeaks her ability to retain in simultaneity the eternal and the ephemeral, the mundane and the divine, and it is on the strength of this capacity that she can conjoin past, present, and future in prophecy. Although Tsvetaeva affords the power of negotiation between the two separate realms of existence to her bodiless Ophelia as well, Ophelia remains too closely engaged with Hamlet and the events of the phenomenal world she haunts to attain either the Sibyl's detachment or her interiority. Tsvetaeva's other spokeswomen address male counterparts; the Sibyl preserves her self-sufficiency and needs no complement to attain a wholeness of vision.

With the resolution of the conflict of eros and death that propels Orpheus and which Hamlet is unable to engage, the Sibyl attains that female superiority over male poets that Tsvetaeva described in the passages from "The Living about the Living" cited at the opening of this chapter. The Sibyl poems indicate that the privileged position of the woman derives from her surrender of individual desires to transpersonal ends. We recognize in connection with her female personae that Tsvetaeva's focus is less on doing away with the body itself than on the elimination of personal gratification from the poetic model. The alignment of the Sibyl with the Virgin Mary and her metamorphosis into a cliff emphasize that the entrance of the male, being filled by the male, and even conception are metaphors that point beyond the realm of the flesh to which they commonly refer. (In chapter Six we shall see Tsvetaeva's similar use of erotic metaphor to point beyond the body in her letters to Rilke.) The paradoxes of self-surrender fostering expansion of the self and of virgin conception and birth become emblems of the paradox of artistic creation—the conjugation of the flesh and the spirit, the mortal and the divine, the ephemeral and the eternal. The active Orpheus seeks out Eurydice. The Sibyl must wait passively to be singled out and entered by the male divinity. On the strength of eros Orpheus penetrates forbidden space. On the strength of self-surrender the Sibyl finds new existence within herself. There is no need to belabor the view of male and female sexuality that informs these differences. Translated into the supramundane space of poetic metaphor, these conventional views that oppress the woman in day-to-day life are transformed by Tsvetaeva into marks of the woman's unarguable ascendancy in the transcendent realm of poetry. In this capacity she becomes a model for male and female poets alike. Orpheus's translation of his physical longing for Eurydice into disembodied song is but an approximation of what the Sibyl and the Virgin Mary achieve. In the cycle *Poets* Tsvetaeva undertakes an analogous translation that removes all poets—regardless of gender—from their abject condition in the quotidian to a superior state in the poetic beyond.

Yet for all the differences between Orpheus and the Sibyl, crucial points of similarity remain. We have noted already that the Sibyl loses her body because she neglects to request of Phoebus physical vitality to complement the longevity he grants her. The way Tsvetaeva regards the Sibyl's "forgetfulness" leads us to the intersection between her myth and that of Orpheus. In the course of her correspondence with the critic Aleksandr Bakhrakh which resonates with the central themes and images of *After Russia*, Tsvetaeva relates, in a letter of 30 June 1923:

> Вот эпиграф к одной из моих будущих книг: (Слова, вложенные Овидием в уста Сивиллы, привожу на память:) «Мои жилы иссякнут,

мои кости высохнут, но ГОЛОС, ГОЛОС — оставит мне Судьба! » (Сивилла, согласно мифу, испросила Феба вечной жизни, *забыла* испросить себе вечной молодости! Не случайная забывчивость!)

[Here is the epigraph to one of my future books: (The words put by Ovid into the mouth of the Sibyl, I cite from memory:) "My veins will run dry, my bones will dry up, but my VOICE, my VOICE will be left me by Fate!" (The Sibyl, according to the myth, asked eternal life of Phoebus, but *forgot* to ask for eternal youth! This forgetfulness is not fortuitous!)][15]

We are reassured by this passage that Ovid's *Metamorphoses* is indeed the primary source for the *Sibyl* cycle. It is also significant that later in this letter Tsvetaeva herself identifies with the ancient soothsayer. Yet what interests us here is that, like Orpheus's backward glance that ensures the loss of Eurydice, the Sibyl's "forgetfulness" is recognized to be not an error, but a fateful election of spirit over flesh. Their dedication to the insubstantial and the centrality they accord voice point to the essential unity of their undertaking.

In her writings Tsvetaeva complicates the dichotomy of body and soul by introducing the voice as a third component that mediates between them. Although itself invisible, the voice depends on physiological apparatus for its production. It needs, moreover, a defined space in which to resound even after it leaves the body that has produced it. Thus the voice is in a peculiar situation of simultaneous dependency on the body and the visible world and freedom from them. As such, it becomes a metonymic representation of the poet, who finds himself in an analogous situation mediating between the visible and the invisible world, between his inner space and that of the outside world. The voice, as Tsvetaeva insists in the letter to Bakhrakh, is thus the poet's definitive characteristic:

У меня где-то в записках есть: « У поэта не должно быть « лица », у него должен быть *голос*, голос его — его лицо ». (« Лицо » здесь как *что*, голос — *как*.)

[Somewhere in my notes I have: "A poet should not have a 'face,' he should have a *voice*, his voice is his face." ["Face" here means *what*, voice—*how*.)][16]

Reflected here is Tsvetaeva's marked preference for aural perception over the visual. As she assured another correspondent, D. A. Shakhovskoi, hearing was for her by far the most privileged of the senses. « Вообще, из всех пресловутых пяти чувств, знаю только одно: слух. Остальных — как не бывало и — хоть бы не было! » [In general of all the notorious five senses I know only one: hearing. As for the rest—it is as if they didn't exist and—it scarcely matters whether they do!].[17]

Tsvetaeva regards the visual as conveying merely the surface of the surrounding world and aligns it with that mundane obtuseness against which the poet struggles. The aural—the vehicle for penetrating superficial appearances—is aligned with enhanced perceptivity. The demand for visual verification is, as we have seen, a potentially dangerous failing. Orpheus's backward glance and the overpowering need of Phoebus's son to see the prophetess whose voice he hears in Tsvetaeva's plans for her larger, unrealized Sibyl work underscore the tragic consequences of refusal to accept aural attestation without recourse to visual verification. Implicit in the behavior of Orpheus and of Phoebus's offspring is the correlativity of visual and physical gratification. From this derives a series of analogues that define Tsvetaeva's creative universe: aligned with the phenomenal world are the visual, the physical, and the semantic; appurtenant to the supramundane space from which poetry derives are the auricular, the spiritual, and the acoustic. Poet, voice, and word thus emerge as analogues by virtue of their mediatorial functions in these various but closely interrelated antinomies.

From this emerges Tsvetaeva's conviction that the superiority of poetic language over any other artistic medium is that the associative potential of its acoustic properties which removes it from mundane constraints operates simultaneously with a referential capacity that links it to this world. The innate abstractness of any linguistic sign system generates the potential for imaginative expressivity that retains productive ties with the recognizable world. This attitude to poetic language is reflected in the imperative that Orpheus retain his body and conceded even in the Sibyl myth by the critical function the body assumes as vessel for the divine voice, a function underscored by the metonymic connection of the Sibylline cave and the Virgin Mary's womb in the first poem and the replacement of her body with the cavernous cliff in the second.

Even as Tsvetaeva rejects the Futurist tendency to replace the specific referential attributes of language with its diffuse, exclusively acoustic features, so too does she ultimately reject the possibility of the poet's permanent withdrawal from this world or from the body that ties him to it. On the strength of longing for the other or of intense inward concentration, the poet is removed from the constraints of the self and the mundane world. Yet ultimately the poet is charged with the task of reconstituting the illimitable within the time and space of mortality. The Sibyl, like Orpheus and like Tsvetaeva herself, does not reject the physical world, but seeks only to prevent mundane contingency from overwhelming poetic destiny.

Chapter Five

Poets

So then because thou art lukewarm, and neither cold nor hot, I will spew thee out of my mouth.

—Revelation 3:16

FOR ALL the appropriateness of the Sibyl as a representative of the poet's mediation between the mortal and the divine, it remains for the myth of Orpheus to portray the hostility of the mundane from which the poet cannot effect a permanent departure and whose sacrificial victim he becomes. The surcease of the Sibyl's desires and her alienation from her surroundings are recognized as a mark of her service to a higher cause. This is not so for Orpheus, whose dedication to a higher purpose is perceived only as a rejection of the surrounding world and, as such, elicits severe reprisal. Although Orpheus's refusal of women after his venture into Hades outwardly resembles the repression of eros for which Ophelia takes Hamlet to task, in actuality it fulfills one of Tsvetaeva's central requirements for poets: the simultaneous protraction and sublimation of physical desire. The Maenads' inability to comprehend Orpheus's translation of the desire for a woman into longing for the unattainable results in his violent end. Where there is true poetic transcendence, the Maenads see only rejection. Such misapprehension of the poet's otherworldly allegiance persists in Tsvetaeva's accounts of poetic destiny. The dual nature of the poet which we have witnessed thus far in the internalized conflicts of desires of the mere mortal with the transpersonal demands of song is projected outward. Represented in the poet's clash with his surroundings, this conflict now emerges not from within the person of the poet, but from a divergence of vantage points. The recreation of these two points of vantage and the images of the poet they generate is the central concern of the cycle *Поэты* [Poets, 1923], which is the focus of attention in this chapter.

The cycle *Poets* provides us with the opportunity to consider more fully the causes of the vast separation between poets and nonpoets and to examine the nature and implications of the animosity that prevails between these two incompatible groups.[1] The poet's atypicality is shown both to elevate him above the surrounding world and to bring down upon him the hostility of its denizens. The fragmentary nature of quotidian perceptual norms makes his dismemberment inevitable and leads the nonpoetic world to dismember Orpheus again and again. The radical differences of the poet's values and scale remove him from the concerns of nonpoets who, for their part, ostracize him alternately for his inutility and his venturousness. His alienation from nonpoets is counterbalanced by the powerful bonds that unite him with all other poets.

Here Tsvetaeva's exploration of poet and poetry is rooted in the ethos of the later Romantics, who replaced initial hopes of transforming the world with the notion that it is the perception of it and not the world itself that must undergo transfiguration. Reflected in *Poets* is Tsvetaeva's desire to enhance the way signs of the surrounding world are ordered and decoded. The cycle provides rich material for exploring this aspect of her *ars poetica.*

Tsvetaeva directs her poetic discourse toward the discovery, examination, and application of images adequate to the representation of the poet. In so doing she also takes into account the poet's surroundings—the context in which he is forced to operate and which determines the apprehension of those images applied to him. The lyrics of *Poets* demonstrate that no single representation of the poet is adequate. This is so not simply because of the poet's complexity, but also because of the fruitful lack of fixity in the meaning of any individual sign or image assigned to him.

It is a vital part of Tsvetaeva's mission that fluidity and relativity of meaning remain at the forefront of her readers' awareness. The vast complex of associative and connective potential that such flexibility generates permits transcendence of the world of sense and mere appearance against which the poet rails. The need to preserve this flexibility informs the poet's hostility to perceptual rigidity and the hypesthesia that results from it. The language of the cycle is both demonstrative and richly allusive. A carefully constructed associative network functions in the substratum of the text to replicate Tsvetaeva's argument, and the technical resources of poetry are engaged in an active demonstration of the thematic material of the cycle. We shall first examine the poems sequentially, focusing on the images of the poet. Having defined the central issues, we shall follow the poet beyond the boundaries of this cycle to trace some of the associative networks that operate in the other, invisible world of the text.

The three poems of *Poets* were written in April 1923 and included in *After Russia.* The first describes the poet against a background of common expectations which he has no intention of fulfilling and lists the conventional perceptual categories that he emphatically rejects. The second poem highlights the abject condition of poets in a mundane context. Here the imagery generated to describe the poet reflects a distinctly unpoetical perspective. In the final lyric, we hear the voice of the solitary poet distraught at the incommensurability of her capacities with the narrow restrictions of the world in which they are to be exercised.

ПОЭТЫ

1

Поэт — издалека заводит речь.
Поэта — далеко заводит речь.

Планетами, приметами, окольных
Притч рытвинами . . . Между *да* и *нет*
Он даже размахнувшись с колокольни
Крюк выморочит . . . Ибо путь комет —

Поэтов путь. Развеянные звенья
Причинности — вот связь его! Кверх лбом —
Отчаетесь! Поэтовы затменья
Не предугаданы календарем.

Он тот, кто смешивает карты,
Обманывает вес и счет,
Он тот, кто *спрашивает* с парты,
Кто Канта на̀голову бьет,

Кто в каменном гробу Бастилий
Как дерево в своей красе.
Тот, чьи следы — всегда простыли,
Тот поезд, на который все
Опаздывают . . .
— ибо путь комет

Поэтов путь: жжя, а не согревая,
Рвя, а не взращивая — взрыв и взлом —
Твоя стезя, гривастая кривая,
Не предугадана календарем!

2

Есть в мире лишние, добавочные,
Невписанные в окоём.
(Нечислящимся в ваших справочниках,
Им свалочная яма — дом).

Есть в мире полые, затолканные,
Немотствующие — навоз,
Гвоздь — вашему подолу шелковому!
Грязь брезгует из-под колес!

Есть в мире мнимые, невидимые:
(Знак: лепрозариумов крап!)

Есть в мире Иовы, что Иову
Завидовали бы — когда б:

Поэты мы — и в рифму с париями,
Но выступив из берегов
Мы бога у богинь оспариваем
И девственницу у богов!

3

Что же мне делать, слепцу и пасынку,
В мире, где каждый и отч и зряч,
Где по анафемам, как по насыпям —
Страсти! где насморком
Назван — плач!

Что же мне делать, ребром и промыслом
Певчей! — как провод! загар! Сибирь!
По наважденьям своим — как по мосту!
С их невесомостью
В мире гирь.

Что же мне делать, певцу и первенцу,
В мире, где наичернейший — сер!
Где вдохновенье хранят, как в термосе!
С этой безмерностью
В мире мер?!

POETS

1

The poet brings language from afar. The poet is taken far by language.

By way of planets, omens, the ruts of roundabout parables . . . Between *yes* and *no*, even hurling himself from a bell tower he will extort a detour . . . for the path of comets

Is the poet's path. Scattered links of causality—that is his connection! Head up—you will despair! A poet's eclipses are not predicted by the calendar.

He is the one who mixes up the cards, who swindles weights and sums, he is the one who *questions* from the school bench, who stands Kant on his head.

Who in the stone tomb of Bastilles is like a tree in its beauty. He whose tracks have always grown cold, the train which everyone misses . . . —for the path of comets

Is the poet's path; burning and not warming, tearing and not nurturing, an explosion and a breaking open—your path, long-maned curve, is not predicted by the calendar!

2

In the world there are the superfluous, the additional ones, uninscribed in the horizon. (For those unlisted in your reference books, a rubbish heap is home.)

In the world there are the hollow, the downtrodden, the mute ones—manure, a nail to your silken hem! Dirt from beneath wheels disdains them!

In the world there are the illusory, the invisible ones: (Their sign: the spots of leprosariums!) In the world there are Jobs who would envy Job—if:

We are poets—and rhyme with pariahs, but having overflowed our banks, we contend with goddesses for a god, and with the gods for a virgin.

3

What am I to do, a blind man and stepson, in a world where each is fathered and sighted, where passions go along anathemas as though along embankments! where weeping / lament is called a head cold.

What am I to do with the rib and Providence of a singer!—Like a power-line! sunburn! Siberia! Along my enthrallments as along a bridge! With their weightlessness in a world of weights.

What am I to do, singer and firstborn, in a world where the blackest is gray! Where inspiration is kept in a thermos! With this immeasurability in a world of measures?!] (*SP* 3:67–68; ellipses in original)

The first poem opens with an anomalous couplet that describes the work of the poet and serves as a guide for how poetry in general and this cycle in particular are to be read.[2] The poet both leads and is led by language; so too must be the reader. Their journey in and through language depends on both its allusive and its denotative potentialities. The entire cycle is a compelling demonstration of precisely such a journey.

The stanza that follows describes the scope and nature of the poet's travel. The list of features that mark the poetic journey comprises a diverse set of images in which the leader and the led become indistinguishable. The planets extend the compass of the journey to other worlds. The omens (« приметы ») guiding the poet are those features that reveal their true significance to soothsayers who discern connections among and thus derive meaning from phenomena that remain disjunct and meaningless to the uninitiated. The semantic influence of « приметы » [omens] on the rhyming « планеты » [planets] encourages the reader to regard extraterrestrial space also in zodiacal terms. Thus from the outset the poet is aligned with a mode of thinking that is expressly irrational and unscientific. He proceeds along lines that are indirect, inefficient, and impractical. The pleonasm « окольных / Притч » [roundabout parables] emphasizes the poet's penchant for tracing the longest distance possible between any two points. It suggests also that the stretch between what is said and what is intended is a considerable one. The « рытвины » [ruts]—somewhat startling in this interplanetary context—of those "roundabout parables" underscore the unevenness of the path, link the poet to the earth, and serve as a reminder that the reader must be prepared for the discomforts attendant on the uneven ride toward the apprehension of meaning that underlies those utterances. The swiftness of the poetic gesture can be deduced from the speed with which the poet has moved from the celestial planets to the ruts of our earth, a trip completed here within the course of one and a half lines.

The poet's preference for indirect routes is accompanied by a reluctance to arrive at any final destination. Confronted with a decision, he remains poised between yes and no, not because he is indecisive or lacking in the moral fiber necessary for commitment, but because the many possible perspectives and contexts of which he retains awareness prevent him from responding unequivocally. This awareness—vouchsafed by the jagged course he pursues—precludes direct and categorical reply. Yet this is not the paralysis from which Hamlet suffers. That Tsvetaeva emphasizes yes and no rather than "between" indicates that the "either/or" that captivated the Danish prince is a category the poet seeks ever to displace with "both/and."

The drive to prolong the distance between any two points is a spatial analogue of the protraction of longing championed in the Orpheus myth. Here it is represented in the poet's overcoming of even the laws of gravity to curve the straight line of his precipitous fall from the bell tower. This headlong plunge suggests that the poet's immediately preceding suspension between yes and no is correlative with his position between life and death. In the poet's fall from the bell tower and the detour he accomplishes under even such unlikely circumstances, Tsvetaeva charts with her characteristic poetic velocity the extraordinary life course of the poet —the forces with which he must contend and to which, as we recognize, he must ultimately succumb. Although these lines focus on the victorious curve the poet successfully exacts, the ellipsis that concludes this statement forebodes the poet's tragic end.

The inappropriateness of the poet's behavior is not inherent in his actions. In fact all he does is appropriate, but only to another place—one whose dimensions are capacious enough to accommodate the poet's activity. The conclusion of the second stanza returns to the interplanetary spaces of its opening. The comets that soar across the boundary of stanzas two and three and represent the unpredictable path of the poet are an allotrope of the poet's fall from the bell tower. The arc so inadmissible in that instance is here necessary and correct: comets are within the gravitational field of the sun—Apollo's domain—and not of our own planet.[3]

The poem gathers momentum in the third stanza. Ellipses, which in the preceding stanza suggest uncertainty or a reluctance to complete thoughts, give way to exclamatory assertions as the poet confronts head-on the expectations of the surrounding world. The rebellion of the poet, which is elaborated in the rapid succession of images in the fourth and fifth stanzas, is predicated on the radical break with causality demonstratively proclaimed in the first two lines of stanza three. This rupture is rendered palpable by the line division that intervenes to separate « Развеянные звенья » [Scattered links] from « Причинности » [Of causality]. The poet's abjuration of both causality and the linearity implicit in it opens the way for associations that enlarge the sphere of his activity.

The high course charted by the poet commands an upward gaze from the earthbound who will, as Tsvetaeva disdainfully predicts, despair of comprehending this vision. The poet's incalculable eclipses, as she asserts, defy calendrical predictions. Yet eclipses are the consequence of an orderly procession of planets and are in fact predictable—but only to those capable of comprehending the general law that governs their motion. What appears as lawless willfulness to the narrow vision of the earthbound is in fact adherence to higher law. We are alerted here also to another meaning of « затменье », which in colloquial speech indicates blacking out or insanity. This poetic "madness" is predicated on the derangement of conventional standards of judgment. The "blacking out" is a recognizable permutation of the lowered eyelids of the Sibyl of Tsvetaeva's eponymous cycle, where the mundane is obscured to permit that inward concentration which is the source of expanded vision.

The intensity of the poem, briefly relaxed in the concluding line of stanza three, heightens in the crescendo and acceleration of stanzas four and five. The fourth stanza emphasizes the poet's renunciation of commonly accepted norms determined by causality, quantification, and dependence on exclusively logical connections (represented here by the whipping boy Immanuel Kant). The four rebellious gestures described in the four lines of this stanza mark the poet's superiority and elaborate both his unpredictability and its underlying sources.

The poet is defined by his disconcerting and disruptive behavior. His disarrangement of cards proclaims his refusal to adhere to a predictable, predetermined course. The word « карты » also means maps: « Атлас — что колода карт » [The atlas is like a deck of cards/maps] (*SP* 3:206), Tsvetaeva was to pun in a poem of 1939. On the strength of this coincidence of signifieds the poet is shown simultaneously to flout both temporal and spatial guides. He successfully deludes even the apparently incontrovertible certainty of weight and enumeration (« Обманывает вес и счет ») that the Sibyl too rejects. Rather than obediently provide learned responses to authority, the poet reverses the existing order to hurl out questions from the school bench. Here Kant is vanquished by the poet, whose discourse leads well beyond the world defined by the philosopher's stance. The power Kant ascribed to reason and his union of empiricism and logic win no favor with Tsvetaeva, who regards a world inhabited by his reason as inhospitable to the work of a poet. Kant's placement of rational principles within the realm of experience is deemed too limiting by Tsvetaeva, who would have the poet respond to the higher reason of a heliocentric world view. Kant's reduction of experience to the logical falls in with the broad categories of quantification and causality which the poet struggles to dislodge. Even as Tsvetaeva rejects nonpoetic systems of thinking, the poems she creates attest to the intellectual rigor and technical mastery that prevail at even her most impassioned moments. The poet operates according to a system that defies logic, but that also rejects willfulness in favor of a disciplined and strictly defined set of criteria.

Exemplifying the poet's unpredictability, the fifth stanza expands to five lines. The intensity of the lyric continues to grow. The "Bastilles" create a complex, powerful image that gives new meaning to the assertion that the poet cannot be contained by the restrictions governing the physical world. The renowned fortress conveys explicitly the antagonism of the mundane toward the poet, whom it tries to subjugate to its own narrow confines. The specificity of this reference is expanded by the plural form into a metaphor indicating that these constraints are many, not limited only to prison walls. In the mundane the poet recognizes many Bastilles that otherwise go unnoticed.

Tsvetaeva makes it clear that the poet's energies are directed not simply against physical bondage or even political restrictions. The poet's breaking out of the far more oppressive confines of quantification, causality, and Kantian logic endows him with the capacity to thrive even within the deathly walls of the Bastille: « Кто в каменном гробу Бастилий / Как дерево в своей красе » [Who in the stone tomb of Bastilles / is like a tree in its beauty]. The poet retains his vitality and self-sufficiency, indeed is activated by the dynamism of the opposing forces of his calling and the limitations imposed by his surroundings. The tree is an ancient symbol of poetry to which Tsvetaeva recurs, as we have observed in the Sibyl cycle, when conveying a specifically poetic ethos. Thus, for example, in the nine-poem cycle *Деревья* [Trees], also included in *After Russia*, trees represent an alternative to the very sort of antipoetical narrowness and hostility described in *Poets*.

Besides its broad application to poets in general, the image of the tree thriving in the confinement of the Bastille is also a specific reference to André Chénier, a poet to whom Tsvetaeva dedicated an eponymous two-poem cycle (1918) included in *Лебединый стан* [Demesne of the Swans]. The presence of the unnamed Chénier is important to the entire cycle, as is Pushkin's elegy to the French poet, and is discussed further below. Here we can observe that Tsvetaeva's reference to Chénier underscores the helplessness of those in power before the poet, who remains even in incarceration a free and growing spirit. The reference expands our understanding of the poet's "unpredictability" with a recognition of his allegiance to concepts of truth and justice higher than those generally admissible within the narrow parameters of "yes or no." Although Chénier initially supported the French Revolution, in the wake of its subsequent excesses he did not hesitate to defend Louis

XVI and to attack both the Girondins and the Jacobins for flouting the Constitution. The poet's loyalty, as these historical data suggest, is based not on the label itself—be it the designation of a monarch or a political party—but on the meanings it assumes in different situations. His "unpredictability"—the refusal to follow any course blindly or uncritically—is both the cause and the consequence of his sensitivity to the fluidity of meaning.

The images of absence which complete stanza five translate the commonplace of the poet being ahead of his time into spatial terms as the poet outstrips the inhabitants of his mundane surroundings. In the trope of the train that everyone misses, the temporal and spatial intersect. As the opening couplet of this lyric indicates, the poet goes faster and farther than the nonpoet on the strength of his ability to make connections which carry him to new realms, new perspectives, and new understanding. Those connections are rooted in and dictated by language: the velocity that sets the poet so far ahead of everyone else is generated by his realization of its associative potential. His energy is neither pragmatic nor functional and cannot be harnessed to a specific end. It generates instead the momentum for the circuitous routes characteristic of the poet. As in « Поезд жизни » [The Train of Life], a poem which Tsvetaeva wrote later the same year (6 October 1923) and which similarly takes its persona on an interstellar journey away from the finite world, here too the train is a metaphor for life and thus links the velocity of the poet's course with the consequent brevity of his life.

Like the poet she describes, Tsvetaeva outstrips her readers and recaptures in the final lines of this (fifth) stanza the unexpectedness of being left behind by a departing train. This demonstration of how a poet startles her audience is a fitting example of unpredictability, which has been underscored thematically and which operates also in the arena of poetic technique. Stanzas two, three, and four are each composed of four lines of iambic tetrameter and follow a regular rhyme scheme: aBaB. The fifth stanza proceeds in exactly the same way. Line four, which the reader has been led to expect to be the last, dutifully fulfills the anticipated rhyme. Yet instead of ending the stanza, it unexpectedly expands into yet another line. The natural pause at the rhyme in the place where the reader expects the stanza to end becomes awkward when the sentence is continued in the next line with the word « опаздывают » [are late]. Having given the reader of this "superfluous" line just enough time to regather momentum in the five consecutive syllables of « опаздывают », Tsvetaeva pulls the reader up short with the extended pause demanded by the completion of the sentence, a dash, and a step down. This sudden and pronounced stop allows the reader time to experience the surprise and discomfiture occasioned by the elusive poet.

By engineering a collision between the conditioned expectations and what actually transpires in this stanza, Tsvetaeva draws to the reader's awareness the seductiveness of predictable patterns and the ease and unconsciousness with which we submit to established norms. Here the importance of the poet's unpredictability, its shattering of the tyranny of such norms, and the awkwardness attendant on it emerge palpably. The reader regards with new respect the isolated path of the comet that appears between stanzas two and three and that blazes again between the two final stanzas of the poem. In its second appearance the phrase « ибо путь комет » [for the path of comets] is isolated from the rest of the text in an iconic representation of the distant, solitary poet. Its placement on the page removes it from the rest of the line while the anticipated but unfulfilled rhyme « комет-поэт » [comet-poet] intensifies the isolation and demonstrates once again the poet's unpredictability.

The comparison of poets with comets suggests characteristics that are potentially harmful to the surrounding world. In the concluding stanza the poet's inutility grows into menace. Like the comets, poets bring not warmth and nurture but scorching heat and disjunction. The « взрыв » [explosion] that characterizes the poet's progress evolves paronomastically out of the « развеянные звенья / Причинности » [scattered links / Of causality] described in stanza three. « Взлом » [breaking open, breaking in] too stresses the disruptive activity of the poet who shatters complacency and breaks out of the narrow limits of convention. The elevated, rhetorical « стезя » [path, way] that designates the poet's life suggests stylistically the poet's ascendancy. The metaphor that represents his life's course, « гривастая кривая » [long-maned curve], is born of the visual image of the fiery arc a comet traces across the sky coupled with Tsvetaeva's etymological acuity: "comet" derives from the Greek *komētēs*, literally the long-haired, elliptical for *astēr komētēs*, long-haired star.[4] The poem culminates with an exclamatory reassertion of the inadequacy of scientific prognostications to gauge the actions of the poet. The poet's unforeseeable "eclipses"—those moments of creative "madness" depicted in the concluding line of stanza three—here typify his entire life's course.

The entire poem concentrates on distancing the poet from the mundane world with spatial and temporal images that shatter prevailing norms and expectations. Impelled by the limitations of the finite world, the poet soars well above it. Yet as positive and assertive as this poem is, the impossible situation of the poet cannot be overlooked. Whatever threat he may pose to the earth, and however unpredictable his course may be, there are only two possibilities open to the poet-comet vis-à-vis the earth: he can either pass by it at great remove or, if he comes too close, crash into it. Nor can we ignore the chilling implications of the other images applied to the poet. However rebellious and undauntable, the poet cannot evade indefinitely the consequences of his headlong fall from the bell tower, the execution which terminates imprisonment, or the arrival of the train at its terminus. The fate encoded in the fortuneteller's cards can be altered only as far as the moment of death to which the poet is inexorably drawn by his calling and which he has in common even with the unpoetical brethren his fiery course bedazzles. Ultimately the poet cannot break entirely free of this earth. The remainder of the cycle focuses on his condition within it.

The poet-comet's flouting of mundane restrictions in the first poem gives way in the second to the contempt of the mundane for the poet, now regarded as earth-bound and described in unsavory images that emphasize his dubious, marginal status. The insistence on « есть *в мире* » [there are *in the world*, my emphasis] with which each of the first three stanzas opens counters the image of the celestial poet who soars above the earth and situates him in a quotidian context that denies him any distinction or significance. It is only in the concluding stanza that these unspecified creatures are explicitly identified as poets. This identity is, of course, no secret to the reader from the very outset, and the anonymity functions only to intensify the degradation of the faceless, unrecognized poet. The account of the poet's threatening and rebellious impracticability found in the preceding poem is replaced here with an assertion of his lowliness, helplessness, and uselessness. It is only at the end of the lyric that the poet is afforded a brief moment of self-assertion and emerges in the process of ascendancy.

The dazzling spectacle of the comet traversing the sky gives way to the poets' marked absence from the horizon. The poem opens with a twofold assertion of their uselessness: poets are neither needed nor accepted by that society whose perspective is projected here. Line two describes poets as uninscribed in the field of vision (« невписанные в окоем »). Emphasized is the passivity of the viewers, who must be told what to see, and the resultant narrowness of their scope. The parenthetic observation that completes the stanza excludes poets from the reference guides of this small-minded world where disconnected statistics determine what in the surrounding world is to be seen and how it is to be regarded. Active perceptual faculties are replaced by an abstract, implicitly bureaucratic ordering of the world, and the consequently circumscribed field of vision makes the poets appear useless and devoid of value. They are discarded and relegated to the "refuse" of this narrow view. (As we shall see, the poets find themselves in good company there.) The possessive adjective « ваших » [your] emphasizes the allegiance of the speaker of the poem to the unnamed group of rejectamenta and indicates that the third person plural adopted here in reference to "those who . . ." is a projection of the attitude of the surrounding world and not of the speaker herself.

Yet the poets cannot be so easily disposed of, and their unsavory existence cannot be overlooked entirely. In the second stanza of the poem they emerge, if not as a threat, then at least as an annoyance. The substantivized adjectives describing them—« полые » [hollow, empty] and « затолканные » [downtrodden]—perpetuate the characterization of uselessness and lowliness with which the poem opened. « Немотствующие » [mute] suggests the poets' silence. Like their invisibility, this silence too must be recognized as a mark of the perceptual inadequacy of their audience. The negative designations of the poets are thus a thrust at the nonpoets and not an abuse of the poets. They project the limitations of those uncomprehending denizens of the mundane who squander their poets.

As the stanza unfolds, the condemnation of the *homo vulgaris* is intensified. The essential incompatibility of poets and nonpoets is projected in metaphors that appear unflattering to the poets and threatening to those around them: « навоз / Гвоздь — вашему подолу шелковому! » [manure / A nail to your silken hem]. Little wonder then that, as the last line of this stanza proclaims, they are disdained even by the mud splattering from beneath the wheels of earth-bound conveyances. Yet to regard the metaphors for poets (manure, nail) as indicating a position inferior to that suggested by the synecdochal representation of the nonpoets (silken hem) is to fall into that limited perceptual field which has already been condemned as false. (The fact that the nonpoets are presented as a fragment and the poets as a whole is a telling one.) In fact, manure, which enriches crop-bearing soil, and nails, which have a constructive purpose, are far more useful than the trailing gown they threaten.

If the preceding poem denies any pragmatic function to poets, here their obvious utility is held in contempt. To recognize the system of values informing the latter judgment as palpably false is not to say that manure and nails must give way to the more glamorous comet. These images do not cancel one another out, but serve rather to indicate the different perspectives from which they emerge. The disparate images of the poets coexist as products of different vantage points. There is nothing intrinsically wrong with the humble manure and nail; the problem lies only in the way they are regarded. Tsvetaeva emphasizes repeatedly that poets and nonpoets are distinguished not by a difference in their respective sign systems, but by the meaning they derive from the signs they share. It is easy to discern the grandeur of the poets in the shimmering metaphor of a comet, less easy to recognize those poets in a dull, common thing.

The last line of this stanza, « Грязь брезгует из-под колес! » [Dirt from beneath the wheels disdains them!], arrests our attention because the expected verb « брызгает » [splatters] is replaced with the acoustically similar but semantically startling « брезгует » [disdains]. This verb personifies the mud, thus making it an emblem of the nonpoets. The line reflects the vision of their world, which, to borrow a phrase from Coleridge, is "the very mire of commonplace common-sense," and which Tsvetaeva unequivocally rejects in the opening poem of the cycle. From another vantage point the mud does not disdain the poet but simply fails to sully him (as in the phrase « грязь не пристает к поэту » [mud does not stick to the poet]), and he remains clean of the abuse of the mundane.

Stanza three opens with a variation on the assertions made in the first stanza. Again poets are represented as unreal and invisible. Yet whereas in the first stanza the poets' invisibility was ascribed to the perceptual inadequacy of the populace, here it emerges as the product of an active denial of their discomfiting existence. The subsequent line, enclosed in parentheses (which in Tsvetaeva's writings inevitably contain crucial information and not merely peripheral commentary) draws a parallel suggesting that in the society of nonpoets, poets are considered abnormal and diseased. The splatters of mud that avoid the poets in the preceding stanza materialize here as the spots marking a leper (« лепрозариумов крап »). Attempts to remove poets from the field of vision now also reflect the fear of infection on the part of the populace that banishes its "lepers." The intensity of the nonpoets' denial of poets reflects the magnitude of the perceived threat and thus also the power of the poets.

The allusion to leprosy leads into the subsequent comparison of poets with Job. This comparison focuses and foregrounds the underlying suggestion that what appears to be the pitiable condition of the poets is in fact a mark of their superiority. Job is singled out to endure great suffering not because he is weak, guilty, or deserving of punishment, but because he is one of the elect—recognized for the endurance of his spirit in the face of the devastating worldly misfortunes by which he is tested. Manifested in his abject state is the unshakable strength of his faith and integrity, which are reaffirmed and celebrated in those very miseries he endures. So too the poets' alienation from earthly goods and station both elevates them and strengthens their faith and integrity in their art.

The identity of the denigrated group described in the poem is made explicit only in the final stanza. Here the unspecified "they" and "those who" are replaced with an emphatically asserted first person plural. This grammatical change signals a shift of vantage point from that of the populace to that of the poets with whom the auctorial voice now unequivocally aligns itself. The metaphorical "rhyming" of poets with pariahs reiterates their status as social outcasts and becomes the launching pad for the poem's radical departure from the disenfranchised image of the poets that occurs precisely at this juncture. Having been identified, the poets rise above the riverbanks to a position of contending with the gods. The image of floodwaters accords well with the metaphor for inspiration that was common currency among the Romantics and that Wordsworth formulated as the "spontaneous overflow of feelings."[5]

In Tsvetaeva's writings the flowing river is a recurring metaphor both for life and for the process of poetry. Here poets are likened to the river.

Condensed in the image of the riverbanks are all the restraints and restrictions—all the "Bastilles"—of the world through which they course. In this lyric Tsvetaeva represents the poets' actions focusing not on their superabundance of emotion (as she does in the last lyric of the cycle) but on the constricted circumstances of the surrounding world. Too narrow to contain them, these circumstances compel the poets literally to expression. The subdued tone in which she announces the event suggests how natural and inevitable it is that the poets rise above those banks. Certainly the descriptions of the poets' unpredictable, circuitous path in the preceding poem indicate how unlikely it would be for them to remain tamely within the confines of the course charted for them. It is emphasized here that the attainment of their new position among the gods does not satisfy the poets, whose essential contentiousness endures. Only among supramundane beings can the "pariahs" of the mundane find worthy adversaries. Having superseded quotidian restrictions, they vie for what the gods hold dearest and guard most jealously.

As in the first poem, the image associated with poetic creativity carries a distinct threat to the surrounding world. It takes the calamitous, self-assertive floodwaters of the poets to rupture the nonpoets' complacent attitude and counter their scornful disregard. Yet once the river has receded the lesson of the powerful waters will doubtless be forgotten and the common citizenry will return to its trivial ordering of life.

The sudden, radical transformation in the description of the poets that occurs in the final stanza appears to suggest two separate states—inspired and uninspired. This is the situation described in Pushkin's well-known lyric «Поэт» [The Poet], which is a subtext for Tsvetaeva's poem. In Pushkin's lyric the abject state of the uninspired poet, «И меж детей ничтожных мира, / Быть может, всех ничтожней он» [And amidst the insignificant children of the world, / he is perhaps the most insignificant], gives way to ascendancy born of Apollonian inspiration: «Но лишь божественный глагол / До слуха чуткого коснется, / Душа поэта встрепенется, / Как пробудившийся орел» [But the divine word / has only to touch his sensitive hearing / and the soul of the poet starts up, / like an awakened eagle].[6] For all the outward similarity of what transpires in "The Poet" and Tsvetaeva's lyric, an important distinction remains: the double image of the poet Tsvetaeva presents is not based on the opposition inspired/uninspired, but rather on the antinomy of the values and constant perceptual norms of the poet and the surrounding populace. Tsvetaeva translates Pushkin's inherent duality of the poet into a duality of possible readings of the sign "poet." The poet, in other words, is a signifier whose various signifieds are ever present, to be elicited by those capable of doing so. Put another way, the abject and the exalted states that succeed one another in Pushkin's poet are held in simultaneity in Tsvetaeva's lyric. The emergence of one or another of these aspects is not the effect of a change in the poet himself as it is in Pushkin's "Poet." It is rather determined by the context in which the poet is perceived and by the perceptual acuity, the perspective, and the decoding process of his perceiver. As we see in this poem, the nonpoets do not recognize in those signs they assume to be indicators of inferiority the marks of the poets' exaltation over the narrow confines of their world. They are oblivious to the fact that disconcerted Hamlet: one and the same sign can indicate vastly different meanings. This oblivion is the direct consequence of the inflexibility of their perspective and their ignorance of the powerful effect of context on the derivation of meaning.

Characteristically, Tsvetaeva replicates this central theme at the level of language. The second stanza of the poem, as we have seen, opens with the designation of the yet-unnamed poets as « полые ». In the given context this is readily understood as "empty" or "hollow" and, as such, perpetuates the lowly guise of the poets. Yet when in the last stanza the poets overflow their banks, the reader recalls that the same adjective can be applied to floodwaters (« полая вода »). Like the two images of the poet, the two meanings of this word are present simultaneously.

Yet however inadequate the perspective of the mundane on the poets, it determines the conditions in which they must live and act. The anguish of the concluding poem of the cycle with its refrain « Что же мне делать » [What am I to do] arises not from the sense of exclusion from the surrounding world detailed in the preceding poem, but rather from despair at having to function within that world. Here we recognize the frustration that will culminate in creative effluence. Here the "uselessness" determined by the nonpoets is sensed by the poet herself. The narrowness of vision and the shallowness of feeling and understanding seen already in the preceding poem make the world too small, too weak, and too anemic to accommodate the intensity and scale of the poet. The solitary poet bemoans the incommensurability of her gift with the narrow emotional and perceptual bounds in which she finds herself. The insufficiency of that world of quantification and of weights and measures emphatically rejected in the first poem is here brought to bear on the poet. The poet's difficult destiny is foregrounded with references to the emotional intensity of her calling and to the poet's own helplessness before it. In her rich analysis of this lyric Antonina Gove notes that "although the poem is written in the first person, the speaker presents herself as a nominative subject 'I,' but obliquely in subjective and appositive datives."[7] This permits Tsvetaeva to speak for poets in general and yet retain an intensely personal tone. Gove further observes: "It is my impression that this oblique presentation of the speaker's person with a concentration on her bardic qualities, contributes to making the statement in the poem appear less egocentric and more substantive and generalizable than they would be in a direct declaration from the speaker."[8]

The poem rephrases the irreconcilable differences separating the poet from the surrounding world. The opening lines, which seem initially to express the poet's dejection at her own inadequacy, emerge once again to be signs of poetic superiority. The blindness and the poet's comparison of herself to a stepchild reiterate the theme of the poet's isolation and marginality of the preceding lyric, yet are at the same time recognizable as those very characteristics that gain Tsvetaeva's Sibyl her superior oracular status. In the mythopoetic world, blindness to the surrounding world inevitably translates into a superior vision that goes well beyond the constructs of the ready-made world.

The condition of orphanhood similarly suggests a removal from physiology and genealogy and thus also freedom from ties to the physical world. In the absence of a father, there is neither surname nor patronymic. This anonymity—a sign of the poet's lowliness in the preceding poem—delivers the poet from the familial destiny to which she would have been bound. The poet thus once again eludes that fate she disarranges in the opening poem of the cycle. Yet in a world where everyone else is sighted and possessed of flesh-and-blood ties, the marks of the poet's electedness are inevitably misapprehended. Mundane sightedness is suggested by the discernible echo of « очи » [eyes] in the epithet « отч » [possessing a father], while its uselessness is suggested by the « зря » [in vain] heard in « зряч » [sighted]. Inasmuch as the remainder of the lyric shows the poet's dejection as arising from the inadequacy of the surrounding world, her "deficiency" described at the outset of the poem is recognized as an asset. The disposition of the lines in the first stanza indicates that the very absence of sightedness and familial ties elevates the poet above the mundane citizenry possessed of them.

The poet's marginal position gains her a breadth of perspective which generates dynamic, ever new interconnections. The cardinal failing of non-poets is the inflexibility of context that impedes their recognition of the rich polyvalence of signs. An outgrowth of this failing is, as we have seen, their ineptitude in reading signs. From this also follows, as the lyric under discussion discloses, the reciprocal incapacity to find appropriate designations for what they encounter. In the resultant imprecision of language, the intensity of life itself is dulled, as momentous events, emotions, and drives are rendered inconsequential by the litotes in which they are couched. To refer to weeping or lament as a mere "head cold" is to deny the scope and intensity of underlying feelings, to reduce them, in Sibelan Forrester's words, "to pathology and physiology."[9] To treat an anathema as an embankment—something that can be gotten over—is both to undercut the passions that elicited it and to trivialize its consequences. Tsvetaeva's use of the plural—"anathemas"—underscores the degradation of the momentous to the commonplace.[10]

The question that opens the second stanza shifts attention to the more specific and urgent problem of what she is to do with her poetic destiny, described here as « ребро и промысл певчей » [the rib and Providence of a singer]. The rib and Providence suggest the inextricability of her very being and her vocation and represent the poet's ties to both mortality and divinity. In the rib we recognize the biblical origin of her physical being and a part of the ribcage into which breath for song is drawn. It appears here in place of the acoustically, metrically, and thematically plausible « крыло » [wing] to assert the poet's ties to the earth and imply the impossibility of flight from either her mortal self or the demands of her art. The word « промысл » signifies « действие верховного сверхбестественного существа в мире а так же само это существо. »[11] As can be seen from this definition, this single word comprises both the actions of a supreme or supernatural being and the higher being itself. It thus indicates the loftiness of the poet and her calling and counterbalances the earth-bound aspect represented by the rib. The poet acknowledges and bows to this destiny, in which we recognize the dual citizenship of Orpheus.

The similes « как провод! загар! Сибирь! » [like a power line! sunburn! Siberia!] create a stark outline of the poet's course. "Power line" conveys the velocity and intensity of the poet's message, which this image frees from physiology. "Sunburn" is a variant of the scorching heat of the comet in the first poem of *Poets*, where the narrow limits of the quotidian are incinerated. At the same time it is an echo of the « Вечности / Бессмертный загар » [The immortal sunburn / of eternity] of poem two of *Jairus's Daughter* and can thus be construed as a mark of the poet's experiences in the other world. Poetic ardor leads to the frigid expanses of Siberia—the distant site of banishment for dangerous criminals and poets, yet at the same time a frontierland rich with promise. Thus this reference to Siberia suggests the harsh punitive measures to which the poet is subjected for her explorations beyond the pale of conventional norms and expectations.

As the despised pariah is promoted to the status of dangerous criminal, poetic inspiration is accordingly described as « наважденье »—« то, что по суеверным представлениям, внушено злой силой с целью соблазна; обман чувств; призрак » [that which according to superstitious beliefs is instilled by evil power with the goal of temptation; deception of feelings; an apparition]. This designation highlights the irrational aspect of the poet which is documented in the first poem of the cycle and underscores once again the absence of the poet's volition before the force of her art. Suggested here is the transgressive, dangerous aspect of the poet's vocation. Her surrender to the "delusions" of her art elevates her above the reaches of the quotidian and she becomes that "conductor" (« провод ») through which higher forces reveal themselves to the commonplace world.

Tsvetaeva was to elaborate on the peculiar interdependency of complete self-surrender and full responsibility entailed in her art in her 1932 essay « Искусство при свете совести » [Art in the Light of Conscience]. The poet, in her account, is subsumed by the poetic imperative—that higher force that depends on her for its own realization:

> Состояние творчества есть состояние наваждения. Пока не начал — obsession, пока не кончил — possession. Что-то, кто-то в тебя вселяется, твоя рука исполнитель, не тебя, а того. Кто — он? То, что через тебя хочет быть.
>
> [The creative state is a state of enthrallment. Until you begin—*obsession*, until you finish—*possession*. Something, someone seizes you, your hand does not your own bidding, but another's. Who is he? That which wants to be through you.] (1:398)

We recognize such surrenders in the abandonment of Orpheus to his longing for Eurydice, of Marusia to her love for the vampire swain, of the Sibyl to the all-consuming fire of the divinity, and see that the "enthrallment" of these personae leads them away from the limiting conditions of the finite world toward greater freedom. Evident too, however, is the potential danger of such surrenders to the poet herself.

In the lyric under discussion the poet describes herself moving « По наважденьям своим — как по мосту! » [Along my enthrallments as along a bridge!]. At first glance this account appears disconcertingly similar to the nonpoets' undervaluations of significant occurrences that are criticized in the preceding stanza and once again in the final one. Yet in fact this phrase signals not a capitulation to those paltry standards, but their reversal. It indicates not the poet's reduction of vast phenomena to niggardly proportions, but rather her own growth to the expansive dimensions of the phenomena she describes here. The nonpoets and the poets attain the same end—an equivalence between self and experience. Yet they are distinguished sharply by the means to this end: the nonpoets reduce anything of magnitude to their own Lilliputian proportions; the poets expand to its scope. The cause and consequences of these antithetical approaches are presented in the conclusion of the stanza. Crystallized in the opposition of weightlessness and weights is the opposition of the creative, abstract, and metaphorical path of "song" to the leadenly pragmatic, literal application of language where the thing is valued more highly than the word that names it. The opposition of limitlessness and measurement that concludes this poem reiterates this criticism. The poet's dangerous but liberating "delusions" that carry little weight in the mundane permit her to rise above it.

With the third repetition of "What am I to do?" in the final stanza, the poet describes herself as bard and firstborn. The first of these designations links the "blindness" of stanza one to Homer and privileges the aural over the visual. The second is suggestive of a divine lineage not apparent in the mundane world, where the poet appears to be fatherless. It implies the connection between the poet and Christ, of whom Tsvetaeva writes in one of the lyrics of *Poems to Blok* (« Ведь тот был тоже сирота, — Сынок безотчий ») [After all that one was an orphan too,— / A fatherless son] (*SP* 2:53).[12] In this concluding stanza the poet's ascendancy is highlighted—much as it had been in the first stanza. Against the mere grayness—the mediocrity—of her surroundings the poet appears black.

In Tsvetaeva's poetic system "blackness," when applied to the art of poetry, is an emblem of purity. This purity is projected in a broad range of examples, including, predictably, Pushkin's negritude, the elevation of the denigrated poet, and the virtue vouchsafed a text by the fertile blackness of its rough draft (« черновик »).[13] The antipode to this "blackness" is gray—that Hamlet of the color charts, which, neither black nor white, is situated somewhere in-between.

In the lyric under discussion Tsvetaeva underscores yet again—as she did in the Hamlet poems—that stymied perceptual and emotional capabilities radically restrict expression. Clearly, the safekeeping of inspiration in thermos bottles precludes that "spontaneous overflow of powerful feelings" that results in poetry. The difference between poet and nonpoet is summarized in the final juxtaposition of the poet's boundlessness with the measures of the mundane, a contrast in which the opposition of wholeness and fragmentation is implicit.

The question that concludes this lyric is the only one followed by a question mark. « Что же мне делать . . . / С этой безмерностью / В мире мер?! » [What am I to do . . . / With this immeasurability in the world of measures?!] No longer rhetorical, this question demands an answer and that answer may be found in the opening poem of this cycle: the poet is to soar, cometlike, well above the confines of this small world—she is to write poetry. Coming full circle to that celestial image, we arrive with greatly enhanced understanding of the dynamism of the opposing forces that activate it. The poet's flight is a metaphorical one that comes about in direct response to the mundane world's restrictions and denigration. The specifically poetic apprehension and application of language fuel travel beyond the limitations of the immediate environment.

If we return now to the opening couplet of the cycle, we recognize in it an adumbration of central concerns articulated in its lyrics and a valuable indication of how the text is to be approached. Following its suggestion, we can discover in the substratum of *Poets* a coherent system of signification that is the function of a poetic ordonnance of subtext, paronomasia, polysemy, and their complex interreactions.[14] If we trace even a few examples of such associations, our reading of this cycle is significantly enriched. The textual substratum serves to reinforce and augment the arguments Tsvetaeva advances in the cycle. More importantly, it functions to create not only illustrative, but also constitutive analogues for the cycle's central themes as the technical resources of poetry are engaged in a demonstration of its thematic material.

Appropriately, the starting point is language itself. Thus, for example, we find in the opening couplet of the cycle that different meanings carried by the verb « заводить » open multiple readings which correspond precisely to the poet's situations subsequently outlined in the text. Given Tsvetaeva's assertion that poetry derives from the poet's peregrinations between worlds, the first line can be understood to represent the poet drawing poetic discourse to our world from afar, the verb functioning in its meaning of « заставить прийти, войти куда-л., ввести » [to force to come to or enter some place, to lead into]. If « заводит » is understood in its meaning "to initiate something" (as in « завести разговор »), there emerges an image of the poet speaking at a great remove from his audience and the emphasis of the description falls on the poet's remoteness from this world and its dwellers. The application to this line of the meaning of the verb « увести далеко или не туда, куда нужно » reveals the circuitous, impractical nature of the poet's progress.[15]

The three readings generated by these distinct meanings of заводить fall into ready coincidence with the images of poets and poetry projected in the cycle. The first and last of the applied meanings of « заводить » function in line two of the couplet to generate simultaneously the notion that the poet goes far in a positive sense *and* that he is led astray by his art, thus encapsulating a central theme elaborated in the cycle. The text is supportive of and in turn supported by these coincidences. We observe here not only the intense condensation characteristic of lyric poetry, but also a demonstration of the central argument of the cycle—that one sign comprises disparate meanings and that the penetration of surface appearances is dependent on the recognition of those underlying meanings.

We have already noted a specific instance of this in the reference to poets as полые in the second poem of the cycle. In the second stanza, the epithet is understood to signify "empty" or "hollow." When in the last stanza the poets overflow their banks, the reader recognizes the dual meaning of the adjective. Recognition of this word's ambiguity entails the recognition of both aspects of the poet.

Here we must enlarge our understanding of the context in which everything discussed thus far takes place. The surface of the text focuses on the marginality of the poets and their isolation from the mundane world, which are encoded in a series of images that range from the soaring comet to the abject leper. Limited perceptual capacities and understanding lead to a misapprehension of the poets and the signs by which they are designated. The mundane perspective from which the poets are regarded determines a context too rigid to admit the multiple meanings generated by the polyvalence of signs. Yet there is another perspective from which to contemplate the poets—one that removes them from the narrow parameters of the thermos-bottle world and appropriately leaves the confines of the text itself to refer us to other poets and texts. This all-inclusive point of vantage springs from the implied presence of André Chénier and Aleksandr Pushkin.

Chénier is evoked, as we recall, in the first poem of the cycle by the lines « Кто в каменном гробу Бастилий / Как дерево в своей красе » [Who in the stone tomb of Bastilles / is like a tree in its beauty], which appear in the series of images conveying the antagonism between the poet and the pillars of the established order he overturns. Although Chénier is never named, his presence becomes a catalyst for the creation of a complex network of expanding interconnections.

The second poem, by virtue of its subtext, Pushkin's "The Poet," draws *the* poet of Russia—also unnamed—into the cycle. The conjunction of Pushkin and Chénier is a fruitful one. As P. V. Annenkov notes, Pushkin was the first Russian to take note of Chénier and one of the first in Europe to appreciate his gift. Chénier became for Pushkin a poetic model no less important than Byron.[16] To this poet-hero Pushkin devoted the long poem *André Chénier* (1825). In it he presents the condemned poet's soliloquy just before execution, framed in an introduction and conclusion in Pushkin's own voice. Chénier is seen writing poetry in prison while awaiting execution and reciting verse on his way to the guillotine. Even at the moment of execution he remains undaunted. The brief faltering of spirit Pushkin depicts in his elegy is overcome by Chénier's recognition that not only he himself but also his executioners will be outlived by his poetry, which will continue to proclaim the larger cause of truth and justice he championed.[17] Pushkin's emphasis on the poetic voice surviving the beheaded poet yields a modern metamorphosis of the prototypal poet Orpheus, one with definite political relevance.

The destinies of Pushkin's elegy and of Pushkin himself are also important to Tsvetaeva's cycle. The censor excised from Pushkin's *André Chénier* some forty-four "subversive" lines that described revolutionary activity in France. This forbidden passage circulated in manuscript after the abortive Decembrist uprising with the superscription « На 14 декабря » [On the Occasion of 14 December]. The power of these lines can be gauged by the anxiety and reprisals they elicited from the government. An officer implicated in their circulation was condemned to death, while Pushkin was subjected to rigorous interrogation on their meaning and then placed under surveillance.[18] The conditions projected on the surface of Tsvetaeva's text are validated and intensified by this substratum. The poet, no longer a mere outcast, constitutes a serious threat to the existing order: the writing of poetry is recognized as both an empowering and a dangerous act.

The ties between Chénier and Pushkin must be expanded to include Tsvetaeva herself, for she too dedicated a work to Chénier. The two lyrics of her *André Chénier* cycle differ significantly from Pushkin's elegy. They focus not on the victory of poetry over its hostile surroundings, but on the unspeakable horror of those surroundings that denies the very act of creating poetry: « И не певец, кто в порохе — поет » [And he who sings in gunpowder is not a singer] and question the validity of the poet's very existence:

Андрей Шенье взошел на эшафот.
А я живу — и это страшный грех.

[André Chénier mounted the scaffold. But I still live and that's a dreadful sin.] (*IP* 2:70)

The first poem conflates the revolutionary periods of France and Russia. In the second, the voice of Chénier on the eve of his execution is also Tsvetaeva's own. It expresses the terror-inspired alienation and sense of impending death which will curtail poetic activity. The poem ends not with poetry's transcendence of death as in Pushkin's elegy, but with an image that foregrounds the brevity of the poet's life:

Утро крадется как тать.
Я дописать не успею.

[Morning steals in like a thief. I won't have time to finish.] (*IP* 2:70)

In both its depiction of Chénier's impending execution and its metaphorical expression of Tsvetaeva's own sense of doom in the inimical setting of postrevolutionary Russia, this statement focuses on the helplessness of the poet before his mortality. Whatever his insights into immortality, the poet must also suffer as a mortal. This is not to say, however, that he must succumb to the hostile forces besieging him. In Tsvetaeva's *André Chénier* the victory of the poet and of poetry is an implicit one—demonstrated by the very creation of the two lyrics of the cycle. Pushkin's exalted image of the poet in his *André Chénier* is complemented by Tsvetaeva's all-too-human one in her work, a situation replicated in her account of poets in this cycle.

The historical, biographical, and textual interconnections among Chénier, Pushkin, and herself that Tsvetaeva establishes in this text play a central role in the characterization of poets. We find here a specific instance of the insignificance of those temporal and spatial divisions which operate in the mundane and which are despised by the poet. Described variously as a lone comet, an outcast, a leper, and a pariah, the poet is found at a deeper level to be not an isolated creature, but a member of a tragic, yet closely connected and threatening Pleiad. In light of this interrelationship the plural of the title *Poets*, which could potentially carry the suggestion of disdain (as does, for example, Tsvetaeva's reference to "Bastilles"), is recognized as an affirmation of that underlying bond.

Throughout her cycle Tsvetaeva insists on the incongruence of essential meaning and appearances and demonstrates that deeper understanding may be derived from a recognition of the capacity of signs to point beyond themselves. Acoustic associations, predictably, are another important means for the radical expansion of perception and intellection that she demands from her readers. It is helpful to trace one such example, which depends on the allusions to Pushkin and Chénier.

The underlying presence of Pushkin in the second poem draws into it the image of Chénier. In the third poem Chénier's presence influences a paronomastic network that further emphasizes the coincidence of what appear to be mutually exclusive images of the poet. In the third line of the second stanza the poet traverses the "enthrallments" of her art: « По наважденьям своим — как по мосту! » The prepositional phrase « по мосту » bears a striking acoustic resemblance to the word « помост »—the wooden platform of a stage or place of execution. This paronomastic association is triggered by and in turn strengthens the presence of Chénier. It evokes both the theatrical final gesture that is recorded by Pushkin in the notes he appended to his elegy (« На месте казни он ударил себя в голову и сказал: pourtant j'avais quelque chose là » [At the place of execution he struck his head and said, "Still, I had something there"] and the execution itself.[19] The fact that « помост » signifies a place of both performance and execution underscores the proximity of poetic utterance and death, thus intensifying the intimations of danger entailed in the practice of poetry.

In this line another readily discernible paronomastic connection enhances the characterization of the poet and provides a link with a central image of the preceding poem. The word « наважденье » that Tsvetaeva uses to characterize poetic inspiration implies that the poetic calling is fraught with danger and echoes the reference of the crestfallen Chénier of Pushkin's elegy to his « враждебный гений » [malevolent genius]. « Наважденье » suggests « наводнение », and this paronomastic link is reinforced metonymically by the image of the bridge which follows it and, acoustically by the « вод » of « провод » in the immediately preceding line. « Наводнение » echoes the Romantic metaphor of overflowing, which is linked in turn to the second meaning of « полые ». The underlying presence of « наводнение » thus expands and strengthens the interconnections between the second and third poems of the cycle and enriches their imagery. Moreover, « наважденье » and « наводнение » overlap not only in their acoustic properties but also in their capacity as metaphors for poetic creation. This draws together once again two complementary perspectives on poetic inspiration: « наважденье » suggests its threat to the poet himself, « наводнение » its threat to the surrounding world. Both threats, as the poem vividly conveys, are real.

In the course of tracing the various connections opened by the text, the reader comes to recognize that the central thematic design of the cycle is replicated subtextually by the particular constellation of texts that are drawn into its orbit. This design is reproduced at the level of language, specifically in the word whose semantic and acoustic properties act as points of linkage for a plethora of ever expanding connections. Tracing the path of poetic discourse does indeed take one far, by the circuitous route promised in the opening couplet of the cycle. Clearly the text of *Poets* is inexhaustible, but even this initial foray into its complexity and integrity reveals the cycle itself to be a demonstration of the process of conjoinment and discovery that poetry is for Tsvetaeva and that is made possible by the transgression of conventional boundaries. The reader is given to understand that a crucial difference between poet and nonpoet lies in the aptitude for reading signs and that this aptitude is directly related to the scope and flexibility of perspective that govern it. To look beyond a single contextually determined meaning of any sign and to follow its acoustic promptings is to pierce appearances in order to arrive at a deeper level of signification in which a broader range of interconnections is possible, indeed, demanded. This expanded apprehension is attained when superficial, conventional delimitations are shuffled off to reveal a realm of infinite potential.

The role of the poet that is both described and demonstrated in the lyrics of this cycle is a cardinal one. In all the guises he assumes, it is a glorified poet who is represented here—one who remains well out of reach of his detractors. Both the censure and the praise of the mundane citizenry are equally insignificant to him. Restrictive measures only fuel his expressivity, while any violence done him testifies to his indisputable power. He is vulnerable only to indifference, for it alone can impede his mission to alter the way the world is perceived. However impossible his situation, the only real danger to the poet-comet is that his flight above the earth or his crash into it will pass unnoticed. Underlying Tsvetaeva's insistence on the poet's suffering at the hands of his unpoetical neighbors is an attempt to forestall that dreaded indifference to poets that invades our century. In Tsvetaeva's vision the cessation of the poet's dismemberment is the death of poetry. In the following chapter we shall see Tsvetaeva's translation of these terrifying conditions into her own life as a poet.

Chapter Six

Orpheus-Rilke

> Manchmal mein ich, was zwischen zwei Menschen möglich ist, ist im Grunde doch nicht viel; alles Unendliche ist innerhalb des Einzelnen . . .
>
> I often think that what is possible between two human beings is not really very much in the long run; everything that is infinite is inside the individual . . .
>
> —Rainer Maria Rilke in a letter to Maria von Thurn und Taxis, 31 May 1911

> Und jene himmlischen Gestalten
> Sie fragen nicht nach Mann und Weib.
> [And those heavenly forms
> They do not concern themselves with man and woman.]
>
> —Johann Wolfgang von Goethe, *Wilhelm Meister's Years of Apprenticeship*

AMONG THE issues that emerge from Tsvetaeva's account of the poetic act is the paradoxical manifestation of the self through the complete self-surrender to song. In "Thus Floated Head and Lyre" we have encountered a poet who, caught unawares, gives himself up to inspiration and yet retains personal responsibility for the consequences of that surrender. In "Eurydice to Orpheus" we have observed Orpheus's challenge to Eurydice's newfound existence in the underworld, leading to a reaffirmation of her own identity and a deepened comprehension of his. We have noted at the end of chapter 3 that Marusia gives herself up to the vampire swain in full knowledge of the price that she must subsequently pay for her surrender. In the opening *Sibyl* poem we have seen the annihilation of self demanded by the god culminate in the expansion of the self that gives her voice and enables her to prophesy. Hamlet's inability to give himself up either to love or to revenge is represented as a sign of his essentially antipoetical nature. The ability to rise to the challenges posed to individual identity becomes for Tsvetaeva a hallmark of the poet. This identity must withstand not only the creative process by which the poet is "obsessed" and "possessed," but also confrontations with the responses of other poets to this essential transpersonal power.

Even as she creates personae who assimilate productively the threats posed to their individual identities, Tsvetaeva herself reenacts the situations she depicts in her lyrics. We have seen the importance of Tsvetaeva's struggle with Aleksandr Blok for the development of her own artistic identity. As we pursue the Orpheus theme further in her writings, we arrive at Tsvetaeva's encounter with Rainer Maria Rilke, a contemporary poet crucial to her development, whom she held in the same high esteem she accorded Blok.

The rich topic of Tsvetaeva's relationship with Rilke has attracted considerable scholarly attention.[1] This chapter considers only one facet of this complex theme: the creative process that fosters the interrelationship of Orpheus, Blok, Rilke, and herself in Tsvetaeva's correspondence with Rainer Maria Rilke in the spring and summer of 1926. Tsvetaeva's recognition of Orpheus in Rilke marks a continued development of her reading of the myth and reflects the importance she ascribed to Rilke's writings. Her near-native command of the German language and her comprehensive knowledge of German letters enabled her to read Rilke's works with penetration.

In Orpheus-Rilke, Tsvetaeva realizes—at least briefly—a personal and artistic contact that takes the place of the meeting with Orpheus-Blok she had demonstratively foregone some five years earlier. From her epistolary contact with Rilke, Tsvetaeva derived much-needed solace and a reaffirmation of her artistic legitimacy, a reaffirmation particularly welcome in the increasingly hostile environment she was confronting and to a significant extent creating herself. At the same time the correspondence became an important proving ground for her own poetic identity and artistic credo. Unwittingly, Rilke posed a challenge that elicited anxiety, conflict, and ultimately growth in Tsvetaeva, a sequence, as we have seen, she deemed essential. As we consider Tsvetaeva's letters to Rilke, we recapitulate major themes she associated with poetry and prepare for the next chapter, in which she herself assumes the role of Orpheus to confront Rilke's death.

Rilke, as we have already observed, left an unmistakable stamp on the lyrics of *After Russia*. The lyrics of this collection reveal that Tsvetaeva had assimilated the philosophical stance projected in his writings. Her personal correspondence of that time similarly reflects the degree to which Rilke shaped her thinking and expressivity. We should recall here that as she worked on the lyrics of *After Russia* Tsvetaeva was also immersed in the writings of Hölderlin, a poet from whom she learned a great deal and who was tremendously important for Rilke as well. Their admiration of Hölderlin serves as a convenient reminder of the broader patrimony shared by the two poets. Rilke's influence cannot be so simply distinguished from Tsvetaeva's independent development of collateral ideas rising from shared cultural ground.

It is safe to speculate that among the forces of attraction that Rilke's verse held for Tsvetaeva was a sense of recognition, for in his poems she could discern a preoccupation with problems similar to those addressed in her own work. As for so many modern poets, the central issue was poetry itself, situated in a world irrevocably divided by the Romantics, who usurped divinity even as they undermined the conviction that it could be attained. Broadly speaking, Rilke and Tsvetaeva were both engaged in overcoming perhaps not so much German Romanticism itself as the problems which it had formulated and which became its legacy to future poets. Neither poet considered Romantic irony an appropriate means for responding to those issues. Each confronted directly the divided world and sought to assimilate the challenges of Romanticism productively into their imaginative searchings. If not expressly a guide, Rilke was at the very least a traveling companion for Tsvetaeva in the search for a way out of the Romantic labyrinth.

Like Tsvetaeva, Rilke affirmed the validity of poet and poetry in the modern age. He too negated the paralysis and ineffectuality of the poet that were admitted with increasing frequency into twentieth-century poetic discourse, and which Tsvetaeva rejected with her attack on Hamlet. Her immersion in his earlier writings and her own thorough familiarity with the poetic sources that nurtured his development contributed to the emergence of artistic conclusions consonant with those Rilke himself developed and expressed ultimately in the *Sonnets to Orpheus* and the *Duino Elegies*, which, although completed in 1922 (just as Tsvetaeva was beginning the lyrics of *After Russia*), did not come into Tsvetaeva's purview until 1926, when he sent them to her.

Their brief but intense correspondence was rooted in fertile artistic ground. Certainly Tsvetaeva's own poetic project of engaging poetic language to mediate between the visible and the invisible, the personal and the universal, between inner creative space and the external world, is consonant with Rilke's poetic stance, particularly as expressed in the *Sonnets to Orpheus*. Yet there were significant differences as well. Because these differences could not be smoothed away, they reactivated Tsvetaeva's insecurities, and her epistolary relationship with Rilke ran aground.

The circumstances in which the correspondence began can be outlined briefly. Boris Pasternak's father, the painter Leonid Osipovich Pasternak, numbered among Rilke's Russian friends. (It was he who painted one of the best-known portraits of Rilke.) Thus when Rilke discovered Boris Pasternak's poems in French translations and in the original he read them with particular interest,[2] despite the fact that his Russian had suffered from disuse. In a letter to Leonid Osipovich dated 14 March 1926, Rilke, who was in Paris at the time and experiencing a resurgence of interest in Russia, praised Pasternak's poems.[3] Leonid Osipovich communicated the happy contents of this letter to his son, who had avidly admired Rilke's verse since boyhood. Boris Pasternak's ecstasy at learning of Rilke's favorable response to his poetry found exuberant expression in what proved to be his only letter to Rilke (12 April 1926). In this letter Pasternak proclaims his love for and gratitude to Rilke and introduces to him another Russian poet, explaining,

> daß es eine Dichterin betrifft, die Sie nicht weniger und *nicht anders* liebt, als ich, und (wie eng oder wie weit man das nicht verstehen wollte), ebenso wie ich selbst, als ein Teil Ihrer eigenen Dichter-Geschichte—Dispansion und Wirkung—betrachtet werden kann. . . . Die Dichterin ist Marina Zwetajewa, eine Dichterin von Geburt, ein großes Talent vom Schlage einer Desbordes-Valmore. . . . Ich stellte mir vor, was für sie ein Buch von Ihnen, vielleicht die Duineser Elegien, deren Name ich nur vom Hörensagen kenne, mit Ihrer Aufschrift, wäre.
>
> [that it concerns a (female) poet who loves you no less and *no differently* than I and (however narrowly or broadly one may wish to construe this) can, just as I myself, be considered a part of your own poetic history—sphere of influence and effect. . . . The poet is Marina Tsvetaeva, a poet from birth, an immense talent of the type of a Desbordes-Valmore. . . . I could imagine what a book from you, perhaps the *Duino Elegies*, whose name I know only from hearsay, with your dedication would mean to her.][4]

Rilke responded to this request at once and on 3 May 1926 wrote his first letter to Tsvetaeva, introducing himself and telling her that his last two volumes of verse, the *Duino Elegies* and the *Sonnets to Orpheus*, were on their way.

Although Rilke did not recognize Tsvetaeva as one of the poets who was also represented in the Ehrenburg anthology where he had noticed Pasternak's poems, to her he was no stranger when his first letter arrived. Well before Rilke was to exert his influence on lyrics of *After Russia* Tsvetaeva had accorded him a prominent position in German letters. Already in her 1919 diary excerpt « О Германии » [About Germany] she had singled him out as a representative of "the best Germany" and had placed him next to Blok, who stood for "the best Russia": « Был бы убит Блок — оплакивала бы Блока (лучшую Россию), был бы убит Рильке — оплакивала бы Рильке (лучшую Германию) » [If Blok were killed, I would mourn Blok (the best Russia), if Rilke were killed, I would mourn Rilke (the best Germany)] (*IP* I: 130). The identification of Rilke with Orpheus prompted by the *Sonnets to Orpheus*, where Rilke himself forges such an equation, was adumbrated *already* in this pairing of Rilke and Blok as the finest representatives of their respective cultures. We learn from Tsvetaeva's letter to Rilke of 9 May 1926 that she had read his collection *Die frühen Gedichte* in Prague (as she was working on poems of *After Russia*).[5] In Pasternak's Peredelkino library is a copy of *Die Weise von Liebe und Tod des Cornets Christoph Rilke* with the inscription "1924, M. Ts. and A. Ts.," apparently a gift from Marina and her sister Anastasia.[6] In 1925 quotations from Rilke's Russia-inspired *Das Stundenbuch* [The Book of Hours]—which were to surface again in Tsvetaeva's correspondence with him—appeared in Tsvetaeva's letters and in the essay « Герой труда » [A Hero of Labor]. In a letter to Gleb Struve dated 25 November 1925, she had expressed her great admiration for the poet with the remark: « Рильке необычаен. Уже нездешние слова » [Rilke is extraordinary. Already otherworldly words].[7]

Between April and August of 1926 Rilke wrote six letters to Tsvetaeva and sent her, in addition to the *Duino Elegies* and the *Sonnets to Orpheus*, his French collection *Vergers*. Each of the latter two volumes was inscribed with poems dedicated to Tsvetaeva and his letter of 8 June was accompanied by the exquisite "Elegie an Marina Zwetajewa-Efron."[8]

From Tsvetaeva, Rilke received nine letters between May and August of 1926, followed by a postcard in November. Although written in German, these remarkable letters retain the hallmarks of Tsvetaeva's style. The paronomasia, etymologically motivated constructions, antitheses, assonance, alliteration, rhythm, parallelism, and anaphora that characterize her Russian writings emerge with equal force in her German of these letters. To acquaint Rilke with her verse, she sent him the collections *Психея* [Psyche] and *Стихи к Блоку* [Poems to Blok].

It is scarcely possible to exaggerate the significance of this brief correspondence to Tsvetaeva, for it extends well beyond the temporal frame of the letters themselves. In addition to these letters, which Konstantin Azadovskii aptly designates "epistolary lyric,"[9] the results of her contact with Rilke include the *poèma Новогоднее* [New Year's, February 1927], analyzed in detail in the following chapter, the prose essay « Твоя Смерть » [Your Death, February 1927], and « Несколько писем Р. М. Рильке » [Some Letters of R. M. Rilke," early 1929], Tsvetaeva's introduction to and translation of six letters—five of Rilke's own (although not to her) and one written about him. These are the only works dedicated expressly to Rilke, but references to him surface in various contexts, including notably the long poems *С моря* [From the Sea, 1926], *Поэма воздуха* [Poem of the Air, 1927], and the essays « Поэт и время » [The Poet and Time, 1932], « Эпос и лирика современной России » [The Epic and the Lyric of Contemporary Russia, 1932], and « Поэт-альпинист » [The Poet-Mountaineer, 1934]. Although the book Tsvetaeva had thought to write about Rilke never materialized, he became for her a frame of reference, much as Blok was, and allusions to him continued to appear in her writings.

We have seen that while Blok was alive, Tsvetaeva had not yet attained the artistic maturity that would have permitted her to address him on equal terms.

By the time she had gained that maturity, Blok was dead and Tsvetaeva could only attempt to equalize their relationship through the persona of Eurydice. Yet when Tsvetaeva distinguished in Rainer Maria Rilke a new incarnation of Orpheus, she was already a mature and recognized writer. Her poetry and her notion of the poet's mission had been formed by some of the very influences that had shaped Rilke's, and Rilke himself had figured as a teacher. In the years intervening between her conscious decision to refrain from contacting Blok directly and May of 1926, when she threw herself fervently into an epistolary exchange with Rilke, Tsvetaeva had grown as a poet and had gained confidence in her own poetic voice.

Even as the association of Blok and Rilke began to take shape, Tsvetaeva, who was no longer prepared to adopt a role of complete passivity and self-effacement, determined an important, exclusive link between herself and Rilke. Her inscription in the copy of *Poems to Blok* she sent him draws attention to what she believed to be an indissoluble link between them: the acoustic similarity of their names: "(Mein Name ist der verkürzte Deine,—merkst Du's nicht?)" [My name is yours shortened—haven't you noticed?].[10] Tsvetaeva appraised Rilke of the mythic significance she ascribed to names in her first letter to him, which opened with an exposition of the destiny she could read in his name. Now, with her inscription, she distinguished the onomastic link between them as a sign of their fated communion.[11]

Tsvetaeva integrated similarities, coincidences, and contrasts she perceived between herself and Rilke into an interrelationship that drew on both Orpheus and Orpheus-Blok. The adulation expressed in the *Poems to Blok*, which she sent to Rilke was presumably to be extended to him as well. Once again the poems of that collection were presented as artistic credentials attesting not only to her own mastery, but also to her artistic acuity and her capacity for complete surrender to poetry.

Here we must digress briefly in order to recall that the shadow of Blok was also present at the launching of her relationship with Boris Pasternak. In response to his enthusiastic letter of praise for her collection *Версты* [Versts], which initiated their correspondence, Tsvetaeva sent Pasternak a copy of her *Poems to Blok*,[12] the collection that included those very poems on the strength of which she had hoped to win Blok's attention and which she was now sending to Rilke. In the initial stages of her correspondence with Pasternak, Tsvetaeva described her missed meeting with Blok in a passage that elevated it to tragic proportions and revealed the intensity of the emotion it continued to evoke in her. In that letter, cited in chapter 2, she writes:

> Пастернак, я в жизни — волей стиха — пропустила большую встречу с Блоком (встретились бы — не умер), сама — 20-ти лет — легкомысленно наколдовала: — « И руками не потянусь ». И была же секунда, Пастернак, когда я стояла с ним *рядом*, в толпе, плечо с плечом (семь

лет спустя!), глядела на впалый висок, на чуть рыжеватые, такие некрасивые (стриженый, больной) — бедные волосы, на пыльный воротник заношенного пиджака. — Стихи в кармане — руку протянуть — не дрогнула.

[Pasternak, in life I—at the will of a verse—missed a momentous meeting with Blok (had we met—he would not have died), I myself—at 20—frivolously augured: "And I will not reach out my hands." And yet there was a second, Pasternak, when I stood *next* to him, in a crowd, shoulder to shoulder (7 years later!), gazed at his sunken temple, at his slightly reddish, so ugly (he was shorn, ill)—thin hair, at the dusty collar of his worn coat.—My poems in my pocket—I had only to reach out my hand—I didn't waver].[13]

The appearance of Blok's shade at the beginning of her correspondence with Pasternak suggests that Tsvetaeva saw in her contact with him a potential fulfillment of the unrealized meeting with Blok. This possibility could only be enhanced by the fact that Pasternak—enthralled by her poetry—had sought her out and had thus successfully played the role Blok failed to realize (a lapsus for which she punishes him with death in the passage cited above). Yet significant as her relationship with Pasternak became for Tsvetaeva, his alignment with Blok and thus also his identification with Orpheus remained unaccomplished. It fell to Rilke to embody the Greek bard, a circumstance that was perhaps "augured" (« наколдован ») by the 1919 essay in which she first paired him with Blok.

Rilke, one of the greatest poets of the time, a poet she held on par with Blok, and who was also, as it emerged, near death, now wrote Tsvetaeva with no prompting on her part. His proffered hand could realize the failed expectation that Blok reach out to her.[14] A passage from her first letter to Rilke reveals that the very reserve that had prevented her from initiating a personal acquaintance with Blok was very much in evidence in her attitude to Rilke. In her explanation as to why she had not paid her respects to Rilke when she arrived in Paris in November 1925 is that familiar hybrid of profound admiration and aching pride:[15]

Warum ich nicht zu Ihnen kam? Weil Sie mein liebstes sind—in der ganzen Welt. Ganz einfach. Und—weil Sie mich nicht kennen. Aus leidendem Stolz, aus Ehrfurcht vor dem Zufall (Schicksal, eins). Aus—Feigheit, vielleicht, um nicht Ihren fremden Blick bestehen zu müssen—auf der Thürschwelle Ihres Zimmers. (Nicht fremd konnten Sie mich doch nicht ansehn! Und wenn auch—der Blick wäre ja für Jedermann, da Sie mich nicht kannten!—das heisst: *doch* fremd!)

[Why I did not come to you? Because you are my most beloved—in the entire world. Just as simple as that. And—because you do not know me. Out of injured pride, out of awe before the coincidence (fate, the same thing). Out of cowardice, perhaps, so as not to have to withstand your glance of unrecognition—at the threshold of your room. (After all, you could not regard me as anything but a stranger! And even if [you could have]—the glance would, after all, have been for just anyone, since you did not know me!—that means: a stranger *after all*.][16]

Tsvetaeva's joy at receiving an unsolicited letter from Rilke could only be enhanced by the fact that it came just when her relations with her Russian readers both in Parisian emigration and in the Soviet Union had reached a nadir.[17] In book II (March-April 1926) of the Brussels journal *Благонамеренный* [Well-Intentioned] Tsvetaeva had just delivered what was perhaps a more stinging slap to the public taste of Parisian émigré circles than even the Futurists could have conceived: the essay « Поэт о критике » (which means both "The Poet on Criticism" and "The Poet on the Critic") and the appended « Цветник » [Flower Garden]. The former essay sets forth *expressis verbis* her attitude toward criticism and her exacting criteria for what a critic's approach to poetry should be. Not surprisingly, the critics Tsvetaeva confronted fell short of the standards she set. "Flower Garden" is a compendium of passages from « Литературные беседы » [Literary Conversations], an essay by the influential critic Georgii Adamovich which had appeared in 1925 in the journal *Звено* [The Link], which he edited. Tsvetaeva subjects his essay to merciless, yet unarguably precise analysis that reveals the critic's insensitivity to language and thus also to poetry. The passages Tsvetaeva selects for her "Flower Garden" exemplify failings she discusses in "The Poet on Criticism." Neither essay shows signs of the benevolence suggested by the name of the journal in which they appeared.

With the publication of these pieces Tsvetaeva accomplished a number of things. First and foremost they constitute a transpersonal, uncompromising defense of poetry. At the same time these essays are a sharp rejection of a community that had hailed her as a leading poet and had regarded her arrival in Paris in 1925 as a major literary event. As such they were a goad to arouse—successfully, as it emerged—the hostility of that community. The targets of Tsvetaeva's essays could scarcely be expected to rise to the challenge of transforming their entire outlook on language and poetry. Accordingly, they met her reproofs and lofty demands with fierce animosity. Tsvetaeva's quixotic challenge, as she was doubtless aware, was to a duel from which she would emerge victorious from that larger perspective of eternal poetic truth she championed, but which in actual day-to-day life, in which her entire family depended on her literary income, would result in severe deprivation.[18] Moreover, Tsvetaeva's alienation of the Parisian émigré literary circles, as Simon Karlinsky notes, "was happening at the very same time when the publication of her memoir 'My Jobs,' with its angry denunciations of the Soviet system, brought down on Tsvetaeva the wrath of the Soviet ideologues and cut off the further possibility of the appearance of her work or any favorable mention of it in her native country."[19] Tsvetaeva's behavior precipitated that very hostility on which the poet's identity is predicated in her reading of the Orpheus myth. On the strength of this hostility she draws herself into that configuration of Orphic personae who accede to the violence of the uninitiated.

Here we may ruefully observe that Tsvetaeva was being torn apart by her critics both in the Soviet Union and in France more for the prose which she appears to have written with the express purpose of inciting animosity than for her poetry. She refused to join the ranks of poets inclined to regard the inefficacy of poetry in the modern world as a failing of poetry itself. Indeed, as she would have it, this was a failing of the surrounding world. Yet the fact that she had to resort to prose to enrage her Maenads bespeaks a tacit admission of the legitimacy of such concerns. Her transition to prose in the latter part of her artistic career carries with it a similar suggestion.

Tsvetaeva's insistence on the difficulty of her situation was motivated by a desire to fulfill the Orphic condition, but also by a need to forestall interpretations of her emigration as flight from an extremely difficult life in her homeland to an easier one abroad. Indeed, it would appear that her emphasis on the unbearable circumstances in which she found herself and on the hostility and indifference she endured, particularly in France, is motivated by a reluctance to appear better off than those poets who had chosen to remain in Russia.

Whatever the psychological implications of her self-perpetuated alienation, her correspondence with Rilke began at a difficult juncture in her career. As Karlinsky trenchantly summarizes, "From being the most praised of Russian poets at the beginning of 1926, she was moving by spring of that year to the position of one of the most berated, both in the Soviet Union and abroad."[20]

Rilke's first letter arrived just as Tsvetaeva was being dismembered on the pages of the émigré press, and her sense of poetic communion with him was doubtless heightened by the surrounding hostility. Tsvetaeva applied her creative energy to align herself with Rilke. The circumstances described in the cycle *Poets* were now to be specifically reenacted in life. In that cycle, as we have seen, the inimical mundane world represented on the surface of the text is superseded by the powerful confederation of poets beneath its surface. In the context of the antipoetic mundane Tsvetaeva emphasized her aloofness and alienation from mundane hostility, but in her epistolary dialogue with Rilke she focused on the plight of her human condition as a way of legitimizing her poetic identity.

Tsvetaeva was quick to create configurations that highlighted her interconnectedness with Rilke. Within the symmetrical framework of complementary opposites by which she habitually ordered details and events of the surrounding world, Rilke, as a male German poet on whom Russia had exerted a profound cultural influence, was a perfect complement to the female Russian poet Tsvetaeva, whose artistic schooling drew heavily on Germanic culture. The fact that *The Book of Hours*, generally considered Rilke's first great poetic achievement, was inspired by his discovery of Russia and imbued with the spirituality he believed to have discovered there is seen by Tsvetaeva as complementary to the inspiration she herself derived from the German Romantics.

Even as Tsvetaeva highlights the importance of Germany to her development, she emphasizes her own Russianness, proclaiming herself not merely a representative of Russia, but that very Russia itself that had stirred Rilke so deeply. In her letters to him she projects herself s a sort of Psyche, « Но с русским именем и в шубке меховой » [But with a Russian name and wearing a fur coat] to borrow Osip Mandel'shtam's felicitous description.[21] She seeks, in other words, to secure for herself the same position vis-à-vis Rilke that she had assigned Blok in her essay "About Germany."

Her adoption of the informal address ("Du") in the latter part of her first letter to him presupposes intimate ties with Rilke. "Aber schreiben will ich Dir—ob Du willst oder nicht," she informs Rilke in her first letter to him, "Über *Dein* Russland (Tsarenkreis und anderes)" [But I want to write you [informal]—whether you want me to or not. About *your* Russia (the Tsar cycle and other things)].[22] The Russia Tsvetaeva describes in her letters is consciously shaped to fit the image of Russia Rilke had developed in his writings, and the statement that concludes her first letter to him is a distillation of his attitude: "Rußland ist für mich noch immer so eine Art Jenseits" [Russia for me is still a sort of beyond].[23]

As important as the reciprocal Russian-German connection is, however, it is superseded by the nexus of interrelationships generated by Orpheus. The privileged position both poets granted the Greek bard provided a meaningful point of intersection whose significance is summarized by Konstantin Azadovskii:

> Die Idee der unsterblichen Seele, beschlossen im Kreis von Geburt und Tod, hatten die Romantiker aus der Lehre der Orphiker entnommen. Orpheus, als Dichter und Prophet dieser Religion, war Rilkes und Zwetajewas Lieblingsheld.
>
> [The Romantics had derived the notion of an immortal soul locked into a cycle of birth and death from the teaching of the Orphists. Orpheus, as poet and prophet of this religion, was Rilke's and Tsvetaeva's favorite hero.][24]

Tsvetaeva integrates the Orpheus myth into her epistolary exchange and draws on it to structure the ties she perceived between herself and Rilke.

Yet while the images of the mythic hero held by Rilke and Tsvetaeva overlap, they do not coincide. In the *Sonnets to Orpheus* Tsvetaeva encounters a joyous, life- and death-affirming poet who differs significantly from the tragic figure she herself envisioned. Rilke leads her to recognize the essential difference between the Orpheus she designates as reincarnated in Rilke and the Orpheus with whom he himself identified. The discrepancy between their images of Orpheus reflects underlying differences that result in the lapse in their correspondence.

We must now consider the persona of Orpheus-Rilke that Tsvetaeva fashions in the course of the correspondence. Although this persona relies on Rilke's conception of poetry, it expresses above all Tsvetaeva's own views. The Orpheus-Rilke she creates originates in the alignment of Rilke with the phenomenon of poetry itself. Her first letter to him, dated 9 May, designates him as "die verkörperte Dichtung," "eine Naturerscheinung," "das verkörperte fünfte Element: die Dichtung selbst," "das, woraus die Dichtung entsteht, und das grösser ist als sie (Sie)" [poetry incarnate, a natural phenomenon, the fifth element incarnate: poetry itself, that from which poetry emerges and which is greater than it (you)].[25] These characterizations bring her to a quintessentially Orphic conclusion that resonates with her admiration of Rilke and elevates him above all other poets:

> Was nach Ihnen ein Dichter noch thun kann? Einen Meister (wie Goethe z.B.) überwindet man, aber Sie überwinden—heisst (würde heissen) die Dichtung überwinden. Ein Dichter ist der, der das Leben überwindet (überwinden soll).
>
> Sie sind eine unmögliche Aufgabe für künftige Dichter. Der Dichter, der nach Ihnen kommt, muss *Sie* sein, d.h. Sie müssen noch einmal geboren werden.
>
> [What more can a poet do after you? One overcomes a master (like Goethe, for example), but to overcome you means (would mean) to overcome poetry. A poet is he who overcomes (should overcome) life.
>
> You are an impossible task for future poets. The poet who comes after you must be *you*, that is, you must be born once again.][26]

In a letter to Anna Teskova written shortly after Rilke's death, Tsvetaeva was to describe him along similar lines as « Германский Орфей, то есть Орфей, *на этот раз* явившийся в Германии. Не Dichter (Рильке)—Geist der Dichtung » [A Germanic Orpheus, that is, Orpheus who has *this time* appeared in Germany. Not a poet (Rilke), but the very essence of poetry].[27] The individuality of both Orpheus and Rilke is subsumed by the higher force which makes its presence known through them, even as these essential poets themselves subsume all poetic production.

In her second letter, written before she had received a reply to the first, Tsvetaeva records her responses to Rilke's *Sonnets to Orpheus*. The terms in which she couches these responses are prompted by Rilke's first letter to her, where he explained, "Geographie ist keine Wissenschaft für mich, sondern ein sofort in Gebrauch genommenes Verhältnis" [For me geography is not a science, but rather a relationship which is immediately put into effect]. He assured Tsvetaeva that she was now allotted a space on his "internal map." Tsvetaeva describes the relationship Rilke's Orpheus suggests to her in similar terms. Yet before she does so she skillfully creates her own "map" and inscribes herself not in the vaguely defined space "between Moscow and Toledo" Rilke had assigned her, but specifically in the realm of Rilke's Orpheus that she sees projected in the *Sonnets*.[28] Rilke's *Sonnets* become a map of the poet's internal poetic space which Tsvetaeva undertakes to explore. "Zwei Nächte les ich in Deinem Orpheus," she writes in her letter of 12 May, "(Dein Orpheus ist ein Land, darum: *in*)" [For two nights I have been reading in your Orpheus. (*In* because your Orpheus is a country)].[29]

The course Tsvetaeva charts through the *Sonnets* is, as befits a poet, intricate, indirect, and idiosyncratic. What it reveals of her Orpheus-Rilke and of her self-image vis-à-vis this poetic phenomenon is central to this study. At the same time, to follow it closely is to participate in the immediacy of the unfolding associative networks of Tsvetaeva's creative process. She prefaces her tour of the *Sonnets* with an account of her own unshakable faith in the eternity of the poetic voice, which she describes against the backdrop of the hostility her defense of poetry had elicited. As she berates her obtuse, inimical critics, Tsvetaeva registers her objection to conventional notions of genre whereby certain ideas are uncritically swallowed if they are couched in poetry but rejected when, as in the instance of "The Poet on Criticism," they are expressed in prose. The critics' failure to recognize the consistency of Tsvetaeva's arguments in their different generic guises constitutes proof of their inability to comprehend her message. Both the censure and the praise of these critics are of no consequence to the poet, who, as Tsvetaeva concludes in her account to Rilke, must remain indifferent to the response of herd animals, be they the literary critics of Paris or the sheep who trailed along after Orpheus.

At the time she wrote this second letter to Rilke, Tsvetaeva's critics could have been more readily compared to the enraged Maenads who dismembered Orpheus than to the dumb animals who followed him. Tsvetaeva, however, comments on their hostility only obliquely, remarking that inasmuch as she is not merely "Frau Z" [Mme. Ts.] but a poet, she is impervious to their attacks, which serve only to confirm her poetic legitimacy.

As the tragic proportions of the *sparagmós* are reduced to the trivial scale of the mundane, Tsvetaeva roots her contention with the critics in their divergent response to Orpheus. This divergence results from the difference in perspective that distinguishes poets from nonpoets represented in the cycle *Poets*. The passage in which this is described bears quoting in full; it is Tsvetaeva's presentation to Rilke of poetic credentials that encourage him to recognize her as an initiate of the Orphic realm who is capable of apprehending his *Sonnets*. The account of her own situation also implies a similarity between herself and the misapprehended Greek bard.

> Ein Kritiker sprach von Blok: "Die vier Jahre, die uns von seinem Tode trennen, haben uns mit seinem Tod versöhnt, ja—beinahe über ihn getröstet."
>
> Ich parierte: "Wenn vier Jahre genug sind, um sich über den Tod eines Dichters wie Blok zu trösten, wie steht's mit Puschkin (†1836). Wie stehts mit dem Orpheus (†?) Jeder Dichter-Tod, ob möglichst natürlich, ist widernatürlich, d. h. *Mord*, darum unaufhörlich, ununterbrochen, ewig—im Moment—dauernd, Puschkin, Blok—und, um alle zu nennen—**Orpheus**—kann nie gestorben sein, weil er jetzt eben (ewig!) stirbt. В каждом любящем — заново, и в каждом любящем — вечно. Darum—kein Trost, bis wir nicht selber 'gestorben sein' werden." (Ungefähr so, russisch war's besser.)[30]

> [A critic said of Blok: "The four years which separate us from his death have reconciled us to his death, indeed have almost brought consolation."
>
> I parried: "If four years are enough to provide consolation for the death of a poet like Blok, how do things stand with Pushkin (†1836). How do things stand with Orpheus (†?) Every death of a poet, even the most natural, is unnatural, that is, *murder*, therefore interminable, uninterrupted, lasting eternally in the moment, Pushkin, Blok—and to name them all—**Orpheus** can never have died, because he is just now (forever!) dying. In each who loves him—anew, and in each who loves him—eternally. Therefore—no consolation until we ourselves will 'have died.'" (Something like that, it was better in Russian.)][31]

The focus shifts from the nonpoets' inability to value the poet to their correlative inability to comprehend his death. The expansion of the moment of death Tsvetaeva describes here and which she was ultimately to accomplish in *New Year's*, her *poèma* written on the occasion of Rilke's death, is essentially a prose rendering of the situation depicted in "Thus Floated Head and Lyre." In that lyric, Tsvetaeva focuses on the moment of transcendence, where the creative process and the process of dying overlap. The locus of transcendence is at the juncture of life and death—the only moment, as she was subsequently to explain in *New Year's*, in which the universe can be seen in its entirety. This juncture is reproduced when the "unnatural" and yet always expected and inevitable moment of the poet's death is internalized by those who love him. Here it is not poetry itself that holds in eternity the transcendent moment, but rather those genuine readers like herself whose lives are coterminous with the deaths of the poets they continue to love and mourn. Thus, by effecting the eternal return of the poet's death, the ideal reader—here Tsvetaeva herself—gains a place within the infinite Orphic realm. The eternal return that she represents in her first letter to Rilke as successive reincarnations of Orpheus is here described in terms of an ever replenishing series of readers. From this perspective transcendence resides not within the individual poem or poet, but rather in the inexhaustible potential of the contexts and connections brought to it by its successive readers. It is situated, in other words, at the interpenetration of the realm of the poem and that of its reader. In arguing that the poet's moment of dying is made to endure by his readers, Tsvetaeva suggests an alternative also to the notion of his death. Thus she discovers an alternative also to the notion of the poet's own reincarnation that attempts to forestall the finality of his death.

In so arguing Tsvetaeva seeks to prove herself necessary to Rilke. Moreover, she unwittingly lays the groundwork for the project she was masterfully to accomplish upon learning of Rilke's death. Particularly in the *poèma New Year's* and in the prose piece "Your Death" she draws Rilke's death into the fabric of her own life and thereby accomplishes within her own poetic terrain that crucial intersection of life and death that she designates as the locus of transcendence in this letter.[32] Yet however successful Tsvetaeva's subsequent translations of Rilke's death into the world of the living, in the face of the yet-living Rilke her insistence on the poet's dependency on an ideal reader like herself resembles suspiciously a territorial claim on Rilke's solitary creative space.

Having contextualized her own attitude toward the Orpheus myth and situated herself in it, Tsvetaeva launches into a rhapsodic response to a series of individual lines she culls from the *Sonnets to Orpheus*. Here her reading of recognition expands into a reading of inclusion, and at times even of intrusion, as she augments her endorsement of what she perceives to be Rilke's artistic intent with indications of how closely the lines she chooses define her own existence—the extent to which those lines are expressly about her. The movement from the specific to the universal that obtains in the detection of mythic patterns is reversed in Tsvetaeva's responses to Rilke's Orpheus poems, which in her treatment yield up intimate personal connections that reaffirm her ties with the admired poet. Eurydice's chastisement of Orpheus in the 1923 lyric "Eurydice to Orpheus" appears to be forgotten—at least for the moment—as Tsvetaeva embraces Rilke in the image of what she construes to be a shared Orpheus.

By way of an introduction to the series of quotations from sonnets 1, 3, 5, 6, and 11 of part I that appear in her letter, she quotes the opening lines of the collection, replacing Rilke's past tense with the present to heighten their actuality: "Da steigt ein Baum. O reine Übersteigung" [There rises a tree. O pure transcendence].[33] Rilke's lines announce the centrality of transcendence in the *Sonnets* and in the myth of Orpheus that informs them. Tsvetaeva's affinity for aligning the image of the tree with poet and poetry that has already been noted parallels Rilke's. Both poets perceive a metaphoric connection between their mediating art and the tree whose roots draw sustenance from the invisible chthonian realm to soar upward in ever expanding branches. The secret nurture necessary to the visible growth and fruition is for Rilke a particularly cogent representation of the poet's work. In his First Sonnet Rilke establishes the tree specifically as an emblem of Orpheus, who, as Walter Strauss notes, "is truly the reconciler of opposites: he is the fusion of the radiant solar enlightenment of Apollo and the somber subterranean knowledge of Dionysus."[34] Tsvetaeva avows to Rilke her direct knowledge of the parallel between prototypal poet and tree: "Und *wie ich das kenne*" [And *how I know that*].[35] She goes on to elaborate that it is the tree's transcendence of itself that permits its growth into the very heavens, and yet she refrains both from developing this idea further and from establishing any connections she could well have made with her own writings. Instead she interpolates at this juncture a digression on the prominence of the number seven in Russian culture.

This digression takes its impetus from the "seventieth heaven" into which Tsvetaeva describes the tree as growing and refers back to a passage from Rilke's preceding letter (10 May). In it he writes that a number seven was written next to her name and address on the letter he received from her and notes that seven was his "segnende Zahl" [blessed number].[36] We may recall here that Orpheus's lyre had seven strings that corresponded to the seven spheres of the universe and that he spent seven days seeking reentry into Hades after his loss of Eurydice. Yet what is especially important for Tsvetaeva in this passage is that Rilke recognizes what appear to be trivial details to be important carriers of meaning. In the ability to discern the capacity of even humble signs to point beyond themselves—something Rilke taught and Tsvetaeva mastered—she rightly feels their proximity most strongly. In discussing the *Sonnets to Orpheus,* Tsvetaeva bases the kinship she seeks to establish with Rilke not only on the many coincidences of their poetic thinking and imagery, but also on similarities she perceives in their creative methods. Indeed, an important message of the letters lies in the correspondents' demonstration of the processes by which they generate and derive meaning. Hence that intimate, conspiratorial tone of the Tsvetaeva-Rilke dialogue noted by Azadovskii, who observes that "in places it creates the impression that its partners are conspirators, accomplices who know something of which the surrounding world has no inkling."[37]

It is not surprising that Tsvetaeva should attempt to find a deeper, underlying unity between herself and Rilke, for the *Sonnets* in general and the First Sonnet in particular could be used more readily to mark the differences than the similarities of the images of Orpheus the two poets project. Rilke's Orpheus represents a transcendence based on the transformation of loss and suffering into joy, an attitude derived to significant measure from his observation of Russian spirituality. Tsvetaeva elevates loss and suffering to mythic proportions as a *sine qua non* of becoming a poet. Through resignation, self-surrender, and sacrifice her poet can attain victory over the mundane to arrive at eternity but not at joy. That Rilke sensed this difference in their views is apparent from his attempt in the "Elegie an Marina Zwetajewa-Efron" (8 June 1926) to apprise Tsvetaeva of the essential unity he perceived between mourning and jubilation:

Wir beginnens als Jubel, schon übertrifft es uns völlig;
plötzlich, unser Gewicht dreht zur Klage abwärts den Sang.
Aber auch so: Klage? Wäre sie nicht: jüngerer Jubel nach unten.

[We begin it as jubilation, already it exceeds us completely; all of a sudden our weight turns the song downward to lament. Yet even so: lament? Could it not be: younger jubilation downward?][38]

The first of the *Sonnets to Orpheus* presents two themes Rilke and Tsvetaeva share: the creative potential of silence and the importance of hearing. At the same time, however, it demonstrates the essential difference in the two poets' reading of the Orpheus myth and in their representations of the poet. Rilke opens the *Sonnets* with Orpheus's song and the gathering of animals who are drawn to it. These animals become the bearers of that space of silence in which Orpheus's song accomplishes metamorphosis. Poetry, as Rilke suggests, affects the internal space of other creatures. Metamorphosis is accomplished as poetry transforms the *Innenraum* of each individual.

As we have seen already in the discussion of the *Sibyl* cycle, the concentration on interiority and on the transformation of internal space is by no means alien to Tsvetaeva. Indeed, both she and Rilke had been urged to exploration of this space by their mutually admired predecessor Hölderlin. Tsvetaeva, however, refused to countenance Orpheus's capacity to move animals, stones, and trees with his song. Not even Rilke's exquisite sonnet dislodges her disdain for this unseemly miracle. The dumb creatures of the Orpheus myth remain for her representations of unthinking readers incapable of experiencing and responding to her works directly and as individuals. "(Die alte Fabel von Orpheus und den Thieren, zu denen auch—Schaafe gehörten?)" [(The old fable of Orpheus and the animals among which were also sheep)] she parenthetically concludes her complaints.[39]

Clearly Tsvetaeva seeks to distinguish herself from Rilke's crowd of admirers. At the same time this particular choice of imagery suggests a desire to insist on her own reading of the myth. Her rejection of the responsive animals is informed by her conception of the poet as a martyr to the hostilities of the mundane rather than their mitigator. Tsvetaeva's poet is a rebel who disrupts existing norms and who is made to suffer in consequence; he is not the bearer of harmony and accord. Implicit in her stance is also a refusal to admit tangible confirmation of the ineffable power of poetry. Indeed it can be argued that it is precisely such an expectation—fostered and nurtured by those responsive animals, stones, and trees—that impels Orpheus to turn his head and lose his beloved. It can hardly be appropriate to lavish on Orpheus such vast testimony of the power of his song on earth and yet to punish him so severely for expecting similar proof of its efficacy as he guides Eurydice homeward. The true transformations accomplished by the poet lie much deeper. However abstractly the dumb beasts drawn to Orpheus are regarded, they remain to Tsvetaeva's understanding of poetry what sleight of hand is to alchemy. The only verification of his powers her poet can rightfully expect is the hostility of the surrounding world.

Tsvetaeva's next four citations—from the Third, Fourth, Fifth, and Sixth Sonnets of part I—limn an Orpheus who projects her understanding of the poet and the poetic imperative. Characterized in the lines she selectively isolates are the equation of essential existence with the production of verse, the difficulty of the task confronting the poet, Orpheus's duality, and his eternal dismemberment and return. Although these broad issues are concerns Tsvetaeva and Rilke hold in common, in the new context of her letter, interspersed with sparse, highly condensed, intimate commentary, the quoted lines stray from their author's intent. Tsvetaeva uses them to spark an active dialogue with Rilke as she develops, expands, reinterprets, and to a significant measure also appropriates the cited passages. Here is a vivid demonstration of the reader's expansion of textual and auctorial bounds that Tsvetaeva described earlier in her letter.

"Gesang ist Dasein" [Song is existence (being there)] is Tsvetaeva's next quotation. This is the controlling idea of the Third Sonnet, which focuses on the difficult situation of the mortal who can only divide the universe even as he seeks its wholeness. Song and being are one, and the self must be subsumed by song. Tsvetaeva connects this statement with the First Sonnet, where silence is represented as potential—presence rather than absence, fullness rather than emptiness—with a laconic parenthetical remark: "(da sein, wer nicht singt ist noch nicht da, kommt noch!)" [(to be there, he who does not sing is not yet there, is yet to come!)].[40] This brief remark highlights Tsvetaeva's preference for anticipation over fulfillment, a position we have seen represented for her, in specifically verbal form, by the Annunciation.

From the Fourth Sonnet Tsvetaeva couples the line that acknowledges the overwhelming weight of the world: "Schwer sind die Berge, schwer sind die Meere . . ." [Heavy are the mountains, heavy are the seas . . .] with the one describing liberation from that weight that concludes the poem: " . . . Aber die Lüfte . . . aber die Räume . . ." [. . . But the airs . . . but the expanses . . .]. She comments on the gentle tone of the first of these and of the last writes: "Diese Zeile ist *reine Intonation* (intention), also reine Engelsrede.

(Intonation: eine intention, die Laut wurde. Verkörperte intention)" [This line is *pure intonation* (intention), that is, pure angel's speech. (Intonation: an intention that became sound. Intention incarnate)].[41] In essence, this acoustically grounded formula is a variation on Tsvetaeva's definition of lyric verse as translation between the visible and the invisible. Underscored here are Rilke's ties with the other world—already emphasized in the opening of her letter—and his similarity to the angels of the *Duino Elegies*. Tsvetaeva focuses here specifically on the acoustic properties of the line to draw attention away from the referents of its individual words. Because his intentions are conveyed through sound rather than meaning, Rilke, she argues, is closer to the other world. Here once again Tsvetaeva aligns the semantic properties of a word with the body and this world and its acoustic characteristics with the spirit and the other world. We have already observed the centrality this alignment assumes in her thinking about poetry and have seen it represented positively by the Sibyl and negatively by Hamlet. It is important in her response to Rilke as well. Indeed, after Rilke's death, which was imminent, Tsvetaeva construed this "intonational" quality of his verse as marking his transition from our world to the one beyond. If for Tsvetaeva Blok's verse thematically presaged his impending death, Rilke's poetry conveyed aurally the gradual loosening of earthly ties in which he was engaged.

Rilke's Third Sonnet locates poetry at the tangency of divinity and mortality. In the Fifth he contemplates the analogous adjacency of the eternal and the ephemeral. The significance of monumental permanence is usurped by flux and metamorphosis. It is in the nature of the poet, these sonnets suggest, to disappear and reappear on the strength of his transcendent word that surpasses existence and leads him where others cannot go. Indeed, the disappearance of the poet signals his cognizance of that which lies beyond *Hiersein* [being here]. The creative process and death are drawn together in the recognition of the parallel between Orpheus's descent for Eurydice and that final descent that followed his dismemberment. The poet's death, Rilke intimates, is to be regarded no differently from that disappearance from the here-and-now effected in the process of writing each poem. Upon completing a poem, the poet is no longer as he was before writing it. Inasmuch as the poet is altered with each return, it comes to matter little when he dies and another poet appears in his place. Thus in Rilke's definition of the archetypal poet, metamorphosis modulates imperceptibly into reincarnation and the eternal into the ephemeral.

We recognize the similarity of the themes addressed in these sonnets to those discussed in connection with Tsvetaeva's definition of the poet. Their culmination is the assertion of Orpheus's primacy, which Rilke highlights in the central passage of the Fifth Sonnet. Tsvetaeva quotes this passage in her letter:

> . . . Wir sollen uns nicht mühn
> Um andre Namen. Ein für alle Male
> Ist's Orpheus, wenn es singt.
>
> [. . . We should not trouble ourselves for other names. Once and for all it is Orpheus when there's song.][42]

Her laconic response appears parenthetically: "(wenn es stirbt—unter Dichtern, das, was ich—im Seitenumwenden—meinte)" [when there's dying—among poets, just what I thought in turning the page].[43] Here she draws together the root idea of Rilke's sonnet and what she herself sought to express in the passage about the death of the poet from "The Poet on Criticism" which she had paraphrased for him earlier in this letter. Her replacement of Rilke's "when there's song" with "when there's death" is terrifying in the intensity of its equation of writing poetry with dying.

Tsvetaeva's qualifying statement "among poets" that accompanies this replacement of "sings" with "dies" carries the further implication that only the poet can discern the signs of death with which each poem is imbued and can recognize the catabasis necessary to its genesis. Tsvetaeva's main point remains that whatever guise their work assumes, all poets—and specifically she and Rilke—engage in the same deadly activity.

The next passage Tsvetaeva quotes is the deceptively simple question posed at the opening of the Sixth Sonnet: "Ist er ein Hiesiger?" [Is he of this world?]. The sonnet amplifies the Orphic apprehension of both this world and the other. Rilke's concern here is not merely to determine the poet's allegiance to one or another of these realms, but to consider the broader implications of the Orphic knowledge of both. The designations "this" and "other" are elaborated in the sonnet. The former includes visible, present, living; the latter applies to invisible, nonpresent, dead. The overriding intent in making these distinctions is to proclaim their necessary interpenetration. Ultimately they are joined within the poet, who must prevent the visible and the here-and-now from taking precedence over the other, invisible, nonpresent world.

In reply to the opening query of Rilke's sonnet, Tsvetaeva signals her accord with this view and responds as if Rilke were addressing the question specifically to her:

> Und man fühlt schon das kommende (nahende) Nein. O, Rainer, ich will nicht wählen (wählen ist wühlen und wüst sein!), ich kann nicht wählen, ich nehm die ersten besten Zeilen, die noch mein Ohr enthält. Ins Ohr schreibst Du mir, mit dem Ohr bist du gelesen.
>
> [And one already feels the approaching (nearing) No. Oh, Rainer, I don't want to choose (to choose is to rummage and be barren!), I cannot choose, I take the first best lines that my ear still holds. You write into my ear, with the ear you are read.][44]

The passage demonstrates again the dependency of her writing on acoustic associations and reveals her penetration of Rilke's creative process. The anticipation of a negative response to Rilke's question as to whether Orpheus is of this world—expressed in the third person—gives way immediately to the first person which signals Tsvetaeva's own identification with Orpheus. As her Hamlet persona conveyed, the impossible choice between antithetical realms must never be made; the energy of their tension must instead be engaged to generate momentum. The argument of her Hamlet poems is captured in the semantic richness that underlies the paronomastic unfolding of the passage in which she now concurs with Rilke's sonnet.[45]

Having registered her own resistance to such choices, Tsvetaeva forces a shift of perspective that transforms the question of deciding between the visible and the invisible into that of selecting the excerpts from the *Sonnets* she includes in her letter. Once again the large poetic process is recognized in the individual lyric. The lines she cites chose themselves, as she explains, and she is simply recording those her ear has retained. The slight errors Tsvetaeva makes in her quotations of Rilke's verse suggest that she is indeed citing what her ear holds without recourse to visual verification. Even as she pays homage to the exquisite acoustics of Rilke's poetry, Tsvetaeva registers the keenness of her own hearing and suggests how finely attuned it is to Rilke's poetry. The writing into the ear that she notes here derives from the First Sonnet, to which she referred in opening her discussion of Rilke's poems. In that sonnet, the tree of transcendence couched in the ear is both Orpheus and his song:

> Da stieg ein Baum. O reine Übersteigung!
> O Orpheus singt! O hoher Baum im Ohr!
>
> [There rose a tree. O pure transcendence!
> Oh Orpheus sings! O lofty tree in the ear!] (2:487)

Tsvetaeva's remark not only equates Rilke with Orpheus, but also makes her the space within which Orpheus and his song come about. Even as she once again seeks to make Rilke and his poetry dependent on her, she acknowledges the changes wrought within her by his verse. She, in turn, seeks to effect a change in the author of these *Sonnets*. Her quotation from the Eleventh Sonnet, "dieser Stolz aus Erde" [this pride of earth], she introduces—for the first time—one of her own works. Promising to send Rilke her collection *Ремесло* [Craft, 1923], she draws his attention to St. George, who appears in it and who, like the rider of Rilke's sonnet ("Und die zwei sind eins" [And the two are one]), fuses with his horse to achieve the unity of rider and steed.

The horse and rider form a common trope in Tsvetaeva's writings. Here she alludes to her seven-poem cycle *Георгий* [George]. In this work St.

George and his steed are differentiated by color and by temperament and yet drawn together by the interdependency essential to the accomplishment of their lofty deed. Indeed, their conjoined dissimilarities are instrumental to the success of the endeavor (e.g., « Стыдливости детской / С гордынею конской / Союз » [The union / of childlike shyness / with the pride of a steed]) The fusion of horse and rider generates the centaurian figure of "horserider" that Tsvetaeva discusses in her letter to Rilke and that represents poetry itself. In both Rilke's sonnet and Tsvetaeva's cycle the image of carrying steed and guiding rider is a complex metaphor for poetic creation that portrays the poet's simultaneous control over, surrender to, and dependence on the creative force. Just as in the opening couplet of the cycle *Poets* the poet both leads and is led by language, here the rider is both guide and passenger of the steed that carries him. In the complex unity they achieve, it becomes no longer possible or necessary to distinguish between them.

Tsvetaeva's last direct reference to the *Sonnets to Orpheus* in this letter is to the Sixteenth Sonnet of part I, over which Rilke had penciled in the explanation, "to a dog."[46] The sonnet deals, as Rilke notes in his commentary, with the interrelationship of poet, dog, and humankind. This is a variation on the theme of the presence of an invisible world within the space of the one visible to us. By virtue of its acute sense of smell, the dog is able to experience an entire stratum of being that remains imperceptible to humans. Its perception of the world it shares with humans is thus significantly different from theirs. Tsvetaeva's oblique response to this sonnet once again translates its message into specific personal detail as she proclaims her great love for dogs. Yet even as she makes this commonplace assertion we recognize that the dog of the sonnet has drawn into Tsvetaeva's present consciousness the now no longer visible yet clearly extant world of her childhood. The poet's associative capacities are thus shown to draw different temporal planes into simultaneity, thereby expanding the world inhabited by the poet. Beneath the surface of her apparently casual remark is the complex world of the creating poet.

Tsvetaeva isolates no further passages from the *Sonnets* for commentary. The main themes of those lyrics, however, continue to resonate in her correspondence with Rilke. In the next letter, dated "Ascension Day," Tsvetaeva returns to the impossibility of choosing between worlds in order to stress the productive unity of the dissimilar that is projected in the rider-steed metaphor. The references now appear as part of her attempt to qualify the distinction she made in her first letter (9 May) to Rilke between "Rilke-Mensch" and "Rilke-Dichter" [Rilke-man and Rilke-poet].

Rilke's response to Tsvetaeva in his letter of 10 May makes it clear that he himself does not acknowledge this distinction. He indicates that he considers the tension between man and poet a sign of illness and not a crucial feature identifying the poet.[47] As it becomes evident that her own reading of the

Orpheus myth as a representation of the tension between human desires and poetic criteria differs significantly from the harmonious balance between them that Rilke strives to attain, Tsvetaeva retreats from her position.

We have seen already the extent to which Tsvetaeva grounded her own poetic credentials in the incompatibility of human and poet. It now emerges that she had recommended herself on the basis of criteria that ran contrary to Rilke's reading of the myth. The animosity of the surrounding world on which Tsvetaeva predicates the poet's identity is entirely absent from Rilke's account. His Orpheus is freed from dependency on mundane hostility even as his creative urge is separated from erotic beginnings. Tsvetaeva's poet, however, remains dependent on both eros and the hostility of the multitude. Her focus on their shared image of rider-steed is an attempt to distract Rilke from this crucial difference between them.

Yet the difference is not so easily bridged. In the *Sonnets*, as Walter Strauss outlines, "Rilke, as the Orphic poet, is not trying to redeem Eurydice from the dead; his mandate is to know what Eurydice knows, to understand it, and to transpose it into song."[48] As Strauss's observation implies, Rilke's success in his project is predicated largely on eliminating eros from that configuration of forces that propel the Orphic mission. Elizabeth Sewell speaks of "the long, loving, cherishing utter rejection of sex and fertility" in Rilke's description of Eurydice in the lyric "Orpheus. Eurydike. Hermes."[49] Important too is Rilke's own "identification with the woman rather than the man" that Sewell notes.[50] In "Orpheus. Eurydike. Hermes" the notion of an erotically driven conjoinment of opposites is replaced with the all-encompassing image of a virginal Eurydice pregnant with death. For Rilke, Orpheus's violation of the boundary between life and death has repercussions that Tsvetaeva does not acknowledge. The descent overrides not only the antinomy of life and death, but also all the lesser antinomies which it subsumes. Thus, as Charles Segal observes, "the destabilizing of familiar boundaries between states of being continues in the fusion of nubile virginity, pregnancy, and death in Eurydice herself. She is both freshly virginal and expectantly pregnant."[51]

Already in that early lyric Rilke is well beyond the reproaches of Tsvetaeva's Eurydice, for he has absorbed into himself precisely those antinomies that make the situation of Tsvetaeva's Orpheus impossible. The tensions propelling her poet are subsumed by and resolved within the poet envisioned by Rilke.

Tsvetaeva was aware of this difference in their essential poets—also their self-portraits. Indeed, in her first letter to him she had already acknowledged Rilke's replacement of dependency on the other with a self-sufficiency born of the internalization of opposites. In it she maintained, "Ich glaub nur an Muttersöhne. Sie sind auch ein Muttersohn. Ein *Mann* nach der *weiblichen* Linie—darum so *reich*. (Zwiefaltigkeit)" [I believe only in mother-sons. You too are a mother-son. A *man* along the *feminine* line—therefore so *rich*. (Duality)].[52] The simultaneity of male and female that Tsvetaeva discerns in Rilke suggests the solitary inward journey as an alternative to the erotically motivated quest for the other that propels her Orpheus and Tsvetaeva herself. It is only after Rilke's repudiation of the split between man and poet in his letter of 10 May, however, that Tsvetaeva becomes fully cognizant of the inapplicability of her own poetic model to Rilke.

That she was taken aback by this recognition is clear from her attempt to smooth over their differences, but it was not long before her project suffered a significant setback. The *coup de grâce* came in Rilke's letter of 17 May, which noted two circumstances that precipitated Tsvetaeva's fierce and sudden, although temporary, retreat from her epistolary outpourings. The first was Rilke's intimation that he might not be able to respond to all of Tsvetaeva's letters. The second was his admission that his Russian had proved inadequate to the poems Tsvetaeva had sent him, even with the assistance of her annotations.[53] Rilke had no intention of injuring Tsvetaeva, but she read these two remarks as an assertion of his unattainable superiority and as a rejection of her own poetic identity. Although the blow existed only in her imagination, the correspondence never fully recovered from its consequences. Tsvetaeva concluded that it would remain impossible for Rilke to regard her as an equal, and that she was destined therefore to remain in that dreaded role of the unrecognized stranger at his door she had described in her first letter.

The overwhelming emotional intensity in the beginning of her correspondence with Rilke now gave way to Tsvetaeva's attempt to reassert herself and to compensate for her vulnerability. She returns to the lyric "Eurydice to Orpheus" to take stock of the persona she had adopted earlier to overcome Orpheus.

In her letter of 25 May 1926 to Boris Pasternak, whom thus far she had by and large excluded from the correspondence with Rilke, Tsvetaeva gives vent to her bitterness at her "rejection" and enlarges the powers she had ascribed to Eurydice. She includes a series of complaints about Rilke and claims to be resigned to the end of their epistolary exchange. It is telling that in this context she assigns Eurydice full responsibility for Orpheus's fateful turn of the head and reinstates that eros which the lyric itself rejects:

> — Оборот Орфея дело рук Эвридики. (« Рук » — через весь коридор Аида!) Оборот Орфея — либо слепость ее любви, невладение ею (скорей, скорей!), либо — о Борис, это страшно — помнишь 1923 год, март, гору, строки:
>
> Не надо Орфею сходить к Эвридике,
> И братьям тревожить сестер —

либо *приказ* обернуться — и потерять. Все, что в ней еще любило — последняя память, тень тела, какой-то мысок сердца еще не тронутый ядом бессмертья, помнишь?

. . . С бессмертья змеиным укусом
Кончается женская страсть!

все, что еще отзывалось в ней на ее женское имя — шло за ним, она не могла не итти, хотя, может быть, уже не хотела итти.

[Orpheus's turning is the work of Eurydice's hands. ("Hands"—through the whole length of the corridor of Hades!) Orpheus's turning is either the blindness of her love, her lack of control over it (faster, faster!), or—oh, Boris, this is terrifying—remember the year 1923, March, the mountain, the lines:

Orpheus must not descend to Eurydice,
And brothers disturb sisters —

or the *command* to turn around—and lose. Everything in her that yet loved—the last memory, the shade of the body, some bit of the heart not yet touched by the poison of immortality, do you remember?

. . . Female passion ends
at immortality with the bite of a snake!

everything in her that still responded to her female name—followed after him, she couldn't not go, although, perhaps, she no longer wanted to go.][54]

Nevertheless, the conclusion of Tsvetaeva's letter to Pasternak reveals a sense of inadequacy—both in herself and in her Eurydice—before Orpheus-Rilke. She expresses the need to create a new Eurydice and assumes a fairly low position on the scale of spiritual development, on the basis of her cognizance of Hades, presumably in lieu of the upper reaches of Rilke's poems:

До страсти хотела бы написать Эвридику: ждущую, идущую, удаляющуюся. Через глаза или дыхание? *Не* знаю. Если бы ты знал, как я *вижу* Аид! Я, очевидно, на еще очень низкой ступени бессмертия.

[I passionately would like to write Eurydice: waiting, walking, disappearing. Through eyes or breath? I *don't* know. If only you knew how I *see* Hades! I am, apparently, still at a very low stage of immortality.][55]

Tsvetaeva's anxiety was well founded, for she was beginning to recognize that her Orpheus did not coincide with Rilke's. The transitions between realms, their tensions, and the *sparagmós*—those external conditions that propel Tsvetaeva's poet—are internalized by Rilke's Orpheus, in whom all is fused. The arguments advanced by Rilke and Tsvetaeva's excessive umbrage at them imply their awareness of the irreconcilable difference between them. Of the passage "Ist er ein Hiesiger? Nein, aus beiden Reichen erwuchs seine weite Natur" [Is he of this world? No, his broad nature sprang from both realms], the opening line of the Sixth Sonnet (part I), which Tsvetaeva too had singled out for comment, Walter Strauss writes:

> This is the doctrine of the double realm, life and death. Orpheus, as a result both of his descent and dismemberment, is perfectly at home in both realms and unites them. Thus he abolishes the 1904 poem, surpassing Eurydice at the same time. His being-here and being-beyond are coextensive because the thread joining them has been restored. Everything now becomes explicable under the category of "der klarste Bezug"—the clearest connection.[56]

The *Sonnets to Orpheus*, like the *Duino Elegies*, present the summation of Rilke's view of the poet's central and, of necessity, solitary position within a complete, yet ever changing universe. In much they concur with Tsvetaeva's views, but they also suggest an alternative solution to some of the issues she confronted. Within his universe Rilke presents the poet not at the juncture of the visible and the invisible, but at the very center where these two realms interpenetrate completely—that "unerhörte Mitte" [unheard-of center] to which he refers in Sonnet 28 (part II) of the *Sonnets to Orpheus*. Walter Strauss describes Rilke as a poet in whose work "everything moves toward fusion and metamorphosis and the image is inward-bound." He contrasts Rilke's deliberate treatment of *coincidentia oppositorum* with what he designates as Mallarmé's essentially Heraclitian dialectics—dialectics, as we may remark, in terms of which Tsvetaeva too perceived existence.[57] For Rilke the fusion of a divided universe takes place within the poet.

Tsvetaeva approximates Rilke's vision in her rejection of a fixed set of truths in favor of process and the fluidity of signification as expressed, for example, in the kaleidoscope metaphor she adopts to define lyric poetry. Her emphasis, however, as this metaphor suggests, remains on the relativity of discrete phenomena whose protean meaning is demonstrated by the shifting perspectives and ever changing contexts that the poet affords her reader and that the reader brings to the poem. The dynamic intensity of her verse derives, as we have seen, from carefully engineered collisions of antinomies and mutually exclusive points of vantage. Her orchestration of tensions and clashes highlights the process of creating connections to reveal the interdependency of apparently antithetical phenomena. Tsvetaeva demands of the poet not that he transfigure the world, but that he enlarge on the perceptual possibilities it affords. In providing a bridge to the other world, the poet encourages not escapism, but the admission of new frames of reference. Travel to the other world that poetry makes possible enhances the returning wayfarer's capacity to recognize in the earthly signs surrounding him indicators of that other world. The ability to derive transcendent meaning from the signs of this world is one that—as Tsvetaeva was at pains to underscore in her letters—she shared with Rilke. In her vision of the universe, however, the Rilkean emphasis on the interpenetration of visible and invisible worlds is regarded specifically in terms of the overlapping of the systems of signification by which they are indicated. Her metamorphoses are dynamic processes taking place within the perceptual space of the poet and her readers. Fueling this process is a carefully structured imbalance that demands the poet's ceaseless peregrinations between worlds.

In her letters to Rilke thus far Tsvetaeva, as we have seen, repeatedly appropriated symbols of universal poetic proportions to her immediate condition, using them to establish intimate connections with Rilke. Now this appropriation, which minimized their differences, prompted stirrings of conscience. In her letter to Rilke of 3 June, Tsvetaeva describes the pain his "rejection" caused her and goes on to offer her own semiapologetic, semiassertive analysis of what must have prompted it. In her assessment of the situation she assumes that Rilke's rejection was brought on by the "translation of the eternal into the now" in which she engaged in her letters to him. She writes:

> Vor dem Leben is man *immer* und *alles*, wie man lebt—ist man *etwas* und *jetzt*. (Ist, hat,—gleich!)
>
> Meine Liebe zu Dir zerstückelte sich in Tage und Briefe, Stunden und Zeilen. Daher die Unruhe. (Daher batest Du um Ruhe!) Brief heute, Brief morgen. Du lebst, ich will Dich sehen. Eine Überpflanzung aus Immer ins Jetzt. Daher die Pein, das Tage-Zählen, jeder Stunde Umwert, die Stunde nur noch als Stufe—zum Brief.
>
> [Before life one is *everything* and *all*, as one lives—one is *something* and *now*. (Is, has,—it's all the same!)
>
> My love for you fragmented itself into days and letters, hours and lines. Hence the agitation. (That is why you asked for peace!) A letter today, a letter tomorrow. You are alive, I want to see you. A transplanting from always into now. Hence the torment, the counting of days, the reassessment of each hour, the hour only as a step—toward a letter.][58]

In the reduction of potential to actuality and the fragmentation of time Tsvetaeva describes we hear a distinct echo of what her own *Sibyl* lyrics condemned. She follows this passage with a denigration of earthly, time-bound love, love not yet made transcendent: "So bin ich. So ist die Liebe—in der Zeit. Undankbar und selbstvernichtend. Liebe ehre und liebe ich nicht" [That is how I am. That is how love is—in time. Ungrateful and self-destructive. I do not respect or love love].[59] Her desires, as she now explains, have been relinquished: "Also, Rainer, vorbei. Ich will nicht zu Dir. Ich will nicht wollen" [So, Rainer, it is over. I do not want to come to you. I do not want to want].[60]

Rilke's response (8 June) and especially the "Elegie an Marina Zwetajewa-Efron" which he enclosed with his letter poured oil on the troubled waters of their epistolary relations. Rilke assures Tsvetaeva that he intended no slight. Yet his conciliatory statements also include approval of Tsvetaeva's decision to surrender her desire for him. His elegy enlarges on the dangers inherent in the need to possess, however abstractly. It concludes with a reiteration of the imperative of the poet's solitude, the only path, in Rilke's philosophy, toward a wholeness of vision.

In the letter with which the elegy was included Rilke relates that he composed this piece sitting on a wall in the midst of hilly vineyards and adds that he "riveted the lizards with its resonance" thus subtly but unmistakably assuming for himself a guise of Orpheus that Tsvetaeva had specifically rejected.[61] Aside from Rilke's fleeting reference to the Orphic constellation Lyra in his letter of 28 July, this is the last direct allusion to Orpheus in the correspondence. Orpheus was no longer a symbol of their unity.

In her reaction to Rilke's letter and the "Marina Elegy" Tsvetaeva says that she is overcome:

> Deine Elegie. Rainer, mein lebenlang verschenkte ich mich in Gedichten—allen. Dichtern auch. Doch ich gab immer zu viel, ich übertönte immer die mögliche Antwort. Die Antwort erschrak. Ich nahm den ganzen Widerhall vorweg. . . .
>
> Und, Rainer, Dein Gedicht, Rilke's Gedicht, des Dichters, der Dichtung—Gedicht. Und, Rainer,—mein Stummsein. Umgekehrte Lage. Rechte Lage.
>
> [Your elegy. Rainer, my entire life I gave myself to everyone in poems. To poets too. Yet I always gave too much, I always drowned out any possible response. The response took fright. I took away the entire resonance in advance. . . .
>
> And, Rainer, your poem, Rilke's poem, the poet's, poetry's—poem. And, Rainer—my silence. The reverse situation. The true situation.][62]

And yet, this avowal notwithstanding, Tsvetaeva resists becoming one of the lizards Rilke enthralls. In her remaining letters to him she continues to assert the primacy of eros in poetic discourse. Thus, for example, in her letter of 2 August she situates the possible meeting they had spoken of in their letters in the realm of dreams and expresses her desire to sleep with Rilke. Tsvetaeva's bare statement in that letter, "ich will mit Dir schlafen" [I want to sleep with you],[63] has been understood as a demand for excessive intimacy by some readers of the correspondence.[64] Yet this letter projects, in fact, both Ophelia's insistence on sexuality and Eurydice's assertion of the asexual fraternity of poets. Once again it is language that successfully unites these antithetical demands. The Eurydice-like lack of interest in bodies Tsvetaeva describes to Rilke and the accounts of her "translations" from body to spirit demand that her expressions of erotic desire be construed as characteristically paradoxical, metaphoric manifestations of a powerful urge for disembodiment. Her seduction is one of language and not of body, "ein

Eros," as Azadovskii has summarized, "der nur in Worten lebt" [an eros that lives only in words].[65] Tsvetaeva claims ultimately to be a champion of the spirit rather than the body, of the word rather than the deed. She provides Rilke with an explicit statement of her position:

> Ich habe den Körper immer in die Seele übersetzt (*ent*körpert!), die "physische" Liebe—um sie lieben zu können—so verherrlicht, dass plötzlich nichts von ihr blieb. Mich in sie vertiefend, *sie* ausgehöhlt. In sie eindringend, *sie* verdrängt. Nichts blieb von ihr, als ich selbst: Seele (so heiss ich, darum das Staunen: Namenstag!).
>
> [I have always translated the body into the soul (*dis*embodied!), have so glorified "physical" love—in order to be able to love it—that suddenly nothing remained of it. Immersing myself in it, have hollowed *it* out. In penetrating it, have displaced *it*. Nothing remained of it but I myself: the soul (that is what I am called, hence the amazement: nameday!).][66]

At the same time, however, Tsvetaeva uses this poetic platform to justify the demands she continues to place on Rilke to grant or to say he grants her significant space in his creative world. In what was destined to be her last letter to him (22 August) she pleads that he simply say yes to all her requests without fearing any consequences. Tsvetaeva's argument that words replace deeds is extended to include now not only erotic love, but all the claims and demands with which she besieges him. Rilke chose not to respond to this letter.

Tsvetaeva too apparently sensed the inevitable termination of what had begun as correspondence but had evolved into a one-sided epistolary contest in which Rilke appeared to be an unwilling participant. It was not until 7 November that Tsvetaeva's brief postcard—asking whether he still loves her—punctuated the ensuing silence. Rilke did not respond.[67]

Like Orpheus's miscarried attempt at earthly union with Eurydice, the Rilke-Tsvetaeva relationship was destined to fail according to those very mythopoetic laws out of which it originated. Underlying the two poets' reaffirmations of poetry and conscious acceptance of poetic responsibility are fundamental differences in their approaches to the rift in the universe created by the Romantics and thus also in their positioning of the poet within that universe—a positioning that shaped their own poetic personalities. As we have seen in the course of this study, Tsvetaeva makes her poet dependent on the unbearable tension that arises from the need to connect what is irreparably sundered. In so doing she translates potentially destructive Romantic divisiveness into a source of creative energy. Yet in this view the need for the poet and poetic activity persists only as long as the essential impossibility of his project remains in effect. It is this that drives the poet to language—the unique site where impossible resolution and regeneration are ultimately accomplished.

What Tsvetaeva's poet achieves in the privileged space of language Rilke's poet attains within himself, arriving at a harmony, equilibrium, and self-sufficiency alien to Tsvetaeva. Thus too Rilke seeks peace and solitude while Tsvetaeva seeks wrenchingly impossible encounters—meetings to be realized only in poetry. Her poet must ever resist the realization of any but such unions. Accordingly, she engineers the "failures" of three momentous encounters in her life. The strict conditions she sets for her meeting with Blok prevent its realization. Her avoidance of a meeting with Pasternak in Berlin is followed by the even greater decision to leave unrecognized his fulfillment of all the requirements that could permit him to enter the Orpheus role left vacant by Blok. Thus in spite of Pasternak's unsolicited, highly appreciative response to her poetry, his recognition of her as a great poet, and the powerful surge of mutual eros expressed in their letters, she admitted no Orpheus-Pasternak. Orpheus-Rilke materializes briefly, but myth and poetry dictate that such unions cannot endure within the bounds of this world:

Не суждено, чтобы сильный с сильным
Соединились бы в мире сем.

[It is not fated for strong to unite with strong in this world.][68] (SP 3:108)

The correspondence between Rilke and Tsvetaeva did not resume again, that is, not until Rilke's death, an apotheosis that opened the way for a transcendent conjoinment. Tsvetaeva, in a fervent denial of the finality of his death much like the one Blok's demise had elicited, reopened the correspondence that had run aground on the shoals of this world.[69] Like Rilke's Eurydice, Tsvetaeva now experienced what it was to be pregnant with death. Appended to a letter of 1 January 1927 to Boris Pasternak, who was invited to witness her supramundane union with Rilke, is a message addressed directly to the deceased poet and written, like all of her letters to him, in German. This missive came to be the blueprint for the intense, far-reaching text of Tsvetaeva's *poéma Новогоднее* [New Year's], which she designated as a letter to Rilke and which demonstrated that she had emerged from her one-sided struggle with him strengthened in voice and vision. The themes of the proximity of the creative act to death, the reconciliation of the ephemeral and the eternal, and the continuity of lament and jubilation now inform her personal Orphic journey into Rilke's death. The aggressive tone that crept into her letters and suggested insecurity gives way now to an earnest search for the means to overcome their separation. Within the inner space of her grief Tsvetaeva takes up the project of Rilke's latter period: accomplishing the union of life and death.

Chapter Seven

New Year's

—Aber Lebendige machen
alle den Fehler, daß sie zu stark unterscheiden.

[But the living all make / the mistake that they distinguish too sharply.]

—Rainer Maria Rilke, The First Duino Elegy

Еще скажу тебе, что ни одной секунды не ощутила тебя мертвым — себя живой. . . . Если ты мертвый — я тоже мертвая, если я живая — ты тоже живой, — и не все ли равно, как это называется!

[I will tell you also that not for a single second did I experience you as dead—myself as alive. . . . If you are dead—I too am dead, if I am alive—you are alive too—and is it not all the same what this is called?]

—Marina Tsvetaeva, "Your Death"

Нам остается только имя—
Чудесный звук, на долгий срок.

[Left to us is only the name / A miraculous sound for a long stretch of time.]

—Osip Mandel'shtam, "Not Believing in the Miracle of Sunday"

TSVETAEVA'S CONFRONTATION of Rainer Maria Rilke's death (29 December 1926) was the creative impetus for the *poèma Новогоднее* [New Year's]. In writing *New Year's* Tsvetaeva addressed the very problem that has generated the ambivalence in treatments of the Orpheus myth through the ages "between the power of art over death and its futility before death."[1] She engages the transpersonal force of language in her urgent, intensely personal search for a means to interweave Rilke's death with her own life. Her quest expands beyond this one particular loss to become an inquiry into the nature of the poetic work.

To relate what the poem is about is to say a great deal and yet not nearly enough, for this *poèma* focuses above all on the process itself of Tsvetaeva's quest to comprehend, articulate, and forge contact with the dead poet. *New Year's* at once traces her noumenal Orphic quest to overcome the boundaries separating life and death, narrates its own becoming, and demonstrates the creative process from which all poems spring. It is also a process of education in the sense of *Bildung*. The intensity of feeling that propels the development of this poem is matched by the incisiveness of the intellect that guides the reasoning it advances. For all its mediumistic intent, *New Year's* is as logical as it is anagogic.

New Year's also compellingly demonstrates the extent to which Tsvetaeva assimilated the philosophical concerns of Rilke's *Sonnets to Orpheus*, *Duino Elegies*, and "Marina Elegy." Characteristically, her emotionally charged quest is cognitively grounded. Here she herself assumes a guise of Orpheus not to retrieve her beloved from the bourne of death, but to learn what he knows. To that end she subjects to intense reexamination the interrelationships of life and death, permanence and impermanence, lamentation and jubilation, and considers the necessary interrelatedness of antinomies that variously define existence. Undone by death, poetry, and being-a-poet, physicality, eros, and gender are no longer the ruling distinctions. The body is abstracted entirely into poetic language and sexual union is superseded by the concept of rhyme. The Orphic quest for the other is accomplished within the space of the word.

Tsvetaeva's immediate response to the news of Rilke's death was denial, which took the form of a letter, penned—like all of her correspondence with Rilke—in German, which—again like all of her letters to him—demanded a reply.[2] This posthumous epistle to Rilke, which Tsvetaeva enclosed with her letter to Pasternak of 1 January 1927, opens with a motif that was to prevail throughout *New Year's*: "Das Jahr geht mit Deinem Tod? Ende? Anfang an" [The year goes with your death? End? Beginning].[3] The refusal to regard death as a termination lends plausibility to the direct communication between herself and Rilke that she attempts to establish. She refers to specific details from their correspondence and concludes with the greeting, "Freudiges Neujahr und eine schöne Himmelneujahrslandschaft" [Joyful New Year and a lovely new year's landscape in heaven]. Condensed in this letter is a recapitulation of themes that had evolved in the course of her epistolary exchange with Rilke, themes which were now destined to serve as the foundation of the mighty *poèma* that followed.

Thus Rilke's death opened the new year and reopened the personal correspondence which had come to an end while he was alive. Tsvetaeva's repeated references to *New Year's* as a "letter" to Rilke endow the new beginning implicit in the title of this work with a personal intensity. Rilke's death provided a new context, a new light, in which to test, reevaluate, and expand the ideas that arose during their brief correspondence. Indeed, in retrospect it is already possible to discern in Tsvetaeva's first letter to Rilke the poetic platform of *New Year's*, for even then her praise of the poet extended well beyond the boundaries of life and death that she now rejects in her poem. There, as we have seen, she identified Rilke as the source and essence of poetry itself. Her request in that letter, "dass Du mir es gönnst, jeden Augenblick meines Lebens zu Dir aufblicken—wie auf einen Berg der mich schützt (so ein steinerer Schutzengel!)" [that you allow me to look up to you every moment of my life—as up to a mountain that protects me (like a stone guardian angel)], continues to inform her stance in *New Year's* as well.[4] Lauding Rilke in that first letter, Tsvetaeva posed the serious, anxious question: "Was nach Ihnen ein Dichter noch thun kann?" [What more can a poet do after you?]. Yet her response makes it clear that for all of Rilke's unattainable superiority, her own position was no longer that of distant worshiper as it had been with Blok. Tsvetaeva now presents herself as a poet who struggles not against other poets, but against their common enemy, the mundane: "Einen Meister (wie Goethe z.B.) überwindet man, aber Sie überwinden—heisst (würde heissen) die Dichtung überwinden. Ein Dichter ist der, der das Leben überwindet (überwinden soll)" [One overcomes a master (like Goethe, for example), but to overcome you means (would mean) to overcome poetry. A poet is he who overcomes (should overcome) life].[5] The course the correspondence took shows that the lines of battle were not as clearly drawn as this passage suggests. Yet the concept of a confederacy of poets united by their struggle against the mundane remained crucial for Tsvetaeva. Rilke's death does not alter the nature of her praise. It constitutes a realization of the deadly metaphoric battle with life in which the poet engages, and which must now undergo further metaphorization.

The fact that her relationship with Rilke was devoid of physical contact and existed exclusively in the realm of language informs Tsvetaeva's argument that contact between them can persist even after his death. The letters, devoted, as we have seen, primarily to the inner poetic geography of the two poets, obviated the need for physical encounters. Although she did not shy away from using overtly erotic imagery to describe both her human and her poetic needs, her imagery served in a metaphorical rather than a literal capacity. Tsvetaeva had, in other words, already accomplished that necessary Orphic replacement of presence with the language of yearning while Rilke was yet alive. What in this aspect of their relationship could death disrupt? As she describes in her (prose) letter responding to his death,

> An ein hieriges Zusammenkommen haben wir beide nie geglaubt;—wie aufs Hier sein, ja? Du bist mir vorangegangen und ordnest—Stube nicht, Haus nicht—die Landschaft zu meinem Bewillkommen.
> [We two never did believe in a meeting here;—just as we don't believe in being here, right? You have preceded me and are arranging—not a room, not a house—but a landscape for my welcome.][6]

With Rilke's death the longing for an improbable meeting in this world had only to be translated into the certainty of a meeting in the other. From the role of organizer of an earthly rendezvous Tsvetaeva had assigned Rilke in her letter of 22 August,[7] he was now promoted to the role of psychopomp, guide to the other world.[8]

Initially the persistence in *New Year's* of central themes of the correspondence and the demands for a response to her "letter" arise as a denial of Rilke's death. Soon, however, they also become homage to the changes death has effected. Tsvetaeva seeks to alter the face of Rilke's death by imbedding it in the context of the living. She insists, however, that the living too have been changed by that death. The transition from the old year (1926) to the new (1927) which constitutes the immediate temporal setting of the *poèma* takes on metaphysical proportions to emblematize the transformation of death into a (re)generative force. After Rilke's death it is not only a different year, but also a different world in which Tsvetaeva finds herself. The novelty of Rilke's situation is also stressed repeatedly. It is as if life and death are born anew with Rilke's passing.

Tsvetaeva's assertion in *New Year's* « как места / Несть, где нет Тебя, нет есть: могила » [just as there is / No place where you are not, no, there is: the grave](lines 64–65) makes it clear that Rilke is for her no Lazarus who can be led from his place of entombment back into life. Her position in *New Year's* is closer to that of the angel who inquires of the myrrh-bearing women approaching Christ's tomb, "Why seek ye the living among the dead?" (Luke 24:5). The temporary disruption of the fixed relationship between the realms of life and death accomplished by Orpheus's journey to the underworld is now replaced by the complete and permanent transmutation of the meaning of both life and death like the one brought about by the death and resurrection of Christ. This is not to say that Tsvetaeva finds in Christian doctrine consolation for Rilke's death or even the terms in which to describe it. Indeed, she rejects a Russian Orthodox image of the afterlife very early in the poem. Although there are moments when Rilke's visage modulates into a Christ-like image, we do not find here that direct equation of poet and savior that permeates her cycle to Blok. Most important is the fact that Rilke's death, like Christ's, is regarded not simply as a condition to be either accepted or denied, but rather as an intransigent demand for the complete reevaluation of the meaning of both life and death. At a crucial moment in *New Year's* Tsvetaeva arrives at the realization:

Если ты, такое око смерклось,
Значит жизнь не жизнь есть, смерть не смерть есть.
Значит — тмится, допойму при встрече! —
Нет ни жизни, нет ни смерти, — третье,
Новое.

[If you, such an eye has dimmed,
That means life is not life, death not death.
That means—it's darkening, I'll understand fully when we meet!—
There is neither life, nor death,—a third,
New thing.] (lines 111–15) (1:265)

Death must be acknowledged as distinct from life, yet even as the difference between them receives its full due, some means for interrelating the two separate states of being must be found. It is for the poet to establish a common ground between the two realms of existence without violating the integrity of either. Given the poet's role of negotiating between the visible world and the invisible, it comes as no surprise that it is in the process of writing *New Year's* that Tsvetaeva seeks genuine contact between the separate realms she and Rilke now inhabit.

If in Rilke's "Elegie an Marina Zwetajewa-Efron" the poet is designated as a *Zeichengeber*, a giver of signs, the role Tsvetaeva assumes in *New Year's* is rather that of a *Zeichenleser*, a reader of signs, as she seeks to comprehend what has transpired by drawing the various tokens of death into ever new configurations with those of life. The problem of finding terms adequate to comprehend, describe, and ultimately override the rift between life and death continues throughout the *poèma*, and the reader follows the struggles and the setbacks the poet suffers on this Orphic mission.

New Year's loosens the ties of the mundane to move toward the transcendent, where life and death can join hands. This takes place against an intense backdrop of rapidly alternating images of this world and the other, addressed from ever varying vantage points and focused on an entire inventory of oppositions, including here-there, near-far, below-above, ephemeral-eternal, mortal-divine, earthly-celestial, impermanent-permanent, all correlative with the ultimate opposition of life and death. Tsvetaeva's primary intent in developing these oppositions is not to emphasize the paradoxical, often oxymoronic nature of existence, but to demonstrate the dependency of the discrete elements of the antinomies on one another for their meaning.[9]

Eurydice of Tsvetaeva's lyric "Eurydice to Orpheus" may be thrown off balance by Orpheus's appearance in Hades that demands she entertain simultaneously the realm of eternal shades and that of mortal bodies. Tsvetaeva, however, is prepared to confront both. *New Year's* is a compelling demonstration of the virtuosity with which Tsvetaeva attains and reproduces the perspectives of these separate worlds. Her agility in alternating the points of vantage of heaven and earth in the *poèma* could be regarded as an unseemly display of her own vivacity in the face of Rilke's quietus, were it not undertaken as part of a vehement denial that his death terminates creative activity. The recreation of the deceased poet's newly acquired way of seeing becomes a means of bridging the two realms of existence far preferable to any attempt at literal resurrection.

In her description of lyric poetry in a letter to Pasternak of 11 February 1923, Tsvetaeva had noted that death is to be found in the "airless expanse" («безвоздушное пространство») between poems.[10] Translated into the vocabulary of the Orpheus myth, this statement suggests that the poet arrives in Hades at the completion of each poem and in preparation for the next. In the descent of Orpheus we thus discern a metaphor for the process of poetic creation, specifically in the sense that any completion constitutes the simultaneous reopening of creative potential. In this regard Tsvetaeva reads the myth in a way Walter Strauss describes as peculiar to poets of our own century who see in Orpheus's descent into hell a "renewal" of the poet.[11] For Tsvetaeva this instauration of creative potential is a direct consequence of the poet's initiation into a new perspective afforded by his sojourn in the other world. From the other world the poet brings back not Eurydice, but a new vantage point on the world to which he returns—and thus also the opening of a new poem. In confronting Rilke's death Tsvetaeva confronts the impossible problem of reconciling the metaphorical death that describes the creative act with the literal one that marks the surcease of creative activity.

In her essay "Flower Garden," we recall, Tsvetaeva singled out as particularly objectionable the remark made by Adamovich that four years had reconciled readers with Blok's death. In the passage she subsequently paraphrased in her second letter to Rilke, she had pronounced reconciliation to the death of a poet to be impossible:

> (Плохо же тогда дело обстоит с Пушкиным (†94 года назад), не лучше с Шенье (†133 года назад), совсем безнадежно с Орфеем († ?).
>
> Смерть поэта — вообще незаконна. Насильственная смерть поэта — чудовищна. Пушкин (собирательное) будет умирать столько раз, сколько его будут любить. В каждом любящем — заново. И в каждом любящем — вечно.)
>
> [(Things are bad then when we are dealing with Pushkin (†94 years ago), no better with Chénier (†133 years ago), and utterly hopeless with Orpheus († ?).

The death of a poet is always unlawful. The violent death of a poet is monstrous. Pushkin (collective) will die as many times as he will be loved. In each who loves him—anew. And in each who loves him—eternally.)] (1:247).

It is clear that Tsvetaeva herself engaged in that loving suspension of death which this passage describes. Her responses to the deaths of admired poets emerge in compelling works of poetry and prose and throughout her correspondence. Through the matrix of the many paradoxical features of the poet's death—at the same time inevitable, necessary, true, and yet also impossible, unacceptable, monstrous—Tsvetaeva pursues her mission of drawing the poet into perpetual presence.[12] This project, as she described it to Rilke, depends largely on the particular context she provides for her subject, a contextualization that removes both spatial and temporal restrictions and overcomes linear time. Demand for visible presence cedes to an acceptance of invisible signs of being.

Thus Rilke's death engendered a powerful creative energy that Tsvetaeva poured into *New Year's*, the prose piece "Your Death," and her translation "Some Letters of Rainer Maria Rilke." It reverberates also in other works, including *Поэма воздуха* [Poem of the Air, 1927], and in her private correspondence. Rilke's continued existence is made manifest not only in the "elsewhere" of these texts, but also in the creative vitality of which they were born. Indeed, Tsvetaeva felt Rilke's presence so strongly as she worked on *New Year's* that she named him co-author of the piece. Describing her work on the *poèma* in a letter of mid-January to Rilke's personal secretary Evgeniia Chernosvitova she writes:

Открытое письмо от меня — ему. . . . Письмо, которое будут читать *все*, кроме него! Впрочем, может быть, отчасти сам его пишет — подсказывает. Хотите одну правду о стихах? Всякая строчка — сотрудничество с « высшими силами », и поэт — *много*, если секретарь! — Думали ли Вы, кстати, о прекрасности этого слова: секретарь (secret)?

Роль Рильке изменилась только в том, что, пока жил, сам сотрудничал с — , а теперь — сам « высшая сила ».

— Не увидьте во всем этом *русской мистики*! Речь-то ведь о *земных* делах. И самое *небесное* из вдохновений — ничто, если не претворено в *земное* дело.

[An open letter from me—to him. . . . A letter *everyone* will read, except he! Or perhaps he is in part writing it himself—prompting me. Do you want one truth about poetry? Every line is a collaboration with "higher powers," and the poet is a *great deal* if he is a secretary! Incidentally, have you ever thought about the beauty of this word: secretary (secret)?

Rilke's role has changed only in that while he lived he himself collaborated with—whereas now he is himself a "higher power."

> Don't see all this as *Russian mysticism*! We are, after all, speaking of *earthly* things. And the most *heavenly* of inspirations is nothing if it is not transformed into an *earthly* deed.][13]

However we construe the active participation of Rilke himself in the genesis of *New Year's* that Tsvetaeva alleges, we cannot fail to recognize that it is fully in concert with Rilke's own way of thinking about his creative process. We may recall here by way of brief example Rilke's assertion that the lyrics of *Aus dem Nachlaß des Grafen C. W.* were dictated to him from the other world.[14] In speaking of the *Sonnets to Orpheus*—written in response to the death of the dancer Wera Ouckama Knoop—he persistently referred to his work as taking dictation, a characterization which, as Elizabeth Sewell observes, "removes inspiration, poetic or otherwise, from the ordinary run of human experience and ranges it among extrahuman or superhuman experiences."[15] The redefinition of the parameters of life and death that Tsvetaeva undertakes in *New Year's* is launched under the auspices of Rilke himself, now named as that higher force guiding the poet.

Tsvetaeva describes the completion of her arduous work on *New Year's* along similar lines. In a letter to Pasternak dated 9 February 1927, she writes of a tremendous creative breakthrough granted her by Rilke himself and apparently connected with her first dream of him.

> Этот сон воспринимаю, как чистый подарок от Р[ильке], равно как весь вчерашний день (7-ое — его число) давший мне *все* (около 30-ти) невозможных, неосуществимых места Письма. Все стало на свое место — сразу.
>
> [I perceive this dream as a pure gift from R(ilke), just like all of yesterday (the 7th—his number) which gave me *all* (about 30) the impossible, unrealizable places of the Letter. Everything fell into place—at once.][16]

This date, Rilke's beloved number seven, is especially significant for, as Azadovskii observes, it marks the fortieth day after Rilke's death—the day on which, according to the Russian Orthodox Church, the soul of the deceased departs from this world.[17] The completion of *New Year's* coincides with the departure of Tsvetaeva's collaborator.

That her views are not in fact the product of "Russian mysticism" is evident from the intellectual rigor that propels Tsvetaeva's undertaking. She leads her reader to recognize that analogous to the contextual influences that shape our approach to matters of universal proportions (including life and death, this world and the other around which *New Year's* centers) are those influences that hold sway in our determination of the meaning of a single word. Central to Tsvetaeva's artistic platform is the generation of an awareness that beyond the dictates of any immediate context or perspective there exist ever more ways of seeing and decoding. Such awareness of ever present, other meanings approximates that unlimited potential Tsvetaeva situates in the other world. It is precisely to the expansion of her reader's conceptual framework that so many of her artistic texts are devoted. What appear on the surface to be contradictions and incongruities derive in fact from her highly controlled use of contrasts, paradoxes, and oppositions. In her essentially Hegelian approach, oppositions are not simply synthesized but are shown instead to be products of a circumscribed perspective, which is escaped when the opposition is pressed far enough to reveal its limitations.

The integrity and success of Tsvetaeva's program result from the virtually exhaustive—often exhausting—consistency with which it is applied. The thematic material of *New Year's*—consideration of life and death, of this world and the other, from various perspectives that provide ever new insights into how they can be interrelated—is guided by the acoustic and semantic possibilities of words which are extended to their broadest to support, indeed to shape, the conception of the universe Tsvetaeva represents in this poem. We have observed already that she was not in the habit of tracing acoustic associations at the expense of the semantic attributes of the word. In *New Year's* too the acoustically determined connections she marshals toward attaining her artistic goals are inevitably accompanied by judicious deployment of semantic possibilities.

Both leading and led by language, Tsvetaeva sets out to explore and map out the topology of the other world in order to coordinate it with our own. Although both in *New Year's* and in Tsvetaeva's description of its genesis death is drawn into the larger process of existence by virtue of its effect on the yet-living, Tsvetaeva does not make the vitality of the other world entirely dependent on our own. The afterlife she describes is one of continual becoming and not a termination. Death emerges not as an isolated event but as an integral part of that larger process of existence which is analogous to the process of lyric poetry, in which each completion is also a reopening, a return to the locus of infinite potential. From this it follows—and the very existence of *New Year's* confirms the conclusion—that Rilke's death does not preclude contact, but demands instead new means for establishing it.

New Year's presents a labyrinthian exploration of the particular form such contact should take. Death itself is baffled by the intricacy and intensity of the myriad interconnections Tsvetaeva creates between herself and Rilke, between the realm of life and the domain of death. This quest shows the work of the poet to entail both brief contacts with death—the writing of individual poems—and steady progress toward it—participation in the larger poetic process. Tsvetaeva overwhelms her reader with her seemingly effortless transitions among incongruous perspectives, stylistic levels, and diction. At times her progress to the dizzying heights of Rilke's new abode suffers setbacks, but the larger sweep of *New Year's* is steady ascent—toward the transcendent qualities she had discerned already in the yet-living Rilke, which now constitute his otherworldly image, and which she recognizes to be the essence of poetry.

Новогоднее

С Новым годом — светом — краем — кровом!
Первое письмо тебе на новом
— Недоразумение, что злачном —
(Злачном — жвачном) месте зычном, месте звучном
Как Эолова пустая башня.
Первое письмо тебе с вчерашней,
На которой без тебя изноюсь,
Родины, теперь уже с одной из
Звезд . . . Закон отхода и отбоя,
По которому любимая любою
И небывшею из небывалой.
Рассказать как про твою узнала?
Не землетрясенье, не лавина.
Человек вошел — любой — (любимый —
Ты). — Прискорбнейшее из событий.
— В Новостях и в Днях. — Статью дадите?
— Где? — В горах. (Окно в еловых ветках.
Простыня.) — Не видите газет ведь?
Так статью? — Нет. — Но . . . — Прошу избавить.
Вслух: трудна. Внутрь: не христопродавец.
— В санатории. (В раю наемном).
— День? — Вчера, позавчера, не помню.
В Альказаре будете? — Не буду.
Вслух: семья. Внутрь: всё, но не Иуда.

С наступающим! (Рождался завтра!) —
Рассказать, что сделала узнав про . . . ?
Тсс . . . Оговорилась. По привычке.
Жизнь и смерть давно беру в кавычки,
Как заведомо-пустые сплёты.
Ничего не сделала, но что-то
Сделалось, без тени и без эха
Делающее!
Теперь — как ехал?
Как рвалось и не разорвалось как —
Сердце? Как на рысаках орловских,
От орлов, *сказал*, не отстающих,
Дух захватывало — или пуще?
Слаще? Ни высот тому, ни спусков,
На орлах летал заправских русских —
Кто. Связь кровная у нас с тем светом:

На Руси бывал — тот свет на этом
Зрел. Налаженная перебежка!
Жизнь и смерть произношу с усмешкой
Скрытою — своей ея коснешься!
Жизнь и смерть произношу со сноской,
Звездочкою (ночь, которой чаю:
Вместо мозгового полушарья —
Звездное!)
                    Не позабыть бы, друг мой,
Следующего: что если буквы
Русские пошли взамен немецких —
То не потому, что нынче, дескать,
Все сойдет, что мертвый (нищий) все съест —
Не сморгнет! — а потому что *тот* свет,
Наш, — тринадцати, в Новодевичьем
Поняла: не без- а все-язычен.

Вот и спрашиваю не без грусти:
Уж не спрашиваешь, как по-русски
Nest? Единственная, и все гнезда
Покрывающая рифма: звезды.

Отвлекаюсь? Но такой и вещи
Не найдется — от тебя отвлечься.
Каждый помысел, любой, Du Lieber,
Слог в тебя ведет — о чем бы ни был
Толк (пусть русского родней немецкий
Мне, всех ангельский родней!) — как места
Несть, где нет тебя, нет есть: могила.
Всё как не было и всё как было,
— Неужели обо мне ничуть не? —
Окруженье, Райнер, самочувствье?
Настоятельно, всенепременно —
Первое видение вселенной
(Подразумевается, поэта
В оной) и последнее — планеты,
Раз только тебе и данной — в целом!
Не поэта с прахом, духа с телом,
(Обособить — оскорбить обоих)
А тебя с тобой, тебя с тобою ж,
— Быть Зевесовым не значит лучшим —
Кастора — тебя с тобой — Поллуксом,
Мрамора — тебя с тобою, травкой,
Не разлуку и не встречу — ставку
Очную: и встречу и разлуку
Первую.

На собственную руку
Как глядел (на след — на ней — чернильный)
Со своей столько-то (сколько?) мильной
Бесконечной ибо безначальной
Высоты над уровнем хрустальным
Средиземного — и прочих блюдец.
Всё как не было и всё как будет
И со мною за концом предместья.
Всё как не было и всё как есть уж
— Что списавшемуся до недельки
Лишней! — и куда ж *еще* глядеть-то,
Приоблокотясь на обод ложи,
С этого — как не на тот, с того же
Как не на многострадальный этот.
В Беллевю живу. Из гнезд и веток
Городок. Переглянувшись с гидом:
Беллевю. Острог с прекрасным видом
На Париж — чертог химеры галльской —
На Париж — и на немножко дальше . . .
Приоблокотясь на алый обод
Как тебе смешны (кому) « должно-быть »,
(Мне ж) *должны* быть, с высоты без меры,
Наши Беллевю и Бельведеры!

Перебрасываюсь. Частность. Срочность.
Новый Год в дверях. За что, с кем чокнусь
Через стол? Чем? Вместо пены — ваты
Клок. Зачем? Ну, бьет — а при чем я тут?
Что мне делать в новогоднем шуме
С этой внутреннею рифмой: Райнер — умер.
Если ты, такое око смерклось,
Значит жизнь не жизнь есть, смерть не смерть есть.
Значит — тмится, допойму при встрече! —
Нет ни жизни, нет ни смерти, — третье,
Новое. И за него (соломой
Застелив седьмой — двадцать шестому
Отходящему — какое счастье
Тобой кончиться, тобой начаться!)
Через стол, необозримый оком,
Буду чокаться с тобою тихим чоком
Стекла о стекло? Нет — не кабацким ихним:
Я о *ты*, слиясь дающих рифму:
Третье.
Через стол гляжу на крест твой.
Сколько мест — загородных, и места
За городом! и кому же машет

Как не нам — куст? Мест — именно наших
И ничьих других! Весь лист! Вся хвоя!
Мест твоих со мной (твоих с тобою).
(Что с тобою бы и на массовку —
Говорить?) что — мест! а месяцов-то!
А недель! А дождевых предместий
Без людей! А утр! А всего вместе
И не начатого соловьями!

Верно плохо вижу, ибо в яме,
Верно лучше видишь, ибо свыше:
Ничего у нас с тобой не вышло.
До того, так чисто и так просто
Ничего, так по плечу и росту
Нам — что и перечислять не надо.
Ничего, кроме — не жди из ряду
Выходящего, (неправ из такта
Выходящий!) — а в какой бы, как бы
Ряд вошедшего б?
                Припев извечный:
Ничего хоть чем-нибудь на нечто
Что-нибудь — хоть издали бы — тень хоть
Тени! Ничего, что: час тот, день тот,
Дом тот — даже смертнику в колодках
Памятью дарованное: рот тот!
Или слишком разбирались в средствах?
Из всего *того* один лишь *свет* тот
Наш был, как мы сами только отсвет
Нас, — взамен всего сего — весь *тот* свет!

С незастроеннейшей из окраин —
С новым местом, Райнер, светом, Райнер!
С доказуемости мысом крайним —
С новым оком, Райнер, слухом, Райнер!

Всё тебе помехой
Было: страсть и друг.
С новым звуком, Эхо!
С новым эхом, Звук!

Сколько раз на школьном табурете:
Что за горы там? Какие реки?
Хороши ландшафты без туристов?
Не ошиблась, Райнер — рай — гористый,
Грозовой? Не притязаний вдовьих —
Не один ведь рай, над ним другой ведь
Рай? Террасами? Сужу по Татрам —
Рай не может не амфитеатром

Быть. (А занавес над кем-то спущен . . .)
Не ошиблась, Райнер, Бог — *растущий*
Баобаб? Не Золотой Людовик —
Не один ведь Бог? Над ним другой ведь
Бог?
Как пишется на новом месте?
Впрочем *есть* ты — *есть* стих: сам и есть ты —
Стих! Как пишется в хорошей жисти
Без стола для локтя, лба для кисти
(Горсти).
— Весточку, привычным шифром!
Райнер, радуешься новым рифмам?
Ибо правильно толкуя слово
Рифма — что — как не — целый ряд новых
Рифм — Смерть?
Некуда: язык изучен.
Целый ряд значений и созвучий
Новых.
— До свиданья! До знакомства!
Свидимся — не знаю, но — споемся.
С мне-самой неведомой землею —
С целым морем, Райнер, с целой мною!

Не разъехаться — черкни заране.
С новым звуконачертаньем, Райнер!

В небе лестница, по ней с Дарами . . .
С новым рукоположеньем, Райнер!

— Чтоб не залили держу ладонью. —
Поверх Роны и поверх Rarogn'a,
Поверх явной и сплошной разлуки
Райнеру — Мария — Рильке — в руки.

New Year's

Happy New Year—light—realm—shelter!
The first letter to you in a new
— A misconception that it's a fertile—
(Fertile—ruminant) a sonorous place, resonant place
Like Aeolus's empty tower.
The first letter to you from yesterday's,
In which I will pine away without you,
Birthplace, now already with one of
The stars . . . The law of departure and retreat,
According to which the beloved becomes anyone
And the extraordinary nonexistent.
Should I tell you how I learned of yours?

Not an earthquake, not an avalanche.
A person entered—anyone—(the beloved is
You).—The most sorrowful of events.
—In News and Days.—Will you give us an article?
—Where?—In the mountains. (A window of fir branches.
A bedsheet.)—After all you don't read newspapers?
So an article?—No.—But . . . —Please excuse me.
Aloud: it's difficult. Inwardly: [I'm] not a Christ-seller.
—In a sanatorium. (In a rented paradise).
—The day?—Yesterday, the day before, I don't remember.
Will you be at the Alcazar?—No, I won't.
Aloud: family. Inwardly: anything but a Judas.

Happy approaching year! (Was to be born tomorrow!)—
Should I tell you what I did having found out about . . .
Shh . . . I misspoke. Out of habit.
I've been putting life and death in quotation marks for a long time now,
As rumors well-known to be empty.
I didn't do anything, but something
Acting with no shadow and no echo
Happened!
                    Now—how did you travel?
How did your heart tear and yet not tear
To pieces? As on Orlov coursers,
Who don't fall behind eagles, *you said*,
Were you breathless—or more?
Sweeter? There are neither heights, nor descents for one
Who has flown on genuine Russian
Eagles. We have a blood tie with the other world:
You've been to Russia—that world ripened/you saw that world
In this one. An arranged desertion!
I pronounce life and death with a
Hidden smile—you will touch it with your own!
I pronounce life and death with a footnote,
An asterisk (night, of which I expect:
Instead of the cerebral hemisphere—
A stellar one!)
                    Before I forget, my friend,
The following: that if Russian
Letters replace German—
It is not because now, so to say,
Anything will do, that a dead person (a pauper) will eat anything—
Without batting an eyelash!—but because *that* world,
Ours,—at thirteen, in Novodevich'e (cemetery)
I understood: is not non- but omni-lingual.

And so I ask not without sorrow:
You no longer ask how to say *Nest*
In Russian? The only rhyme, one that covers
All nests: stars.

Am I distracted? But such a thing
Could not be found—to distract me from you.
Every thought, any, Du Lieber,
Syllable leads into you—whatever its
Sense (even if German is closer than Russian
For me the angels' is closer than all the rest!)—just as there is
No place where you are not, no, there is: the grave.
Everything as it wasn't and everything as it was,
—Didn't you—just the slightest bit about me?
Your surroundings, Rainer, your spirits?
Urgently, without fail—
The first vision of the universe
(Meaning of the poet
In it) and the last of the planet,
Given to you only once—in its entirety!
Not a poet with dust, spirit with body,
(To separate them is to insult them both)
But you with you, you with your very self,
—To be of Zeus does not mean being best—
Castor—you with you—with Pollux,
Marble—you with you—with grass,
Not a parting and not a meeting—a
Confrontation: both a first meeting and
A first parting.
                        How did you look at your own
Hand (at the trace of ink on it)
From your so-many-(how many?)-mile
Endless because beginning-less
Height above the crystal level
Of the Mediterranean—and other saucers.
Everything as it wasn't and everything as it will be
With me too beyond the suburbs.
Everything as it wasn't and everything as it already is
—What is an extra week to a
Correspondent!—and where *else* is there to look,
Leaning on the edge of the loge,
From this—but at the other, from that other
But at this much-suffering one.
I live in Bellevue. A town of nests and
Branches. Exchanging glances with the guide:
Bellevue. A prison/fortress with a splendid view

Of Paris—that palace of the Gallic chimera/gargoyle—
Of Paris—and a little farther . . .
Leaning on the scarlet edge
How funny must seem to you (for whom) there "may be,"
(But for me) there *must* be, from that immeasurable height,
Our Bellevues and Belvederes!

I'm disconcerted. Detail. Urgency.
The New Year is at the door. For what, with whom will I toast
Across the table? With what? Instead of foam—a wad
Of cotton. What for? So, it strikes—but what has that to do with me?
What am I to do in New Year's noise
With this internal rhyme: Rainer—died.
If you, such an eye has dimmed,
That means life is not life, death not death.
That means—it's darkening, I'll understand fully when we meet!—
There is neither life, nor death,—a third,
New thing. And for it (strewing straw
over the twenty-seventh for the departing
Twenty-sixth—how fortunate
To begin with you, to end with you!)
Across the table, endless to the eye,
I'll clink glasses with you in quiet clinking
Glass with glass? No—not their public-house kind:
I with *you*, flowing together giving the rhyme:
A third.
I gaze across the table at your cross.
How many places on the outskirts, and space
In the outskirts! And to whom does the bush wave
But to us? Places—specifically ours
And no one else's! All the foliage! All the firs!
Places, yours and mine (yours and yours).
(Should I say that I would even go to a mass meeting
With you?) the places are nothing! what about the months!
And weeks! And rainy suburbs
Without people! And mornings! And everything taken together
Not even begun by the nightingales!

I must see badly, for I'm in a pit,
You must see better—from on high:
Nothing worked out for us.
To such an extent, so purely and so simply
Nothing, so appropriate
To us—that there's no need even to enumerate.
Nothing, except—do not expect anything
Out-of-the-ordinary (whoever gets off beat is
Wrong!)—but into what order and how

Would you have fit?
The eternal refrain:
Nothing with at least something indicating something.
Something—at least from afar—at least the shadow
Of a shadow! It doesn't matter that it's that hour, that day
That house—and granted even to a condemned man in shackles
By memory: that mouth!
Or did we inquire too much into means?
Of all *that* only that *light*
Was ours, just as we ourselves are only the reflection
Of ourselves,—instead of all this—all *that* world!

From/Congratulations on the most undeveloped of outskirts—
Congratulations on your new place, Rainer, light, Rainer!
Congratulations on the extreme promontory of demonstrability!
Congratulations on your new eye, Rainer, hearing, Rainer!

Everything was a hindrance
To you: passion and friend.
Congratulations on new sound, Echo!
Congratulations on new echo, Sound!

How many times at the school desk:
What mountains are these? What rivers?
Are the landscapes nice without tourists?
I wasn't mistaken, Rainer—paradise is mountainous,
Thunderous? Not widow's demands—
There is, after all, not just one paradise, there is after all another
Paradise above it? Terraced? I judge by the Tatras—
Paradise cannot but be an
Amphitheater. (And the curtain is lowered before someone . . .)
I was not mistaken, Rainer, God is a *growing*
Baobab? Not a Golden Louis—
There is, after all, not just one God? There is, after all, above him, another God?
How's writing in the new place?
Actually if you *are*—there *is* verse: you are yourself
Verse! How's writing in the good life
Without a table for the elbow, forehead for the hand
(Hollow of the hand).
—A little note in the usual code!
Rainer, are you rejoicing in the new rhymes?
For correctly interpreting the word
Rhyme—what if not a whole series of new
Rhymes—is Death?
Nowhere to go: the language has been learned.
A whole series of new meanings and

Consonances.
Good-bye! 'Til our acquaintance!
Whether we'll see each other, I don't know, but we'll conspire to sing together.
Congratulations on the land unknown to me myself—
Congratulations on the whole sea, Rainer, the whole me!

Let's not miss each other—drop me a line beforehand.
Congratulations on the new sound-sketchings Rainer!

In the heavens is a ladder, along it with Gifts . . .
Congratulations on your new ordination, Rainer!

—So they don't flood I hold with my palm.—
Over the Rhône and over the Rarogne,
Over the obvious and total separation
Into Rainer—Maria—Rilke's hands.[18] (*SP* 263–67; ellipses in original)

The new beginning of Rilke's death is emphasized from the very start, where the commonplace greeting « с Новым годом » [Happy New Year]—destined to reappear in a series of variations at the conclusion of the poem—undergoes a metaphysical expansion. For all its apparent simplicity, this beginning provides the impetus for interconnections that serve as the ideational matrix of the poem and establish signposts that help to chart a course through its densely laden, intricate development.

In a discussion of *New Year's*, Joseph Brodsky observes that the opening line, which begins already on a high note, moves ever higher and thus indicates the vast space separating Rilke from the world of the living.[19] Here Tsvetaeva takes stock of and acknowledges the distance she must traverse in the poem. In analyzing the complexity of this line, Brodsky notes,

> . . . только « год » в « С Новым годом » употреблен в своем буквальном значении; все остальные слова в этой строчке нагружены — перегружены — ассоциациями и переносным смыслом.
>
> [. . . only "year" in "Happy New Year" is used in its literal meaning; all the other words in this line are loaded—overloaded—with associations and figurative meaning.][20]

Tsvetaeva uses the polysemy of key words in the poem to represent the difference between the two distinct worlds of existence but also to highlight their contiguity in language. The eduction of the various meanings of these words that come into play in the course of the poem highlights the function of context and becomes emblematic of travel between the two realms. If we look ahead to consider briefly the course of development that the words of the opening line set into motion, we arrive at a helpful outline of some of the principle themes and strategies of *New Year's*.

Beginning with the very first word of the poem, we may observe the marked frequency with which the preposition « с » [with, or down from] appears and the variety of its possible meanings Tsvetaeva deploys. With the series of greetings it introduces (lines 1, 153–56, 159–60, 185–86, 188, and 190), she underscores the all-pervasive novelty of space, place, and perspective afforded Rilke by the other world. In using « с » to designate point of origin or of vantage she highlights the vast difference in the perspective of the two different worlds she and Rilke now inhabit (cf., e.g., « Со своей столько-то (сколько?) мильной/ . . . Высоты » and « С этого — как не на тот, с того же / Как не на многострадальный этот »). Alternately the preposition « с » draws together separate attributes and entities. It reconnects the deceased poet with those qualities that Tsvetaeva refuses to surrender to death (see especially lines 74–79), signals a meeting with Rilke (line 120), and helps to project a place where she and Rilke can meet (line 128). The certainty of union with Rilke is ultimately attained when с appears as a verbal prefix in line 184 (« Свидимся—не знаю, но — споемся »).

« Свет » and « край » too are demonstratively presented as the meeting ground for divergent significations. Tsvetaeva draws out and develops the polysemic potential of these nouns with the express purpose of delineating and relating the two separate realms of existence for which « свет » and « край »—by virtue of the meanings they comprise—emerge not merely as indicators, but as models.

Tsvetaeva ascribes great significance to the confluence of the meanings "light" and "world" in the signifier « свет ». In the 1 January 1927 letter to Pasternak with which she had enclosed her posthumous letter to Rilke, she described his death expressly in terms of this duality of meaning: « Тот свет, ты только пойми: свет, освещение, вещи, *инако* освещенные, светом твоим, моим » [The other world/light, only understand: light/world, illumination, things illuminated *differently*, with light that is yours, mine].[21]

Tsvetaeva's use of the word « край » proceeds along similar lines. In the opening of *New Year's* she draws on its meaning of "land" or "realm" to designate the new world Rilke has now attained and to suggest its remove from her own. The other meaning of « край » which surfaces later in the text—"edge" or "rim"—serves to underscore both that the two separate realms are coterminous and that the domain of the poet is always peripheral to the mundane world. Like « свет », « край » functions in this poem both to distinguish and to conjoin this world and the other. Its semantic potential is augmented by the acoustic configurations into which the word is drawn. Because « край » rhymes with « рай » [paradise] and « Райнер » [Rainer] and because acoustically and semantically it resembles « окраина » [outskirts] and « крайним » [outermost, extreme], it suggests the translation of the poet's marginal situation in this world to the ultimate marginality of the other. The expression « на краю света », which means a distant or remote region and which is evoked by the acoustic and semantic texture of *New Year's*, represents the difference between Rilke's and Tsvetaeva's realms and yet also strengthens the parallel between the two poets, both of whom are removed from the mundane.

That her own tangential relation to this world is comparable to Rilke's position is projected by Tsvetaeva's use of the word « край » and underscored by « место », a substantive that indicates both the specificity of place associated with the physical world and the spacious, undelineated expanse of the other. In lines 89 and 131 « место » [place, space] becomes « предместье » [suburb] and, like « окраина » [outskirts] (line 153), expands into an analogue for Rilke's situation in the other world.

As is evident from even this cursory sketch, the deceptively simple opening line of *New Year's* harbors the seeds of the further development of the entire *poèma*. In Tsvetaeva's own formulation from the cycle *Poets*,

Поэт — издалека заводит речь.
Поэта — далеко заводит речь.

[The poet brings language from afar.
The poet is led far by language.] (*SP*, 3:67)

Tsvetaeva follows the expansive opening greeting of *New Year's* with her own account of the other world, which, as she makes clear, is at odds with the concept of the afterlife suggested by the Russian Orthodox requiem prayer with its appeal that the deceased be granted eternal rest in a fertile place (« в месте злачном »). For Tsvetaeva this image of fecundity is too reminiscent of our own world and denigrates eternal life to little more than a repetition of life on earth—a "chewing of the cud"—as she laconically summarizes in the disdainful parenthetic observation « (Злачном—жвачном) » [Fertile—ruminant]. Her own corrective, « месте зычном, месте звучном » [a sonorous place, resonant place] for all its acoustic proximity to the rejected phrase from the prayer, suggests a much more significant difference between this world and the other in the implied transformation of physical attributes into pure sound. The epithets « зычный » and « звучный » and the immediately following comparison of the other world to an empty Aeolian tower present us not with a place (« место »), but with space (also « место ») uncluttered by the detritus of earthly life and possessed of ideal acoustics. Thus very early in the poem the other world is determined to be a realm of unlimited acoustical potentiality rather than an improved version of our own world from which, as the prayer suggests, pain, sorrow, suffering, and want have been removed. The new potential for resonance augments the new light (« свет ») that the other world (« свет ») provides in which to regard things. The "placeness" of this world is counterposed to the expanse of the other, by the insistent repetitions of the word « место », which yields up alternately the meanings "place" and "space."

The empty Aeolian tower that stands in anticipation of the breath of wind which will cause its resonance suggests that this is a place not of rest but of anticipation, where something is demanded of the poet. Introduced here is that expectant silence in terms of which Tsvetaeva described creative potential and which is central to the Orphic realm of Rilke's *Sonnets to Orpheus*.[22] On the strength of this silence, the other world of her account becomes the poet's workshop and the poet a familiar in it.

It is interesting to observe that in the essay "Natal'ia Goncharova" (1929) Tsvetaeva's description of the ideal working space she perceived that artist's studio to be depends on the very imagery aligned in *New Year's* with the other world. This passage—the first two paragraphs of a section titled « Мастерская » [The Studio]—describes both paradise and the artist's work place as sites of unlimited potential in yet another assertion of the proximity of the creative act to death. Tsvetaeva writes:

> Первое: свет. Второе: пространство. После всего мрака — весь свет, всей стиснутости — весь простор. Не было бы крыши — пустыня. Так — пещера. Световая пещера, цель всех подземных рек. На взгляд — верста, на стих — конца нет . . . Конец всех Аидов и адов: свет, простор, покой. После этого света — тот.
>
> Рабочий рай, *мой* рай, и, как рай, естественно здесь не данный. В пустоте — в тишине — с утра. Рай прежде всего место пусто. Пусть — просторно, просторно — покойно. Покойно — светло. Только пустота ничего не навязывает, не вытесняет, не исключает. Чтобы все могло быть, нужно, чтобы ничего не было. Все не терпит *чего* (как могло бы — есть).

> [First: light. Second: space. After all the gloom—all the light, after all the constriction—all the expanse. If it didn't have a roof it would be a desert. As it is it's a cave. A cave of light, the goal of all subterranean rivers. To the eye—a mile, for poetry—endless . . . The end of all Hades and hells: light, space, tranquillity. After this world—the other.
>
> A paradise for work, *my* paradise, and, like paradise, naturally not given here. In emptiness, in silence—first thing in the morning. Paradise is first and foremost an empty place. Spacious, if you will—spacious—tranquil. Tranquil—bright. Only emptiness does not intrude, does not crowd anything out, does not exclude. For all to be possible it is necessary for there to be nothing. All is incompatible with *what* (like "could be" with is).] (*IP* 1:286; ellipsis in original)

Here the physical space of Goncharova's studio disappears altogether, having provided the impetus for Tsvetaeva to move through Hades to arrive at a personal paradise of unbounded possibility identical to the one in which she had situated Rilke. Her paradise is a place where she is freed not *from* work, but *to* work. Removed from it are all mundane temporal, spatial, and perceptual constraints against which the poet struggles and all the physical impediments to the writer's work. The passage is characterized by the pointed transformation of chthonian images into those visions of light and openness that also prevail in the description of Rilke's other world.

Yet in *New Year's* the space thus delineated does not become Tsvetaeva's own. Having limned Rilke's new setting, she interjects a reminder of her own distance from it. However natural it is that she write Rilke, this is no mere continuation of their earlier correspondence, but her first letter, as she underscores, written in the particular circumstances of Rilke's death. The point of reference of line 2 is its addressee: « Первое письмо тебе на новом » [The first letter to you in a new]. In line 6, the point of reference is transferred to Tsvetaeva herself: « Первое письмо тебе с вчерашней » [The first letter to you from yesterday's]. In the series of rapid juxtapositions of Rilke's situation with her own, particularly pronounced in the opening of the poem, Tsvetaeva reveals the extent of her own distress at the immensity of the abyss separating them, as she now finds herself alone in what was but yesterday also Rilke's homeland. Her recognition of him among the stars—a trope that glimmers with the constellation of Orpheus's lyre and which was prominent in their correspondence—brings with it the realization that Rilke's death effects not only his spatial remove but also a painful qualitative change in their relationship. While Tsvetaeva's upward gaze can be directed at individual stars, it is clear that the vantage point of a celestial body affords no such specificity for the perception of our own world. For Rilke the distinctive features of this earth are blurred, and a beloved becomes just anyone even as an extraordinary person is rendered as "never having existed" (« . . . Закон отхода и отбоя, / По которому любимая любою / И небывшею из небывалой ») [. . . The law of departure and retreat, / according to which the beloved becomes anyone / and the extraordinary nonexistent] (lines 9–11). It is ultimately the creation of *New Year's* that enables Tsvetaeva to bridge the gulf separating them and to distinguish herself from the undifferentiated populace of our planet. But that distance has yet to be traversed.

The imbalance of the situation that prevails between them is replicated in Tsvetaeva's description « Человек вошел — любой — (любимый — / Ты) » [A person entered—anyone—(the beloved is / you)] (lines 14–15). Here the « любимая любою » of line 10 is reversed. This reversal, together with the marked emphasis (achieved by the line division) on « любимый » [beloved] and « Ты » [You], signals a powerful reassertion of her own love for Rilke which the momentous transformations accompanying his death cannot efface. Such chiastic groupings of images and phrases serve throughout the poem to represent the crossing-over from one world to the other and to alert the reader to the effect of this transition between realms on perspective.

Given the unfathomable distance between herself and Rilke, it is doubtless of some comfort to Tsvetaeva that other denizens of earth are at even greater remove from him—or, more accurately, that she herself, having distanced herself from the surrounding world, is thus closer to Rilke. She describes how she learned of Rilke's death not only to relive the blow—to which the mourner ever returns—of receiving news of a beloved's death, but also to dissociate herself from the surrounding world.

We know that Marc Slonim was the bearer of both the news of Rilke's death and an invitation to the New Year's Eve celebration to which Tsvetaeva alludes.[23] This pairing of missions is held up as proof that he has failed to recognize the significance of Rilke's death. Tsvetaeva finds his business-as-usual air highly offensive. Her private condemnation of her interlocutor's indifference to Rilke's death is born of her own recognition of its significance. She apprises her reader (and above all Rilke) of the true feelings she harbors but does not reveal to her callous visitor.

Slonim objected to the harshness of Tsvetaeva's characterization, which, he believed, misrepresented what had actually transpired.[24] Yet it is clear that she is not interested in providing a factual account of the event. Her description of the anonymous interlocutor, designated in *New Year's* as "anyone" (« любой »), shapes not a real person, but a spokesman of the mundane, a carrier of precisely that misapprehension of death she intends to combat in the *poèma*. In referring to Rilke's death as if it were an isolated, completed event, the Slonim persona displays his inability to recognize its capacity to engage the living. He remains blind to the magnitude both of the death itself and of the changes it continues to effect. The very coincidence of the New Year and the New Death which becomes the foundation for Tsvetaeva's bridge between the two worlds is lost on "Slonim." In dissociating herself from him she simultaneously charts the course of her own response to Rilke's death. Even as she gives the differences between life and death their due, she reasserts above all the poet's mission to draw them together.

To rise above "Slonim's" antipoetical mundane world, however, is not yet to attain Rilke's. Tsvetaeva herself must still arrive at an adequate definition of both life and death. Her studied circumvention of the word "death" thus far in the poem gives way to the growing awareness of a need to confront and redefine it specifically in the context of the word "life." In line 12 she simply leaves out the offending substantive: « Рассказать как про твою узнала? » [Should I tell you how I learned of yours?]. In lines 26 and 27 she comes closer to naming it, but breaks off suddenly to explain her near articulation of the taboo word as a slip of the tongue, a force of habit: « Рассказать, что сделала узнав про . . . ? / Тсс . . . Оговорилась. По привычке » [Should I tell you what I did having found out about . . . ? / Shh . . . I misspoke. Out of habit].

Tsvetaeva first names death specifically in conjunction with life. She then repeats this pair of antinomies three times in close succession to underscore that even before Rilke died, her comprehension of life and death had differed from that of the average person and had always to be qualified: « Жизнь и смерть давно беру в кавычки » (line 28); « Жизнь и смерть произношу с усмешкой / Скрытою » (lines 42–43); and « Жизнь и смерть произношу со сноской » (line 44) [I've been putting life and death in quotation marks for a long time now; I pronounce life and death with a / Hidden smile; and I pronounce life and death with a footnote]. Having rejected the conventional pairing of life and death, Tsvetaeva now seeks to discover the true significance of this antinomy.

Tsvetaeva's entire platform for the subsequent examination of "life and death" is concentrated not in the weighty substantives, but rather in the "and"—specifically in its ability to function as either a conjunctive or a disjunctive conjunction. The entire *poèma* oscillates between the two possible relations the conjunction "and" establishes between "life" and "death"—now melding them to emphasize their interdependency, now distinguishing sharply between them in homage to their incommensurable differences.

Interpolated between the first and second references to life and death (between lines 28 and 42) is Tsvetaeva's reference to Rilke's trip to Russia, described as a rehearsal for his ultimate escape from this world: « На Руси бывал — тот свет на этом / Зрел. Налаженная перебежка! » [You've been to Russia—that world ripened/you saw that world / in this one. An arranged desertion!]. She refers here to the formative influence of Russian spirituality and culture on Rilke's artistic development. Now the profound ties Rilke felt with Russia are construed as his preparation for departure from the world. The purpose of this reference is twofold. Most immediately it recalls an important cultural intersection between herself and Rilke and suggests that by virtue of her own Russianness—which she underscored in her letters to him—she too is an initiate of that other world to which the poet is drawn. Once again Tsvetaeva implies that creative activity leads the poet ever closer to death and thus facilitates the final transition. Her line « На орлах летал заправских русских — » (38) [Who has flown on genuine Russian eagles] refers to Rilke's lyric "Nächtliche Fahrt. *Sankt Petersburg*" [Nocturnal Ride. *Saint Petersburg*] and indicates that he himself had seen his departure from this world prefigured in his Russian experiences. In the observation « Связь кровная у *нас* с тем светом » [*We* have a blood tie with the other world, my emphasis] we recognize a variation on Eurydice's insistence on the kinship of all poets with the dead which concludes the poem "Eurydice to Orpheus." The image of Russia that united Tsvetaeva with Rilke in his lifetime now serves to link him both with death and with the living poet who analyzes it.

Tsvetaeva's second qualification of "life and death"—that hidden smile with which she utters these words—is the smile of an initiate. It surfaces from the space that housed the internal commentary accompanying her conversation with Slonim. The ties to Rilke implied in the reference to Russia evolve now into a knowing intimacy of the sort we saw already in their correspondence—here captured in the image of Rilke touching her life with his death, her hidden smile with his own (« своей ея коснешься »). This metaphorical taction of ineffable smiles becomes the first of a series of ephemeral contacts that develop in the course of the poem to culminate in rhyme and the touching of the poets' hands.

The third repetition of "life and death" is followed by a breathtaking expansion of scale as the hemisphere of the cranium becomes the vault of the heavens in which the qualifying asterisk is now set as a star. A similar transposition of physiology into cosmology appears in Tsvetaeva's 2 August letter to Rilke, in which she observes: "Den Mund hab ich immer als Welt gefühlt: Himmelsgewölbe, Höhle, Schlucht, Untiefe. Ich habe den Körper immer in die Seele übersetzt (*ent*körpert) . . ." [I have always felt the mouth to be a world: vault of heaven, cave, ravine, abyss. I have always translated the body into soul (*dis*embodied) . . .].[25] Both passages reflect Tsvetaeva's capacity to distinguish the universal in the minute and her penchant for analogical thought, which guide her project in *New Year's*.

Inasmuch as Tsvetaeva referred to this poem as a "letter" to Rilke, it is highly appropriate that it develop the vocabulary, imagery, symbols, and thematic constructs of their correspondence. This provides her the obvious means for creating a private space within the open forum of this "letter" and serves at the same time as an insistence on the continuity between life and death. Yet even as this continuity is underscored in the perpetuation of the correspondence, the poetic form in which this particular "letter" is couched and the fact that German is now supplanted by Russian demonstrate Tsvetaeva's recognition of the profundity of change wrought by death. She explains in the poem that her shift to Russian must be regarded not as a liberty taken in the face of the powerlessness of the deceased, but rather as a mark of her own familiarity with the other world.

Не позабыть бы, друг мой,
Следующего: что если буквы
Русские пошли взамен немецких —
То не потому, что нынче, дескать,
Все сойдет, что мертвый (нищий) все съест —
Не сморгнет! — а потому что *тот* свет,
Наш, — тринадцати, в Новодевичьем
Поняла: не без- а все-язычен.

New Year's

> [Before I forget, my friend,
> The following: that if Russian
> Letters replace German—
> It is not because now, so to say,
> Anything will do, that a dead person (a pauper) will eat anything—
> Without batting an eyelash!—but because *that* world,
> Ours,—at thirteen, in Novodevich'e (cemetery)
> I understood: is not non- but omni-lingual.] (lines 47–54)

The most immediate subtext of this passage is to be found in the poets' correspondence. In that fateful letter of 17 May, where Rilke admitted that he was unable to read Tsvetaeva's poetry, he referred to Russian as the most poetic of all languages and spoke of "*das* Licht . . . in dem alle Sprachen *eine* Sprache sind: (und diese, Deine, die russische, ist ohnehin so nah, *alle* zu sein!)" [*that* light . . . in which all languages are *one* language: (and this one, yours, Russian, is already so close to being *all* [languages]!)].[26] On the strength of the fact that свет—the Russian equivalent for "Licht" (light)—also carries the meaning "world," Tsvetaeva applies Rilke's words to the present situation. At the same time she underscores that her own comprehension of that omnilingual other world derives not from Rilke's letter or even his death, but from a childhood experience that launched her first Orphic quest into death and thus also into poetry. The source of Tsvetaeva's thirteen-year-old comprehension is another death—that of her passionately beloved "cousin" Nadia Ilovaiskaia, who died of tuberculosis in 1905.[27]

In 1933 Tsvetaeva was to describe the impact of this event in the memoir «Дом у Старого Пимена» [The House at Old St. Pimen's] in terms that recall vividly and specifically the emotional and philosophical thrust of *New Year's*. Like so many of Tsvetaeva's memoirs, "The House at Old St. Pimen's" is largely devoted to analyzing the poet—again specifically in the context of death. We shall dicuss this essay more fully in the conclusion. Here we shall simply consider a series of brief passages that describe Tsvetaeva's reaction to her cousin's death and express emotions and ideas central also to *New Year's*.

> Первый ответ на удар было: сорваться с места. Но куда? Новодевичье кладбище далёко, да там ее и нет. . . . не обнаружив ее нигде, обнаружив, что ее нет — *везде*, я стала в тупик. Где же мне ее искать, чтобы сказать . . . Что? Да то самое. . . .
>
> У — мер — ла. Значит нигде?
>
> И вот, начинаются упорные поиски ее — везде. . . . Как же я не сообразила, что здесь слишком светло? Что здесь можно только *быть*, или *не*-быть. . . .
>
> Нади я не увидела никогда, как ни вызывала, как ни умоляла, как ни подстерегала. . . .

Нади я глазами не увидела никогда. . . .

Но знаки — были. . . . Знаки — были. Любовь всегда найдет. Все было знак.

Может, в моем повествовании не увидят главного: моей тоски. Тогда скажу, эта любовь была — тоска. Тоска смертная. Тоска по смерти — для встречи. Нестерпимое детское « сейчас »! А раз здесь нельзя — так не здесь. Раз живым нельзя — так — « Умереть, чтобы увидеть Надю », так бы я со сна ответила на вопрос: чего я всего больше хочу.

[The first response to the blow was: to go tearing off. But where? Novodevich'e cemetery is far, and besides she isn't even there. . . . not having found her anywhere, having found that she wasn't *everywhere*, I came to a dead end. Where then can I look for her to tell her . . . What? Why that very same thing. . . .

She—has—died. So she is nowhere?

And so begins my stubborn search for her—everywhere. . . . How is it that I didn't realize that it is too bright here? That here it is possible only to *be* or *not* to be.

I never did see Nadia, no matter how I summoned her up, how I pleaded, how I stood on guard for her. . . .

I never saw Nadia with my eyes. . . .

But there were signs. . . . There were signs. Love will always find them. Everything was a sign.

Perhaps the main thing in my narrative will remain unseen: my longing. Then I will say that this love was—longing. A deathly longing. A longing for death—for a meeting. The child's unbearable "now"! And since it's impossible here—then not here. Since the living cannot—then—"To die in order to see Nadia," that is how, from half sleep, I would have answered the question as to what I wanted most of all.] (*IP* 2:236–38)

It is clear that Tsvetaeva's reminiscences of her adolescent confrontation with Nadia's death come filtered through her adult experience of engaging Rilke's. It is clear too that although Tsvetaeva designates Rilke as her personal psychopomp she is careful to establish her own familiarity with the other world as having been gained independently of him. Like the series of qualifications of "life and death," the allusion to Nadia's death is a reminder that the other world is no *terra incognita* for Tsvetaeva. Indeed her very ability to describe in considerable detail that landscape in which Rilke now finds himself constitutes proof of the journeys she herself has accomplished to that realm. The possessive adjective "our"—which she appends to « тот свет » [the other world] after a line break that gives it particular emphasis—reiterates the notion of the two poets' mutual citizenship in the realm of death that we have already noted in the line « Связь кровная у нас с тем светом » [We have a blood tie with the other world].

The designation of the other world as omni-lingual is rooted in the notion of unlimited potential that Tsvetaeva suggests at the opening of *New Year's* with the image of the empty Aeolian tower. Language itself, for all its power to indicate the vast potentiality of the beyond, is recognized in this context as limiting. Predictably, this aspect of language received some attention in her correspondence with Rilke. In the letter of 6 July in which she responded to Rilke's French collection of poetry, *Vergers*, she advanced the following definition of poetry:

> Dichten ist schon übertragen, aus der Muttersprache—in eine andere, ob französisch oder deutsch wird wohl gleich sein. Keine Sprache ist Muttersprache. Dichten ist nachdichten.
>
> [To write poetry is already to translate, from the mother tongue into another—whether into French or German matters little. No language is the mother tongue. To write poetry is to translate.][28]

Implicit in this characterization is the notion that poetry is but a limited, imperfect realization of the potential from which it stems. The language in which it is ultimately couched is thus a matter of indifference.

Yet Tsvetaeva is far from denying various languages their individual characteristics. "Doch jede Sprache hat etwas nur ihr Gehörendes, was *sie* ist" [Yet every language has something that belongs exclusively to it, that is *it*], she remarks in the same letter. She concludes her discussion of the difference between French and German with the observation, "Denn deutsch ist doch der Muttersprache am nächsten. Näher als russisch, glaub ich. Noch näher" [For German is after all closest to the mother tongue. Closer than Russian, I think. Even closer].[29] This conclusion emerges from her assessment of German as a language of promise and becoming rather than fulfillment and being. (To the latter category Tsvetaeva relegates French.) She observes apropos *Vergers*: "Rainer, ich erkenne Dich in jeder Zeile, doch klingst Du kürzer, jede Zeile ein abgekürzter Rilke, etwa wie ein Konspekt. Jedes Wort. Jede Sylbe" [Rainer, I recognize you in every line, yet you sound shorter, every line an abbreviated Rilke, like a synopsis. Every word. Every syllable].[30] After his death this transition to French was recognized by Tsvetaeva as a sign of his imminent departure from this world. In her letter to Pasternak of 1 January 1927 she explains:

> Он устал от всемощности, захотел ученичества, схватился за неблагодарнейший для поэта из языков — французский («poésie») — опять смог, еще раз смог, сразу устал. Дело оказалось не в немецком, а в человеческом. Жажда французского оказалась жаждой ангельского, тусветного. Книжкой *Vergers* он проговорился на ангельском языке.
>
> [He grew tired of omnipotence, wanted apprenticeship, grasped at the most ungrateful of languages for a poet—French ("poésie")—again was able,

was able once again, grew tired immediately. The problem turned out to be not in the German, but in the human. The thirst for French turned out to be a thirst for the angelic, the otherworldly. With the book *Vergers* he gave himself away in the language of angels.][31]

In these passages Tsvetaeva highlights the reciprocal influence that prevails between the poet and the medium of his art. Here is a variation on the image of horse-rider from Rilke's *Sonnets to Orpheus* which had captured her attention during their correspondence. Even as a language carries the perceptual and expressive capabilities of the poet, so too is it guided by the poet and made to reflect his particular vision. Yet for all its potential, language itself imposes preconditions on perception and restrictions on expression. The erosion of its delimitations expands perceptual possibilities much as does the "new light" of the other world.

In that omni-lingual space the restrictions inherent both in language and in the peculiarity of the individual poet are removed. It emerges from the cited passages that the metalanguage to which Tsvetaeva refers alternately as « всеязычность » and "Muttersprache" is that of silence—a state which increasingly attracted the attention of modern poets. She regards this silence as neither threatening nor daunting. Rather, she perceives in it a call to action characterized by intense anticipation and by the demand that the poet tap its endless promise. The abstracted "mother tongue" precludes the barren void and indicates an imaginative region rich with possibility. In this context death is not voicelessness, but the ultimate transcendence of the limitations of both self and language—a return to the very source of poetry.

Here emerges also Tsvetaeva's analogy—one made more explicit in lines 61–65 of *New Year's*—between language and place. Just as the space of the other world gives way to the place of this one, so too is its omni-lingualism replaced with linguistic specificity. In any event, as Tsvetaeva observes, Rilke need no longer wonder how to say "Nest" in Russian as he had in his letter of 19 August.[32]

Whatever the personal and metaphysical implications of the omni-lingual other world, in *New Year's* this descriptive detail also carries the immediate function of justifying Tsvetaeva's incorporation of German words into the poem, where they are made to interact fully with the Russian of the text. Thus "Nest" is drawn into the acoustic chain « Nest-несть-нет есть », while "Du Lieber" is preceded by « любой » and rhymed with « ни был » and thus made to enter into a semantic and acoustic configuration with « любимая любою » (line 10) and « любой — (любимый — / Ты) » (lines 14–15).

The convergence of all earthly languages in the other world is paralleled by the convergence of all earthly signs in Rilke. « Отвлекаюсь? » [Am I distracted?] Tsvetaeva asks and immediately proceeds to explain why this is impossible:

Но такой и вещи
Не найдется — от тебя отвлечся.
Каждый помысел, любой, Du Lieber,
Слог в тебя ведет — о чем бы ни был
Толк

[But such a thing
Could not be found—to distract me from you.
Every thought, any, Du Lieber,
Syllable leads into you—whatever its
Sense] (lines 59–63)

The intensity of Tsvetaeva's preoccupation with Rilke manifests itself in her receptivity to signs of his continued existence. Every thought and every syllable, regardless of meaning, generate associations with him. Far from removing Rilke from her purview, his death has vouchsafed his omnipresence in her life.

Tsvetaeva goes on to claim particular affinity with that "language of angels" to which she referred in the passage cited earlier from her letter to Pasternak. Here we come to understand that even as Rilke's *Duino* angels mediate between the visible and the invisible, within the metaphysical landscape Tsvetaeva creates in *New Year's* the "language of angels" mediates between the unbounded potentiality of the other world and the narrow pragmatic function assigned to language in our own. Her designation distinguishes poetic language from ordinary discourse and draws attention to its capacity to mediate between the two extremes of unfathomably too much and pitifully too little meaning. The "language of angels" is that of a poet who has attained both keen sensitivity to and full mastery over his earthly tongue and who moves now toward the broader proving grounds of the other world. The dual sense of "translation" Tsvetaeva deploys in defining her art is applied in the context of *New Year's* specifically to the project of reaching Rilke.

It is significant that Tsvetaeva now claims for herself the "language of angels" (« Мне, всех ангельский родней! ») which in her letter to Pasternak she had described as Rilke's. In so doing she yet again underscores her personal familiarity with his new domicile, asserts her own poetic credentials, and prepares for the attainment of Rilke himself with which the poem culminates.

Here it is helpful to reconsider the differences in Tsvetaeva's and Rilke's cosmogonies, for these differences too affect the course of *New Year's*. In the opening of his "Elegie an Marina Zwetajewa-Efron" Rilke sets life and death within a universal scheme which is fixed and yet in flux:

O die Verluste ins All, Marina, die stürzenden Sterne!
Wir vermehren es nicht, wohin wir uns werfen, zu welchem
Sterne hinzu! Im Ganzen ist immer schon alles gezählt.
So auch, wer fällt, vermindert die heilige Zahl nicht.

[O the losses into the All, Marina, the falling stars!
We do not increase it wherever we hurl ourselves,
toward whatever star! In totality everything is always
already counted. Thus too whoever falls does not
diminish the sacred number.][33]

Cyclical change and the fluidity of relationships shape the universe of the elegy. The incessant regrouping of parts Rilke describes calls to mind the kaleidoscope metaphor Tsvetaeva evokes to define lyric poetry. We have seen already that, although their cosmogonies and the ultimate purpose they assign poetry have much in common, Rilke and Tsvetaeva differ in their positioning of the poet within the divided space of the universe. Rilke's poet stands at the center, absorbed into the eternal cycle of death and regeneration. He dissolves into and conversely contains within himself the universe in its entirety. Tsvetaeva's poet is not accorded a position of such harmony. The wholeness of vision that Rilke grants to the poet is one that Tsvetaeva admits to be possible only at the moment of transition between life and death. In *New Year's* she demands from Rilke an account of this unique transitory moment in which all antinomies coincide:

Первое видение вселенной
(Подразумевается, поэта
В оной) и последнее---планеты,
Раз только тебе и данной — в целом!

[The first vision of the universe
(Meaning of the poet
In it) and the last of the planet,
Given to you only once—in its entirety!] (lines 70–73)

Tsvetaeva's poet is a dromomaniac. The need to bridge the two worlds drives her to ceaseless peregrinations between them. Each poem represents the attainment of different points of vantage afforded by those worlds. It bears testimony to the poet's journey to the bourne of death and back.

Implicit in Tsvetaeva's construct of two separate realms of existence is an entire series of antinomies that delineate the universe. Her interrelation of the constituent parts of these antinomies reflects her larger intent in *New Year's* to unite life and death. Thus, for example, although the parallelism of the line « Не поэта с прахом, духа с телом » [Not a poet with dust, spirit with body] (line 74) suggests that poet and spirit be regarded apart from the mortal body, Tsvetaeva pointedly refuses to make such a distinction. To do so, as she explains parenthetically, is to denigrate both: « (Обособить — оскорбить обоих) » [(To separate them is to insult them both)] (line 75). Accordingly, Tsvetaeva likens the poet to the twins Castor—the mortal son of Tyndareus—and Pollux—the progeny of Zeus, who after his brother's death shared with him his own immortality. The twins, whose devotion won celestial celebration in the constellation Gemini, spend alternate days on Mount Olympus and in the world below and, taken together, provide a fitting image for the poet Tsvetaeva seeks to define. With the line « —Быть Зевесовым не значит лучшим— » [—To be of Zeus does not mean being best—] (line 77) she insists that the mortal not be undervalued in the face of the immortal. The insistent variations on the refrain « тебя с тобой » [you with you] demand that the mutual interdependency of the mythical twins be recognized and that the poet's inescapable duality be acknowledged.

The paired images of grass and marble develop further what is essentially the demand that the "and" of distinction be replaced with the "and" of conjoinment. The fragile, ephemeral existence of the poet on earth is not simply supplanted by the enduring permanence of marble—be it monument or tombstone. The poet must recognize both aspects of being. He must devote his life to shaping the enduring monument of poetry in the face of his own impermanence. Tsvetaeva concurs with Rilke in recognizing this as a definitive feature of the poet and the goal of poetry. As Segal summarizes: "On the one hand the poet seeks to capture and monumentalize the timeless. On the other hand he seeks to convey the flowing, passing moment in all of its transient beauty, relinquishing any hold on it."[34] Tsvetaeva's reference to Castor and Pollux and her pairing of the images of grass and marble recapture these Orphic demands.

In her insistence that these paired antinomies constitute the poet's union with himself, Tsvetaeva emphasizes that she is not endowing Rilke with new attributes on the strength of his death, but is rather drawing his different aspects into simultaneity. Implicit in this characterization is an attempt to capture and prolong that unique moment of death at which the divergent images come together.

The problem Tsvetaeva now faces is that her definition of the poet whose creative act depends on both realms applies to a living poet rather than to one who is dead. Rilke's death accomplishes that ultimate escape which he—like all poets—had already rehearsed in his lifetime (« налаженная перебежка ») and he is now spared from having to return to our earth. Attaining the other world provides a new light in which to see things, but only at the expense of the perspective offered by our world. As Strauss notes,

"Only he who is at home in both realms can know the relation of change to permanence and can preserve that which is really lasting."[35] The renewal of perspective and thus also of perception demands the repeated movement between realms in which Rilke is no longer engaged.

The very qualities that are brought together in the images of Castor and Pollux and of grass and marble also serve to distinguish the two separate worlds. Tsvetaeva acknowledges the distance between herself and Rilke as they gaze into one another's worlds, but shows too that they share the poetic trait of always looking beyond their immediate surroundings.

> . . . — и куда ж *еще* глядеть-то,
> Приоблокотясь на обод ложи,
> С этого — как не на тот, с того же
> Как не на многострадальный этот.
>
> [. . . and where *else* is there to look,
> Leaning on the edge of the loge,
> From this—but at the other, from that other
> But at this much-suffering one.] (lines 92–95)

She leans on the edge of her theater box, Rilke on the crimson edge of the horizon (« Приоблокотясь на обод ложи » and « Приоблокотясь на алый обод »). From Rilke's perspective the features of our world are ludicrously small, and even prominent landmarks become indistinguishable. Much as in the opening of the poem Rilke's death renders the beloved just another person (line 10), so here the Mediterranean Sea becomes simply one of the many "saucers" that dot our earth (lines 84–87). Bellevue, where Tsvetaeva lives and Belvedere, the site of Rilke's death, are also rendered indistinguishable. Their names do after all mean the same thing and it is inevitable that the difference between them be lost in that omni-lingual world Rilke now inhabits. Tsvetaeva's couching of these proper nouns in the plural emphasizes that from Rilke's new perspective these sites lose their uniqueness. In the context of the space he now inhabits such distinction of place is meaningless.

That for Rilke the geographic features of our world are a mere "*may* be" (« должно-быть »), while for Tsvetaeva they are the "*must* be" (« *должны* быть ») of inescapable necessity (lines 102–4), encapsulates the central difference between their respective realms. Yet even as this difference is underscored, the fact that it is depicted by a minimal pair indicates the power of language to draw these antithetical conditions into close proximity. Here the two realms stand but one letter apart and we are reminded that in language life and death are coterminous. The uniqueness of the poet's peculiar position vis-à-vis both life and death modulates now into images of the poet's solitude and motivates the three assertions Rilke's death leads Tsvetaeva to make. These assertions, which span past, present, and future, emerge specifically out of the poetic correlativity of life and death: « Все как не было и все как было » (line 66), « Все как не было и все как будет » (line 88), and « Все как не было и все как есть уж » (line 90) [Everything as it wasn't and everything as it was; Everything as it wasn't and everything as it will be; Everything as it wasn't and everything as it already is]. For all its newness, Rilke's death is possessed of a familiar inevitability. Its magnitude is subsumed by universal poetic law. In these lines we may recognize Tsvetaeva's stark reformulation of a central theme that permeates the *Duino Elegies* and which finds specific expression in the already cited opening lines of Rilke's "Elegie an Marina Zwetajewa-Efron," with their resignation to the poet's inability to effect a substantive transformation within the ever changing universe.

The poet's proximity to and contacts with the other world while he is yet alive figure importantly in Tsvetaeva's attempt to comprehend Rilke's death. This proximity serves in the *poèma* as a counterbalance to her repeated insistence on the newness of Rilke's recently attained state. Thus we have seen Tsvetaeva discern in his contact with Russia a preparation for the afterlife. To develop as a poet is to come closer to death. With each return from the beyond where the creative process leads, the poet finds himself more of the other world and less of this one. His repeated transitions between worlds are accomplished against the backdrop of a gradual but steady movement toward transcendence of our own world, a situation replicated in the process of Tsvetaeva's own development in *New Year's*.

Yet as the Orpheus myth predicts, it is not only the poet's own orientation toward the other world that leads him to death, but also the animosity of the mundane. The reference to Paris in this section of *New Year's* perpetuates the theme of the poet's contacts with death in his lifetime, but presents it now in terms of inimical surroundings rather than of spiritual nourishment as provided, for example, by Russia. Tsvetaeva mentions Paris when she juxtaposes her own dwelling place to Rilke's celestial home.

> Беллевю. Острог с прекрасным видом
> На Париж — чертог химеры галльской —
> На Париж — и на немножко дальше . . .
>
> [Bellevue. A prison/fortress with a splendid view
> Of Paris—that palace of the Gallic chimera/gargoyle—
> Of Paris—and a little farther . . .] (lines 98–100)

This simple description of her setting takes on deeper significance if regarded in a context broader than that of the mundane world. In his essay on this poem Joseph Brodsky notes that such treatment of concrete detail is characteristic of Tsvetaeva's poetry:

> Действительность для нее — всегда отправная точка, а не точка опоры или цель путешествия, и чем она конкретней, тем сильнее, дальше отталкивание.
>
> [Reality is for her always a point of departure rather than a point of rest or the goal of a journey, and the more concrete it is, the stronger, the further the repulsion.] (*SP* 1:[65])

Thus here too « острог » is both the fortress of Bellevue and an emblem of the poet's captivity in the quotidian, a captivity which, as the cycle *Poets* maintains, cannot contain the poet. The view of Paris serves to locate Tsvetaeva with geographic specificity on the outskirts of the imposing French capital. At the same time it intimates that by virtue of being a poet she is ever an outsider rather than a participant in the "glories" of the mundane world. This gives rise to the parallel she develops in *New Year's* between her suburb and the other world inhabited by Rilke.

The reference to Paris also carries the suggestion of mundane hostility endured by the poet and the sacrificial death in which that hostility culminates. André Chénier was executed in Paris. Tsvetaeva herself was calumnied in that metropolis. These negative associations could only be intensified by the famous opening line of Rilke's *Notebooks of Malte Laurids Brigge*, which describes Paris: "So, also hierher kommen die Leute, um zu leben, ich würde eher meinen, es stürbe sich hier" [So this is where people come to live, I would sooner have thought that what one does here is die].[36] Here is a very different "rehearsal" of the poet's death. Embedded in the image of Paris is a grim alienation born of a materialism that was antithetical to the spiritual harmony both Rilke and Tsvetaeva discerned in distant Russia. Even as the poet is drawn closer to the other world by the creative act, he is driven toward it by the malevolence of his surroundings. Bellevue affords Tsvetaeva a view of the latter aspect of the poet's death, yet she has only to look "a bit farther" to see also the transcendence of death beyond it. We encounter here once again the ellipses which in Tsvetaeva's poetic system so often signal departure from the mundane world.

Thus far in *New Year's* we have found Tsvetaeva's direct addresses to Rilke set in an elaboration of her personal attitude toward life and death. The poet's familiarity with the other world and her own intimate ties with Rilke which cannot be severed by death stand at the center of her exposition. This provides a philosophical prelude, but not yet a solution to Tsvetaeva's personal dilemma: coming to terms with Rilke's death. Upon completing her description of his view of our world she returns to the vantage point of the living, having recaptured his newly-attained perspective but not Rilke himself. Her masterful achievement of the distinct perspectives of the two separate realms of existence in which she and Rilke now find themselves has not yielded an undoing or a redefinition of Rilke's death. Indeed it has underscored the difference that prevails between their respective worlds. Nor can Tsvetaeva escape the pain that she as a human being must suffer at this loss.

The heightened urgency of the subsequent section reflects her agitation. As Brodsky summarizes,

> И естественным образом с этого места — с этого конца Вселенной и с этого взгляда, мельком брошенного на свое «настоящее» — на себя — начинается в стихотворении разговор о самом немыслимом и невозможном; начинается самая главная, сугубо личная тема — тема любви автора к адресату. Всё предшествующее есть, в сущности, гигантская экспозиция, отчасти пропорциональная той, которая и в реальной жизни предшествует признанию в сильных чувствах.
>
> [And naturally from this place—from the end of the Universe and from this glimpse, fleetingly thrown at her "present"—at herself—there begins in the poem a discussion of the most unthinkable and impossible; there begins the major, purely personal theme—the theme of the love of the author for the addressee. All that precedes it is essentially a gigantic exposition, in part proportional to the one that precedes a confession of powerful feelings in real life as well.] (*SP* 1:[65])

The acceleration and intensity so strongly felt at the opening of this section underscore the importance of the question Tsvetaeva poses:

> Что мне делать в новогоднем шуме
> С этой внутреннею рифмой: Райнер — умер.
>
> [What am I to do in New Year's noise
> With this internal rhyme: Rainer—died.] (lines 109–10)

Having surveyed both this world and the other in the light of Rilke's death, she now turns inward to consider the changes that death has wrought upon her. The internalization of the death now alienates her from her surroundings and renders them incomprehensible to her. In the new context of her own inner space, life and death must yet again be reevaluated and reformulated:

> Если ты, такое око смерклось,
> Значит жизнь не жизнь есть, смерть не смерть есть.
> Значит — тмится, допойму при встрече! —
> Нет ни жизни, нет ни смерти, — третье,
> Новое.
>
> [If you, such an eye has dimmed,
> That means life is not life, death not death.
> That means—it's darkening, I'll understand fully when we meet!—
> There is neither life, nor death,—a third,
> New thing.] (lines 111–15)

Her confrontation with Rilke's death forces Tsvetaeva to expand her previous designation of hallmarks of life and death as complementary opposites.[37] She implies that her own comprehension will be perfected only after she dies, but it is clear that her sojourn in Rilke's new realm (lines 101–4) has already expanded her understanding. Rather than simply discrediting conventional views of "life-and-death" as she had earlier in the poem, Tsvetaeva now sees in Rilke's death a denial of each of the two components of the phrase: «Значит жизнь не жизнь есть, смерть не смерть есть» [That means life is not life, death not death]. She goes beyond her earlier rejection of the either/or relationship between life and death expressed in the series of three qualifications (lines 28–29, 42–43, and 44–45) and supersedes the notion of conjoinment suggested by the Castor-and-Pollux, grass-and-marble images (lines 74–82) to postulate a new "third state."

Tsvetaeva's assertion that life and death are coterminous within each poet does not ease sufficiently the living poet's dilemma of how to embrace the death of a beloved poet and how to touch not only that death but the poet himself. No longer content with her own masterful travels between the vastly different perspectives afforded by the separate realms, Tsvetaeva now focuses on making the disparate worlds coextensive. She seeks, in effect, a prolongation of that instance of simultaneity of the two realms that she described as taking place only at the moment of dying (lines 70–72). She develops a "third state" in which the unique wholeness of vision is reconstituted from the two halves of the universe each poet respectively inhabits. The rhyme accomplished here between «при встрече» [upon meeting] and «третье» [third thing] adumbrates the meeting of Tsvetaeva and Rilke accomplished in the last line of the text.

Tsvetaeva determines to bring her own life into contact with Rilke's death. The approaching New Year suggests the metaphor for this contact. A New Year's toast across the table at which she is seated is transfigured into the touching not of glasses, but of herself and Rilke. The internal rhyming of Rainer with death that Tsvetaeva described in line 110 evolves now into a rhyme of herself with Rilke that leads her to postulate a third state which is neither life nor death and yet is also both («*Я* о *ты*, слиясь дающих рифму: / Третье») [*I* with *you*, flowing together giving the rhyme: / a third]. We shall return to examine more fully the implications of this metaphorical "rhyming." Here we must observe that Tsvetaeva's contact with Rilke, as the image of the toast suggests, is a brief one that—like life itself—presupposes parting.

Yet having arrived at this "third state," Tsvetaeva is apparently not yet prepared to grasp it fully. The perspective that affords her this vision is difficult for a living, sentient being to maintain. Her contemplation of a photograph Rilke had sent her of the Château de Muzot, where he was living at the time of the correspondence (« Через стол гляжу на крест твой », line 123), precipitates an urgent consideration of places, based on the premise articulated earlier in the poem: « как места / Несть, где нет тебя » [just as there is / No place where you are not] (lines 64–65).[38] In the space of nine lines (124–32) we find a fourfold repetition of the word « мест » [places] bolstered by the appearance of « места » and shored up further by the acoustic support of the related words « предместий » and « вместе ».

The urgency of the repetitions suggests that Rilke is at once in all and in none of the places she considers. These repetitions reveal the desperation underlying Tsvetaeva's attempt to convince herself that all the locations that had served as projected meeting places while Rilke was yet alive, like those she shared with him in the imagination, remain unaltered by his death. Here emerges the mortal, human side of the poet. Her attempt to situate Rilke in her own surroundings suggests a temporary slip on her part into the all-too-human desire for tangible presence that led Orpheus to the underworld, but that caused him also to look back at and lose his beloved. Here the metaphysical table (« стол, необозримый оком ») of the preceding section becomes suddenly once again a common object of the everyday world, even as the otherworldly Rilke is reduced to an image of his last dwelling place on earth. The immeasurable distance separating Tsvetaeva from Rilke has reasserted itself.

It is instructive here to digress briefly to consider the symbolic significance that "table" assumes in this context. In Tsvetaeva's writings the table often appears as a concrete emblem of the dedication, hard work, and *Sitzfleisch* which she persistently wedded to the images of creative flight and divine dictation that described the inspired moments of her creative process. The table, to which she pays homage in the lyric « Тише, хвала » [Softer, Praise, 26 January 1926] and the cycle *Стол* [Table, 1933–35], is the humble vehicle of translations from the beyond into signs comprehensible to our own world. If otherworldly phenomena can be couched in the lowly signs of our own world, then it follows that those humble signs can themselves become indicators of the other world. In Tsvetaeva's threefold repetition of « через стол » [across the table] in this section of *New Year's* (lines 107, 119, 123) we see this particular sign—table—waver between its earth-bound and its transcendental possibilities. The prepositional phrase first occurs in the interrogative « За что, с кем чокнусь / Через стол? » [For what, with whom will I toast / Across the table?]. The line break isolates and highlights « Через стол » and suggests that it is not only the wherefore and with whom of the proposed toast but also the table across which it can be made that is questioned. The answer to the latter query follows in line 119, which qualifies the nature of that table: « Через стол, необозримый оком » [Across a table, endless to the eye]. The modification of the toast is demanded by a further question in which a paronomastic link with стол is readily discerned: « Стекла о стекло? » [Glass with glass?]. The answer, as we have seen, is in keeping with the metaphysical qualities this particular table has taken on: « Нет — не кабацким ихним: / *Я* о *ты*, слиясь дающих рифму: / Третье » [No—not their public-house kind: / *I* with *you*, flowing together giving the rhyme: / Third]. Yet just as Tsvetaeva arrives at the notion of "rhyming" herself with Rilke, her faith in the transcendent power of poetry apparently wavers and the table returns to the literal, nonsymbolic proportions of the everyday world even as she contemplates Rilke's photograph of Muzot.

Tsvetaeva's realization of the fact that she has lost ground in her ascent toward Rilke and the all-encompassing vision she seeks leads her to confront once again the distance between them and the difference in their perspectives. Conspicuously absent from this passage is the playfulness and ironic humor of the earlier section in which she described herself and Rilke gazing at one another's worlds. Here she senses keenly the inferiority of her own position: « Верно плохо вижу, ибо в яме, / Верно лучше видишь, ибо свыше » [I must see badly, for I'm in a pit / You must see better—from on high] (lines 134–35). Missing also are the points of similarity and intersection between them that were highlighted earlier. Having received an intimation of the higher truth of the "third state," Tsvetaeva once again finds herself in the everyday world. Now she is alienated not from her immediate surroundings as before (« Что мне делать в новогоднем шуме » [What am I to do in New Year's noise]) but rather from her recently attained vision. This perspective admits only the concrete reality of the physical world according to whose laws her letters and artistic ties with Rilke amount to no*thing*: « Ничего у нас с тобой не вышло » [Nothing worked out for us].

How can the meeting that had failed to materialize under the ordinary circumstances of the sensible world take place now in the extraordinary circumstances of Rilke's death? Tsvetaeva is faced with the dilemma—signaled by the metrical awkwardness and the unwieldy enjambments of lines 140–44—of how to fit an extraordinary expectation into the narrow parameters of the ordinary world.

> Ничего, кроме — не жди из ряду
> Выходящего, (неправ из такта
> Выходящий!) — а в какой бы, как бы
> Ряд вошедшего б?
>
> [Nothing, except—do not expect anything
> Out-of-the-ordinary (whoever gets off beat is
> Wrong!)—but into what order and how
> Would you have fit?] (lines 140–44)

Earlier in the poem Tsvetaeva acknowledged her own sense of helplessness and passivity in the face of the vast and silent working of death: « Ничего не сделала, но что-то / Сделалось, без тени и без эха / Делающее! » [I didn't do anything, but something / Acting with no shadow and no echo / Happened!] (lines 30–32). Here she acknowledges the all-too-human pain Rilke's death causes her and surrenders briefly to a need for some tangible sign, however faint, of his intangible being (lines 144–45).

The specific details—the hour, day, and place—that would have to be determined for their projected meeting to materialize remain unaltered and yet seem no longer appropriate to the situation (lines 146–47). Indeed, Tsvetaeva appears to question briefly even the significance of her own writing in the context of Rilke's new state of being. In the image of a shackled person condemned to death who is yet granted his own expressive and communicative capacities (lines 147–48) we discern a miniature portrait of Tsvetaeva's poet and recognize André Chénier, who writes poetry in the impenetrable confines of the Bastille and recites verse on the way to his execution. Yet we also see all poets who are condemned to mortality in the constricting circumstances of this world and who transcend those confines by means of the creative act. Tsvetaeva's use of the mouth here, in place of the trope of voice she more commonly aligned with poetry, intensifies the connection of poetic production with physiology and thus also with death—that giving up of the ghost which in the Orpheus myth is described as the soul departing through the mouth. Her inclusion of memory in this complex configuration suggests both the poet's awareness of the unbounded other world—that very realm to which the Sibyl promises a return in her consolation of the infant. At the same time it implies the memory of the deceased poet; a memory not of preservation, but of creation that stimulates poetic activity.

Rather than give up on the possibility of a meeting with Rilke, Tsvetaeva now reformulates the nature of her contact with him. The specificity of place of this world is translated into the expansiveness and luminosity of the other:

> Или слишком разбирались в средствах?
> Из всего *того* один лишь *свет* тот
> Наш был, как мы сами только отсвет
> Нас, — взамен всего сего — весь *том* свет!
>
> [Or did we inquire too much into means?
> Of all *that* only that *light*
> Was ours, just as we ourselves are only the reflection
> Of ourselves,—instead of all this—all *that* world!] (lines 149–52)

Here the powerful connective force of polysemy manifests itself to determine the ground Tsvetaeva shares with Rilke both before and after his death. She briefly pulls apart the two meanings of « свет » only to emphasize the confluence of light and the other world in this word. The shared light in which, as poets, she and Rilke regarded their universe suggests a similarity of vision that outweighs the fact that their plans for an actual meeting never materialized. Here Tsvetaeva succeeds in making up for lost ground as she recognizes that everything in this world is superseded by the other. What is ineffable light here becomes a concrete, essential feature of the other world.

Sensing perhaps the need for a fresh start, Tsvetaeva continues *New Year's* with an elaboration of the gratulant exclamation of its opening. The subsequent development of the poem leaves no doubt that the brief period of desperation she experienced has served to test and to temper her faith in the capacity of her art to achieve union with Rilke and has strengthened her poetic and reflective muscle.

The desperate repetitions of "place" in Tsvetaeva's urgent but ineffectual attempt to locate Rilke in our world can now be understood as a brief plea for respite from the demands of her art that she herself attain the other world. As such it is similar to the reluctance expressed by Orpheus' head to leave the world of the living in the lyric "Thus Floated Head and Lyre." The « свет », « край », and « кров »of the first line of the poem now undergo an expansion that reveals the progress Tsvetaeva has made in her quest. The four lines in which these nouns reappear are a recapitulation of the major points arrived at in *New Year's* thus far and a rededication to the task she has undertaken. As such, they constitute a sort of stocktaking that helps to dispel her doubts. This assessment of what has been achieved generates the impetus for pressing on.

С незастроеннейшей из окраин —
С новым местом, Райнер, светом, Райнер!
С доказуемости мысом крайним —
С новым оком, Райнер, слухом, Райнер!

[In the most undeveloped of outskirts—
Congratulations on your new place, Rainer, light, Rainer!
Congratulations on the extreme promontory of demonstrability!
Congratulations on your new eye, Rainer, hearing, Rainer!] (153–56)

This brief passage determines the course of the subsequent exposition. The fourfold repetition of "Rainer" marks the renewed intensity of Tsvetaeva's attempt to reach Rilke and—together with the word « окраин » (lines 153–56)—acoustically prepares the way for the examination of « рай » [paradise] which is soon to follow. The replacement of « край » [edge, land] with « окраин » [outskirts] in the first of the lines cited above reasserts the parallel Tsvetaeva suggested earlier between her suburb and Rilke's other world and reaffirms the similarity she perceived in their respective conditions. The second line underscores the novelty of the place/space and world/light of Rilke's newly attained realm. Tsvetaeva, as the third of these lines suggests, situates herself at the most extreme point of the *terra firma*, which juts into the uncharted seas that separate her from Rilke's new world. From that position she no longer demands that the existence of this new world be proved to her, but rather assumes the responsibility of testifying to its reality. Her attempt to pinpoint the place of Rilke's new location gives way to more productive efforts to describe the space of that new world. She now considers more closely the new inhabitant of the domain of the empty Aeolian tower, focusing specifically on the effect of that new space on Rilke's perceptual capacities.

Tsvetaeva has not yet succeeded in getting beyond the obvious and apparently incontrovertible problem that, attendant on the achievement of the ideal realm of the other world, is the bitter irony that in it the writing of poetry is precluded. She directs the balance of her *poèma* toward dealing with this situation. In the four lines in truncated meter of the section that follows, Tsvetaeva fortifies herself for this task and sets out her first argument toward its fulfillment.

Всё тебе помехой
Было: страсть и друг.
С новым звуком, Эхо!
С новым эхом, Звук!

[Everything was a hindrance
To you: passion and friend.
Congratulations on new sound, Echo!
Congratulations on new echo, Sound!] (lines 157–60)

The first two lines refer to the jealously guarded solitude Rilke regarded as vital to his creativity. Tsvetaeva herself, as we have seen, had taken umbrage at the gentle but firm insistence on solitude with which he countered her demands on him. In her letters to Pasternak of that time she had described Rilke in a particularly bitter tone as needing no one, not even his own family.[39] Yet in the light of his death, Rilke's pursuit of solitude becomes another sign of his progress toward the other world as did his Russian journeys and his French collection *Vergers*. Rilke's death has taught Tsvetaeva herself to see things in a new light. His rejection of physical contact—amorous or amicable—implies, in Tsvetaeva's expanded vision, a rejection not of her, but of the physical world and of his own bodily presence in it. As such it presages his transformation from a physical entity into the purely acoustic phenomenon she describes in *New Year's*. Rilke is not only situated in that realm of pure sound described in the opening of *New Year's*, but becomes himself the Sound and Echo reverberating in the new space.

Having provided this characterization, Tsvetaeva goes on to explore the topography of the other world. Rilke—very likely under the influence of Verlaine—frequently relied on geographic metaphors in his descriptions of inner poetic space. This imagery, as we have seen, found its way into his letters to Tsvetaeva and she in turn adopted it in her responses. Here she arrives at last at a specific designation for the space/place she has been struggling to come to terms with in the course of *New Year's*. It is paradise—« рай » in which « Райнер » resounds and which, in turn, can be heard sounding in his name. That Rilke's visible body is to be replaced with his audible name is subsequently borne out. His name, which is conspicuously late in making its appearance in *New Year's* (not until line 154), permeates paronomastically the remaining forty lines of the poem where it is invoked directly no fewer than eleven times.[40]

Just as Tsvetaeva bans the adjective « злачное » (fertile) from her description of the other world in the opening of the poem, here she rejects the notion of a static, unchanging paradise from her chorography of Rilke's space. Into the other world she projects favored features of her own poetic landscape. The paradise she describes is a mountainous one, rumbling with Jehovian thunder. As catabasis is replaced with anabasis, Tartarus gives way to the terraced Tatras to which she likens Rilke's new setting. This comparison provides a subtle reminder of the familiarity with the Czech landscape she shared with Rilke but indicates above all that attainment of the other world does not preclude continual upward striving.

As we have seen, the fact that Tsvetaeva transforms the German Romantics' nocturnal, chthonian image of death into one of light and ascent does not weaken the association between the creative act and death. Having attained—with Rilke and Tsvetaeva—the paradise described here, it is helpful to reformulate the problems she confronts in associating writing poetry with dying in order to understand better her solution in the closing sections of the poem.

We have seen thus far in *New Year's* that the most prominent feature of the poet's entry into death is the new perspective it affords. We have already noted, for example, Tsvetaeva's playful reference to the Mediterranean and "other saucers" that Rilke contemplates from the elevation of his newly attained point of vantage. Yet she is by no means oblivious to the fact that in this immense transition something is also lost. The price exacted for this new scope of vision is specificity. Even as we witness the loss of the individual characteristics of our world, so too we see the erosion of distinctiveness as the beloved becomes "anyone" and the exceptional individual ceases to exist (lines 9–11). We may distinguish in these examples the reason for the demand that the poet ever return to our world. In *New Year's* Tsvetaeva makes it clear that she finds in the humble nests of this world a perfectly appropriate rhyme for the lofty stars of Rilke's (lines 57–58). Indeed, wedding the humble and the lofty, the specific and the universal that we have also seen in the images of Castor and Pollux and of grass and marble, is the particular provenance of poetry.

The impossibility of Rilke's return to our world is rendered all the more painful and difficult to accept in the context of Tsvetaeva's definition of a poet as someone who must engage in perpetual movement between the two realms of existence in order to connect divergent perspectives and thereby to expand and correct the false, narrow, and fragmented view of existence that prevails in the mundane. She is faced with the dilemma of finding a way to incorporate the dead poet into her definition of what a living poet accomplishes. In her attempt she neither retreats from her position that poetry is of both worlds nor shies away from demonstrating her own virtuosity in representing them. Instead, Tsvetaeva first recognizes in Rilke's death the attainment of an ideal state—one which does not simply preclude the writing of poetry, but rather obviates the need to do so. Rilke's death has vanquished the triviality of our world and has thus itself fulfilled the major end of poetry.

So regarded, Rilke's death is itself a poem. Not only does it free him from the Lilliputian concerns of our world, but it also rectifies the petty falsehoods that characterize it, as we can recognize from a juxtaposition of the rumbling mountain paradise in which Tsvetaeva situates Rilke with the world he left behind as it is characterized in the opening of the poem (lines 15–24). To the triviality of *News* and *Days*—newspapers whose names reflect the smallness of the mundane temporal framework—is juxtaposed the unprecedented eternity of the other world. However appropriate a setting the mountainous terrain mentioned in line 17 is for the last days of a poet, the vitality of the evergreens outside his window is leeched by the bedsheet—a reminder of Rilke's ailing body, bedridden condition, and that threat of impending death which only death itself can lift. The scale of the thunderous mountain paradise that is his present home serves as a corrective to what Tsvetaeva disdainfully describes as the "rented paradise" (« в раю наемном ») of the sanatorium where he spent the last days of his life and permits the accomplishment of the true rhyme, « Райнер-рай ». Here we may note parenthetically that the place where his death occurred can be of interest only to antipoets like Hamlet and nonpoets like Slonim. Tsvetaeva knows not to seek Rilke at the site of his death any more than at the site of his grave.

Thus Slonim's comments, recorded at the beginning of the poem to represent the narrowness of vision Tsvetaeva ascribed to the mundane, undergo a twofold correction: they are first discredited by the narrator's internal commentary in the opening of *New Year's* and then translated into the boundlessness of the other world in the latter part of the *poèma*. Rectification of the petty falsehoods of the mundane, such as the one accomplished here by Rilke's death, is the duty and the privilege of poetry. His death becomes the poetic gesture that has made things "as they should be."

Yet in this transformation of Rilke's inability to write poetry into a freedom from needing to do so, Tsvetaeva does not yet find an entirely adequate solution to her dilemma, particularly since it implies a termination that offers little hope of reopening—a view she is at pains to eliminate from the concept of Rilke's death. She is not content to see in his death his ultimate poem; nor is she entirely satisfied with having situated Rilke in a resonant paradise superior to our own world. This discontent urges her to press further in her exploration.

Above all, Tsvetaeva is intransigent in her refusal to let Rilke rest in peace. She describes him—indeed even the gods of the paradise he inhabits—engaged in continued growth and aspiration. That Rilke's attainment of the celestial realm is not to be regarded as a grand finale to his life is underscored by her development of the images that define his setting. The amphitheater which evolves metonymically out of the terraced Tatra Mountains modulates into the image of a theater suggested in the parenthetical remark « (А занавес над кем-то спущен . . .) » [And the curtain is lowered before someone . . .)].[41] The image of the lowered theater curtain is in turn metonymically connected with the loge from which Tsvetaeva had regarded the other world earlier in the poem (line 93).

In a letter to Tsvetaeva of 10 May 1926 Rilke described the difficulty of accepting finality: "Drängen nicht die Leute deshalb so aus dem Theater, weil sie, nach so viel angebotener Gegenwart, den Vorhang nicht ertragen? [Do not people press out of the theater so because after so much proffered presence they can not bear the curtain?].[42] In *New Year's* she transforms this image of ending into highly charged anticipation of a new beginning. In keeping with her platform she urges us to recognize the fallen curtain as one that is about to rise. The image is a dense and powerful one, to which Tsvetaeva had dedicated the 1923 poem « Занавес » [Curtain]. In his penetrating analysis of that lyric, Tomas Venclova elaborates on the profundity of this image in a passage that contributes to our understanding of its function in *New Year's*:

> *Занавес* есть субститут: для мифопоэтического воображения он в ослабленном виде отображает, обозначает *завесу в храме* (« мощная завеса нас отделяет от другого мира »), ту самую завесу, которая по евангельскому преданию разверзлась и упала в миг мировой трагедии.
>
> [The *curtain* is a substitute: for the mythopoetic imagination it refers in weakened form to the *curtain in the temple* ("a mighty curtain separates us from the other world"), that very curtain which according to the Gospels was rent and fell at the instant of the world tragedy.][43]

In *New Year's* too, Tsvetaeva's curtain denies finality to Rilke's death and situates it instead within the space of revelation and expectancy. Demanded here is a radical reevaluation of life and death.

The escalating levels of the terraced terrain of the other world and the sense of expectation that characterizes it are augmented by the image of a presiding deity who is himself continually growing and who is moreover superseded by a hierarchy of gods:

> Не ошиблась, Райнер, Бог — *растущий*
> Баобаб? Не Золотой Людовик —
> Не один ведь Бог? Над ним другой ведь
> Бог?
>
> [I was not mistaken, Rainer, God is a *growing*
> Baobab? Not a Golden Louis—
> There is, after all, not just one God? There is, after all, above him, another
> God?] (lines 170–73)

Thus even after death the poet is engaged in continual process which is analogous to poetry itself. The earlier suggestion that death obviates the need for writing poetry is now augmented by the notion that the process persists in the disembodied setting of the other world. In this context the reflexivity of the verb "to write" becomes especially significant in the questions Tsvetaeva poses to Rilke: « Как пишется на новом месте? » and « Как пишется в хорошей жисти / Без стола для локтя, лба для кисти » [How's writing in the new place; How's writing in the good life / Without a table for the elbow, forehead for the hand]. Rilke has now attained the realm of poetic origin, the aphysical realm where both table and body—vehicles of poetry—are superfluous.

The sentence Tsvetaeva interpolates between these two questions insists that Rilke is not removed from poetic process: « Впрочем *есть* ты — *есть* стих: сам и есть ты — / Стих! » [Actually if you *are*—there *is* verse: you are yourself / Verse!]. The notion that Rilke's death be regarded as a poem has modulated here into the more satisfying idea that his very existence—which death has but translated into another realm and not undone—is itself the essence of poetry. Thus Tsvetaeva's assertion in her first letter to Rilke that he is "die Dichtung selbst, oder (noch zu wenig) das, woraus die Dichtung ersteht, und das grösser ist als sie (Sie)" [poetry itself, or (still too little) that from which poetry originates, and that is greater than it (You)] is fully realized by his death.[44]

Once Rilke's continued existence and participation in poetic process are ascertained, it makes perfect sense to expect a sign from him. The request — « Весточку, привычным шифром! » [A little note in the usual code] shows clearly the extent to which Tsvetaeva's own progress in understanding his death has developed since the earlier plea, « Ничего хоть чем-нибудь на нечто / Что-нибудь — хоть издали бы — тень хоть / Тени! » [Nothing with at least something indicating something. / Something—at least from afar—at least the shadow / Of a shadow!]. (lines 144–46) The loss of faith marked by that outcry now gives way to a wise certainty that Rilke will respond.

The epithet « привычный » [usual, customary] indicates the poet's familiarity with the disembodied state. The noun « шифр » [cipher or code] that appears here in place of the expected paronomastic cousin « шрифт » [handwriting] indicates the linguistic possibility the new world opens to Rilke, but suggests too that all poetry originates in the "language of angels" that demands deciphering. The paronomastic prompting of « шифром » leads Tsvetaeva to define death as a series of new rhymes:

> Райнер, радуешься новым рифмам?
> Ибо правильно толкуя слово
> *Рифма* — что — как не — целый ряд новых
> Рифм — Смерть?
>
> [Rainer, are you rejoicing in the new rhymes?
> For correctly interpreting the word
> *Rhyme*—what if not a whole series of new
> Rhymes—is Death?] (lines 178–81)

The specificity of the internal rhyme with which Tsvetaeva struggled earlier in the poem (« Райнер-умер ») undergoes a significant transformation. If the capacity of death to expand possible connections and rhymes is recognized, the rhyme of Rilke's name with death (« Райнер-умер ») and with the afterlife (« Райнер-рай ») can be expanded into the rhyming of life and death, of herself with Rilke.

Tsvetaeva's formulation in lines 122–23 « *Я* о *ты*, слиясь дающих рифму: / Третье » [*I* with *you*, flowing together giving the rhyme: / A third] spoke of this possibility but had not yet accomplished a rhyme. The realization of the rhyme of life and death becomes possible only after she herself has grown in understanding. Rilke's death thus becomes a vital force that not only demands his continued growth, but also exacts upward striving from those who contemplate it. The theme we encountered earlier (line 54) of the relation between language and the other world is here powerfully condensed in the representation of death as an escape not simply from the conditions of the finite world and the body, but from the limitations of language itself. Tsvetaeva—a staunch champion of allusive over denotative language—represents death as an expansion of both its acoustic and semantic possibilities:

> Некуда: язык изучен.
> Целый ряд значений и созвучий
> Новых.

[Nowhere to go: the language has been learned.
A whole series of new meanings and
Consonances.] (lines 181–83)

Accordingly, she expresses certainty not in visual contact but in an expressly unmystical consonance with Rilke, conveyed by an expression that in colloquial usage suggests conspiracy: « Свидимся — не знаю, но — споемся » [Whether we'll see each other, I don't know, but we'll conspire to sing together].

The urgent repetitions of "Rainer" in the latter part of *New Year's* bring us to the climax and mark Tsvetaeva's own ascent toward Rilke. The greetings with which she now hails him continue to reflect her certainty in their meeting rather than to acknowledge the distance between them. Her exclamatory congratulations—which up to now referred only to Rilke's newly attained afterlife—expand to encompass her own world and herself as well. The preposition « с » which appears in the gratulant phrases goes on to function in its capacity to conjoin, and the bearer of the greetings is united with her addressee.

That a significant shift occurs in Tsvetaeva's perspective on Rilke is indicated by the lines:

С мне-самой неведомой землею —
С целым морем, Райнер, с целой мною!

[Congratulations on the land unknown to me myself—
Congratulations on the whole sea, Rainer, the whole me!]

If earlier in the poem (line 155) she was the peninsula jutting into the uncharted seas of Rilke's new existence, here Marina becomes the sea washing the coast of Rilke's *terra incognita*.

Tsvetaeva prompted Rilke to identify her with the sea in the initial stages of their correspondence, despite her own frequently expressed dislike of its formless horizontality, to which she preferred the solid verticality of mountains. Introducing herself, she wrote in her letter of 9 May that she would admit only the ocean (she was then in St. Gilles) as a co-reader of his letters to her.[45] This, together with the emphasis she placed on the significance of names and acoustic associations in that letter, led Rilke to refer to the "Andrang Deines Ozeans" [pressure of your ocean] in his response.[46] This association of Tsvetaeva with the sea was to persist in his letters and in the "Marina Elegy." That Tsvetaeva should encourage Rilke to link her with an image she herself resisted aligning with poetry may be understood as a characteristically hyperbolized expression of homage and self-effacing humility. Her sea washed the foothills of Rilke's momentous accomplishments and she could only beg that he grant her the privilege "jeden Augenblick meines Lebens zu Dir aufblicken—wie auf einen Berg der mich schützt" [to look up to you every moment of my life—as up to a mountain that protects me].[47] When Rilke, taken aback by the demands her self-surrender placed on him, interjected into the correspondence the cautionary remarks she interpreted as rejection, Tsvetaeva realigned the images of sea and mountains so as to connect herself with the latter and Rilke with the former. In two letters to Pasternak (25 and 29 May 1926) she demoted Rilke from the lofty status she had accorded him and compared him to a "cold" and "unfeeling" sea.[48] (Her reference to "Eurydice to Orpheus" discussed in the previous chapter occurs in the first of these letters.) Tsvetaeva's reinstatement of her earlier equation of herself with the sea in *New Year's* retracts her harsh characterization of Rilke and betokens a resurgence of the humility she had expressed earlier. Yet for all the associative and psychological implications of the alignment of herself with the sea, in *New Year's* Tsvetaeva uses it first and foremost to evoke her own given name, which she must prepare the reader to discern in the concluding line of the poem.

Up to now Tsvetaeva has characterized the other world with a specificity that testifies to her intimate knowledge of it. Her admission in line 185 that it is a "land unknown" to herself is intended not as a retreat from her earlier position, but as a direct confrontation of the fact that—whatever knowledge of death the creative process affords the poet and whatever contiguity she can establish between their respective worlds—an incontrovertible difference prevails between her and Rilke. Here that difference is particularized by the designation of the other world as « земля » [land] rather than as « свет » [light, world] as she has referred to it up to now. Because Tsvetaeva is herself a poet, she can attain the perspective afforded by the other world and can perceive her earthly surroundings in that peculiar light in which it bathes this world. The beyond remains for her the quintessential representation of that unlimited potentiality which is the source of all poetry. For the poet who has died, however, this abstract space becomes concrete terrain. Rilke can stand on the earth of the other world. Its terraced mountains and hierarchy of deities suggest the need for a continual process of achieving similar actualizations of abstractions and realizations of metaphors in endless, successive stages.

The most significant accomplishment of the couplet we are considering is the rhyming of « неведомой землею » with « с целой мною ». Given the importance rhyme assumes in *New Year's* as a poetic image, this *act* of rhyming establishes a significant point of contact between herself and Rilke's new domain and suggests once again the contiguity of their respective worlds. Here Tsvetaeva has revised the perspective she projected earlier in the poem. The vast distance separating her world from Rilke's no longer prevails. From the undifferentiated mass of "anyone" (« любые ») emerges the "beloved"

(« любимая ») who now includes herself in the series of congratulations she addresses to him.

The line « Не разъехаться — черкни заране » [Let's not miss each other—drop me a line beforehand] (line187) lowers the elevated tone of the preceding lines and suggests in a deceptively casual tone that even as she is embarking on her journey to meet Rilke, he may well be undertaking a similar project to visit her. Rilke is here afforded an independent, active role in planning their meeting. Sound and cipher fall together in the neologism « звуконачертанье » [sound-sketching] Tsvetaeva creates in elaborating on the motif of the new possibilities Rilke now has at his disposal for tracing sound and meaning.

The stage for their encounter has been set. Tsvetaeva has only to designate the mode of her conveyance to Rilke's new abode. The concentration on linking the two separate realms that has prevailed throughout the poem leads her to the image of a ladder connecting heaven and earth: « В небе лестница, по ней с дарами . . . » [In the heavens is a ladder, along it with Gifts . . .] (line 189). There is no dearth of precedent for such linkage. By way of example we can cite Plato's *Symposium*, where Diotima urges that we dissolve ties to the inhabitants of this world and its surroundings and, by a ladder of ascending abstractions, achieve the highest good in an otherworldly "contemplation of beauty absolute." The *Klimax* (Ladder of Divine Ascent) of St. John Climacus sums up the teachings of the desert fathers from renunciation of life on the first rung to faith, hope, and charity on the thirtieth and topmost rung. In the Old Testament Jacob dreams of gift-bearing angels ascending and descending a ladder that links heaven and earth. Jacob's ladder comes to be regarded as a prototype for the Virgin Mary, the means for Christ's descent from heaven to earth, and thus uniter of mortal and divine. In the Russian Orthodox Church the Virgin Mary is hailed as the ladder between heaven and earth during services on Tsvetaeva's favorite Holy Day—the Annunciation. In the Gospel according to St. John faith in Christ provides access to the vision of the ladder that joins heaven and earth: "And He saith unto him, Verily, verily, I say unto you, Hereafter ye shall see heaven open, and the angels of God ascending and descending upon the Son of Man" (1:51).

The ladder—the central image shared by these various texts—conflates the notion of communication between the earthly and the divine with the attainment of higher reaches of individual development. In *New Year's* Tsvetaeva must similarly first perfect her own understanding before she can reach Rilke. The completion of the poem marks her attainment of the uppermost rung, and it is in turn her arrival at that rung that permits the completion of the poem. *New Year's* is both the vehicle by means of which she ascends to Rilke and the gift she places in his hands. Tsvetaeva herself becomes, like the Virgin Mary and the Sibyl she compares her to, a uniter of heaven and earth.

The final gratulant exclamation that precedes the delivery of Tsvetaeva's gift is «С новым рукоположеньем, Райнер!» [Congratulations on your new ordination, Rainer!]. It would appear that she has arrived at a parallel between priest and poet based ostensibly on their roles as mediators between the earthly and the divine and that the monk of *Das Stundenbuch* [The Book of Hours] is here elevated to priesthood. Yet the actual situation is more complex. Submerged in this brief greeting is a personal subtext which removes Rilke from Christian tradition and heightens significantly the role she ascribes to him. In her second letter to Rilke (12 May 1926) Tsvetaeva wrote eloquently of his familiarity with the topography of the other world. She referred in this context to *The Book of Hours*, remarked on Rilke's highly individualistic approach to God, and then went on to say:

> Priester sind nur Störer zwischen mir und Gott (Göttern). Du, Du bist der Freund, der die Freude (ob Freude?) einer grossen Stunde zwischen Zweien (den ewigen Beiden!) *tieft* und höht, ohne den man den anderen nicht mehr fühlt und den man, wie man's schliesslich merken muss, *einzig liebt*.[49]
>
> [Priests are only intruders between me and God (Gods). You, you are the friend who *deepens* and heightens the joy (if that's what it is) of a great hour between two (the eternal both!) without preventing one from sensing the other any longer and whom one, as one must finally notice, *loves exclusively*.][50]

In *New Year's* Rilke emerges similarly not merely as a mediator, a guide who directs her upward journey, but as that lofty goal itself with which she seeks to merge—both the subject and the object of the poem.

Her new comprehension of his death frees her completely from that only place where Rilke no longer exists. She rises above the Rhône River over which looms the cliff Rarogne, on which Rilke is buried. The thunderous rumblings of the "R" of Rilke's name with which this passage reverberates herald Tsvetaeva's approach to that resonant realm («рай — гористый / Грозовой», lines 164–65) Rilke now inhabits and her transcendence of the "obvious and complete separation" of his death. The intense repetitions of his name and the density of its paronomastic presence in this passage demonstrate the space of the other world to be Rilke himself.[51]

To understand more fully what the closing line of the poem accomplishes, it is helpful to recapitulate the central conclusions at which Tsvetaeva has arrived thus far. We shall therefore remain balanced on the penultimate rung of the ascending ladder of *New Year's* in order to reconsider how it has been attained before taking the final upward step.

Certainly it is possible to recognize that the text of *New Year's* is itself a fitting metaphor for the coming together of the living poet and the one deceased. This rich and exquisite poem goes well beyond a quotidian understanding of life and death to establish an enduring link between Tsvetaeva and Rilke, as the two poets' separate worlds are comprised by the text. The participation of Rilke in the composition of *New Year's*, which Tsvetaeva noted in her letter to Evgeniia Chernosvitova of mid-January 1927 and described also in her letter to Pasternak of 9 February 1927, can only intensify the notion that *New Year's* is a specific manifestation of an Orphic journey to the other world and a paradigm for the function Tsvetaeva ascribes to all poetry of bridging the separate realms of existence.

This monumental aspect of *New Year's* is complemented by Tsvetaeva's recognition of the ephemeral. We have already seen that in the course of examining the relation between this world and the other, she draws on a series of images that suggest brief moments of taction. This series includes the touching of the poets' smiles (line 43), the brief entertainment of both worlds at the moment of the poet's death (line 73), Castor and Pollux in whom mortality and immortality alternate, the tenuous link of the ephemeral and the lasting suggested by the images of grass and marble, the New Years' toast in which the two poets themselves touch briefly, and finally the concept of rhyme.

In the course of the poem we have observed how the "internal rhyme" « Райнер-умер » evolves into the suggestion that a rhyme could perhaps be accomplished between the two poets themselves. There emerges then the rhyme of Rilke and paradise (« Райнер-рай »), a rhyme that could not materialize in the context of the false paradise of the sanatorium Tsvetaeva referred to in the beginning of the poem (line 21). Death, according to her pursuit of this train of thought, demands new connections. It opens the possibility for new consonances and rhymes and thus permits her to rhyme herself with Rilke's world.

It is important to recognize here that Tsvetaeva regarded rhyme not as a casual contingency, but as a profound and revealing union. What is perhaps the strongest lyrical manifestation of this belief appears in the poem « Есть рифмы в мире сём » [There Are Rhymes in This World, 1924]. In this lyric she presents a compelling argument for the power of fate implicit in the consonances of names—in this instance Helen and Achilles (« Елена-Ахиллес »)—whose conjoinment is both necessary and inevitable and whose sundering results in severe reprisals. Rhyme, in other words, although dependent on the common acoustic ground shared by two words, is also capable of yielding unique and powerful semantic revelation. The realization of a rhyme draws two words into a third state that transcends not only their individual existence, but even the pairing itself. A characteristically laconic formulation of this idea appears in a letter to Anna Teskova of 12 December 1927: « . . . ничто *четное* добра не дает. А рифма? Рифма есть *третье*! » [. . . nothing *even* leads to good. And rhyme? Rhyme is the *third*!].[52] In this « третье » we recognize that "third state" which Tsvetaeva postulates as a replacement for life and death in *New Year's* (lines 114–15).

A letter to Charles Vildrac written in 1930 helps to further our understanding of the esteem in which Tsvetaeva held rhyme. In this letter she responds to Vildrac's question as to why she persists in writing rhymed verse when it is no longer in vogue in French poetic circles of the day. She characterizes herself as « влюбленная в рифму более, чем кто-либо » [more than anyone in love with rhyme] and goes on to emphasize that rhyme is not an artifice, but the fulfillment of a natural, spontaneous creative and communicative urge:[53] « Почему я рифмую! Словно мы рифмуем « почему »! Спросите народ — почему он рифмует; ребенка — почему рифмует он; и обоих — что такое « рифмовать »! » [Why I rhyme! As if we rhyme "why"! Ask the people why they use rhymes; a child why it uses rhymes; and both what it is "to rhyme"].[54]

Somewhat later in the letter Tsvetaeva explains her artistic goals specifically in terms of her attitude to the relation between the acoustic and the semantic properties of words: « Я пишу, чтобы *добраться до сути*, выявить суть; вот основное, что могу сказать о своем ремесле. И тут нет места звуку вне слова, слову вне смысла; тут триединство » [I write in order to *arrive at the essence*, to reveal the essence; this is the fundamental thing I can say about my craft. And here there is no place for sound outside of the word, for the word outside of meaning; here is a triunity].[55] This passage makes it clear that for Tsvetaeva rhyme—more than any other single poetic device—heightens specifically the interaction of semantic and acoustic properties of any given word. We have already observed her marked tendency to align the former with the visible world and the latter with the invisible realm. Particularly in light of this distinction, rhyme—which accomplishes a profound interaction between those two discrete worlds of the word—provides a compelling analogue for the bringing together of life and death and of herself and Rilke that complements the role the text itself seeks to achieve.

The appropriateness of the analogy to the central thematic construct of the poem is obvious. Even as the rhyming of two words draws attention to their acoustic similarity, it simultaneously throws into sharper relief any existing semantic differences. Conversely, whatever the semantic differences between two words, they can be drawn together on the strength of shared acoustic properties. Thus rhyme emphasizes simultaneously the affinity and the disparity of the two words it conjoins, demanding and accomplishing unprecedented connections in much the same way that Tsvetaeva draws out both the congruence and the vast dissimilarity of this world and the other, of her own situation and Rilke's. It is no mere coincidence that in the letter to Vildrac in which she discusses rhyme she emphasizes her kinship with « Рильке, который не поэт, а *сама поэзия* » [Rilke, who is not a poet, but *poetry itself*].[56]

The subject of rhyme came up in Tsvetaeva's first letter to Rilke (9 May 1926). Interwoven with her expansive praises of him in that letter are manifold examples of the high esteem in which she holds names and acoustic associations—features she had accurately recognized as crucial also to Rilke's poetics. The letter culminates with her assertion that mountains and nights rhyme.[57] Here "rhyme" takes on a metaphorical function, for neither German nor Russian provides any acoustic justification for taking this assertion literally. In this particular context she uses the word "rhyme" to establish a common ground for two images she and Rilke associated with poetry and used to define poetic space. Tsvetaeva is not prepared to surrender, in either that first letter or this final one of *New Year's*, the mountain which was also Hölderlin's root image of poetry in favor of Rilke's more traditionally German Romantic night. Yet she was ready, indeed eager, to discover a similarity in the metaphysics and poetic values out of which these images emerged. Accordingly, "rhyme" is used in an abstract sense to suggest, in place of an acoustic semblance, a similarity of symbolic function the images "night" and "mountain" take on in their respective poetic systems.

In *New Year's* we see the word "rhyme" used to an analogous end, but with the marked difference that the symbolic contiguity of the rhymed words is upheld, indeed dictated, by their shared acoustic features. In the context of the exploration of Rilke's death, "rhyme" serves both as a metaphor highlighting the consonance of their artistic systems and as a metonymic representation of the contact between this world and the other that Tsvetaeva projects in the writing of this poem.

That a specific poetic device should serve as the root image of an issue of universal proportions—the nature of the interrelationship between the worlds of the living and of the dead—is a direct manifestation of the analogical relationship between Tsvetaeva's poetics and metaphysics. As is highly characteristic of her writings, the weighty symbolic significance she accords rhyme in *New Year's* is accompanied by a concrete example of the way in which one specific rhyme can—on the strength of the referential aspects of its components—successfully represent the two separate realms of existence in which Tsvetaeva and Rilke now find themselves, and at the same time—by virtue of the shared associative potential of those components—create a common ground between the separate states of being. The specific rhyme in question appears relatively early in the poem. It leads to and reenforces Tsvetaeva's conclusion, but at the time of its appearance cannot yet be fully appreciated as the carrier of meaning we subsequently recognize it to be. Having arrived at an understanding of the text in its entirety, we can now better appreciate the line of argument it unfolds.

The rhyme in question is « звезды-гнезда », which Tsvetaeva introduces in lines 55–59. This rhyme shelters the entire universe being explored in and generated by the text.

Вот и спрашиваю не без грусти:
Уж не спрашиваешь, как по-русски
Nest? Единственная, и все гнезда
Покрывающая рифма: звезды.

[And so I ask not without sorrow:
You no longer ask how to say *Nest*
in Russian? The only rhyme, one that covers
All nests: stars.]

The fact that this rhyme refers specifically to the private correspondence of the two poets adds an important personal dimension and accomplishes the intersection of the universal with the specific. In his last letter to Tsvetaeva (19 August) Rilke had expressed his desire to recall the Russian word for "nest."[58] In what proved to be her last letter to him (22 August), Tsvetaeva responded, adding that the word « гнездо » [nest] has no rhyme in the singular, but that its plural rhymes with stars—« звезды ».[59] In *New Year's* this rhyme expands to span the actual and the ideational boundaries of the poem. In lines 8 and 9 Tsvetaeva describes Rilke as being among the stars. The image of the star then reemerges from the asterisk of the footnote qualifying "life and death" (lines 44–45) and participates in the dramatic escalation we have already noted from the hemisphere of the skull to that of the starry heavens (lines 45–47). Once the "stars" are rhymed with the "nests" (lines 57–58), they disappear from the poem. The "nest," however, reappears in Tsvetaeva's representation of the two disparate perspectives offered by their respective dwelling places: « В Беллевю живу. Из гнезд и веток / Городок » [I live in Bellevue. A town of nests and / branches] (lines 96–97). There is no explicit mention of stars here, but the previously established « звезды–гнезда » rhyme and the context in which it appears draws this description of her own situation into a rhyme with Rilke's as described in lines 8–9 (« теперь уже с одной из / Звезд . . . »). The coincidence of case and number (genitive plural) in these particular instances of "nests" and "stars" makes the rhyme both perfect and inevitable—this despite the distance that intervenes between the two words in the poem. The lofty, lasting stars are fixed above the humble impermanence of the earthly nests, and the two words become emblems of the two separate realms even as the fact that they rhyme presupposes the rhyming of life and death and of herself and Rilke at which Tsvetaeva ultimately arrives.

Here we must recall also the powerful acoustic unfolding generated by the German word for гнездо, *Nest*, in lines 64–65: « — как места / Несть, где нет тебя, нет есть: могила », which blossoms in line 112: « Значит жизнь не жизнь есть, смерть не смерть есть », and leads finally to the overriding conclusion: « Нет ни жизни, нет ни смерти, — третье, / Новое » (lines 114–15) [just as there is no place where you are not, no, there is: the grave; / That means life is not life, death not death; There is neither life, nor death—a third, / New thing]. The specific rhyme of stars and nests, together with the acoustic series engendered by the German word *Nest* (a trace of that omni-lingual quality Tsvetaeva ascribes to the other world), generates a true poetical representation of the universe, one that remains rooted firmly in the specific details of our world and of her correspondence with Rilke even as it points well beyond them.

The broader context of *New Year's* and the central thematic concerns it articulates motivate the conjunction of the metaphor of text and the metonymy of rhyme in Tsvetaeva's project to bridge the "obvious and complete separation" occasioned by Rilke's death: the text of *New Year's* is her lasting monument to Rilke within which the metonymy of rhyme represents the ephemeral, a necessary complement to permanence. In her ultimate "letter" to Rilke she succeeds in demonstrating that, like Orpheus, she too "both inhabits the transient sense world and reaches toward the permanence of art." Like the Greek bard she "spans and joins the living and the dead."[60]

Tsvetaeva's contemplation of Rilke's death has deepened her understanding and has made possible her own ascent, which closes the vast distance between them represented in the opening of *New Year's*. Although her mourning remains unabated and she must shield the poem she carries aloft from her flowing tears (« Чтоб не залили держу ладонью »), she succeeds in completing her journey. The final step takes what appears already to be the crowning point of the poem even higher: the delivery of the completed poem: « Райнеру — Мария — Рильке — в руки ». The tension generated by the intense paronomastic presence of "Rainer" in the latter part of the poem is relieved by the emphatic articulation of the poet's full name, which appears—each of its parts highlighted by the separating dashes—with weighty inevitability in the decelerated conclusion of the poem. Brodsky has commented on the "prosaic" quality of this final line, which provides the name of the addressee and the directions for how this "letter" is to be delivered.[61] We recognize again that Tsvetaeva is not engaging in "Russian mysticism," but in a carefully delineated and scrupulously monitored journey of discovery.

Realized at the end of the poem is that conjoinment of hands she had eschewed with Blok and Pasternak and that had failed to materialize with the living Rilke. The ultimate rhyme is accomplished as their hands meet. The last line of the poem provides a closure not only for Tsvetaeva's "letter" *New Year's*, but for her entire correspondence with Rilke which now comes full circle. Her first letter to him (9 May 1926) had opened with Rilke's full name. The salutation was followed by Tsvetaeva's praise of that name and culminated in her equation of it with poetry itself:

> Rainer Maria Rilke!
>
> Darf ich Sie so anrufen? Sie, die verkörperte Dichtung, müssen doch wissen, dass Ihr Name allein—ein Gedicht ist. Rainer Maria, das klingt kirchlich—und kindlich—und ritterlich. Ihr Name reimt nicht mit der Zeit—kommt von früher oder von später—von je*her*. Ihr Name hat es gewollt, und Sie haben den Namen gewählt. (Unsere Namen wählen wir selbst, was kommt—das folgt).
>
> [Rainer Maria Rilke!
>
> May I call you that? You, poetry incarnate, must know, after all, that your name is itself a poem. Rainer Maria, that sounds ecclesiastical—and childlike—and chivalrous. Your name does not rhyme with time—it originates earlier or later—from time immemorial. Your name desired it, and you chose the name. (We ourselves choose our names, what comes—follows).][62]

In arriving at Rilke's full name Tsvetaeva accomplishes not simply a rhyme but a fated confluence with her beloved poet. Although she refrains from interjecting her own name outright in the poem, the concluding section which resonates with "Rainer" is filled with Marina's own paronomastic presence as well. We have already noted that in line 186 the parallel she suggests between herself and the sea evokes her given name. To this we may add the strong acoustic prompting provided by the rhyming of « Дарами » with « Райнер » (lines 189–90). « Дарами » is the least perfect of the rhymes that Tsvetaeva finds in *New Year's* for « Райнер », which has been coupled up to now with « окраин », « крайним », and « заране », yet it is also the most significant inasmuch as « дарами » is a near anagram of « Марина ». Its rhyming with « Райнер » adumbrates that ultimate acoustic confluence of Marina and Rainer Maria which the reader must subsequently discern in the final line of the *poèma*. Tsvetaeva had already drawn Rilke's attention to the acoustic proximity of their given names in her inscription in the gift copy of *Стихи к Блоку* she sent him in the early stages of their correspondence. We recall her parenthetic observation, "(Mein Name ist der verkürzte Deine,—merkst Du's nicht?) [(My name is yours shortened—haven't you noticed?)].[63]

Rilke's death can obviate physical and—for all of Tsvetaeva's protestations to the contrary—epistolary contact between them. It cannot, however, undo the acoustic confluence of their names, which transpires well beyond the parameters of "life and death." "Marina" continues to resound in "Rainer Maria" even after the collaborative effort of writing *New Year's* is completed. This resonance endures beyond the "letter" and its delivery and thus counteracts the closure of the text. Moreover, it forfends the inevitable drifting apart of any two words that have been rhymed. Here is the acoustic « взаимопроникновение » [mutual interpenetration] of which she speaks in the essay to Rilke « Твоя смерть » [Your Death]:

Как рука в руке, да, но еще больше: как река в реке.
 Проникаясь, проникаю.

[Like hand in hand, yes, but even more: like river in river.
 Becoming penetrated, I penetrate.] (*IP* 1:273)

Having followed Tsvetaeva's own Orphic journey, we, like the poet herself, arrive at a nearer understanding of the question posed earlier: what, if not the retrieval of the beloved, must the poet accomplish with the departures from and returns to this world? We have seen that the first step of the poetic act is the attempt to achieve the impossible. Thus Orpheus undertakes Eurydice's retrieval. Yet Tsvetaeva's poet is neither mystic nor thaumaturge. The prerequisite of impossibility carries the specific and concrete function of guaranteeing the irremediable frustration that fuels the creative act. The second criterion necessary for the production of poetry is that the poet ensure the failure of his quest whenever its success appears to be at hand. Demanded here is the gesture that brings about irreparable loss, and thus both prolongs and intensifies desire. Now loss may be transformed into gain as powerful frustrated needs overflow the narrow banks of the concrete world. The unbearable tension generated by peregrinations between irreconcilable antipodes forces the poet to break the oppositions that tyrannize the ready-made world. Orpheus's dismemberment may be regarded as a ritualistic representation of this stage. The poet leaves this world to enter not death, where desire must cease, but rather the alternative "third state" of song. The tensions that have created disjunction must now be productively assimilated into a reconstitution of what has been torn asunder. The privileged space in which this can take place is language. In it the sensuous incarnation of desire—impossible in the other world and prohibited to the poet in this world—can be accomplished, accomplished, moreover, in a way that would prolong desire rather than satisfy it. Language neither replaces nor reconstitutes what has been lost. The poet sees in it the space where impossible unions can be actualized with an otherwise unattainable profundity and endurance.

« « Живой » никогда не даст себя так любить, как « мертвый » » [A "living person" will never allow himself to be loved like a "dead one"] (*IP* 1:115) Tsvetaeva had written in her "Excerpts from the Book *Earthly Signs*" (1919). At the time of its writing, this statement suggested a desire for control. *New Year's*, however, demonstrates that she now recognizes in death not simply a license to manipulate the beloved or love itself, but the imperative to enter that poetic space in which the living and the dead can unite and in which love and death can endure in simultaneity.

Rilke's death is an extreme test case of the hypothesis Tsvetaeva advanced in the material studied in the preceding chapters: that the impossible can be actualized in language. The test case is won when she succeeds in achieving her impossible union with Rilke not only in language, but also specifically in the worlds of the word itself.

Tsvetaeva's conduct in *New Year's* reaffirms her own description of the poet in the first lyric of her *Poets* cycle as someone « Кто Канта наголову бьет » (Who stands Kant on his head), for this poem falls in readily with post-Kantian philosophical searchings. Tsvetaeva's final "letter" to Rilke is a highly instructive example of Hegelian *Aufhebung*—a concept that emerged from and remained central to the metaphysical strivings of the Romantics. The poem's central opposition of life and death—together with the entire constellation of oppositions grouped around it—is "at the same time annulled, preserved, and raised to a higher level," to apply M. H. Abrams's trenchant definition.[64] That this quintessentially Romantic vehicle for understanding should remain crucial to Tsvetaeva's artistic probings can come as no surprise in the face of her own readily acknowledged biographical, spiritual, and artistic ties to that movement. Her remarkable originality and forcefulness emerge in her recognition that this can take place even within an individual word. She extends this philosophical construct to the very materiality of her art and finds consistent, concrete application for this dialectic throughout the hierarchy of poetic units, each of which is made to reflect consummately the larger scheme of the universe she projects. Tsvetaeva's Orphic quest is achieved as death is transformed into an epiphenomenon of the creative process.

Conclusion

Но бывает —
жизнь
встает в другом разрезе,
и большое
понимаешь
через ерунру.

[But it happens—
life
appears in another perspective
and you understand
big things
through trivialities.]

—Vladimir Maiakovskii

Ибо что же все художество, как не нахождение потерянных вещей, не увековеченье — утрат?

[For what then is all art if not the finding of lost things, not the perpetuation—of losses.]

—Marina Tsvetaeva, "House at Old St. Pimen's"

TSVETAEVA'S ORGANIZATION of experience places the conditions of reality into a mythic framework in which cosmogony and mythopoeia coincide. Myth, the "untrue story imaging truth,"[1] points the way to the uncovering of profound meaning that underlies mere surface appearances. By aligning signs of mundane reality with preexisting myths Tsvetaeva could show that these signs point beyond the present world rather than confirm it. Imbedded in myth, the apparently trivial details of our surroundings become signs of future destiny rooted in an originary past. Linear temporality is replaced with synchrony on the strength of which the ephemeral is drawn into the ever present.

In « Живое о живом » [The Living about the Living], Tsvetaeva presents the following definition: « Мифотворчество: то, что быть могло и быть должно, обратно чеховщине: тому, что есть, а чего, по мне, вовсе и нет » [Mythopoeia: that which could have been and should be, the reverse of Chekhovitis: that which is, but which in my opinion does not exist at all] (*IP* 2:66). she assigns not only a higher value, but a higher reality to myth-making. Her epigraph to *After Russia*—a slightly misquoted passage from the eighteenth-century poet and theoretician Vasilii Trediakovskii—defines the role of the poet along similar lines:

> От сего, что поэт есть творитель не наследует, что он лживец: ложь есть слово против разума и совести, но поэтическое вымышление бывает по разуму так, как вещь *могла* и *долженствовала* быть.
>
> [From the fact that the poet is a creator it does not follow that he is a liar: a falsehood is a word that goes counter to reason and conscience, but poetic invention is in accordance with reason—the way that something *could* and *ought to* have been.][2] (*SP* 3:9)

In "Les Nuits florentines" (1933) she articulates this attitude with greater specificity: « Великий мастер может создать нечто идеальное, ибо он создает то, что долженствует быть, реальность в потенции. Высокую реальность » [A great master can create something in its ideal form, for he is creating that which ought to be: reality in potential. Lofty reality].[3] This essentially neo-Platonic justification for the deviation of art from reality recurs throughout Tsvetaeva's writings. We have seen that the potentialities to which she refers here become accessible through a radical alteration in the way the world is perceived. This essentially Romantic undertaking of transforming not the world itself but our perception of it is advanced by Tsvetaeva's structuring of her surroundings according to mythic patterns. Such structuring informs all of her mature writings and receives explicit attention in her prose essays—a genre to which she turned with increasing frequency in the thirties.

Although external pressures—including the need for income and the diminishing number of readers capable of following her increasingly difficult verse—certainly contributed to Tsvetaeva's inclination toward prose, it is clear too that more profound personal artistic needs were simultaneously at work. Her prose is dedicated above all to explicating her verbal art, to demonstrating the creative process, and to defining the poet as she confronts the question that looms ever larger in our century as to what need there can be for poetry in the modern age. The essays do more than describe poetic activity; they guide the reader through the poet's thought process and into that peculiarly poetic attitude to the surrounding world which is determined by language and shaped by a mythic apprehension of the universe. Here Tsvetaeva is often frankly didactic—her use of language is more demonstrative and instructive, the connective tissue of logic is more overt, and the mythopoeia more explicit.

In her essays Tsvetaeva also examines, analyzes, and takes stock of her own poetic development. She presents her poetic credentials in accounts of her own becoming and in the homage she pays to the achievements of fellow poets in essays written as epitaphs commemorating not their deaths, but their creative vitality. Life itself becomes a poetic text, not in the exuberant Pasternakian mode which transforms natural phenomena into creators of verse, but in the more intellectually controlled recognition of commonplace signs as indicators of meaning well beyond the bounds of habitual norms. If, as is customary, we accept Tsvetaeva's poems as a lyrical diary of her life, we may regard her essays as a record of the process of becoming a poet and a reaffirmation of her poetic destiny. In these essays she reassesses images and details retrieved from her childhood and youth from the vantage point of a mature poet to whom their genuine meaning reveals itself. Her own poetic prowess is demonstrated in the process of comprehending that meaning. What appear to be relatively unimportant details of her biography and family situation are recognized now to be signs of momentous import, of destiny itself.

The guises in which the poet appears in the essays are so many and various as to warrant a separate study. Here we note only that the myth of Orpheus continues to shape Tsvetaeva's characterization of poets in general and informs particularly the accounts of her own artistic identity. An exhaustive account of the rich and allusive permutations of this pivotal myth in Tsvetaeva's prose would take considerably more space than remains. This brief conclusion focuses on only a few examples that are particularly well suited for recapitulating and complementing the essential features of the poet considered thus far. This will lead us to the closing: two final appearances of Orpheus from among Tsvetaeva's later lyrics, the poems «Разговор с гением» [Conversation with a Genius, 1928] and «Есть счастливцы и счастливицы» [There Are Fortunate Men and Women, 1935].

In her essays Tsvetaeva persistently cites the imperative to counteract death as the impetus for the creative process. The memoir «Дом у Старого Пимена» [The House at Old St. Pimen's] provides a particularly intense and detailed representation of the struggle with death undertaken by the poet. Tsvetaeva began the essay in 1928, prompted by her newly begun correspondence with Vera Bunina (neé Muromtseva) with whom, as Karlinsky describes, she "shared reminiscences [that] brought into existence several of Tsvetaeva's memoirs of the 1930's."[4] The death of her half-brother Andrei in 1933 urged the essay to its completion.

At the center of this memoir is the death of the beautiful Nadia Ilovaiskaia. As Tsvetaeva's reference to Nadia's death in *New Year's* has already suggested, it was this particular death that first awakened in the young Marina an overwhelming longing for the other world. She describes her attachment to Nadia and the effect of her death in a letter to Bunina of 23 May 1928. The passage provides a revealing background for the essay:

> Вы мне пишете о Наде Иловайской, любовью к которой — нет, просто КОТОРОЙ — я болела — дайте вспомнить! — год, полтора. Это было мое наваждение. Началось это с ее смерти — я тогда была в Германии, в закрытом учебном заведении, мне было 10 лет. « Умерла Надя Иловайская » (письмо отца). . . . Но дружны мы не были — не из за разницы возраста — это вздор! — а из за моей робости перед ее красотой, с которой я тогда в стихах не могла справиться (пишу с 6-ти лет, в Нерви мне было 8 л[ет]) — проще: дружны мы не были, потому что я ее любила. И вот — неполных 2 года спустя — смерть. Тут я дала себе волю — полную — два года напролет пролюьила, *про-видела* во сне — и сны помню! — и как тогда не умерла (не сорвалась в след) — не знаю.
>
> . . . Эту любовь я протаила в себе до — да до нынешнего часа! и пронесла ее сквозь весь 1905 г. Она затмила мне смерть матери (июль 1906 г. — от того же).
>
> « Надя Иловайская » для меня — вся в 10 лет: БЕЗДНА. С тех пор я — что? научилась писать и разучилась любить. (И первое не совсем, и второе не совсем, — даст Бог на том свете — первому разучусь совсем, второму научусь зȧново!)
>
> [You write me about Nadia Ilovaiskaia, with love for whom, no, simply FOR WHOM I suffered—let me think!—a year, a year and a half. That was my obsession. It began with her death—I was then in Germany in a boarding school, I was ten years old. "Nadia Ilovaiskaia died" (a letter from my father). . . . But we had never been friends—not because of the difference in our ages—that's nonsense!—but because of my timidity before her beauty, which I could not then deal with in my poetry (I have been writing since the age of six, in Nervi I was eight)—more simply: we were not friends because I loved her. And then—less than two years later—death. Here I gave myself complete freedom—I loved her a full two years and *fore-saw* her in my dreams—and I remember those dreams!—and how I did not die then (didn't take off after her) I do not know. . . . I harbored this love within myself until—why until now! and carried it through all of 1905. It obscured my mother's death for me (July 1906—from the same cause).
>
> "Nadia Ilovaiskaia" was for me at ten: an entire ABYSS. What have I done since then? I learned to write and unlearned how to love. (The first not entirely and the second not entirely—God grant that in the other world I will unlearn the first completely and will learn the second anew!)][5]

In these excerpts from Tsvetaeva's letter to Bunina we recognize that interrelation of love, death, and longing for the other world that in the

Orpheus myth culminates in poetry, but which is here construed along somewhat different lines. The futile attempts to convey in verse Nadia's beauty and her own love for her are replaced by the freedom to love unrestrainedly that the child Marina gains from Nadia's death. The liberating quality of death and the irresistible pull of the other world she now experiences constitute a vital step in the transformation of the infatuated young scribbler of verse into the full-fledged poet.

The confrontation of Nadia's death becomes a rite of passage into the realm of poetry that leads the child to recognize the inadequacy of construing existence in terms of being or not being: «Как же я не сообразила, что . . . здесь можно только *быть* или *не*-быть» [How is it that I didn't understand that . . . here one can only *be* or *not* be] (*IP* 2:237). It is this insight that provides intimations of an elsewhere and prompts Tsvetaeva to seek beyond Hamlet's inadequate ontology to arrive at the "third state" so compellingly represented in *New Year's*. The "resurrection" of her cousin accomplished on the pages of "The House at Old St. Pimen's" emerges as the fulfillment of her own inescapable poetic destiny:

> Может быть, милая Надя, ты, оттуда сразу увидев все будущее, за мной, маленькой девочкой, ходя — ходила за *своим поэтом*, тем, кто воскрешает тебя ныне, без малого тридцать лет спустя?
>
> [Perhaps, dear Nadia, you, having at once seen the entire future from there, in following me, a little girl—followed *your poet*, the one who is now resurrecting you some thirty years later?] (*IP* 2:240).

Tsvetaeva's own poetic becoming within the framework of Nadia's death is imbedded in the mature poet's attempt to counteract the terrifying, deadly fate that hangs over the entire Ilovaiskii family.

In the ill-starred house at St. Pimen's, time and space act as correlative powers of destruction. In this moribund setting the historian Dmitrii Ilovaiskii reigns over time, whose flow he reverses. To his miserly spouse (his second wife, Aleksandra Aleksandrovna) is relegated the governing of space which she steadily constricts. In place of the poet's vigorous rejection of temporal and spatial restrictions, we find here their inexorable imposition and thus the undoing of life itself. In "The House at Old St. Pimen's" Tsvetaeva confronts an antipoet far grimmer than Hamlet—one who engages in activity directly retrograde to her own. In the context of Ilovaiskii's death-dealing existence, the poet's capacity to return the members of the household to life and the means she employs to that end emerge all the more forcefully. Their retrieval is predicated largely on the generative spatialization of mental processes and the unfolding of temporal metaphors we have come to associate with Andrei Belyi—that consummate student of Gogol', Dostoevskii, and Rudolf Steiner. Onto a spatio-temporal matrix Tsvetaeva superimposes what appears to be a Nietzsche-inspired concept of history. The mythopoeic projections of the poet regenerate precisely those life-giving connections that historicity severs.

In the Ilovaiskii house Tsvetaeva discerns a model of the universe: in the oppressive lower floor with its vaulted ceilings the children are forced to support the upper reaches of the Olympian parents presiding over them. In her account Tsvetaeva establishes an analogical relationship between the powers of destruction determining the destiny of this family and the forces at work in Russia during this time. Implicit in a central passage of the essay is the identification of the inflexible patriarch Ilovaiskii and his devoted spouse, who translates his "ideas" into "methods," with the autocrat of Russia and his regal consort (*IP* 2:226). It emerges that the poet's intensely personal, idiosyncratic psychological probing illuminates a broad spectrum of human experience with the recognition of the organic relationship of parts to whole.

Very early in the essay the reader is made to understand that the reversal of the spatial disposition of the Ilovaiskii house—the only one, as Tsvetaeva notes, she has ever seen in Russia in which the parents' quarters are above stairs and the children's below—is correlative with the horrific reversal of the natural temporal process, codified here in terms of death prevailing over life, age over youth, Ilovaiskii over his children. All that is young and vivacious in the Ilovaiskii home dies while the old patriarch persists in unseemly longevity:

> Это был смертный дом. Все в этом доме кончалось, кроме смерти. Кроме старости. Все: красота, молодость, прелесть, жизнь. Все в этом доме кончалось, кроме Иловайского.
>
> [This was a house of death. Everything in that house was in the process of ending, except death. Except old age. Everything: beauty, youth, charm, life. Everything in that house was in the process of ending, except Ilovaiskii.] (*IP* 2:220)

Her search for an appropriate designation for Ilovaiskii leads Tsvetaeva to try out Charon, Chronos, Zeus, and to conclude finally «Не Зевес, а Гадес» [Not Zeus, but Hades]. This well-motivated association engenders an expanding network of associations, and their centripetal impetus in itself serves as a powerful antidote to the constriction of life in which Ilovaiskii and his spouse engage. To trace even briefly some of the branchings of this network is to experience the vivacity of poetic thinking which interrelates fragments of existence in an approximation of the organic world.

An attribute of Hades is the staff which, as Tsvetaeva notes, is also wielded by St. Pimen, whose nearby church gives the house its name. Out of this metonymic linkage of Hades and St. Pimen develops the connection between the patriarch of the house and the chronicler monk Pimen of Pushkin's drama *Boris Godunov*. Tsvetaeva reenforces this connection with a myriad of details, including those vaulted ceilings which had prompted her to compare the children's quarters with Hades and a funeral vault. The central connection is the fact that Ilovaiskii is, like the monk Pimen, a historian. This alignment with the chronicler monk highlights his total absorption in the past and complete oblivion to the present. (It emerges in the course of the essay that Ilovaiskii has never heard of Lenin and Trotskii [*IP* 2:243].) At the same time—in the context of the analogy between the fate of the house and the destiny of the nation—this association intimates that Ilovaiskii's historical records, like those of Pushkin's monk, entail a condemnation of the usurpers of power ruling Russia at the time.

Yet, like Pimen, Ilovaiskii is himself not aware of this. His alienation from his own time and surroundings is stressed repeatedly and projected both in the physical properties of his house and in his bearing toward his family connections. Tsvetaeva's recollections of a visit yield a concrete image of his isolation not only from the world around him, but from life itself:

> Единственное, что у меня осталось от единственного моего посещения дома Иловайских — это стопы «Кремля» в глубоких нишах окон, стопы, доходившие до оконного креста и не аллегорически, а физически застилавшие жителям и посетителям Божий свет и мир. Комнату эту, полуподвальную, с годуновскими сводами, прошу запомнить.
>
> [The only thing I have retained from my only visit to the Ilovaiskii home are the stacks of [the journal] *The Kremlin* in the deep niches of the windows, stacks reaching the window casements and not allegorically, but physically blocking out God's light and world from its inhabitants and visitors. I ask that you remember this semi-basement room with its Godunovian vaults.) (*IP* 2:220)

For the ruler of Hades it is the shades of the past that constitute reality. The flesh-and-blood inhabitants of the surrounding world remain for him nameless and thus also nonexistent:

> И не узнавал он нас не потому, что он нас столько-то лет не видел, а потому, что он нас вообще никогда ни разу не увидел, т.е. лица с именем не связал, а не связал, потому что ему было все равно.
>
> [And he failed to recognize us not because he had not seen us for so-and-so many years, but because he had never once actually seen us, that is, had never connected the name and the face, and he didn't make that connection because it was all the same to him.] (*IP* 2:218)

His failure to establish the connection between name and person, like his complete disjunction of then-and-there from here-and-now, emerges as a destructive force, counterposed to which is the generative power that springs from the poet's recognition of their interrelatedness.

Tsvetaeva was to elaborate more fully on the differences that prevail between historical and poetical perception in her Pushkin essays of 1937.[6]

Here in "The House at Old St. Pimen's" she intensifies the disparity between poet and historian by presenting their differences against a backdrop of significant shared characteristics. Prominent among these common features is Ilovaiskii's "blindness" to the surrounding world and what Tsvetaeva refers to as his « нечеловечское одиночество служения » [inhuman solitude of service], descriptions she applies in this essay to Ilovaiskii, but which are—as, for example, the *Sibyl* poems indicate—also singularly appropriate for defining the poet. She notes his poetlike ceaseless labor and commitment to exposing truth at any cost. Even his dedication to the past is characterized in terms that Tsvetaeva habitually reserves for the poet: « целиком и отродясь отдавшись миру не менее потустороннему: былому » [having given himself totally and from birth to a realm no less otherworldly: the past]. (*IP* 2:242) Indeed the Tolstoian motto « против течения » [against the current] which Tsvetaeva claims in this essay to be the leitmotif of her mother's and her own lives (*IP* 2:229) is fully applicable to the temporal and spatial reversals effected by Ilovaiskii in his home.

Yet if the historian shares in features crucial to Tsvetaeva's poet, this only underscores the fated and fateful difference in the consequences of their respective enterprises. The spatial and temporal constructs that determine their apprehension of existence also determine whether the force they wield is the death-dealing one of disjunction or the life-giving one of (re)generation. Tsvetaeva alerts her reader to this essential difference between herself and Ilovaiskii early in the essay with the observation:

> Но очи его видели другое. Они не видели смысла сменяющихся на столе тел. *Истории* в своем доме и жизни историк не ощутил. (А может быть и не истории, а Рока, открытого только поэту?)
>
> [But his eyes saw something else. They did not see the significance of this succession of bodies on the table. The historian did not sense the *history* in his own home and life. (Or perhaps not even history, but Fate, revealed only to the poet?)] (*IP* 2:221)

The poet perceives not sequentially but synchronically and can thus comprehend the interrelatedness of the deaths whose significance is lost on Ilovaiskii, who sees only a series of bodies. Where Ilovaiskii's perception of isolated events sunders past from present and thus also from future, the poet's discrimination of fate conjoins past, present, and future and fosters the recognition of analogues between the individual and the universal. Characters and events do not remain fixed by linearity in one temporal space. Instead they are drawn into synchrony within a protensive mythic dimension to create wellsprings of life where the historian sows seeds of death. It is on the strength of her ability to detect mythic patterns and to use them to forge complex interconnections that Tsvetaeva can counteract Ilovaiskii's unnatural, fragmenting, and death-dealing linearity. Unlike Ilovaiskii's permanent withdrawal from his time, the poet's departures from this world presuppose her return; she does not remain permanently apart from the surrounding world (as does Ilovaiskii), but learns to recognize in it intimations of mythic time and space.

Ilovaiskii's disjunction of time is complemented by the fragmentation of space accomplished by his second wife, Aleksandra Aleksandrovna, whom Tsvetaeva describes as buried alive in her marriage. If her husband is the reverser of time, Aleksandra Aleksandrovna is the constrictor of space. In the course of the memoir her existence, conveyed in geographic metaphors, narrows steadily from Nervi—the Italian seaside resort that provides tubercular patients a last hope for life—to the cluttered subterranean vaulted room where she meets her violent end at the hands of would-be robbers. Her merciless restriction of her children's sphere of activity emerges as a grim metaphor for the curtailment of their very lives. Fueling her strangulation of vitality is an obsession with material possessions. Opposite Ilovaiskii's role of the monk Pimen, his wife plays the role of the Covetous Knight. To her morbid compulsion to guard and preserve her belongings she sacrifices her children, her love, and her life.

As in her portrait of Dmitrii Ilovaiskii, so too in the description of Aleksandra Aleksandrovna Tsvetaeva highlights an important point of intersection with the poet. The possessions to which Aleksandra Aleksandrovna sacrificed life cast a spell on the child poet as well. Marina too is awestruck by treasures the Ilovaiskii trunk yields up during the annual airing of its contents. The story of Aleksandra Aleksandrovna demonstrates them to be inimical to life, and we recognize the gravity of Marina's mother's injunction against touching any of the things that emerge from the trunk, or indeed any Ilovaiskian belongings.

We have seen that mythic apprehension saves the poet from the deadliness of linearity. The preeminence she assigns the verbal sign over what it designates preserves her from the constriction of existence by the rigid boundaries material things impose. Language enables her to subvert the conventional rank of perceived objects to expand the domain of sensibility which those objects otherwise contract. Marina becomes enamored not of the things themselves, but of the words that name them. She is saved by the magic of their sound: «Никакого смысла, чистейшая магия» [No meaning, purest magic] (*IP* 2:216 and again on 217). The relative insignificance to which the things themselves are relegated permits the acoustic and symbolic associative potentialities of words to extend existence into the endless domain of myth. Thus, for example—on the strength of the acoustic and metonymic connections that prevail between them—Tsvetaeva recognizes in the garnets («гранаты») that emerge from Valeriia's opulent, forbidden trunks the seeds of Persephone's pomegranate («гранат»). The events described in the essay prove that this association, far from being merely whimsical, is profoundly revelatory.

Tsvetaeva's essay demonstrates that the becoming of the poet and the counteracting of those forces that are associated with Nadia's removal from life are correlative. A reintegration of past and present willfully sundered by Ilovaiskii also promotes the creation of a vital interrelationship between the living and the dead. The unnaturally straitened bounds of materialism imposed by Aleksandra Aleksandrovna are made to give way to an expansive associative realm in which Nadia is an active participant.

The poet urges the perceptual faculties and thought processes of her readers into those mythic channels that enlarge the scope of vision and engender life-creating connections in an effort to counteract the destructive forces of fragmentation. To this end the poet seeks not to create new myths, but rather to draw on the vital structuring capacity of existing ones to reveal an organic interrelationship among what appear to be the random contingencies of the mundane. In this essay Tsvetaeva pays homage to the universality of myth and to the poet's participation in it: «так как все — миф, так как не-мифа — нет, вне-мифа — нет, из-мифа — нет, так как миф предвосхитил и раз навсегда изваял — все» [since everything is myth, since there is no non-myth, no extra-myth, nothing that falls outside myth, since myth has anticipated and shaped everything once and for all] (*IP* 2:221).

In "The House at Old St. Pimen's" Tsvetaeva redefines and elaborates the Orphic mission of counteracting death, applying it to her own poetic activity. In "The Living about the Living," written the same year (1933) and dedicated to the Russian Symbolist poet Maksimilian Voloshin, she interweaves features of the Orpheus myth with biographical details to shape a symbolic framework that reaffirms her poetic destiny. Here too she emerges as a profound reader of signs. In a recollection of her 1911 sojourn at the Voloshins' home in the Crimean town of Koktebel', she evokes its ancient, mythical quality and discusses Voloshin's own close ties with this land, with myth and with myth-making. It is in this context that she describes an outing to what Voloshin designated as the entrance to Hades.

Characteristically, Tsvetaeva draws this event into the larger mythic structure she created for her own life, where it functions as a counterbalance to the world's contempt for the poet. In juxtaposition with the entrance to Hades the perfidy of the mundane is trivialized and rendered ineffectual:

> Что я в жизни видела, кроме черного хода? И чернейших людских ходов?
>
> А вот что: вход в Аид.

[What have I seen in life besides back doors? And the blackest of human dealings?
Why this: the entrance to Hades!] (*IP* 2:58)

Having thus formulated the difference in scope of the mundane and the mytho-poetical, Tsvetaeva explains that she had come to Koktebel' to forget her first love. She does not name this beloved and refers to him only as the man who had introduced her to Orpheus, "the translator of Heraclitus and the Orphic hymns" (*IP* 2:58). Vladimir Nilender, whom we recognize in this description, is pointedly excluded from Tsvetaeva's subsequent account of the associations Orpheus holds for her—this in spite of her later admission that she did not in fact succeed in forgetting him.

> И каждый раз, будь то в собственных стихах, или на « Орфее » Глюка, или просто слово Орфей — десятисаженная щель в скале, серебро морской воды на скалах . . .
>
> [And each time whether in my own poems, or at Gluck's *Orpheo*, or simply the word Orpheus—a twenty-yard fissure in a cliff, the silver of saltwater on the cliffs . . .][7] (*IP* 2:58)

Tsvetaeva consciously chooses to link the myth of Orpheus specifically with her poetic rather than her erotic nascency. The Greek bard is conjoined not with the image of an earthly love, but with the site of her own apprehension of an outlet from this world. The destiny implicit in her visit to the entrance to Hades is described in terms not of descent but of high cliffs, not of Hades itself but of a fissure that opens the possibility for departure.

Maksimilian Voloshin, her guide on this expedition, was among the early discoverers of the poet Tsvetaeva. He welcomed the appearance of ***Вечерний альбом*** [An Evening Album]—her first book of poetry, which was addressed to Nilender—with a very encouraging review and brought her into a flourishing and dynamic artistic community.[8] Even as she distances herself from Nilender in this essay, Tsvetaeva draws a connection between him, the guide to the Orphic hymns, and Voloshin, the guide to the entrance of Hades.

That her own entrance into poetry is flanked by a poet and a philologist is a detail of great import. We may observe that in the essay « Пленный дух » [A Captive Spirit, 1934], written on the occasion of Andrei Belyi's death, Tsvetaeva accords the same philologist mythic status and makes manifest the significance of what she has gained by the act of relinquishing that earthly love for him she describes in "The Living about the Living." In "A Captive Spirit" Tsvetaeva maintains that Nilender's account of the parting of Belyi and his beloved Asia Turgeneva also sheds light on her own parting from Nilender:

и весь рассказ об Асе и Белом — *о нас* рассказ, если бы один из нас был хоть чуточку безумнее или преступнее другого из нас. Но зато — и какое в этом несравненное сияние! — знаю, что если я, сейчас, столько лет спустя, или еще через десять лет, или через все двадцать войду в его филологическую берлогу, в грот Орфея, в пещеру Сивиллы, он правой оттолкнет молодую жену, левой обвалит мне же на голову подпотолочную стопу старых книг — и кинется ко мне, раскрывши руки, которые будут — крылья.

Это нам и всем подобным нам награда за все нами отвергнутые Монреалы.

[and the entire story about Asia and Belyi was a story *about us*, had either one of us been even just the tiniest bit more insane or criminal than the other. But then—and what an incomparable radiance there is in this!—I know that if now, so many years later, or in still another ten years, or even a full twenty years more I walk into his philological den, that grotto of Orpheus, that Sibylline cave, he will push his young wife away with his right hand and with his left will sweep the nearly ceiling-high stack of old books right onto my head—and will rush toward me with open arms which will be—wings.

This is the reward for us and all those like us for all the Montreals we have spurned.] (*IP* 2:90)

The primacy Tsvetaeva accords the word manifests itself in her equation of the philologist's study with the grotto of Orpheus and the cave of the Sibyl. The reference to her relationship with Nilender provides her with the opportunity to draw attention to her own profound respect for the word, and to foreground the unrequited love whose energy prevails over the many years and events that have come between them. The merely momentary coupling afforded by the body is sacrificed to the lasting union born of unfulfillment which is inscribed in poetic language.

That she should find herself in the myth of Orpheus even as she seeks to elude the man who introduced her to the Greek bard is not mere chance, but a stroke of destiny. She can escape Nilender, but not her poetic calling. Indeed that very flight is to be recognized as a true sign of the emerging poet who eschews physical gratification and transforms it instead into the verse of her first poetry collection. Such renunciation became Tsvetaeva's motto and the organizing principle of her biography, whether in fleeing marriage with Nilender, foregoing direct contact with Blok and Pasternak, or shaping in words an otherworldly union with Rilke. In the configuration of cliff, sea, and fissure to which Voloshin ferries her and which she persists in associating with Orpheus, we recognize the root images of the poetic destiny Tsvetaeva authored for herself: the sea of Marina, the cliff of fate which forces the waves crashing against it to leap higher,[9] and the mysterious mythical cleft that provides access to creative space—an alternative both to eros and to the hostile and limited world in which the poet appears.

We have seen that for Tsvetaeva poetic creativity is a structuring of life, urged on by the imperative of confronting death—which, subsuming even the power of eros, ultimately becomes the principal force impelling artistic production. Highlighted is the strong sense of the essential unity of all poets in the face of the ominous antagonism of the surrounding world and the nigh unbearable demands of their art. As the poet steadily approaches her own death, references to Orpheus serve to underscore the human pain of the poet who pleads for respite from the intransigent demands of her art. The life-affirming image of the undoer of death is complemented by that of self-sacrificing victim. This is felt with particular poignancy in two of Tsvetaeva's later lyrics that evoke the Orpheus myth and whose consideration will complete this investigation: "Conversation with a Genius" and "There Are Fortunate Men and Women."

The first of these was written in 1928 and appeared initially in the Parisian journal *Современные записки* [Contemporary Annals] under the title « Школа стиха » [School of Verse], which Tsvetaeva later amended.[10] In this poem Orpheus appears as a model for a markedly feminine plaintiff who, in a series of images that emphasize aridity and unproductiveness, bemoans the impossibility of singing only to have each plea for respite countered by the inexorable demand of her genius that she continue her song.

Разговор с гением

Глыбами — лбу
Лавры похвал.
« Петь не могу! »
— « Будешь! » — « Пропал,

(На толокно
Переводи!)
Как молоко —
Звук из груди.

Пусто. Сухà.
В полную веснь —
Чувство сука » .
— « Старая песнь!

Брось, не морочь! »
« Лучше мне впредь —
Камень толочь! »
— « Тут-то и петь! »

« Чтò я, снегирь,
Чтоб день-деньской

Петь? »
— « Не моги,
Пташка, а пой!

Нà зло врагу! »
« Коли двух строк
Свесть не могу? »
— « Кто когда — *мог?!* » —

« Пытка! » — « Терпи! »
« Скошенный луг —
Глотка! » — « Хрипи:
Тоже ведь — звук! »

« Львов, а не жен
Дело ». « *Детей*:
Распотрошен —
Пел же — Орфей! »

« Так и в гробу? »
— « И под доской ».
« *Петь* не могу! »
— « *Это* воспой! »

Conversation with a Genius

[The laurels of praise are clods to the forehead. "I cannot sing!" "You will!" "The sound has vanished from my chest/breast like milk. (Switch the baby to oat gruel!) Empty. I'm dry. In full spring—the sensation of a dry twig." "That's an old song! Forget it, don't bother me!" "It would be better henceforth to grind stone!" "That's just when you should sing!" "What am I, a finch, to sing day in and day out?" "Be unable to, little bird, but sing! To spite the enemy!" "But what if I can't connect even two lines?" "Who ever *could?!*" "Torment!" "Suffer!" "My throat is a mowed field!" "Wheeze: after all that too is a sound!" "It is the task of lions, not women." "Of *children*: dismembered, Orpheus did after all sing!" "So too in the grave?" "Even under the lid." "I cannot *sing*!" "Sing *that*!"] (*SP* 3:138–39).

The genius with whom the despairing poet converses refuses to countenance the excuses for why she can no longer be expected to sing—first by denying her situation any uniqueness (« Старая песнь! // Брось, не морочь! »), then by pointing out that it is precisely in time of extreme hardship that song is most necessary (« Тут-то и петь! »). This elicits the supplicant's protestation that she is no finch who can be expected to sing constantly. In this finch we recognize the famous bird of Gavrila Derzhavin's poem « Снегирь » [The Bullfinch] in which the poet bids his bird to fall silent before the death of General Suvorov. This injunction is refuted by Orpheus himself. Tsvetaeva's own position needs no further rehearsal after our exploration of *New Year's*, that quintessential transformation of death into song. Thus too the genius of her lyric—equally unmoved by pleas and literary allusion—responds predictably that the bird is to sing even when it cannot. As the dialogue continues, the inability to join effectively even two lines of verse is impatiently brushed aside with a question that designates this to be the norm: « Кто когда — *мог?!* » [Who ever *could*?!]. Torture too must be endured and articulated even if it is in hoarse groans. Indeed, singing *is* torture.

In counterargument to the suggestion that the difficult task is more appropriate to lions than women, the genius maintains only that it is the task of children. It is in this aura of powerlessness and helplessness, two characteristics Tsvetaeva had emphasized in connection with her Blok-Orpheus, that the Greek bard enters this poem—again as in the Blok-Orpheus poems—at the moment of *sparagmós*. Yet if in the Blok poems Orpheus's dismembered body serves as the backdrop for the transcendent qualities of the poetic voice, here the emphasis is on the intense suffering attendant on making that voice heard. The designation of Orpheus as « распотрошен » accentuates the markedly down-to-earth tone of the genius's responses and succeeds in capturing simultaneously the idea of "gutting" (« потрошить ») and sundering (« раз- »). Even the grave site, so emphatically denied in connection with Orpheus and in poems written to Blok and to Rilke, is here designated as a locus of song. The very impossibility of poetic production is to become the subject of poetry.

The entire conversation is focused on that crucial incompatibility of human being and poet that divides the poet from both surroundings and self. The stanzaic divisions within this dialogue suggest that this is Tsvetaeva's confrontation with herself, that the two interlocutors in this poem represent a split within her. This divided self—which we have seen projected also in the lyric "Thus Floated Head and Lyre" and in the antipoetical Hamlet's arguments with his conscience—is in itself more poignant than any of her pleas for respite. Unlike the alternation of images of helpless individual and mighty poet that we have noted, for example, in Pushkin's lyric "The Poet," the dialogue Tsvetaeva creates here insists on the simultaneity of antinomic images that was also demanded in the *Poets* cycle. To conjoin implacable genius and hapless supplicant is to conjoin the poet with herself—« себя с собой ». Crystallized here is the ambivalence of the Orpheus myth toward the poet, whom it endows with a power that supersedes mortality, yet whom it makes also a victim of the mortal world. The fierce struggle between poetic genius and mere human, between the Olympian demands of her art and her own needs, effects another sort of *sparagmós*. The very antinomies that Tsvetaeva had wedded with such success in *New Year's* here threaten to pull dangerously and destructively apart.

In the lyric "There Are Fortunate Men and Women" (January 1935), Orpheus represents once again the excruciating difficulties of the poetic calling. In this poem, as in the "Conversation with a Genius," Tsvetaeva describes verse no longer as the much-needed outlet for pent-up emotion, or as the means for sublimating earthly desires and making possible the impossible, or for vanquishing death. Instead she again expresses an acute desire to be spared the demands of her art even as she demonstrates her full cognizance of the impossibility of evading them. The longing for an escape—no longer from the mundane but rather from the poetical—now dominates.

Есть счастливцы и счастливицы,
Петь *не* могущие. Им —
Слезы лить! Как сладко вылиться
Горю — ливнем проливным!

Чтоб под камнем что-то дрогнуло.
Мне ж — призвание как плеть —
Меж стенания надгробного
Долг повелевает — петь.

Пел же над другом своим Давид,
Хоть пополам расколот!
Если б Орфей не сошел в Аид
Сам, а послал бы голос

Свой, только голос послал во тьму,
Сам у порога *лишним*
Встав, — Эвридика бы по нему
Как по канату вышла . . .

Как по канату и как на свет,
Слепо и без возврата.
Ибо раз *голос* тебе, поэт,
Дан, остальное — взято.

[There are fortunate men and women who can *not* sing. It is for them to shed tears! How sweet it is for sorrow to pour itself out in a torrential downpour! So that something trembles under the stone. As for me—my calling like a lash—amidst funereal wailing duty commands me to sing. David did, after all, sing over his friend, though cleft in twain! If Orpheus had not descended into Hades himself, but had sent his voice only into the darkness, he himself standing at the threshold, *superfluous,* Eurydice would have emerged along it as if along a tightrope . . . As if along a tightrope and as if into life, blindly and with no return. For once the *voice* is given you, poet, everything else is taken away.] (*SP* 3:184; elipsis in original)

Song is the fulfillment of a painful duty. The whole point of poetry is to prolong grief, not to mitigate it. To the fortunate condition of those who cannot sing Tsvetaeva juxtaposes the harshness of the imperative under which she herself labors, « —призвание как плеть ». The verb « петь » [to sing], tellingly rhymed with « плеть » [lash], stands alone at the end of the second stanza, representing the isolation of the poet. Her song—that controlled expression of illimitable emotion—stands out from the unbridled funerary wailing surrounding it.

The evocation of David in the stanza that follows powerfully reasserts the elegiac duties of the poet. The profundity of the pain David experiences at the death of his soulmate Jonathan is described here as a split in his very self: « хоть пополам расколот! » We recognize that, as the myth of Orpheus suggests and as Tsvetaeva demonstrates in *New Year's*, the divided selves, like the separated living and the dead, are reunited by song.

Tsvetaeva's reference to David evokes Rilke's lyric "Klage um Jonathan" from *Neue Gedichte II*, a collection which Tsvetaeva knew well and which includes, as we have observed, the poem "Eine Sibylle." In the plaint of Rilke's David are two themes which undergo fuller development both in his "Marina Elegy" and in Tsvetaeva's *New Year's*. The first of these is the interrelation of permanence and ephemerality; the second is the death of one loved so deeply as to constitute a part of the very self of the bereaved.

Even as Tsvetaeva's line "though cleft in twain" participates in this particular thematic configuration, it activates the image of another sort of split, for, as we may recall here, the death of Jonathan meant at one and the same time the loss of an irreplaceable friend and the anointment of David as king over the House of Judah. Moreover, the battle with the Philistines (in which Jonathan perished) took the life of his father, Saul, David's sworn enemy and would-be slayer. Here, then, emerges a concrete image of that interpenetration of jubilation and mourning Rilke describes in his "Marina Elegy."

Tsvetaeva devotes the remainder of her poem—exactly half—to a particularization of this notion. Given the central theme of the poem—an elaboration of the imperative of song—the appearance of Orpheus is appropriate, all the more so because Rilke's "Klage an Jonathan" prefigures the *Sonnets to Orpheus,* where the jubilation expressed in the face of death harks back to the Psalms of David. Yet the Orpheus invoked here is of Tsvetaeva's own making. In this section of her poem we once again encounter the suggestion—familiar to us already from the lyrics "Like One Somnolent, Intoxicated" and "Eurydice to Orpheus"—of the inappropriateness of the intrusion of the flesh-and-blood bard into the realm of shades. Yet here Tsvetaeva's opprobrium at attempts to return the dead to life that she expressed in connection with Eurydice, Lazarus, and Jairus' daughter is mitigated by an acknowledgement of the pain attendant on allegiance to the otherworldly. The emphasis on the unseemliness and inevitable failure of attempted retrieval gives way now to a consideration of how its success might be possible.

Accordingly, the fourth stanza culminates in Eurydice's emergence from the underworld, her return made possible by the replacement of Orpheus's offending body with the voice—that quintessential intermediary between body and soul. Yet the emphasized *лишним* [*superfluous*] of the penultimate stanza suggests acoustically the «лишение» [deprivation] of the poet with which the poem concludes.

The final stanza repeats «как по канату» [as if along a tightrope] of the last line of the stanza preceding it. This is a reference to the tightrope along which Eurydice leaves Hades; yet here the simile is repeated not to reassert the privileged position Tsvetaeva habitually assigns voice, but rather to emphasize the metaphorical quality of that "tightrope." We are led to recognize here that if the tightrope is a metaphor, so too is the world into which it leads Eurydice: «и *как* на свет» [and *as if* into life] (my emphasis). In other words, Eurydice's blind obedience to the summons of the voice and the elimination of her forced return to Hades («Слепо и без возврата») establish her presence not in our flesh-and-blood world, but within that symbolic and metaphoric realm of poetry itself—that "third state" that is both and neither the realm of shades and the realm of mortals. Orpheus can only transform Eurydice into song. They are united when song and poet become one. Direct physical contact is eschewed. Here Apollo's "gift" is not freely given. In return for the voice all else is exacted: «Ибо, раз *голос* тебе, поэт, / Дан, остальное взято» [For once the *voice* is given you, / poet, everything else is taken away]. The cost of poetry is supreme.

Tsvetaeva's emphasis now falls on the sacrifice exacted in return for the gift of voice rather than on the power of that voice. We have already seen the common mortal struggle between life and death modulate for the poet into a struggle between creative powers and death. Death overrides the erotic force that assures procreation, but the poet vanquishes death by transforming it into a generative force out of which poetry is born. Orpheus's song, which before the catabasis is motivated by eros, is after his sojourn in Hades impelled by death.

Mourning turns to jubilation when song vanquishes death. Yet the lyric "There Are Fortunate Men and Women" is an expression of neither jubilation nor lament, but of resignation which lies in the fallow space between them. The tragedy of Tsvetaeva's suicide can be seen ripening as her accounts of her art come to approximate that projected by Anton Chekhov, a writer she disdained as alien to the poetic, and who—in the play she claimed never to have read because she always confused its title with *The Wild Duck*—reduces the entire existence of an artist to mere endurance.[11] Tsvetaeva's cries for respite from the demands of her art are pleas for release from the life of a poet, a release from those struggles with death from which only death itself can free her.

Embedded in the specific context of the Orpheus myth as Tsvetaeva read it, her own death too can be regarded as perpetuating the poetic process. However tragic, death transforms the aridity and barrenness described in

"Conversation with a Genius"—a recurring theme in Tsvetaeva's last years—into a force that continues to impel creativity. The poet is drawn toward death by her art and driven to it by the inimical mundane. This doubly assured death is held in perpetuity by her readers and demands the poet's eternal return. In Tsvetaeva's kaleidoscope metaphor that describes the process of poetry, we recognize a powerful condensation of the Orpheus myth: that particular creative order whose vitality depends on disintegration and the subsequent reemergence of form anew.

Notes

PREFACE

1. Elizabeth Sewell, *The Orphic Voice: Poetry and Natural History* (New Haven: Yale University Press, 1960), 47.

2. Walter Strauss, *Descent and Return: The Orphic Theme in Modern Literature* (Cambridge, Mass.: Harvard University Press, 1971), 219.

INTRODUCTION

1. I borrow this designation from a penetrating study of Tsvetaeva's conception of the other world: Ieva Vitins, "Escape from Earth: A Study of Tsvetaeva's Elsewheres," *Slavic Review* (December 1977), 644–57. See also Vitins's extensive "Escape from Earth: A Study of the Four Elements and Their Associations in Marina Cvetaeva's Work," Ph.D. Diss., University of California, Berkeley, 1974.

2. Marina Tsvetaeva, *Избранная проза в двух томах*, ed. A. Sumerkin, 2 vols. (New York: Russica Publishers, 1979), 1:106. All subsequent references to this edition, henceforth *IP*, appear in the text.

3. « Письма Марины Цветаевой », *Новый мир* 4 (1969), 199.

4. Marina Tsvetaeva, *Неизданные письма*, ed. G. Struve and N. Struve (Paris: YMCA Press, 1972), 278–79.

5. Walter Strauss, *Descent and Return: The Orphic Theme in Modern Literature* (Cambridge: Harvard University Press, 1971), 3.

6. J. Marin King translates the title of this essay as "A Living Word about a Living Man" in Marina Tsvetaeva, *A Captive Spirit: Selected Prose* (Ann Arbor: Ardis, 1980). I retain the less specific character of the original.

7. Strauss, op. cit., 4.

8. For an extensive treatment of Tsvetaeva's use of "inherited texts," which include classical myths, see Michael Makin, *Marina Tsvetaeva: Poetics of Appropriation* (Oxford: Clarendon Press, 1993). Studies that focus on

Tsvetaeva's treatment of specific myths include Jerzy Faryno, *Мифологизм и теологизм Цветаевой (« Магдалина » — « Царь-Девица » — « Переулочки »)*, *Wiener slawistischer Almanach*, Sonderband 18 (Vienna, 1985); K. Medvedeva, « Стихи о Сивилле, Орфее, и Эвридике как звено в концепции поэта в лирике Марины Цветаевой начала двадцатых годов », in *Некоторые проблемы русской и зарубежной литературы*, ed. O. A. Fin'ko (Vladivostok n.p.: 1974), 16–28; Tomas Venclova, "On Russian Mythological Tragedy: Vjacheslav Ivanov and Marina Cvetaeva," in *Myth in Literature*, ed. Andrej Kodjak, Krystyna Pomorska, and Stephen Rudy, New York University Slavic Papers 5 (Columbus: Slavic Publishers, 1985), 89–109; and Laura Weeks, " 'I Named Her Ariadna . . .' The Demeter-Persephone Myth in Tsvetaeva's Poems for Her Daughter," *Slavic Review* 49, no. 4 (1990), 568–84.

9. Jurii Lotman, "The Origin of Plot in the Light of Typology," *Poetics Today* 1, nos. 1–2 (1979), 161–84.

10. Mircea Eliade, *Myth and Reality*, trans. Willard R. Trask (New York: Harper and Row, 1963), 8. See also Eliade's *Myth of Eternal Return*, trans. Willard R. Trask (Princeton: Princeton University Press, 1974).

11. Omry Ronen, "A Functional Technique of Myth Transformation in Twentieth-Century Russian Lyrical Poetry," in *Myth in Literature*, ed. Kodjak, Pomorska, and Rudy, 120.

12. Charles Segal, *Orpheus: The Myth of the Poet* (Baltimore: Johns Hopkins University Press, 1989), 34.

13. Ibid., 4–5.

14. John Block Friedman, *Orpheus in the Middle Ages* (Cambridge: Harvard University Press, 1970), 1.

15. It is interesting to compare this assertion with a passage in Rilke's letter to Nanny Wunderly-Volkart of 29 July 1920:

> . . . es ist dasselbe, es ist der Dichter, denn im letzten Sinne giebt es nur Einen, jenen unendlichen, der sich da und dort durch die Zeiten in einem, ihm unterworfenen Geiste geltend macht.
>
> [. . . it is one and the same, it is the poet, for in the last anaylsis there is only One, that never-ending one who here and there through the ages manifests himself in a spirit that is subordinated to him.]

(R. M. Rilke, *Briefe an Nanny Wunderly-Volkart* [Frankfurt-am-Main: Insel Verlag, 1977], 1:292).

16. « По ту сторону поэтики: К характеристике литературных взглядов М. Цветаевой », *Звезда* 10 (1992), 159 (my translation).

CHAPTER ONE: THE EMERGENCE OF ORPHEUS

1. *Письма к А. Тесковой* (Jerusalem: Versty, 1982), 40.

2. *Rainer Maria Rilke und Marina Zwetajewa: Ein Gespräch in Briefen* (Frankfurt-am-Main: Insel Verlag, 1992), 91 (henceforth *R-Z Corr.*).

3. «Письма М. И. Цветаевой Ю. П. Иваску» (1933–1937 gg.), in *Русский литературный архив*, ed. M. Karpovich and D. Chizhevsky (New York: n.p., 1956), 209.

4. See Anastasia Tsvetaeva, *Воспоминания* (Moscow: Советский писатель, 1983), 313–21. The most extensive biographical account appears in Mariia Razumovskaia, *Марина Цветаева: Миф и действительность* (London: Overseas Publications Interchange, 1983), chapters 5 and 6 (originally published in German under the title *Marina Zwetajewa, 1892–1941: Mythos und Wahrheit* [Vienna: Age d'Homme Karolinger, 1981]). See also among others Simon Karlinsky, *Marina Tsvetaeva: The Woman, Her World, and Her Poetry* (Cambridge: Cambridge University Press, 1986), 29–32, 36, 52, 118; Viktoria Schweitzer, *Быт и бытие Марины Цветаевой* (Fontenay-aux-Roses, France: Syntaxis, 1988), 76, 77, 79, 84, 85, 152; and Jane A. Taubman, *A Life through Poetry: Marina Tsvetaeva's Lyric Diary* (Columbus: Slavica Publishers, 1989), 26–31. Nilender is the focus of Liudmila Polikovskaia, «Мудрец-филолог. Кто он?: К биографии одного лирического героя Марины Цветаевой», *Звезда* 10 (1992), 173–79.

5. Marina Tsvetaeva, *Стихотворения и поэмы в пяти томах*, 5 vols. (New York: Russica, 1980–1993), 1:72. All references to Tsvetaeva's poetry are cited according to this edition, henceforth designated in the text as *SP* with volume and page numbers following.

6. Razumovskaia mentions specifically Heine, Novalis, Bettina von Arnim, and Goethe, op. cit., 67.

7. Walter Strauss, *Descent and Return: The Orphic Theme in Modern Literature*, 21.

8. Ibid., 26.

9. Dorothy Zayatz Baker, *Mythic Masks in Self-reflexive Poetry: A Study of Pan and Orpheus* (Chapel Hill: University of North Carolina Press, 1986), 26.

10. Ibid., 29.

11. Ariadna Efron, *Страницы воспоминаний* (Paris: Lev, 1979), 63.

12. Tsvetaeva's relationship to Blok has attracted the attention of a number of scholars. Among the more prominent are Andrew Field, "A Poetic Epitaph: Marina Tsvetaeva's Poems to Blok," *Triquarterly* (Spring 1965), 57–61; Anna Saakiants, «Марина Цветаева об Александре Блоке», in *В мире Блока* (Moscow: *Советский писатель*, 1981), 416–40; Schweitzer, op. cit., 229–44; Taubman, op. cit., chapter 8, 88–93.

13. Schweitzer, op. cit., 237 (ellipsis in original).

14. Blok's death on 25 July 1921 prompted Tsvetaeva to write seven lyrics and the five-poem cycle *Подруга* [Friend] between 2 August and 28

November of that year. These works were subsequently published together with Tsvetaeva's 1916 lyrics addressed to Blok in a volume titled *Стихи к Блоку* [Poems to Blok] (Berlin: Ogon'ki, 1922).

15. See, for example, John Block Friedman, *Orpheus in the Middle Ages*, 36–37, 40.

16. For penetrating commentary on both this lyric and "Thus Floated Head and Lyre" see Michael Makin, *Marina Tsvetaeva: Poetics of Appropriation*, 189–90.

17. We shall encounter a powerful representation of this criterion in Tsvetaeva's description of the Cumaean Sibyl, a persona of the poet examined in chapter 4.

18. Aleksandr Blok, *Собрание сочинений в шести томах* (Moscow: Pravda, 1971), 3:192 (ellipsis in original).

19. The editors of the Russica edition of Tsvetaeva's poetry cite Ovid's *Metamorphoses* as the source for both this poem and the lyric "Like One Somnolent, Intoxicated" (*SP* 2:374), and Makin, op. cit., 189, echoes this assertion. Yet because Ovid includes neither the detail of the mendacious nightingale nor that of the woman of Lesbos, Tsvetaeva is apparently relying here on Schwab and/or Stoll. The accounts of both authors include these details as well as the responding riverbanks.

20. Cf., for example, the poem « Вскрыла жилы » [I Slashed My Wrists] and the essay dedicated to Rilke, « Твоя смерть » [Your Death].

21. In 1940 Tsvetaeva appended the title "Orpheus" to this poem. See Schweitzer, op. cit., 237.

22. It is interesting to note that Tsvetaeva is suggesting here precisely what Rainer Maria Rilke some five years later was to formulate in the elegy he dedicated to her as "was übermäßig sie biegt, ründet sie reichlich zum Kranz" [richly it rounds them to crowns, that which excessively bends] (Rainer Maria Rilke, *Sämtliche Werke* [Wiesbaden: Insel Verlag, 1958]; trans. J. B. Leishman, *Rainer Maria Rilke: Poems 1906–1926* [London: Hogarth Press, 1957], 347–48).

23. "Daher kommt es, dass jene Insel so herrliche Dichter und Sänger erzeugt hat; ja selbst die Nachtigallen sangen dort lieblicher als anderswo, um das Grab des göttlichen Orpheus zu ehren" [Thus it has come to pass that this island has produced such glorious poets and singers; for there even the nightingales sang more sweetly than anywhere else to honor the grave of the divine Orpheus] (Gustav Schwab, *Die schönste Sagen des klassischen Altertums* [Stuttgart: n.p., 1900], 62). H. W. Stoll describes Lesbos as "der Sängerinsel, wo später Alkaios sang und die gefeierte Sappho, wo die Nachtigallen lieblicher singen, als anderswo sonst auf der Erde" [the island of singers where later Alkaios sang and the celebrated Sappho, where the nightingales sing more sweetly than anywhere else on earth] (*Die*

Sagen des klassischen Altertums [Leipzig: Druck und Verlag B. G. Teubner, 1884], 105).

24. Makin, op. cit., 189.

25. Catriona Kelly reads the dismemberment of Orpheus represented in this poem along gender lines: "The poem averts the power of the male body by reducing it from a (threatening) whole to vulnerable, feminized pieces (both *lira* and *golova* are grammatically feminine). . . . It also places a passive man at the disposal of active women: destroyed by the Maenads' act of violence before the poem opens, Orpheus is reconstituted at its end by a woman of Lesbos, who catches his 'remnants' in her net" (*A History of Russian Women's Writing, 1820–1992* [Oxford: Clarendon Press, 1994], 306).

26. Private communication (1995).

27. It is interesting to note that Tsvetaeva's discussions of Vladimir Mayakovskii in her 1932 essays « Искусство при свете совести » [Art in the Light of Conscience] and « Эпос и лирика современной России » [The Epic and the Lyric of Contemporary Russia] focus primarily on the conflict between man and poet, using this essentially Orphic dilemma to explain Mayakovskii's suicide (see *IP* 1:405–6 and 2:23).

28. *R-Z Corr.*, 56.

29. Strauss, op. cit., 171.

CHAPTER TWO: EURYDICE

1. Antonina Gove, "The Feminine Stereotype and Beyond: Role Conflict and Resolution in the Poetics of Marina Tsvetaeva," *Slavic Review* 36 (1977), 247.

2. Simon Karlinsky, *Marina Cvetaeva: Her Life and Art* (Berkeley: University of California Press, 1966), 193–94.

3. Simon Karlinsky, *Marina Tsvetaeva: The Woman, Her World, and Her Poetry* (Cambridge: Cambridge University Press, 1986), 185.

4. In the aria "E quest' asilo ameno è grato" (scene 2 of act II or III, depending on the version of the opera consulted) Eurydice describes the tranquillity of the underworld, where the realm of the living is completely forgotten. Tsvetaeva refers to Gluck's opera in the essay « Живое о живом » [The Living about the Living], where she describes the associations Orpheus holds for her.

5. Marina Tsvetaeva, *Неизданные письма*, 282.

6. Tsvetaeva was to make a similar statement about Aleksei Aleksandrovich Stakhovich. In a diary entry dated 27 February 1919, devoted to the death of Stakhovich, Tsvetaeva writes: « И скажу еще одно, чего не знает никто: — если бы на Рождестве 1918 г. я, как хотела, зашла к Стаховичу, он бы не умер » [And I will say something else that no one knows: if on

Christmas of 1918 I had dropped in on Stakhovich as I wanted to do, he would not have died] (*IP* 1:76).

7. Marina Tsvetaeva, *Сочинения в двух томах*, ed. and commentary by Anna Saakiants, 2 vols. (Moscow: Художественная литература, 1988), 2:470.

8. That Blok would deliver her *poëma На красном коне* [On a Red Steed] to Akhmatova is not the least flattering aspect of this plan. This particular messenger would grant legitimacy to the poetry he conveyed and would elevate Tsvetaeva to both his own and Akhmatova's status. Although her relations with Akhmatova fall outside the parameters of this particular study it is interesting to recall here that Tsvetaeva's eleven-poem cycle *Стихи к Ахматовой* [Poems to Akhmatova, 19 June–2 July 1916] followed hard on the heels of her 1916 series of poems to Blok (15 April–18 May).

9. Tsvetaeva's emphatic allegiance to Moscow figured prominently in her self-definition, particularly where Petersburg poets were concerned. Her habit of "bestowing" her city on others was both a gesture of generosity and a means of self-assertion (cf., e.g., her poems to Akhmatova and to Mandel'shtam).

10. *Собрание сочинений в шести томах*, 2:237.

11. See Rilke's letter of 17 May 1926, *R-Z Corr.*, 66, 67.

12. *Неизданные письма*, 293–94.

13. The Gospels of Matthew, Mark, and Luke state that Christ takes the girl by the hand to draw her back to life. Only Mark and Luke refer to Christ's utterance of the command that she arise.

14. Here we should note that it is in concert with the thematics of this poem that enjambments assume this function. Elsewhere in Tsvetaeva's poetry enjambments—which occur with high frequency—assume different semantic coloring. For a valuable discussion of this rich topic, see Lev Losev, «Значение переноса у Цветаевой», in *Марина Цветаева: Труды 1-го международного симпозиума (*Лозанна, *30.VI.-3. VII. 1982)*, ed. Robin Kemball (Berne: Peter Lang Verlag, 1991), 272–83.

15. *Неизданные письма*, 293.

16. Elizabeth Sewell, *The Orphic Voice: Poetry and Natural History*, 330–31.

17. Charles Segal, *Orpheus: The Myth of the Poet,* 120, 121.

18. *Неизданные письма*, 294.

19. Segal, op. cit., 10, 11.

CHAPTER THREE: HAMLET THE ANTIPOET AND OPHELIA

1. Charles Segal, *Orpheus: The Myth of the Poet,* 85.

2. The chronological order of the poems under discussion in chapters 2 through 5 is as follows: the first two poems of the *Sibyl* cycle (5 and 6 August 1922); "Ophelia to Hamlet" and "Ophelia—in Defense of the Queen" (28 February 1923); "Eurydice to Orpheus" (23 March 1923); *Poets* cycle (8 and 22 April 1923); the third poem of the *Sibyl* cycle (17 May 1923); and "Hamlet's Dialogue with His Conscience" (5 June 1923).

3. To the same year belong two additional lyrics in which Ophelia figures prominently, but from which Hamlet is absent: « На назначенное свиданье » (18 June 1923, titled « Офелия » in the manuscript), which also appears in *After Russia,* and « По набережным, где седые деревья » (28 September 1923), which Tsvetaeva did not include in that collection.

4. In « Записки наблюдателя » 1 (1924).

5. In her essay « Диалог Марины Цветаевой с Шекспиром: Проблема Гамлета » Anna Tamarchenko treats these three poems as a cycle. See *A Centennial Symposium Dedicated to Marina Tsvetaeva* (Northfield, Vt.: Russian School of Norwich University, 1992), 159–76.

6. Dorothy Zayatz Baker, *Mythic Masks in Self-reflexive Poetry: A Study of Pan and Orpheus,* 5.

7. Walter Strauss, *Descent and Return: The Orphic Theme in Modern Literature,* 130.

8. Eleanor Rowe, *Hamlet: A Window on Russia* (New York: NYU Press, 1976), 116.

9. The literature on *Hamlet* in Russia is too vast to cite here. In addition to Rowe's book, helpful background materials and references can be found in Ernest J. Simmons, *English Literature and Culture in Russia* (Cambridge, Mass.: Harvard University Press, 1935), chapter 7, "The Early History of Shakespeare in Russia," 204–36; A. Anikst, « Гамлет », in *Шекспировский сборник*, ed. A. Anikst and A. Shtein (Moscow, 1961); Boris Eikhenbaum, « К истории Гамлета в России », in *Шекспировский сборник*, ed. A. Anikst (Moscow, 1967); Howard A. Goldman, "Shakespeare's Hamlet in the Work of Boris Pasternak and Other Modern Russian Poets" (Ph.D. Diss., Indiana University, 1975).

10. Rowe, op. cit., 22.

11. Stefan Bodo Würffel, *Ophelia: Figur und Entfremdung* (Bern: Francke Verlag, 1985), 31, 29.

12. Ibid., 27 (my translation).

13. This list of poems is taken from Rowe, who discusses them in chapter 8 of her study (see especially 114–17).

14. The lyrical precedent for Pasternak's suggestion of a parallel between Desdemona and Ophelia can be found in A. A. Fet's poem « Я болен, Офелия » [I am sick, Ophelia, 1847], which was part of the four-poem cycle *K*

Офелии [To Ophelia] and which concluded with a reference to Desdemona as Ophelia's sister.

15. Ihab Hassan, *The Dismemberment of Orpheus* (Madison: University of Wisconsin Press, 1982), 2.

16. Whether Tsvetaeva herself concurred with readers such as her beloved writer Ludwig Tieck, who insisted that Ophelia's loss of innocence preceded even the counseling of her brother Laertes, or with those readers who considered Ophelia a virgin, it is the latter view that she projects in her poems.

17. For a discussion of this episode, see Viktoria Schweitzer, *Быт и бытие Марины Цветаевой*, 201, 202; and Tamarchenko, op. cit., 2:160–61.

18. Pasternak, having decided against emigration, left Berlin on 18 March 1923 to return to Russia. Tsvetaeva, then living in the outskirts of Prague, explained that she received word of his impending departure too late to obtain a visa. Jane A. Taubman suggests that Tsvetaeva may intentionally have foregone this much longed-for meeting. She describes the missed meeting and its consequences in chapter 18 of *A Life through Poetry: Marina Tsvetaeva's Lyric Diary.* Other studies devoted to Tsvetaeva's relationship with Pasternak at this time include Olga Raevsky-Hughes, « Борис Пастернак. Марина Цветаева (К истории дружбы) », *Вестник русского христианского движения* 100 (1971), 281–305; Jane A. Taubman, "Marina Tsvetaeva and Boris Pasternak: Toward the History of a Friendship," *Russian Literature Triquarterly* 1/2 (1972), 303–21; and R. D. B. Thomson, "Cvetaeva and Pasternak, 1922–1924," in *Boris Pasternak and His Times: Selected Papers from the Second International Symposium on Pasternak*, ed. Lazar Fleishman (Berkeley: Berkeley Slavic Specialties, 1989), 58–90. Invaluable material is presented in Jewgenij Pasternak, Jelena Pasternak, and Konstantin Asadowskij, eds., *Rainer Maria Rilke, Marina Zwetajewa, Boris Pasternak: Briefwechsel* (Frankfurt am Main: Insel Verlag, 1983). Ariadna Efron discusses this chapter of her mother's life in *Страницы воспоминаний*, 115–128.

19. Ieva Vitins, "The Structure of Marina Cvetaeva's 'Provoda': From Eros to Psyche," *Russian Literature Journal*, 41, no. 140 (1987), 143–55. Vitins observes that in the cycle *Provoda* Tsvetaeva herself assumes the role of Orpheus.

20. Taubman, op. cit., 189.

21. Tamarchenko reads this phrase as referring to abstract political concerns, op. cit., 163.

22. This statement appears in the 1937 essay « Пушкин и Пугачев » (Pushkin and Pugachev), *IP* 2:297.

23. Simon Karlinsky, *Marina Tsvetaeva: The Woman, Her World, and Her Poetry*, 183.

24. Aleksandar Flaker, «Взбунтованный эрос Марины Цветаевой», in *Марина Цветаева: Труды первого международного симпозиума (Лозанна, 30.VI.-3.VII. 1982)*, ed. R. Kemball, 353.

25. Ibid.

26. Tamarchenko, op. cit., 166.

27. Ibid., 164, 167.

28. Even the alternations of poetic voice are gradually broken down in Shostakovich's setting.

29. Michael Makin, *Marina Tsvetaeva: Poetics of Appropriation*, 230.

30. Private communication.

31. "Alexander died, Alexander was buried, Alexander returneth into dust; the dust is earth; of earth we make loam, and why of that loam, whereto he was converted, might they not stop a beer-barrel?" (V, i).

32. A. Bakhrakh, «Письма Марины Цветаевой», *Мосты* 5 (1960), 315.

33. *Неизданные письма*, ed. G. Struve and N. Struve, 294 (ellipsis in original).

CHAPTER FOUR: THE SIBYL

1. Antonina Gove, "The Feminine Stereotype and Beyond," *Slavic Review* 36, (June 1977), 247.

2. The issue of gender is important in Tsvetaeva's writings and self-image and has been addressed from a variety of perspectives by a number of scholars. Among these are Svetlana Boym, *Death in Quotation Marks: Cultural Myths of the Modern Poet* (Cambridge, Mass.: Harvard University Press, 1991), 191–240; Hélène Cixous, "Difficult Joys," in *The Body and the Text: Hélène Cixous, Reading and Teaching*, ed. Helen Wilcox, Keith McWatters, Ann Thompson, and Linda R. Williams (New York: Harvester-Wheatsheaf, 1990), 5–30; Hélène Cixous, "Poetry, Passion and History: Marina Tsvetaeva," in *Readings: The Poetics of Blanchot, Joyce, Kafka, Kleist, Lispector, and Tsvetayeva*, ed. Verena Conley (Minneapolis: University of Minnesota Press, 1991), 110–51; Sibelan Forrester, "Bells and Cupolas: The Formative Role of the Female Body in Tsvetaeva's Poetry," *Slavic Review* 51, no. 2 (1992), 232–46; Antonina Gove, "The Feminine Stereotype and Beyond: Role Conflict and Resolution in the Poetics of Marina Tsvetaeva," *Slavic Review* 36 (1977), 231–55; Barbara Heldt, *Terrible Perfection: Women and Russian Literature* (Bloomington: Indiana University Press, 1987), 98–102, 130–43; Anya M. Kroth, "Androgyny as an Exemplary Feature of Marina Tsvetaeva's Dichotomous Poetic Vision," *Slavic Review* 38 (1979), 563–82; and Stephanie Sandler, "Embodied Words:

Gender in Cvetaeva's Reading of Puškin," *Slavic and East European Journal* 34, no. 2 (Summer 1990), 139–57.

3. John Block Friedman, *Orpheus in the Middle Ages*, 26.

4. A rudimentary discussion of this cycle can be found in Olga Peters Hasty, "Tsvetaeva's Sibylline Lyrics," *Russian Literature* 19 (1986), 323–40.

5. For a discussion of the image of trees in Tsvetaeva's works, see O. G. Revzina, « Тема деревьев в поэзии М. Цветаевой », in *Ученые записки Тартуского Университета, 576, Типология культуры: Взаимное воздействие культур* (Труды по знаковым системам 15), ed. Ju. Lotman (Tartu: Tartu University, 1982), 141–48.

6. Rainer Maria Rilke, *Sämtliche Werke*, 6 vols. (Frankfurt am Main: Insel Verlag, 1987), 1:568. Unless otherwise noted, all citations of Rilke's verse are from this edition. Volume and page references are given in the text.

7. M. H. Abrams, *Natural Supernaturalism: Tradition and Revolution in Romantic Literature* (New York: W. W. Norton, 1971), 377.

8. In « врасплох » we recognize the adverb that characterizes the unexpectedness of Blok-Orpheus's summons into the creative state in the lyric "Like One Somnolent, Intoxicated."

9. For a penetrating discussion of the distribution of internal rhymes in this and other poems, see Edward Stankiewicz, "The Orchestration of Rhymes in the Poetry of Marina Cvetaeva," *Slavica Hierosolymitana* 5–6 (1981), 334.

10. Although, strictly speaking, not a believer, Tsvetaeva was thoroughly familiar with the liturgical canon of the Russian Orthodox Church.

11. It was doubtless not lost on Tsvetaeva that her "Eurydice to Orpheus" complements Rilke's "Annunciation." In Rilke's lyric the incorporeal angel who appears in the physical world is disconcerted by Mary's corporeal existence, while in Tsvetaeva's lyric the insubstantial Eurydice is disturbed by the appearance of the flesh-and-blood Orpheus in the realm of the shades.

12. Ariadna Efron, *Страницы воспоминаний*, 64.

13. Brigitte Peucker, *Lyric Descent in the German Romantic Tradition* (New Haven: Yale University Press, 1987), 18.

14. Quoted in ibid., 17.

15. Aleksandr Bakhrakh, « Письма Марины Цветаевой », *Мосты* 5 (1960), 306.

16. Ibid., 307.

17. *Неизданные письма*, 350. (The letter is dated 30 December 1925.)

CHAPTER FIVE: *POETS*

1. Part of the material in this chapter appears in "Marina Tsvetaeva's Cycle *Поэты*," in *Marina Tsvetaeva: One Hundred Years*, ed. V. Schweitzer,

J. Taubman, P. Scotto, and T. Babyonyshev (Oakland: Berkeley Slavic Specialties, 1992), 131–46. I am grateful to Jane Taubman and Peter Scotto for their helpful commentary on my analysis of this cycle.

2. Tsvetaeva was to cite these two lines in her essay « Пушкин и Пугачев » [Pushkin and Pugachev, 1937], where she uses them to describe the specifically poetic nature of the prose of *Капитанская дочка* [The Captain's Daughter].

3. Tsvetaeva's lyric, « Косматая звезда » [Shaggy Star], written a year earlier, describes a comet and anticipates thematic concerns articulated in the poem under discussion.

4. Eric Partridge, *Origins* (New York: Macmillan, 1966), 112.

5. M. H. Abrams has pointed out that this image recurs frequently in the Romantics' definitions of poetry. See *The Mirror and the Lamp: Romantic Theory and the Critical Tradition* (New York: W. W. Norton, 1958), 88, 101, 132, etc.

6. Aleksandr Pushkin, *Полное собрание сочинений в десяти томах*, 10 vols. (Moscow: Академия наук, 1963), 3:22.

7. Antonina Gove, "Parallelism in the Poetry of Marina Cvetaeva," in *Slavic Poetics: Essays in Honor of Kiril Taranovsky* (The Hague: Mouton, 1973), 181.

8. Ibid.

9. Private communication.

10. The opposition of the singular and plural in Tsvetaeva's works is given fruitful attention by L. V. Zubova, *Поэзия Марины Цветаевой: Лингвистический аспект* (Leningrad: Leningrad University Press, 1989), 28–30.

11. V. V. Rozanova and I. I. Matveev, eds., *Словарь русского языка*, 4 vols. (Moscow: Государственное издательство иностранных и национальных словарей, 1959), 3:636.

12. These lines appear in the second poem of the *Подруга* [Friend] cycle, whose lyrics laud N. A. Nolle-Kogan and the son she bore two months before Blok's death. Thinking Blok to have been the child's father, Tsvetaeva compares Nolle-Kogan with the Virgin Mary and the infant with Christ, thus according Blok the position of the divine father.

13. The single best example is in the essay « Мой Пушкин » [My Pushkin, 1937], in which "blackness" is a central trope.

14. Zubova, op. cit., provides insightful material relating to Tsvetaeva's use of the polyvalence of linguistic signs in the third chapter of her book, « Синкретизм в поэзии М. Цветаевой », 110–88.

15. Rozanova and Matveev, op. cit., 1:685.

16. P. V. Annenkov, "Materials for Pushkin's Autobiography," in *Russian Views of Pushkin*, ed. D. J. Richards and C. R. S. Cockrell (Oxford: William A. Meeuws, 1976), 30–31.

17. For a sensitive study of Pushkin's "André Chénier," see Stephanie Sandler, "The Poetics of Authority in Pushkin's 'André Chénier,'" *Slavic Review* 42, no. 2 (Summer 1983), 187–203.

18. See Pushkin, op. cit., vol. 10, «Деловые бумаги, показание по делу об элегии «Андрей Шенье»».

19. Pushkin, op. cit., 2:264. It is interesting to note that in a letter to Vera Aleksandrovna Merkurieva that Tsvetaeva wrote on 31 August 1940, exactly one year before her own death, she concluded her expression of resignation to her fate and from her calling with a quotation of these very words uttered by Chénier (*Сочинения в двух томах*, 2:543).

CHAPTER SIX: ORPHEUS-RILKE

1. The work of Konstantin M. Azadovskii [Asadowskij] is pathbreaking. See especially his notes and commentary in *Rainer Maria Rilke, Marina Zwetajewa, Boris Pasternak: Briefwechsel*, ed. Jewgenij Pasternak, Jelena Pasternak, and Konstantin M. Asadowskij (henceforth *Briefwechsel*); *Райнер Мария Рильке, Борис Пастернак, Марина Цветаева: Письма 1926 года* (Moscow: Kniga, 1990); *Rainer Maria Rilke und Marina Zwetajewa: Ein Gespräch in Briefen* (henceforth *R-Z Corr.*); and *Небесная арка: Марина Цветаева и Райнер Мария Рильке* (St. Petersburg: Acropolis, 1992). Other significant contributions to this area of inquiry include Vladimir Admoni, «Марина Цветаева и поэзия XX века», *Звезда* 10 (1992) 163–69; Patricia Pollock Brodsky, "On Daring to Be a Poet: Rilke and Marina Cvetaeva," *Germano-Slavica* 3, no. 4 (1980), 261–69; Olga Peters Hasty, "Marina Cvetaeva's Encounter with Rainer Maria Rilke" (Ph.D. diss., Yale University, 1980); Katherine Tiernan O'Connor, "Reflections on the Genesis of the Pasternak-Rilke Correspondence," in *Readings in Russian Modernism: To Honor Vladimir Markov*, ed. Ronald Vroon and John E. Malmstad, UCLA Slavic Studies, new series, vol. 1 (Moscow: "Nauka," Oriental Literature Publishers, 1993), 260–65; and Irma Rakusa, "Marina Zwetajewa und Rainer Maria Rilke: Auf Grund unveröffentlichter Briefmaterialien," *Neue Zürcher Zeitung*, 1–2 September 1979, 65. Anna A. Tavis has devoted several studies to this theme: "Marina Tsvetaeva through Rainer Maria Rilke's Eyes," in *A Centennial Symposium Dedicated to Marina Tsvetaeva* (Northfield, Vt.: Russian School of Norwich University, 1992), 219–29; "Russia in Rilke: Rainer Maria Rilke's Correspondence with Marina Tsvetaeva," *Slavic Review* 52, no. 3 (Fall 1993), 494–511; and *Rilke's Russia: A Cultural Encounter* (Evanston: Northwestern University Press, 1994), chapter 9.

2. Rilke read Hélène Iswolky's French translations "Nuit accablante" and "Départ" in Paul Valéry's literary almanac *Commerce* (no. 6, 1925) and poems

in the original in Il'ya Ehrenburg's anthology *Портреты русских поэтов* [Portraits of Russian Poets] (Moscow: Аргонавты, 1923).

3. The text of this letter may be found in *Briefwechsel*, 59–61. The Ehrenburg anthology referred to in Rilke's letter came out in Berlin in 1922. The notes to *Briefwechsel* (279) provide a list of Russian poets who appear in this anthology but inexplicably neglect to include Tsvetaeva, who was in fact one of the poets represented in this volume. This omission is rectified in *R-Z Corr.*, 202n.35.

4. *Briefwechsel*, 77. (The complete text of the letter appears on 75–78.)

5. *R-Z Corr.*, 48. She refers here, as Azadovskii notes, to the second, expanded edition of Rilke's *Mir zu Feier* (1899) that appeared in 1909 under the title *Die frühen Gedichte* (*R-Z Corr.*, 214n.15).

6. Marion Böhme, "Rilke und die russische Literatur" (diss., Vienna 1966), 92–93.

7. Gleb Struve, «Из моей переписки с писателями. Письма Г. В. Иванова, М. И. Цветаевой и М. А. Алданова (1923–1925)», *Мосты* 13–14 (1968), 397.

8. Tsvetaeva claimed to have received seven letters from Rilke. Perhaps she counted the Elegy in order to arrive at her own and Rilke's favorite number.

9. *R-Z Corr.*, 27.

10. This passage is cited according to the original manuscript of the letter, Rilke Ms. A 364 1–7, Rilke-Archiv, Landesbibliothek, Bern. An unfortunate error appears in the reproduction of the inscription in *Briefwechsel*, 111.

11. For a discussion of this feature of Tsvetaeva's poetics, see Olga Peters Hasty, "Tsvetaeva's Onomastic Verse," *Slavic Review* 45, no. 2 (1986), 245–56.

12. See letter of 29 June 1922 in Marina Tsvetaeva, *Неизданные письма*, 270.

13. Ibid., 282.

14. The only fly in the ointment was that Rilke wrote not of his own accord to praise her poetry, but as a favor to Boris Pasternak. Tsvetaeva's subsequent exclusion of Pasternak from her correspondence with Rilke suggests a denial of this deviation from her master plan.

15. Tsvetaeva did not know that her visit would in any event have been impossible since Rilke had left Paris at the end of the summer of that year.

16. *R-Z Corr.*, 48.

17. For a full account of Tsvetaeva's situation at this time, see Simon Karlinsky, *Marina Tsvetaeva: The Woman, Her World, and Her Poetry*, chapter 7, "Splendours and miseries of 1926," 148–72. A detailed description of the initial stages of Tsvetaeva's Parisian sojourn appears in Irma Kudrova, « Полгода в Париже — К биографии Марины Цветаевой », in *Wiener slawistischer Almanach*, Sonderband 3, ed. Horst Lampel and Aage A. Hansen-Löve (Vienna: Institut für Slawistik der Universität Wien, 1981), 129–59.

18. For an outline of some of the major reprisals the essay brought, see *Briefwechsel*, 295–96*n*5.

19. Karlinsky, op. cit., 158.

20. Ibid.

21. Osip Mandel'shtam, *Собрание сочинений в трех томах*, ed. G. Struve and B. Filippov, 3 vols. (Washington, D.C.: Inter-Language Literary Associates, 1967), 1:58.

22. *R-Z Corr.*, 49. Tsvetaeva is referring to *Die Zaren: Ein Gedicht-kreis* [The Tsars: A Lyric Cycle] from *Buch der Bilder* [Book of Images].

23. Ibid., 51.

24. *Briefwechsel*, 43.

25. *R-Z Corr.*, 46–47.

26. Ibid., 47.

27. *Письма к А. Тесковой*, 48.

28. *R-Z Corr.*, 52.

29. Ibid., 55.

30. Ibid., 56.

31. *R-Z Corr.*, 56. The actual text from « Цветник » appears in *IP* 1:247.

32. For a discussion of "Your Death," see Olga Peters Hasty, " 'Your Death': The Living Water of Cvetaeva's Art," *Russian Literature* 13 (1983), 41–64.

33. *R-Z Corr.*, 56.

34. Walter Strauss, *Descent and Return: The Orphic Theme in Modern Literature*, 18.

35. *R-Z Corr.*, 56.

36. Ibid., 52.

37. *Briefwechsel*, 52–53.

38. *R-Z Corr.*, 71.

39. Ibid., 56.

40. Ibid., 57.

41. Ibid.

42. Following her own stylistic practice, Tsvetaeva erroneously capitalizes the first words of each line. The editor of *R-Z Corr.* has corrected this error. Here I retain the format of the original letters.

43. *R-Z Corr.*, 57.

44. Ibid.

45. The verb *wühlen* carries the meanings "to root, dig, or grub up (the ground); burrow, turn up the ground; rummage, rake about (in); (fig.) agitate, stir up, foment (dicontent, etc.); (fig.) gnaw (as pain)." The various meanings of *wüst* include "desert, waste, desolate, deserted, uncultivated, fallow; confused, wild, disorderly; dissolute." See Harold T. Betteridge, ed., *The New Cassell's German Dictionary* (New York: Funk and Wagnalls, 1958), 575.

46. That Tsvetaeva's commentary does not extend into part II of the *Sonnets*

may perhaps be explained by the fact that the image of Orpheus fades and all but disappears from those poems.

47. *R-Z Corr.*, 53.

48. Strauss, op. cit., 183.

49. Elizabeth Sewell, *The Orphic Voice: Poetry and Natural History*, 330.

50. Ibid. 331.

51. Charles Segal, *Orpheus: The Myth of the Poet*, 122.

52. *R-Z Corr.*, 48–49.

53. See Felix Philipp Ingold, "M. I. Cvetaevas Lese- und Verständnishilfen für R. M. Rilke," *Die Welt der Slawen* 24, no. 2 (1979): 352–68.

54. *Неизданные письма*, 293–94 (ellipsis in original).

55. Ibid., 297.

56. Strauss, op. cit., 186.

57. Ibid., 142, 144.

58. *R-Z Corr.*, 68–69.

59. Ibid., 69.

60. Ibid.

61. Ibid., 70.

62. Ibid., 75.

63. Ibid., 82.

64. Anna Tavis, for example, refers repeatedly to Tsvetaeva's "demands for personal intimacy (*zhutkaia intimnost'*)," in "Russia in Rilke," 503, 507. Christopher Barnes, in speaking of these letters, notes Tsvetaeva's "surprisingly carnal idiom," in *Boris Pasternak: A Literary Biography* (New York: Cambridge University Press, 1989), 374.

65. *R-Z Corr.*, 26.

66. Ibid., 83.

67. Tsvetaeva was apparently unaware of the gravity of Rilke's illness. He died less than two months later. Yet, inasmuch as Rilke continued writing letters to others even after he stopped writing to Tsvetaeva, the end of the correspondence cannot be attributed entirely to his failing health.

68. These are the opening lines of the second poem of Tsveaeva's cycle *Двое* [The Two, 3 July 1924].

69. Azadovskii notes significant parallels in Tsvetaeva's response to Blok's and Rilke's deaths (*R-Z Corr.*, 31–32).

CHAPTER SEVEN: *NEW YEAR'S*

1. Charles Segal, *Orpheus: The Myth of the Poet*, 34.

2. The German text of this posthumous letter appears in Jewgenij Pasternak, Jelena Pasternak, and Konstantin M. Asadowskij, eds., *Rainer Maria Rilke, Marina Zwetajewa, Boris Pasternak: Briefwechsel*, 247–48. It appears

in English in Margaret Wettlin and Walter Arndt, *Boris Pasternak, Marina Tsvetayeva, Rainer Maria Rilke: Letters Summer 1926* (San Diego, New York, London: Harcourt Brace Jovanovich, 1983), 209–10. The German text also appears in Konstantin M. Asadowski, ed., *Rainer Maria Rilke und Marina Zwetajewa: Ein Gespräch in Briefen*, 92–93. A Russian translation of it can be found in Marina Tsvetaeva, *Неизданные письма*, ed. G. Struve and N. Struve, 319–20, and in the expanded Russian edition of the Tsvetaeva-Rilke correspondence edited by Konstantin Azadovskii, *Небесная арка: Марина Цветаева и Райнер Мария Рильке* (Saint Petersburg: Акрополь, 1992), 113–14. Unless otherwise noted my citations of the letters are from the 1992 Azadovskii edition of the Rilke-Tsvetaeva correspondence (henceforth *R-Z Corr.*). The translations are my own.

3. *R-Z Corr.*, 92.

4. Ibid., 49.

5. Ibid., 47.

6. Ibid., 93.

7. Ibid., 90.

8. In connection with her 1929 translations of some of Rilke's letters (*IP* 1:268–82) Tsvetaeva stated that she wanted not to write about or even to Rilke, but rather to provide him with an opportunity to speak through her. On the strength of the double meaning of "to translate" she created an analogy between her own role of translator and that of psychopomp which she assigned Rilke:

> Я Рильке перевожу на русскую речь, как он когда-нибудь переведет меня на тот свет.
>
> За руку — через реку.
>
> [I am translating Rilke into the Russian language just as he will one day translate me into the other world.
>
> By the hand—across the river.] (*IP* 1:273)

9. Anya M. Kroth has captured the essential significance of this aspect of Tsvetaeva's vision in her insistence that the poet's world is not dualistic but dichotomous in that Tsvetaeva "stresses the close connection and mutual interrelation between any two antithetical poles" ("Towards a New Perspective on Marina Tsvetaeva's Poetic World," *Wiener slawistischer Almanach, Sonderband 3* [Vienna, 1981], 6).

10. *Неизданные письма*, 279.

11. Walter Strauss, *Descent and Return: The Orphic Theme in Modern Literature*, 13.

12. This is a recurrent theme in Tsvetaeva's works. In her essay « Поэт-альпинист » (1934), dedicated to Nikolai Gronskii, she elaborates on it with particular intensity.

13. A. S. Efron, « Письма Марины Цветаевой », *Новый мир* (1969), 199.

14. Indeed, Rilke went so far as to claim that someone was literally guiding his pen.

15. Elizabeth Sewell, *The Orphic Voice: Poetry and Natural History*, 373.

16. *Неизданные письма*, 325.

17. *R-Z Corr.*, 31, 205n62.

18. This English rendering, like the others in this book, is a very basic, not to say primitive, interlinear translation that falls painfully short of capturing the original and makes no pretense at being poetry. Line divisions have been preserved only in order to facilitate the reading of this long text.

19. Joseph Brodsky, « Об одном стихотворении », *SP*, 1:[45–46]. Brodsky's penetrating reading of *New Year's* contributes richly to our understanding of the text and its author.

20. Ibid., [45].

21. *Неизданные письма*, 318.

22. In writing of Rilke's *Sonnets to Orpheus*, Walter Strauss, op. cit., notes the prevalent "metaphors of silence and the attentive ear" in part I and states that "true Orphic space is silent space, and Orphic song is but the celebration of this silence of inwardness" (202).

23. On the day she received the news of Rilke's death Tsvetaeva wrote to Pasternak: « Пришли звать на Новый год и, одновременно, сообщили » (*Неизданные письма*, 316). In a letter to Teskova written 14 November 1936, at the approach of the tenth anniversary of Rilke's death, Tsvetaeva recalls the visit, once again underscoring Slonim's insensitivity, which becomes emblematic of mundane callousness to the poet: « Я помню день: утром 31-го пришел Слоним — приглашать на встречу Нового Года в ресторан — и: — « А Вы знаете? Р. умер » » [I remember the day: the morning of the 31st Slonim came—to invite me to a New Year's celebration at a restaurant—and: "and did you know? R. died"] (Письма к. А. Тескдвой, 146).

24. See his memoirs in *Новый журнал* 104 (1971), 145.

25. *R-Z Corr.*, 83 (ellipsis in original).

26. Ibid., 67.

27. Nadia Ilovaiskaia was in fact a direct relation of Tsvetaeva's half-brother Andrei and half-sister Valeriia, and not of Tsvetaeva herself.

28. *R-Z Corr.*, 76.

29. Ibid., 77.

30. Ibid.

31. *Неизданные письма*, 318.

32. "Wie gern wüßt' ich jetzt wieder, wie Nest russisch heißt (vergessen!)" [How I would now like to know once again what *nest* is in Russian (I've forgotten!)] *R-Z Corr.*, 87.

33. *R-Z Corr.*, 71.

34. Segal, op. cit., 127.

35. Strauss, op. cit., 186.

36. Tsvetaeva was to refer to this passage from *The Notebooks* in a letter to Anatolii Shteiger written nearly ten years later (September 1936), in which she remarks:

> Если бы Вы ехали в Париж — за собственным одиночеством, как 23-летний Рильке, оставивший о Париже бессмертные слова: «Я всегда слышал, что это город, где живут, по-моему — это город, где умирают.»
>
> [If you were going to Paris to seek your personal solitude like the 23-year-old Rilke, who left the immortal words about Paris: "I always heard that this was a city where one lives, in my opinion this is a city where one dies."] (*Новый мир* 4, 210).

37. An elaboration of this notion can be found in «Твоя смерть» [Your Death]: «Если ты мертвый — я тоже мертвая, если я живая — ты тоже живой, — и не все ли равно, как это называется!» [If you are dead—I too am dead, if I am alive—you are alive too—and is it not all the same what this is called!] (*IP* 2:265).

38. On June 8, 1926, Rilke sent Tsvetaeva six photographs of Muzot. On one of them a wooden cross appears in the foreground. (See the photographs in *Briefwechsel*.)

39. See, for example, the letters to Pasternak dated 25 and 29 May 1926 in *Неизданные письма*, 293, 303.

40. For a study of the significance Tsvetaeva ascribed to names, see Olga Peters Hasty, "Tsvetaeva's Onomastic Verse," in *Slavic Review* 45, no. 2 (1986), 245–56.

41. In his essay on *New Year's* Brodsky reminds us that amphitheaters have no curtains (*SP*, 74–75).

42. *R-Z Corr.*, 52.

43. Tomas Venclova, *Неустойчивое равновесие: Восемь русских поэтических текстов* (New Haven: Yale Russian and East European Publications, 1986), 139.

44. *R-Z Corr.*, 47. See also her letter of 12 May (54–59).

45. Ibid., 50.

46. Ibid., 52.

47. Ibid., 49.

48. *Неизданные письма*, 302.

49. *R-Z Corr.*, 54.

50. In the essay «Поэт и время» (1932) Tsvetaeva describes this priesthood in a somewhat different way: «Рильке нашему времени так же

необходим, как священник на поле битвы: чтобы за тех и за других, за них и за нас: о просвещении еще живых и прощении павших — молиться» [Rilke is just as crucial for our time as a priest on the field of battle: to pray for both sides, for them and for us: for the enlightenment of the yet-living and for the forgiveness of the fallen] (*IP* I: 378).

51. It is interesting to recall here the explanation Tsvetaeva gives Nanny Wunderly-Volkart in a letter of 5 July 1930 for why she refrains from using Rilke's name and refers to him only as "R": "(seinen ganzen Namen schreib ich ungern—zu laut, zu ausgeredet—nein, ein grosses, stilles (und steiles) R.—wie ein Fels (Roc) Raron, wie seine Rhône, wenn sie vom Fels fällt, R.—sein Tauf-und-Dichtername in einem, R., einfach *er*)" [I don't like writing his name—too loud, too pronounced—no, a big, quiet (and steep) R.—like a cliff (*Roc*) Rarogne, like his Rhône, when it plummets from the cliff, R.—his baptismal and poetic name in one, R., simply *he*)] (*R-Z Corr.*, 165).

52. *Письма к А. Тесковой*, 57 (ellipsis in original)

53. *Новый мир* 4 (1969), 204.

54. Ibid., 203.

55. Ibid., 204.

56. Ibid.

57. "Ich glaube an Berge. (Die Zeile, in meiner Umänderung—die schliesslich keine ist—denn Berge und Nächte *reimen*—erkennst Du doch?)" [I believe in mountains. (This line, in my transformation—that ultimately isn't one—for mountains and nights *rhyme*—you do recognize it, don't you?)] (*R-Z Corr.*, 51). This is a reference on Tsvetaeva's part to "Du Dunkelheit aus der ich stamme" [you darkness from which I stem] of part I of Rilke's *Book of Hours*, a poem which acclaims the limitless, all-encompassing quality of darkness and ends with the line "Ich glaube an Nächte."

58. *R-Z Corr.*, 87.

59. Ibid., 91.

60. Segal, op. cit., 141.

61. Brodsky notes that «в руки» [into the hands of] was a standard form used at the time in addressing letters (*SP* 1:[80]).

62. *R-Z Corr.*, 46. Tsvetaeva did not know that Rilke had ceased using his given name René, adopting in its stead the name Rainer by which Lou Andreas-Salomé called him. The cited passage of her letter to Rilke reiterates her notion that fate is encoded in a given name, that the name draws a particular fate toward its bearer.

63. *R-Z Corr.*, 215n.24.

64. M. H. Abrams's definition of *Aufhebung* as it appears in *Natural Supernaturalism: Tradition and Revolution in Romantic Literature*, 177, summarizes perfectly what Tsvetaeva accomplishes in *New Year's*.

CONCLUSION

1. This definition of myth by the compiler of the *Suidas Lexicon* is cited in John Block Friedman, *Orpheus in the Middle Ages*, 5.

2. Tsvetaeva draws particular attention to this epigraph in her essay « Поэт — альпинист » [The Poet-Mountaineer, 1934], written on the death of the poet Nikolai Gronskii. See *Сочинения в двух томах*, 2:421.

3. Ibid., 2:255.

4. Simon Karlinsky, *Marina Tsvetaeva: The Woman, Her World, and Her Poetry*, 189.

5. *Неизданные письма*, 402, 403.

6. See « Мой Пушкин » and especially « Пушкин и Пугачев » (*IP* 2).

7. A variation on this image of saltwater washing cliffs appears in a passage from Tsvetaeva's 1937 essay « Мой Пушкин », in which she describes her first encounter with the sea at the age of ten and narrates her attempt to finish writing Pushkin's lyric « К морю » in its entirety on a seaside cliff before a wave can obliterate it (*IP* 2:278–79; ellipsis in original).

8. Tsvetaeva's major biographers have provided accounts of this period of her development. See, for example, Viktoria Schweitzer, *Быт и бытие Марины Цветаевой*, chapter 2; and Mariia Razumovskaia, *Марина Цветаева: Миф и действительность*, chapter 2.

9. This image derives from a passage in Hölderlin's *Hyperion* which Tsvetaeva chose as the epigraph to the cycle *Провода* (1923), dedicated to Pasternak and written after their projected meeting failed to materialize: "Des Herzens Woge schäumte nicht so schön empor, und würde Geist, wenn nicht der alte stumme Fels, das Schicksal, ihr entgegenstände" [The heart's surge would not froth so beautifully upward and become spirit if the old, mute cliff, fate, did not stand opposed to it] (*SP* 3:57). In the notes to the cycle this epigraph is erroneously labeled as a misquotation (*SP* 3:448). It is, in fact, cited accurately.

10. This was to have been the title of the lyric in the collection of verse Tsvetaeva assembled in 1940, an edition that never materialized.

11. In a letter addressed to A. Bakhrakh, Tsvetaeva wrote: « Только слухом (зато с самого раннего детства) слыхала, никогда, по сей 1932 г., августа 31-е, не читала ни « Дяди Вани », ни « Трех сестер », ни « Чайки », которую по детским запечатлениям всегда путала с « Дикой уткой » . . . и *нечаянно* не читала, просто: не пришлось, в полном собрании сочинений, которое в доме было, нужно думать, — всегда пропускала — от заведомой чуждости, в которой, верно, не ошиблась . . . » [Only by hearsay (but from my earliest childhood) I heard about, but never—to this very 31 August 1932—read either *Uncle Vanya*, or *The Three Sisters*, or *The Seagull*, which from childhood impressions I always

confused with *The Wild Duck* . . . and did not read *inadvertently*, simply didn't happen to: in the edition of his complete works that we had at home I suppose I always skipped them—from my certainty in their foreignness, in which I was surely not mistaken . . .] (« Письма Марины Цветаевой », *Новый мир* 4 [1969], 194).

Index

Titles of works are listed under the names of the authors